- Go to **awmi.net/sg442** to download PDFs of the following resources for each lesson in this study guide:
    - Outlines
    - Discipleship Questions
    - Scriptures
- Share as many copies as you'd like.
- These documents are not for resale.

Living in God's Best

in

Study Guide

Andrew Wommack

Living in God's Best Study Guide
ISBN: 978-1-59548-292-1

Copyright © 2018 by Andrew Wommack Ministries Inc.
PO Box 3333
Colorado Springs CO 80934-3333

Published by Andrew Wommack Ministries Inc.

www.awmi.net

Table of Contents

How to Use Your Study Guide

Whether you are teaching a class, leading a small group, discipling an individual, or studying on your own, this study guide is designed for you! Here's how it works:

Each lesson consists of the **Lesson** text, **Outline, Teacher's Guide, Discipleship Questions, Answer Key,** and **Scriptures.** Some lessons also contain recommendations for further study.

Outline for Group Study:
    I.   If possible, briefly review the previous lesson by going over the **Answer Key/ Teacher's Guide** answers for the **Discipleship Questions/Teacher's Guide** questions.

    II.   Read the current **Lesson** text or **Teacher's Guide** aloud.
    A.   Be sure that each student has a copy of the **Outline.**
    B.   While the **Lesson** text or **Teacher's Guide** is being read, students should use their **Outlines** to follow along.

    III.   Once the **Lesson** text or **Teacher's Guide** is read, facilitate discussion and study using the **Discipleship Questions/Teacher's Guide** questions (all questions are the same).
    A.   Read one question at a time.
    B.   The group should use their **Outlines** to assist with answering the questions.
    C.   Have the group read aloud each specifically mentioned scripture before answering the question.
    D.   Discuss the answer/point from the **Lesson** text as desired.
    E.   As much as possible, keep the discussion centered on the scriptures and the **Lesson** text or **Teacher's Guide** points at hand.
    F.   Remember, the goal is understanding (Matt. 13:19).
    G.   One individual should not dominate the discussion; instead, try to draw out the quieter ones for the group conversation.
    H.   Repeat the process until all of the questions are discussed/answered.

Materials Needed:
    Study guide, Bible, and enough copies of the **Outline, Discipleship Questions,** and **Scriptures** for each student. (PDFs of the **Outlines, Discipleship Questions,** and **Scriptures** can be downloaded via the URL located on the first page of this study guide.)

Outline for Personal Study:

    I.   Read the current **Lesson** text or **Teacher's Guide**.
        A. Read additional information, if provided.
        B. Meditate on the given scriptures as desired.

    II.   Answer the corresponding **Discipleship Questions/Teacher's Guide** questions.

    III. Check your work with the **Answer Key/Teacher's Guide** answers.

Materials Needed:
    Study guide, Bible, and a writing utensil.

God Dependent

LESSON 1

And there came an angel of the Lord, *and sat under an oak which was in Ophrah, that pertained unto Joash the Abiezrite: and his son Gideon threshed wheat by the winepress, to hide it from the Midianites. [12] And the angel of the* Lord *appeared unto him, and said unto him, The* Lord *is with thee, thou mighty man of valour. [13] And Gideon said unto him, Oh my Lord, if the* Lord *be with us, why then is all this befallen us? and where be all his miracles which our fathers told us of, saying, Did not the* Lord *bring us up from Egypt? but now the* Lord *hath forsaken us, and delivered us into the hands of the Midianites. [14] And the* Lord *looked upon him, and said, Go in this thy might, and thou shalt save Israel from the hand of the Midianites: have not I sent thee?*

Judges 6:11-14

During the time of Gideon, the Israelites were being oppressed by the Midianites, who would come down and take away all the Israelites' foodstuffs. Gideon was threshing wheat behind a winepress so he could conceal it from these enemies. He was hiding and trying to beat out a little bit of grain so he could have something to eat, when an angel appeared to him and declared, "The Lord is with you, you mighty man of valor!"

Gideon responded, "If I am a mighty man of valor, where are all of God's mighty works that our fathers told us about? You know, how He delivered them from the Egyptians, brought us into this land, and performed all the other miracles?" Some people interpret this as Gideon criticizing the angel and saying, "No, I don't believe You. I don't trust You." Personally, I look at it the opposite way. Gideon had heard about the miraculous beginnings of the nation of Israel and was sick and tired of living a substandard life. Refusing to yield to these enemies who were forcing Israel to live that way, he was doing what he had to do to thresh some wheat. In his heart, Gideon was tired of living under the enemy's oppression. He genuinely wanted God's best. So, the angel responded, saying, "Go with this your might, and God will be with you." In other words, the angel basically rewarded him for wanting more than what life was handing him.

One of the first steps to seeing the supernatural power of God operate in your life is getting to the place where you genuinely say, "I am not going to live like this anymore!" From your heart, you declare, "I refuse to live this way any longer!"

BURNING DAYLIGHT!

Are you in a dead-end job? Do you hate going to work? Maybe you get up on Mondays and talk about "blue" Monday. You drag through your week because you have to do your job, but then on Friday it's TGIF (thank God it's Friday) because you can't wait to get out of there. Why are you living like that? Life isn't a dress rehearsal; this is the real deal. You're burning daylight!

Either you've advanced today and gotten closer to what the Lord has for you in life, or you've just spent another day wasting time. If you don't love what you're doing, if it doesn't give you a buzz, and if it doesn't build you up and excite you, then why are you doing it? You might say, "But Andrew, I have to make a living." Why not make a life?

Do you know why you're living the way you're living? It's because you've accepted it. You're just marching in step and keeping time, not really doing anything significant. You're just tolerating it.

God made you for something special. He's never created a piece of junk. He's never made a failure. God doesn't make people mediocre or what the world would call "normal." He created people to be unique and to accomplish different purposes. Not everybody's going to do what I'm supposed to do; neither will I do what someone else is to do. God made you special, and your life should count. You ought to be excited about your life and about knowing that you're fulfilling God's call and your destiny. Yet many people just settle for less.

> *But he giveth more grace. Wherefore he saith, God resisteth the proud,*
> *but giveth grace unto the humble.* [7] *Submit yourselves therefore to*
> *God. Resist the devil, and he will flee from you.*
>
> James 4:6-7

Humility is submitting yourself to God; it's yielding to Him. According to 2 Chronicles 16:9, the Lord is looking for someone who is humble and submitted to Him. His eyes find the one who is hungry and who desires Him, the one who isn't satisfied with what everybody else is settling for.

SELF-DEPENDENT

To a degree, I'm preaching to the choir right now. Here you are, reading this book written by a hick from Texas. So, either you're a fanatic or you were told to read this by one. You aren't just run-of-the-mill. You desire something more. You're submitting to God. You could be watching "As the Stomach Turns" or something like that on television, but instead, you're reading and considering what I'm saying—what God is saying—through this study guide.

Humility is submitting ourselves to God and resisting the devil. The devil flees from us when we do that. Sadly, most of us aren't submitting ourselves to God. We aren't resisting the devil; we're actually cooperating with him, and much of the time, our cooperation isn't even intentional. We just don't recognize what we're doing.

Humility is being God-dependent instead of self-dependent. It's trusting the Lord instead of your own flesh's strength and ability. When you're trying to live life by your own human strength and effort, you aren't humble, and you aren't submitted to God.

That was King Asa's problem in 2 Chronicles 16:1-6. The kingdom of Israel had broken into two parts. The northern ten tribes were called Israel, and the southern two tribes were called Judah. Asa was king over Judah. The king of Israel came against him and began to build a town called Ramah. The town was strategically located where it could cut off Judah's supplies and prevent communication with any other country. Its purpose was to help bring about Judah's defeat.

The Word says that when the king of Israel built Ramah and began the siege, King Asa took all of the gold, silver, and treasures that were in the house of the Lord—all of his wealth—and sent it to Benhadad, the king of Syria, saying, "Let there be a league between us and you. Go and attack Israel." The idea was that if Israel was busy fighting a war with Syria, they wouldn't be able to also fight with Judah. Benhadad took all of the treasures, listened to Asa's request, and then attacked the king of Israel. So, the king of Israel had to abandon his siege of Judah and discontinue building the town of Ramah.

WHAT'S WRONG WITH THAT?

Taking this opportunity, King Asa commanded all of his people to go to Ramah and scatter all of the stones that were being used to build it. This destroyed everything the king of Israel was doing there. So, Asa basically won this battle without any cost of human life for him or his armies because he hired the Syrians to go and attack Israel for them. In this way, he got out of his problem.

Now, most people would think, *What's wrong with that? His problem was over. No one from Judah lost their life. What could be wrong with that?*

God had a different perspective. Second Chronicles 16:7-8 says,

> *And at that time Hanani the seer came to Asa king of Judah, and said unto him, Because thou hast relied on the king of Syria, and not relied on the* LORD *thy God, therefore is the host of the king of Syria escaped out of thine hand. [8] Were not the Ethiopians and the Lubims a huge host, with very many chariots and horsemen? yet, because thou didst rely on the* LORD, *he delivered them into thine hand.*

Keep this in mind as we turn back to look at a few verses in 2 Chronicles 14 that speak of when Asa first came to power and began to reign as king:

> *And Asa did that which was good and right in the eyes of the* LORD *his God: [3] For he took away the altars of the strange gods, and the high places, and brake down the images, and cut down the groves: [4] And commanded Judah to seek the* LORD *God of their fathers, and to do the law and the commandment. [5] Also he took away out of all the cities of Judah the high places and the images: and the kingdom was quiet before him. [6] And he built fenced cities in Judah: for the land had rest, and he had no war in those years; because the* LORD *had given him rest. [7] Therefore he said unto Judah, Let us build these cities, and make about them walls, and towers, gates, and bars, while the land is yet before us; because we have sought the* LORD *our God, we have sought him, and he hath given us rest on every side. So they built and prospered.*
>
> 2 Chronicles 14:2-7

Judah's peace and prosperity were directly related to King Asa seeking the Lord. That's clearly stated in the verses quoted above.

PRIDE

> *And Asa had an army of men that bare targets and spears, out of Judah three hundred thousand; and out of Benjamin, that bare shields and drew bows, two hundred and fourscore thousand: all these [580,000 total] were mighty men of valour. [9] And there came out against them Zerah the Ethiopian with an host of a thousand thousand [a million], and three hundred chariots; and came unto Mareshah. [10] Then Asa went out against him, and they set the battle in array in the valley of Zephathah at Mareshah. [11] And Asa cried unto the* LORD *his God, and said,* LORD, *it is nothing with thee to help, whether with many, or with them that have no power: help us, O* LORD *our God; for we rest on thee, and in thy name we go against this multitude. O* LORD, *thou art our*

God; let not man prevail against thee.

2 Chronicles 14:8-11, brackets mine

God resists the proud but gives grace to the humble (James 4:6). Asa humbled himself and depended on God: He had 580,000 men, but he was fighting a host of over a million. It was way beyond his ability. So, he cried out to the Lord, saying, "Our eyes are on You. We look to You. We need Your help!" God gives grace to the humble, but He resists the proud.

You aren't humbling yourself when you try to figure everything out on your own. You aren't submitting to God when you just go and do it all yourself. Although most people wouldn't recognize or call such actions "pride," that's exactly what you're operating in. Most people think of pride as someone exalting themselves and considering themselves better than everyone else. However, pride—at its root—is simply depending on self. It's when someone decides they're just going to figure it out and do it on their own.

THE JOURNEY IS MORE IMPORTANT

When Asa humbled himself and cried out to God for help, He came to his aid:

So the LORD smote the Ethiopians before Asa, and before Judah; and the Ethiopians fled. [13] And Asa and the people that were with him pursued them unto Gerar: and the Ethiopians were overthrown, that they could not recover themselves; for they were destroyed before the LORD, and before his host; and they carried away very much spoil. [14] And they smote all the cities round about Gerar; for the fear of the LORD came upon them: and they spoiled all the cities; for there was exceeding much spoil in them. [15] They smote also the tents of cattle, and carried away sheep and camels in abundance, and returned to Jerusalem.

2 Chronicles 14:12-15

This was the multitude referred to in 2 Chronicles 16:8-9 that God delivered into King Asa's hand when he trusted in and called upon Him:

Were not the Ethiopians and the Lubims a huge host, with very many chariots and horsemen? yet, because thou didst rely on the LORD, he delivered them into thine hand. [9] For the eyes of the LORD run to and fro throughout the whole earth, to shew himself strong in the behalf of them whose heart is perfect toward him. Herein thou hast done foolishly: therefore from henceforth thou shalt have wars.

2 Chronicles 16:8-9

Can you see what King Asa was being rebuked for? Previously, when he was outnumbered nearly two to one, he had trusted God, and God delivered him. This time, instead of trusting and following God by going out to fight, he took the treasures from the temple and palace and sent them to the king of Syria to hire him to fight against Judah's enemies. The Lord said to Asa, "I had planned on giving the Israelites into your hand, and you would have conquered the Syrians too. But now you've gone and made a treaty with the Syrians. Not only have the Israelites escaped out of your hand, but the Syrians have too." God's whole plan for King Asa and Judah was thwarted.

Some people think, *Well, King Asa was under attack. He just did whatever it took to get out of the situation.* What we have to understand is that it's not a matter of just obtaining the right result—it matters how you got there. It's not a matter of just getting your needs met—have you trusted God? Ask yourself, have you done all of this through the flesh, in the natural way? In God's eyes, the journey is more important than the destination.

SHOOTING FOR GOD'S BEST

Without knowing it, many of us have compromised. We've chosen the world's way of trying to deal with our lives and problems. By doing so, we've limited what God can do in and through us.

Notice King Asa's response after the prophet Hanani spoke God's message to him:

> *Then Asa was wroth with the seer, and put him in a prison house; for he was in a rage with him because of this thing. And Asa oppressed some of the people the same time.*
>
> 2 Chronicles 16:10

Asa became angry with the Lord's messenger and rejected both him and God's message.

You may not like some of what I'm about to share with you, but be open to let the Lord touch your heart. God's eyes are searching for those whose hearts are totally His. He's looking for people who will humble themselves before Him. He wants to bless you more than you want to be blessed. But you need that same attitude that Gideon had where you are sick and tired of being sick and tired and won't settle for anything less than God's best. There are reasons why the blessing of God isn't manifesting in your life more than it is, and it's never God's fault. The reality is, we're to blame. So, let's not make the same mistake King Asa did and get mad at the messenger, amen? Let's humble ourselves before His mighty hand and receive God's message for us today.

Now, before I start going into specifics, let me preface this by saying that I'm not against anybody. Everything I'm about to call out, I've done. But if God speaks to you about something specific, you need to respond.

GRACE FLOWS

The Lord loves you wherever you are. Even if you aren't seeking the things of God, He loves you. If some of the things I'm about to address are in your life, He loves you. His love is unconditional and doesn't change. But your ability to receive His best for your life is impacted by these things being present in your life. You shouldn't be just surviving, getting by, and trying to make things work. There truly is a difference between God's way and the world's way of doing things.

King Asa obtained his goal. He got the king of Israel to stop building that city. He got out of that bind, but he didn't do it God's way. Because of that, 2 Chronicles 16:9 tells us that from then on, he was plagued by wars.

Now, under the Old Covenant, God judged people and did things that He doesn't do under the New Covenant. Under the New Covenant, He placed all of our judgment upon Jesus, but there are still consequences for our choices. Even though God may not be the one punishing us, what He can do in our lives will be hindered if we don't do things His way. We do reap results from our decisions.

By winning one war, King Asa had many wars come his way that the Lord never intended. We may obtain our goals too, but are we doing it God's way and through God's strength? God resists the proud but gives grace to the humble. Grace flows to those who submit themselves to and depend on Him.

Outline

I. During the time of Gideon, the Israelites were being oppressed by the Midianites, when an angel appeared to Gideon and declared, "The Lord is with you, you mighty man of valor!"

   A. Gideon responded, "If I am a mighty man of valor, where are all of God's mighty works that our fathers told us about?"

   B. Some people interpret this as Gideon criticizing the angel.

   C. Gideon was sick and tired of living a substandard life.

   D. One of the first steps to seeing the supernatural power of God operate in your life is getting to the place where you, from your heart, declare, "I refuse to live this way any longer!"

II. Either you've advanced today and gotten closer to what the Lord has for you in life, or you've just spent another day wasting time.

   A. If you don't love what you're doing, then why are you doing it?

   B. It's because you've accepted it.

   C. You're just marching in step and keeping time, not really doing anything significant.

   D. God made you special, and your life should count.

   E. You ought to be excited about your life and about knowing that you're fulfilling God's call and your destiny.

   F. To a degree, this is preaching to the choir: You desire something more; you're reading and considering all of this—what God is saying—through this study guide.

III. According to 2 Chronicles 16:9, the Lord is looking for someone who is humble and submitted to Him.

   A. Humility is submitting yourself to God; it's yielding to Him and resisting the devil:

But he giveth more grace. Wherefore he saith, God resisteth the proud, but giveth grace unto the humble. [7] Submit yourselves therefore to God. Resist the devil, and he will flee from you.

James 4:6-7

B. Sadly, many Christians are actually cooperating with the devil, and their cooperation isn't even intentional.

C. Humility is being God-dependent instead of self-dependent.

D. When you're trying to live life by your own human strength and effort, you aren't humble, and you aren't submitted to God.

IV. Instead of trusting and following God by going out to fight Israel, King Asa took the treasures from the temple and sent them to the king of Syria to hire him to fight against Judah's enemies.

A. According to 2 Chronicles 16:7-8, the Lord basically said to Asa, "I had planned on giving the Israelites into your hand, and you would have conquered the Syrians too. But now you've gone and made a treaty with the Syrians. Not only have the Israelites escaped out of your hand, but the Syrians have too."

B. God's plan for King Asa and Judah was thwarted.

C. What you have to understand is that it's not a matter of just obtaining the right result—have you trusted God?

D. Ask yourself, have you done all of this through the flesh, in the natural way?

E. In God's eyes, the journey is more important than the destination.

V. Without knowing it, you have probably compromised.

A. You've chosen the world's way of trying to deal with your life and problems.

B. By doing so, you've limited what God can do in and through you.

C. Notice King Asa's response after the prophet Hanani spoke God's message to him:

Then Asa was wroth with the seer, and put him in a prison house; for he was in a rage with him because of this thing. And Asa oppressed some of the people the same time.

2 Chronicles 16:10

D. Asa became angry with the Lord's messenger and rejected both him and God's message.

E. You may not like some of what I'm about to share with you, but be open to let the Lord touch your heart.

F. God's eyes are searching for those whose hearts are totally His; He's looking for people who will humble themselves before Him.

G. He wants to bless you more than you want to be blessed.

H. You need the same attitude that Gideon had, where you are sick and tired of being sick and tired and won't settle for anything less than God's best.

I. There are reasons why the blessing of God isn't manifesting in your life more than it is, and it's never God's fault.

J. The reality is, you're to blame.

K. Don't make the same mistake King Asa did and get mad at the messenger.

L. Humble yourself before God's mighty hand and receive His message for you today.

VI. If some of the things I'm about to address are in your life, God still loves you.

A. Your ability to receive His best for your life is impacted by these things being present in your life.

B. There truly is a difference between God's way and the world's way of doing things.

C. King Asa obtained his goal, but he didn't do it God's way.

D. Because of that, 2 Chronicles 16:9 says that from then on, he was plagued by wars.

E. Under the New Covenant, even though God may not be the one punishing us, what He can do in our lives will be hindered if we don't do things His way.

F. God resists the proud but gives grace to the humble.

G. Grace flows to those who submit themselves to and depend on Him.

Teacher's Guide

1.   During the time of Gideon, the Israelites were being oppressed by the Midianites, when an angel appeared to Gideon and declared, "The Lord is with you, you mighty man of valor!" Gideon responded, "If I am a mighty man of valor, where are all of God's mighty works that our fathers told us about?" Some people interpret this as Gideon criticizing the angel. Gideon was sick and tired of living a substandard life. One of the first steps to seeing the supernatural power of God operate in our lives is getting to the place where we, from our hearts, declare, "I refuse to live this way any longer!"

1a.   Why did Gideon respond the way he did to the angel?
   Because he was sick and tired of living a substandard life
1b.   What is one of the first steps to seeing the supernatural power of God operate in your life?
   Getting to the place where you, from your heart, declare, "I refuse to live this way any longer!"

2.   Either we've advanced today and gotten closer to what the Lord has for us in life, or we've just spent another day wasting time. If we don't love what we're doing, then why are we doing it? It's because we've accepted it. We're just marching in step and keeping time, not really doing anything significant. God made us special, and our lives should count. We ought to be excited about our lives and about knowing that we're fulfilling God's call and our destinies. To a degree, this is preaching to the choir: We desire something more; we're reading and considering all of this—what God is saying—through this study guide.

2a.   Either you've _____ today and gotten _____ to what the Lord has for you in life, or you've just spent another day _____ time.
   Advanced / closer / wasting
2b.   *Discussion question:* How much can you love what you're doing if you're not living in God's best?
   Discussion question

3.   According to 2 Chronicles 16:9, the Lord is looking for someone who is humble and submitted to Him. Humility is submitting ourselves to God; it's yielding to Him and resisting the devil:

>   *But he giveth more grace. Wherefore he saith, God resisteth the proud, but giveth grace unto the humble. [7] Submit yourselves therefore to*

> *God. Resist the devil, and he will flee from you.*
>
> James 4:6-7

Sadly, many of us as Christians are actually cooperating with the devil, and our cooperation isn't even intentional. Humility is being God-dependent instead of self-dependent. When we're trying to live life by our own human strength and effort, we aren't humble, and we aren't submitted to God.

3a. True or false: According to 2 Chronicles 16:9, the Lord is looking for someone who is proud and resistant to Him.
    False

3b. Humility is being what (James 4:6-7)?
    A.   Weak instead of strong
    B.   Sick instead of healed
    C.   Poor instead of rich
    D.   God-dependent instead of self-dependent
    E.   Self-dependent instead of God-dependent
    D.   God-dependent instead of self-dependent

3c. When you're trying to live life by your own human strength and effort, you aren't _____, and you aren't _____ to God.
    Humble / submitted

4.   Instead of trusting and following God by going out to fight Israel, King Asa took the treasures from the temple and sent them to the king of Syria to hire him to fight against Judah's enemies. According to 2 Chronicles 16:7-8, the Lord basically said to Asa, "I had planned on giving the Israelites into your hand, and you would have conquered the Syrians too. But now you've gone and made a treaty with the Syrians. Not only have the Israelites escaped out of your hand, but the Syrians have too." God's plan for King Asa and Judah was thwarted. What we have to understand is that it's not a matter of just obtaining the right result—have we trusted God? We have to ask ourselves, have we done all of this through the flesh, in the natural way? In God's eyes, the journey is more important than the destination.

was God's plan for King Asa and Judah thwarted?
**ause instead of trusting God, King Asa took the treasures from the temple and
t them to the king of Syria to hire him to fight against Judah's enemies**
ue or false: What really matters is obtaining the right result.
alse
In God's eyes, the _____ is more important than the _____.
Journey / destination

5.   Without knowing it, we have probably compromised. We've chosen the world's way of trying to deal with our lives and problems. By doing so, we've limited what God can do in and through us. Let's look at King Asa's response after the prophet Hanani spoke God's message to him:

> *Then Asa was wroth with the seer, and put him in a prison house; for he was in a rage with him because of this thing. And Asa oppressed some of the people the same time.*
>
> 2 Chronicles 16:10

Asa became angry with the Lord's messenger and rejected both him and God's message. We may not like some of what Andrew is about to share with us, but we need to be open to let the Lord touch our hearts. God's eyes are searching for those of us whose hearts are totally His. He's looking for people who will humble themselves before Him. He wants to bless us more than we want to be blessed. But we need the same attitude that Gideon had where we are sick and tired of being sick and tired and won't settle for anything less than God's best. There are reasons why the blessing of God isn't manifesting in our lives more than it is, and it's never God's fault. The reality is, we're to blame. So, we shouldn't make the same mistake King Asa did and get mad at the messenger. We need to humble ourselves before God's mighty hand and receive His message for us today.

5a. True or false: If you've compromised, you've limited what God can do in your life.
     True
5b. God's eyes are searching for those whose _____ are totally His.
     A.   Stomachs
     B.   Hearts
     C.   Riches
     D.   Sundays
     E.   Minds
     B.   Hearts

6.   If some of the things Andrew is about to address are in our lives, God still loves us. But our ability to receive His best for our lives is impacted by these things being present in our lives. There truly is a difference between God's way and the world's way of doing things. King Asa obtained his goal, but he didn't do it God's way. Because of that, 2 Chronicles 16:9 says that from then on, he was plagued by wars. Under the New Covenant, even though God may not be the one punishing us, what He can do in our lives will be hindered if we don't do things His way. God resists the proud but gives grace to the humble. Grace flows to those who submit themselves to and depend on Him.

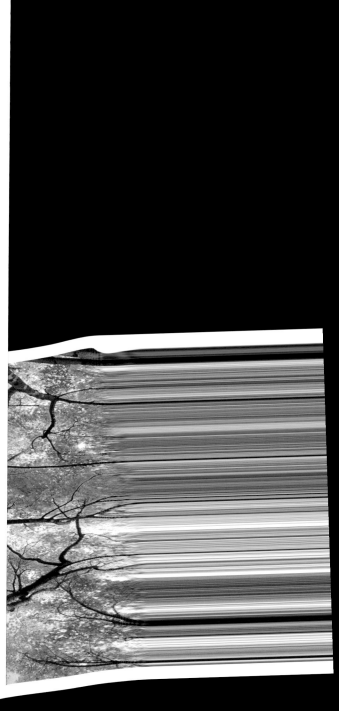

6a. *Discussion question:* What kinds of things in your life are impacting your ability to receive God's best?

Discussion question

6b. There truly is a difference between _____ way and the world's way of doing things.

God's

6c. To whom does God's grace flow?

To those who submit themselves to and depend on Him

God's way is perfect. All the LORD's promises prove true. He is a shield for all who ...

Discipleship Questions

1. Why did Gideon respond the way he did to the angel?

    _____

    _____

    _____

2. What is one of the first steps to seeing the supernatural power of God operate in your life?

    _____

    _____

    _____

3. Either you've _____ today and gotten _____ to what the Lord has for you in life, or you've just spent another day _____ time.

4. *Discussion question:* How much can you love what you're doing if you're not living in God's best?

    _____

    _____

    _____

5. True or false: According to 2 Chronicles 16:9, the Lord is looking for someone who is proud and resistant to Him.

6. Humility is being what (James 4:6-7)?
    A. Weak instead of strong
    B. Sick instead of healed
    C. Poor instead of rich
    D. God-dependent instead of self-dependent
    E. Self-dependent instead of God-dependent

7. When you're trying to live life by your own human strength and effort, you aren't _____, and you aren't _____ to God.

8. Why was God's plan for King Asa and Judah thwarted?

_____

_____

_____

9. True or false: What really matters is obtaining the right result.

10. In God's eyes, the _____ is more important than the _____.

11. True or false: If you've compromised, you've limited what God can do in your life.

12. God's eyes are searching for those whose _____ are totally His.
    A. Stomachs
    B. Hearts
    C. Riches
    D. Sundays
    E. Minds

13. *Discussion question:* What kinds of things in your life are impacting your ability to receive God's best?

_____

_____

_____

14. There truly is a difference between _____ way and the world's way of doing things.

15. To whom does God's grace flow?

_____

_____

_____

Answer Key

1. Because he was sick and tired of living a substandard life

2. Getting to the place where you, from your heart, declare, "I refuse to live this way any longer!"

3. Advanced / closer / wasting

4. *Discussion question*

5. False

6. D.   God-dependent instead of self-dependent

7. Humble / submitted

8. Because instead of trusting God, King Asa took the treasures from the temple and sent them to the king of Syria to hire him to fight against Judah's enemies

9. False

10. Journey / destination

11. True

12. B.   Hearts

13. *Discussion question*

14. God's

15. To those who submit themselves to and depend on Him

Scriptures

JUDGES 6:11-14

And there came an angel of the LORD, and sat under an oak which was in Ophrah, that pertained unto Joash the Abiezrite: and his son Gideon threshed wheat by the winepress, to hide it from the Midianites. [12] And the angel of the LORD appeared unto him, and said unto him, The LORD is with thee, thou mighty man of valour. [13] And Gideon said unto him, Oh my Lord, if the LORD be with us, why then is all this befallen us? and where be all his miracles which our fathers told us of, saying, Did not the LORD bring us up from Egypt? but now the LORD hath forsaken us, and delivered us into the hands of the Midianites. [14] And the LORD looked upon him, and said, Go in this thy might, and thou shalt save Israel from the hand of the Midianites: have not I sent thee?

JAMES 4:6-7

But he giveth more grace. Wherefore he saith, God resisteth the proud, but giveth grace unto the humble. [7] Submit yourselves therefore to God. Resist the devil, and he will flee from you.

2 CHRONICLES 16:1-10

In the six and thirtieth year of the reign of Asa Baasha king of Israel came up against Judah, and built Ramah, to the intent that he might let none go out or come in to Asa king of Judah. [2] Then Asa brought out silver and gold out of the treasures of the house of the LORD and of the king's house, and sent to Benhadad king of Syria, that dwelt at Damascus, saying, [3] There is a league between me and thee, as there was between my father and thy father: behold, I have sent thee silver and gold; go, break thy league with Baasha king of Israel, that he may depart from me. [4] And Benhadad hearkened unto king Asa, and sent the captains of his armies against the cities of Israel; and they smote Ijon, and Dan, and Abelmaim, and all the store cities of Naphtali. [5] And it came to pass, when Baasha heard it, that he left off building of Ramah, and let his work cease. [6] Then Asa the king took all Judah; and they carried away the stones of Ramah, and the timber thereof, wherewith Baasha was building; and he built therewith Geba and Mizpah. [7] And at that time Hanani the seer came to Asa king of Judah, and said unto him, Because thou hast relied on the king of Syria, and not relied on the LORD thy God, therefore is the host of the king of Syria escaped out of thine hand. [8] Were not the Ethiopians and the Lubims a huge host, with very many chariots and horsemen? yet, because thou didst rely on the LORD, he delivered them into thine hand. [9] For the eyes of the LORD run to and fro throughout the whole earth, to shew himself strong in the behalf of them whose heart is perfect toward him. Herein thou hast done foolishly: therefore from henceforth thou shalt have wars. [10] Then Asa was wroth with the seer, and put him in a prison house; for he was in a rage with him because of this thing. And Asa oppressed some of the people the same time.

2 CHRONICLES 14:2-15

And Asa did that which was good and right in the eyes of the Lord his God: [3] For he took away the altars of the strange gods, and the high places, and brake down the images, and cut down the groves: [4] And commanded Judah to seek the Lord God of their fathers, and to do the law and the commandment. [5] Also he took away out of all the cities of Judah the high places and the images: and the kingdom was quiet before him. [6] And he built fenced cities in Judah: for the land had rest, and he had no war in those years; because the Lord had given him rest. [7] Therefore he said unto Judah, Let us build these cities, and make about them walls, and towers, gates, and bars, while the land is yet before us; because we have sought the Lord our God, we have sought him, and he hath given us rest on every side. So they built and prospered. [8] And Asa had an army of men that bare targets and spears, out of Judah three hundred thousand; and out of Benjamin, that bare shields and drew bows, two hundred and fourscore thousand: all these were mighty men of valour. [9] And there came out against them Zerah the Ethiopian with an host of a thousand thousand, and three hundred chariots; and came unto Mareshah. [10] Then Asa went out against him, and they set the battle in array in the valley of Zephathah at Mareshah. [11] And Asa cried unto the Lord his God, and said, Lord, it is nothing with thee to help, whether with many, or with them that have no power: help us, O Lord our God; for we rest on thee, and in thy name we go against this multitude. O Lord, thou art our God; let not man prevail against thee. [12] So the Lord smote the Ethiopians before Asa, and before Judah; and the Ethiopians fled. [13] And Asa and the people that were with him pursued them unto Gerar: and the Ethiopians were overthrown, that they could not recover themselves; for they were destroyed before the Lord, and before his host; and they carried away very much spoil. [14] And they smote all the cities round about Gerar; for the fear of the Lord came upon them: and they spoiled all the cities; for there was exceeding much spoil in them. [15] They smote also the tents of cattle, and carried away sheep and camels in abundance, and returned to Jerusalem.

Resist Debt

LESSON 2

The LORD shall open unto thee his good treasure, the heaven to give the rain unto thy land in his season, and to bless all the work of thine hand: and thou shalt lend unto many nations, and thou shalt not borrow.
Deuteronomy 28:12

Did you know that lending and not borrowing is God's best? The average American has no qualms about going into debt, yet we wonder why we aren't blessed. If you pay for a house on credit, you're going to pay for that thing at least twice—perhaps three times. Suppose you buy a house for $500,000. By the time you get through paying all the interest on a multi-year mortgage, you're going to pay $1.5 million for it. Have I made you uncomfortable yet? If you're in debt, that doesn't mean that God's mad at you. I'm not saying that you're sinning. But the average American doesn't see being debt free as a good thing. They think debt is just fine, and that attitude limits God. That attitude stops God's best from manifesting in our lives because instead of doing things His way concerning lending and not borrowing, we just go into debt.

Many people have credit cards that have been run up to the max. If they got their credit cards paid off, they would just turn around and use them again to expand their lifestyle and buy something else. If they won the lottery, all they would do is get more, buy more, and then eventually end up in the same position they're in now—or worse. They live right up to the limit. If they live in a million-dollar house now and then won the lottery, they would go out and buy themselves a ten-million-dollar house, a yacht, and much more. Statistics show that over time, lottery winners wind up in just the same position as before. They aren't shooting for God's best!

Again, if that's you, there's no condemnation. God loves you, and I do too, which is why I'm telling you the truth (Gal. 4:16). The present American system has made everything available through debt, and as long as you can tolerate living in debt, you'll never get out of it. If you're in this position, don't feel bad about it or get discouraged over it. Instead, recognize the situation for what it is, humble yourself, and trust God to lead you forward toward His best.

A MINDSET

Now, most businesspeople will tell you that there's a difference between good debt and bad debt. They will say that it's not wrong to go into debt when obtaining appreciating items like a home, an investment, or some other income-producing item. However, Romans 13:8 says, *"Owe no man any thing, but to love one another: for he that loveth another hath fulfilled the law."*

Personally, I believe when the Word says *"owe no man any thing,"* this clearly expresses God's best, but I won't argue this with someone who believes that it's okay to go into debt for something that will appreciate in value. The main point I'm making here is that most of the things we spend our money on and go into debt for are depreciating items—things that lose value over time. For instance, when someone buys a new car for $40,000, within five or ten minutes of driving it off the lot, it's only worth $30,000. It's a depreciating item. It's never going to appreciate. Most of the things that we buy are depreciating items. We just go into debt for them and wonder why we aren't experiencing God's best.

You will never prosper with a debt mindset. You must get out of this destructive, limiting mindset. God is looking at your heart as you read this right now. He's asking, "How will you respond?" Are you going to just keep running after the so-called "American dream" where you get all you can, can all you get, and then sit on your can? There's something better than that—God's best. But God's best isn't even a goal for most people.

My wife, Jamie, and I bought a house and went into debt. We used my VA loan and purchased our home. God didn't hate us, and we loved God. We got that loan and— long story short—paid it off in fifteen years. We became debt free over a decade ago. It's been a long time now.

MORTGAGING YOUR FUTURE!

Jamie and I buy all of our cars with cash. If you were to buy a less expensive, good-quality car instead of a fancy one, you could take what you would have spent on car payments and put it in the bank. Within four years, you could go buy another car debt free and not waste all that money on interest. If you'd be willing to drive something less than the newest and best, you could start paying cash for your vehicles. Then you wouldn't be paying for a car two or three times over.

I see these television commercials offering payments for up to five or even six years. Most cars don't last that long. You're tired of them by the time the new car smell wears off or you've damaged them in an accident. I bet you don't usually keep a car five or six years. Even if you do, you end up upside down on it because the worth has depreciated to less than what you still owe on it. Yet you roll that over into your next vehicle's payment and then wonder why God's best isn't working in your finances. It's because you aren't desiring His best. You're settling for immediate gratification. You may be satisfied temporarily, but you're mortgaging your future!

That's what's happening on a national level here in America. We're digging ourselves into a huge hole. We've run up our national debt so high, it's doubtful that we or our children will ever be able to pay it off. It's unrealistic to think that we can keep doing this year after year and that other countries will just continue lending to us and being our friends. Sooner or later, somebody's going to pull the plug on this. Somebody's going to call their payments due, and things are going to crash. Neither governments nor individuals can perpetually live this way; sooner or later debt catches up with us. Everyone who holds a debt mindset is part of the problem. It's wrong, and we aren't seeking God's best!

Most people think credit is just awesome. Instead of having to wait for years to get a decent car, you can have it right now! What the lenders don't tell you is that you're going to pay two or three times what it's worth with all the interest you'll pay. You'll be upside down and in such a mess that you might have to work two or three jobs to pay for it. It used to be that women could stay home and raise their families. Now both spouses have to work because we're living in houses, driving cars, and purchasing things on credit that are more than we can afford. So, we farm our kids out to somebody else and wonder why we're having problems.

I'm not saying that you're of the devil if this is where you are right now. We've had some debt in our ministry. A while back we took out a $3.2 million loan to buy a building in Colorado Springs. On top of that, this building needed another $3.2 million in renovations before we could really use it. I was trying to take out a construction loan for it, but it just kept getting delayed. The bank kept telling me, "Next week you'll have the money…. Next week you'll have the money…." Nine long months later, we sat down with the banker and he said, "It's been so long, let's just get a new appraisal. Let's start the whole process over again." All I could imagine was another nine months of hearing, "Next week…"

"TOO LATE"

I told the banker, "No, I'm going to pray about this." I should have prayed about it in the first place, but I didn't. So, I took some time and prayed in tongues about this earnestly. The Bible says that when we pray in tongues, our spirits pray (1 Cor. 14:14). It also says that we can pray for an interpretation, so I did, and God reminded me of a prophecy that I had received previously. This prophetic word had been about our expansion, saying, "You aren't going to have to take out a loan for your expansion, because you have a bank." At the time the word was spoken, I thought, *What bank do I have?* The brother prophesying continued, saying, "Your partners are your bank. You're going to do this debt free." The Lord reminded me of this specific prophecy when I prayed in tongues over the delayed loan situation. So, I decided—no more debt!

At the rate our ministry was receiving money at that time, added to the amount we had saved, I figured it would have taken us over a hundred years to come up with that $3.2 million. But our Bible school was totally out of space, so our need was immediate. The ministry was bulging at the seams. We were facing imminent disaster if we didn't get this new building purchased and renovated. However, I felt like God was speaking to me, so I made a decision to receive God's best. I declared, "Even if they offer me all the money I want tomorrow, I'm not going to take it." Guess what? The very next day the banker came to me and said, "You don't need $3.2 million— we think that you need $4 million. We are now approved to loan you $4 million." I answered "Too late," and turned down the loan. We committed ourselves to do that project debt free. Over just fourteen months, that $3.2 million came in, and we finished renovating that building debt free. Glory to Jesus!

Then the Lord spoke to me about moving up to Woodland Park, Colorado, and building a Bible college campus to accommodate as many people as possible so we could provide life-changing training to reach the world. So, we've been building this new facility in Woodland Park called *The Sanctuary*. We're already seeing entire nations changed! The first phase cost $32 million and included the acquisition of the property, infrastructure, architect fees, and construction of the first new building—a 72,000-square-foot facility called *The Barn*. All this has been done debt free. Hallelujah!

At the time of this writing, the construction of our second building is well underway. We also have plans for a much-needed parking garage. It will provide parking for up to 1,085 cars. This second facility, *The Auditorium*, is over twice as big as *The Barn*. At this time, we're $27 million into this project. We are about halfway there, and plan to finish it debt free.

Andrew Wommack Ministries has over 400 employees at both our Colorado Springs and Woodland Park offices. *The Sanctuary* property, located just outside of town, is 157 acres and has a beautiful, unobstructed view of Pikes Peak. In 2016, the assets of the ministry in these two locations were valued well over $50 million. Yes, we could go out and borrow money, but I'm shooting for God's best!

IT'S SUPERNATURAL!

One reason people don't receive God's best is because they can live without it. Most folks can live in debt. They've adjusted to it, and it's not a big deal to them anymore.

Recently I was talking with the mayor of Woodland Park. He commented, "Look at all this. Look what you have done. You must have had a lot of money!"

I responded, "Actually, Mayor, I have nothing. I don't have any money at this time, but it's all coming in. You just hide and watch; it'll all be there when we need it." He was shocked that we would be doing this huge construction project without having millions of dollars in the bank. I don't currently have it in the bank, but it'll be there. I'm trusting God. I believe that the eyes of the Lord are running to and fro throughout the whole earth, and He's saying, "There's Andrew. He's trusting Me. I'll show Myself strong in his behalf" (2 Chr. 16:9). As a result, I've already spent over $60 million on these buildings without incurring a single dollar of debt. And we've done all this in addition to raising the $1 million that we need every month just to pay our television and radio bill. Right now we can be seen and/or heard by a potential 3.2 billion people all around the world. It costs a lot of money to do that! Our payroll is also over $1 million per month. Our office recently received around 3,000 calls in one day—and that was just at our USA location! We now have fifteen AWM offices and over 120 more employees around the world. All this, and we still give many of our teaching materials away. Just try to figure it out. It's supernatural!

One reason you aren't receiving God's best is because you're not truly desiring it. You want the results—to be debt free—but you aren't willing to trust God. It's too much effort to depend on Him and much easier to just go get a loan. I'm not trying to hurt you. I just want to elevate your thinking and set your sights on something better. As long as you can live in debt up to your eyeballs, you will. As long as paying for everything you have two or three times over is "normal" to you, you aren't going to see God's best. Think about it—what could you do with all of the interest you've paid out?

A RIGHT AND WRONG WAY

My wife and I have been debt free for more than ten years. It doesn't take much money to live when you're not making payments for everything. What kind of pressure would you be relieved from, how much stress would leave your life if you had no debt? You'd be in an awesome position if you weren't paying any interest. You would be shocked how simply and freely you could live.

We say we want God's best, but if we do, why is it that we keep on doing things that are contrary to the instructions He gave us? If we truly desire to receive God's best, we're going to have to submit ourselves to the Lord and resist debt. There are other applications of this truth, but this is an important one. We must learn to resist the easy way of buying things.

Loan marketing is the classic bait-and-switch. The television commercials say, "Buy this and you can save money!" (If you weren't in debt, you could save much more than what they're promising.) They're asking you to go further into debt while they make tons of money off you in interest. Somehow, they convince you that going into debt equals you "saving" money. You aren't saving a thing. They're bleeding you dry!

You may live in a really nice house and drive a fancy car. You may have a lot of nice things—much more than I do. But have you acquired all this God's way? Can you sleep at night? Or do you live under the crush of constant financial pressure? It's not just about "can I get this?" There's a right and wrong way to prosper.

Asa won the battle, but he was rebuked because he didn't do it God's way. The Lord had something better. If Asa had obeyed, he could have defeated not only the king of Israel but also the king of Syria. He would have won—gaining a whole lot of spoil, instead of losing all of his assets and peace (2 Chr. 16:1-10).

Let's humble ourselves and resist debt. Let's depend on God and receive His best!

Outline

I.   Did you know that lending and not borrowing is God's best?

> *The LORD shall open unto thee his good treasure, the heaven to give the
> rain unto thy land in his season, and to bless all the work of thine hand:
> and thou shalt lend unto many nations, and thou shalt not borrow.*
>
> Deuteronomy 28:12

A. If you pay for a house on credit, you're going to pay for that thing at least twice—perhaps three times.

B. Instead of doing things God's way concerning lending and not borrowing, the average American just goes into debt.

C. If that's you, there's no condemnation.

D. As long as you can tolerate living in debt, you'll never get out of it.

E. If you're in this position, don't feel bad about it or get discouraged over it.

F. Instead, recognize the situation for what it is, humble yourself, and trust God to lead you forward toward His best.

II. Most businesspeople will say it's not wrong to go into debt when obtaining appreciating items like a home, an investment, or some other income-producing item.

A. However, Romans 13:8 says, *"Owe no man any thing, but to love one another: for he that loveth another hath fulfilled the law."*

B. This clearly expresses God's best, but it is hard to argue with someone who believes that it's okay to go into debt for something that will appreciate in value.

C. The main point is that most of the things we spend our money on and go into debt for are depreciating items, and we wonder why we aren't experiencing God's best.

E. We will never prosper with a debt mindset.

F. God is looking at our hearts right now, asking, "How will you respond?"

G. Are we going to just keep running after the so-called "American dream" where we get all we can, can all we get, and then sit on our can?

H. There's something better—God's best—but that isn't even a goal for most people.

III. What's happening on a national level here in America is people are digging themselves into a huge hole.

A. Neither governments nor individuals can perpetually live this way; sooner or later, debt catches up with them.

B. Everyone who holds a debt mindset is part of the problem.

C. Many people think credit is a good thing.

D. What the lenders don't tell them is that they're going to pay two or three times what their purchase is worth once they pay all the interest.

E. They'll be upside down and in such a mess that they might have to work two or three jobs to pay their bills.

F. It used to be that women could stay home and raise their families.

G. Now both spouses have to work because they're living in houses, driving cars, and purchasing things on credit that are more than they can afford.

H. Parents farm their kids out to somebody else and wonder why they're having problems.

I. This is not to say that you're of the devil if this is where you are right now.

IV. One reason people don't receive God's best is because they can live without it.

A. They've adjusted to debt, and it's not a big deal to them anymore.

B. One reason you aren't receiving God's best is because you're not truly desiring it.

C. You want the results, but you aren't willing to trust God.

D. It's too much effort to depend on Him and much easier to just go get a loan.

E. This is not meant to hurt you but to elevate your thinking and set your sights on something better.

F. As long as paying for everything you have two or three times over is "normal" to you, you aren't going to see God's best.

G. Think about it—what could you do with all of the interest you've paid out?

V. It doesn't take much money to live when you're not making payments for everything.

    A. What kind of pressure would you be relieved from, how much stress would leave your life if you had no debt?

    B. You'd be in an awesome position if you weren't paying any interest.

    C. You would be shocked how simply and freely you could live.

    D. If you truly desire to receive God's best, you're going to have to submit yourself to the Lord and resist debt.

    E. There are other applications of this truth, but this is an important one.

    F. We must learn to resist the easy way of buying things.

VI. You may live in a really nice house and drive a fancy car, but have you acquired all of this God's way?

    A. Or do you live under the crush of constant financial pressure?

    B. There's a right and wrong way to prosper.

    C. Asa won the battle, but he was rebuked because he didn't do it God's way.

    D. If Asa had obeyed, he could have defeated not only the king of Israel but also the king of Syria.

    E. He would have won—gaining a whole lot of spoil, instead of losing all of his assets and peace (2 Chr. 16:1-10).

    F. Humble yourself and resist debt.

    G. Depend on God and receive His best!

Teacher's Guide

1. Did you know that lending and not borrowing is God's best?

    The LORD shall open unto thee his good treasure, the heaven to give the rain unto thy land in his season, and to bless all the work of thine hand: and thou shalt lend unto many nations, and thou shalt not borrow.
    Deuteronomy 28:12

    If we pay for a house on credit, we're going to pay for that thing at least twice—perhaps three times. Instead of doing things God's way concerning lending and not borrowing, the average American just goes into debt. If that's us, there's no condemnation. As long as we can tolerate living in debt, we'll never get out of it. If we're in this position, we shouldn't feel bad about it or get discouraged over it. Instead, we should recognize the situation for what it is, humble ourselves, and trust God to lead us forward toward His best.

1a. True or false: Deuteronomy 28:12 reads that borrowing and not lending is God's best.
    False
1b. If you've gone into debt, there's _____.
    A. A price to pay
    B. Refinancing available
    C. No condemnation
    D. A law against that
    E. Judgment coming
    C. No condemnation
1c. True or false: If you tolerate debt, eventually you'll get out of it.
    False
1d. What should you do if you're in debt?
    Recognize the situation for what it is, humble yourself, and trust God to lead you forward toward His best

2. Most businesspeople will say it's not wrong to go into debt when obtaining appreciating items like a home, an investment, or some other income-producing item. However, Romans 13:8 says, "*Owe no man any thing, but to love one another: for he that loveth another hath fulfilled the law.*" This clearly expresses God's best, but it is hard to argue with someone who believes that it's okay to go into debt for something that will appreciate in value. The main point is that most of the things we spend our money on and go into debt for are depreciating items, and we wonder why we aren't experiencing God's best. We will never prosper with a debt mindset. God is looking at our hearts right now, asking, "How will you respond?" Are we going to just keep

running after the so-called "American dream" where we get all we can, can all we get, and then sit on our can? There's something better—God's best—but that isn't even a goal for most people.

2a. According to Romans 13:8, what is God's best concerning debt?
    A. To owe anyone something because of love
    B. To owe someone anything except love
    C. To love someone anywhere, as long as it's real
    D. To find anyone you love and owe them something
    E. To owe no one anything except love
    E. To owe no one anything except love
2b. True or false: You shouldn't go into debt for a depreciating item.
    True
2c. You will _____ prosper with a debt mindset.
    Never
2d. *Discussion question:* How are you going to begin running after God's best?
    Discussion question

3. What's happening on a national level here in America is people are digging themselves into a huge hole. Neither governments nor individuals can perpetually live this way; sooner or later debt catches up with them. Everyone who holds a debt mindset is part of the problem. Many people think credit is a good thing. What the lenders don't tell them is that they're going to pay two or three times what their purchase is worth once they pay all the interest. They'll be upside down and in such a mess that they might have to work two or three jobs to pay their bills. It used to be that women could stay home and raise their families. Now both spouses have to work because they're living in houses, driving cars, and purchasing things on credit that are more than they can afford. Parents farm their kids out to somebody else and wonder why they're having problems. This is not to say that we're of the devil if this is where we are right now.

3a. *Discussion question:* Why is debt appealing, and why is it dangerous?
    Discussion question

4. One reason people don't receive God's best is because they can live without it. They've adjusted to debt, and it's not a big deal to them anymore. One reason we aren't receiving God's best is because we're not truly desiring it. We want the results, but we aren't willing to trust God. It's too much effort to depend on Him and much easier to just go get a loan. This is not meant to hurt us but to elevate our thinking and set our sights on something better. As long as paying for everything we have two or three times over is "normal" to us, we aren't going to see God's best. Let's think about it—what could we do with all of the interest we've paid out?

4a. One reason people don't receive God's best is because they can _____ without it.
    Live

4b. Why is living in debt not a big deal to some people?
    Because they've adjusted to it

4c. In order to receive God's best, what is one thing you have to do?
    A. Desire it
    B. Sample it
    C. Buy it
    D. All of the above
    E. None of the above
    A. Desire it

4d. *Discussion question:* What's wrong with getting a loan so you can have what you want right now?
    Discussion question

4e. Paying for everything you have two or three times over should not be what?
    A. Discouraged
    B. Normal
    C. Foolish
    D. Pardoned
    E. Grievous
    B. Normal

5. It doesn't take much money to live when we're not making payments for everything. What kind of pressure would we be relieved from, how much stress would leave our lives if we had no debt? We'd be in an awesome position if we weren't paying any interest. We would be shocked how simply and freely we could live. If we truly desire to receive God's best, we're going to have to submit ourselves to the Lord and resist debt. There are other applications of this truth, but this is an important one. We must learn to resist the easy way of buying things.

5a. *Discussion question:* What would your life be like without any debt?
    Discussion question

5b. If you truly desire to receive God's best, you're going to have to _____ yourself to the Lord and _____ debt.
    Submit / resist

6. We may live in a really nice house and drive a fancy car, but have we acquired all of this God's way? Or do we live under the crush of constant financial pressure? There's a right and wrong way to prosper. Asa won the battle, but he was rebuked because he didn't do it God's way. If Asa had obeyed, he could have defeated not only

the king of Israel but also the king of Syria. He would have won—gaining a whole lot of spoil, instead of losing all of his assets and peace (2 Chr. 16:1-10). Let's humble ourselves and resist debt. Let's depend on God and receive His best!

6a. True or false: There is a right way and a wrong way to prosper.
True

6b. If Asa had done things God's way, he would have what?
A. Had victory in battle
B. Gained a lot of spoil
C. Kept his assets and peace
D. All of the above
E. None of the above
D. All of the above

6c. _____ yourself and resist debt.
Humble

6d. _____ on God and receive His best!
Depend

Discipleship Questions

1. True or false: Deuteronomy 28:12 reads that borrowing and not lending is God's best.

2. If you've gone into debt, there's _____.
    A. A price to pay
    B. Refinancing available
    C. No condemnation
    D. A law against that
    E. Judgment coming

3. True or false: If you tolerate debt, eventually you'll get out of it.

4. What should you do if you're in debt?

    _____

    _____

    _____

5. According to Romans 13:8, what is God's best concerning debt?
    A. To owe anyone something because of love
    B. To owe someone anything except love
    C. To love someone anywhere, as long as it's real
    D. To find anyone you love and owe them something
    E. To owe no one anything except love

6. True or false: You shouldn't go into debt for a depreciating item.

7. You will _____ prosper with a debt mindset.

8. *Discussion question:* How are you going to begin running after God's best?

    _____

    _____

    _____

9. *Discussion question:* Why is debt appealing, and why is it dangerous?

_____

_____

_____

10. One reason people don't receive God's best is because they can _____ without it.

11. Why is living in debt not a big deal to some people?

_____

_____

_____

12. In order to receive God's best, what is one thing you have to do?
    A. Desire it
    B. Sample it
    C. Buy it
    D. All of the above
    E. None of the above

13. *Discussion question:* What's wrong with getting a loan so you can have what you want right now?

_____

_____

_____

14. Paying for everything you have two or three times over should not be what?
    A. Discouraged
    B. Normal
    C. Foolish
    D. Pardoned
    E. Grievous

15. *Discussion question:* What would your life be like without any debt?

   _____

   _____

   _____

16. If you truly desire to receive God's best, you're going to have to _____ yourself to the Lord and _____ debt.

17. True or false: There is a right way and a wrong way to prosper.

18. If Asa had done things God's way, he would have what?
    A. Had victory in battle
    B. Gained a lot of spoil
    C. Kept his assets and peace
    D. All of the above
    E. None of the above

19. _____ yourself and resist debt.

20. _____ on God and receive His best!

Answer Key

1. False

2. C.   No condemnation

3. False

4. Recognize the situation for what it is, humble yourself, and trust God to lead you forward toward His best

5. E.   To owe no one anything except love

6. True

7. Never

8. *Discussion question*

9. *Discussion question*

10. Live

11. Because they've adjusted to it

12. A.   Desire it

13. *Discussion question*

14. B.   Normal

15. *Discussion question*

16. Submit / resist

17. True

18. D.   All of the above

19. Humble

20. Depend

Scripture

DEUTERONOMY 28:12

The LORD shall open unto thee his good treasure, the heaven to give the rain unto thy land in his season, and to bless all the work of thine hand: and thou shalt lend unto many nations, and thou shalt not borrow.

GALATIANS 4:16

Am I therefore become your enemy, because I tell you the truth?

ROMANS 13:8

Owe no man any thing, but to love one another: for he that loveth another hath fulfilled the law.

1 CORINTHIANS 14:14

For if I pray in an unknown tongue, my spirit prayeth, but my understanding is unfruitful.

2 CHRONICLES 16:1-10

In the six and thirtieth year of the reign of Asa Baasha king of Israel came up against Judah, and built Ramah, to the intent that he might let none go out or come in to Asa king of Judah. [2] Then Asa brought out silver and gold out of the treasures of the house of the LORD and of the king's house, and sent to Benhadad king of Syria, that dwelt at Damascus, saying, [3] There is a league between me and thee, as there was between my father and thy father: behold, I have sent thee silver and gold; go, break thy league with Baasha king of Israel, that he may depart from me. [4] And Benhadad hearkened unto king Asa, and sent the captains of his armies against the cities of Israel; and they smote Ijon, and Dan, and Abelmaim, and all the store cities of Naphtali. [5] And it came to pass, when Baasha heard it, that he left off building of Ramah, and let his work cease. [6] Then Asa the king took all Judah; and they carried away the stones of Ramah, and the timber thereof, wherewith Baasha was building; and he built therewith Geba and Mizpah. [7] And at that time Hanani the seer came to Asa king of Judah, and said unto him, Because thou hast relied on the king of Syria, and not relied on the LORD thy God, therefore is the host of the king of Syria escaped out of thine hand. [8] Were not the Ethiopians and the Lubims a huge host, with very many chariots and horsemen? yet, because thou didst rely on the LORD, he delivered them into thine hand. [9] For the eyes of the LORD run to and fro throughout the whole earth, to shew himself strong in the behalf of them whose heart is perfect toward him. Herein thou hast done foolishly: therefore from henceforth thou shalt have wars. [10]

Then Asa was wroth with the seer, and put him in a prison house; for he was in a rage with him because of this thing. And Asa oppressed some of the people the same time.

Supernatural Health

LESSON 3

And, behold, the acts of Asa, first and last, lo, they are written in the book of the kings of Judah and Israel. [12] And Asa in the thirty and ninth year of his reign was diseased in his feet, until his disease was exceeding great: yet in his disease he sought not to the LORD, but to the physicians.

2 Chronicles 16:11-12

For Asa, seeking the physicians was not the same as seeking the Lord. Many of us today do the same. Culturally, we've developed this mindset that the very first thing we should do when facing sickness is go to the physicians, depend on medicine, and submit to surgery. Seeking God is our last thought—if we even think of it at all. Many people think that God and physicians are equal. They aren't.

Am I against physicians? No, I'm not. Neither am I against bankers. I'm just saying that we ought to rely on them only if we've prayed and the Lord has led us that way. However, most people's default is to always, always go through all of man's ways and resources first and turn to God *only* when the situation gets beyond human ability.

Asa did not seek the Lord and rely on His divine strength and ability. He sought physicians, depending instead upon man's strength and ability. God recorded this in His Word to instruct us (1 Cor. 10:11). It's another indication of how Asa kept doing things in his own might instead of depending on God.

My friend, you need to learn how to depend on God, even for your health.

THEY MAKE MISTAKES

Recently one of our Charis Bible College students went to see a local physician here in Woodland Park, and apparently rebuked him. Being a Christian himself, this doctor came in to see me about the incident. Rather than just getting offended and criticizing us, he stated, "I want to find out what you believe."

We sat down and talked, and I told him, "I'm not against physicians. If it weren't for you doctors, most Christians would be dead because they haven't been believing God. I'm not against you or those in your profession. What I am against is this Godlike attitude that many doctors have. Someone comes in and the doctor tells them that they have something like cancer and that they're going to die. But when the patient responds, 'No, I believe God,' some in your profession ridicule them and make them feel like a fool because they're trying to believe that something can happen beyond human ability."

This man spoke up, saying, "Oh, no, that's not me. I'm a believer. I'm a Christian. I believe God can heal."

I responded, "Well, then, that's great for you. But I do have a problem with doctors when they make a person feel like they're weird for believing God."

I have a doctor on my board of directors. He's a godly man, and we've talked about all of these things. I'm not against physicians, but they are just human beings. They aren't God, and they make mistakes.

FIRST TURN TO GOD

While in England recently, I read an article in a paper there saying that taking too many vitamins and supplements leads to a higher risk of cancer. Now, this isn't saying we shouldn't eat the fruits or vegetables that God provided for us. This was talking about people who take vitamins and supplements in excess. But many people today just take whatever others shove at them. They take a pill to get up and a pill to go to bed; they have a pill for everything! They rely on the flesh and then wonder why they aren't receiving God's best.

Let me make this clear: I'm not against doctors. I believe doctors are fighting sickness, but it's just through human ability. Some of what doctors do is good and some of it's bad. I've had services where I've prayed for twelve people in a row, and everything they needed prayer for was caused by medication or complications from surgery. There's a reason why doctors have the highest malpractice insurance in the world. This doctor on my board, who is a personal friend of mine, operated on a patient and accidentally left three sponges inside of him. The patient nearly died! This doctor had to go back in and take the sponges out because his assistant didn't count right. That doesn't make him of the devil. He's not a bad person, but he is just a man. He made a mistake. Doctors make mistakes, but people think doctors are infallible.

If the Lord tarries, people will look back on our day a hundred years from now and shake their heads at the way cancer is currently being treated. Doctors use chemotherapy and radiation treatments that cause people to get sick and have their faces swell up and hair fall out. Many years from now, people will look back on us and say, "Those twenty-first century people were so primitive. I can't believe people submitted to that kind of treatment. It was so barbaric!" But right now, such treatment is cutting edge, and everyone is so excited about it.

I'm not against veterinarians, but I don't take my dog to the vet. Do you know why? I don't have a dog. I'm not against doctors, but I don't go to a doctor. Do you know why? I don't believe I'm sick. Even when I feel sick, even when some kind of symptom tries to tell me I'm sick, I stand on the Word of God and believe. Now, if you aren't to that place yet, there's no condemnation (Rom. 8:1). Don't sit there and die trying to be like someone else. Do what you've got to do to get well, but you ought to turn to God first.

CEMENT NAIL

Asa didn't turn to God; rather, he depended on the physicians (2 Chr. 16:12). Someone might argue, "Well, those physicians back then weren't any good. Ours are awesome!" Perhaps that is true, but we need to get a better understanding of the proper order of things.

I prayed for a man who had been driving a cement nail. The nail broke, hit the concrete, bounced up, and stuck in his eye. His coworkers brought him over to my house with this cement nail hanging out of his eye so I could pray for him. I prayed, and all of the pain left his body. The bleeding stopped and he was totally pain free. I believed God had healed him, but I told him, "Somebody needs to pull that nail out of your eye. I could do it, but you might want someone who knows what they're doing." He answered, "I think I'll go to a doctor." I said, "I think that would be a wise choice." I actually sent the man to the doctor. I'm not against doctors, but notice that we prayed first and saw the miracle happen. We saw the power of God flow and then, after that, the man did what he needed to do.

Do you want supernatural health? I've been walking in supernatural health now for forty-seven years. I've only been sick twice during that whole period of time, and both occasions were because of my own stupidity. I had ministered forty-one times one week and then forty times the next week. I got so tired, I literally had to crawl to get into bed. I stayed in bed for twenty-four hours trying to recover and after a day of rest, I felt pretty good. So, I went out and split a cord of wood by hand. That was too much, too soon! I got a sinus infection and lay in bed for three days. That was because of my own stupidity, and that's it. I don't get sick. I don't believe in being sick.

You might be thinking, *I don't believe that.* See, you're not believing for God's best. You just accept whatever season they say it is—flu season, hay fever season, allergy season—and suffer with it. You don't expect to walk in divine health, then you wonder why you aren't receiving God's best. It's not your goal. Amen, or oh, me?

DON'T BE COMPLACENT!

Perhaps you've been taught that you'll have heart problems, that it just runs in your family. It's been spoken over you a million times, so you've accepted it. You tell people, "Well, I'm over forty, you know. It's just a matter of time now…" Or maybe you say, "My eyesight is about to start going bad." Why do you accept that? God's Word says:

> *And Moses was an hundred and twenty years old when he died: his eye was not dim, nor his natural force abated.*
>
> Deuteronomy 34:7

And Moses was under an inferior covenant (Heb. 8:6)! What we have in Christ is better than what Moses had. Yet if somebody today goes to believing for good eyesight without glasses, people label them a fanatic, weirdo, or freak. They'll ask, "What's wrong with you?" That's what I'm asking: What's wrong with **you**? You aren't even believing for God's best. You've accepted something inferior. Is God mad at you because you have glasses? No! I'm just saying that you aren't believing for God's best. You've accepted second, third, or fourth best, and you're content to live there. As long as you're content to be less, you will be.

God's eyes are searching to and fro throughout the whole earth right now (2 Chr. 16:9). He's looking for someone who will trust Him for His best—divine health. Why not you? Pray this prayer when you decide to start believing for God's best, and set that as your standard: "God, don't look any further. I want Your best. I don't want second best. I don't want to just cope and survive. Lord, I want to thrive!" If you set reaching the stars as your goal, even if you miss your goal and hit the moon, that's more than most people have ever done.

Most folks are shooting at nothing and hitting it every single time! Am I condemning someone who goes to the doctor? No, not at all. What I'm saying is that it isn't God's best; there's something better than that. If you aren't walking in it yet, don't be condemned. Take advantage of what the doctors can do, but don't be complacent! Don't stay there. Look to God for His best!

Outline

I. For Asa, seeking the physicians was not the same as seeking the Lord (2 Chr. 16:11-12).

   A. Many of us today do the same.

   B. Culturally, we've developed this mindset that the very first thing we should do when facing sickness is go to the physicians, depend on medicine, and submit to surgery.

   C. Seeking God is our last thought—if we even think of it at all.

   D. Many people think that God and physicians are equal; they aren't.

   E. We ought to rely on physicians only if we've prayed and the Lord has led us that way.

   F. Many people's default is to go through all of man's ways and resources first and turn to God *only* when the situation gets beyond human ability.

   G. Asa depended upon man's strength and ability.

   H. It's another indication of how he kept doing things in his own might instead of depending on God.

   I. Friends, we need to learn how to depend on God, even for our health.

   J. Many people today just take whatever others shove at them: a pill to get up and a pill to go to bed; they have a pill for everything!

   K. They rely on the flesh and then wonder why they aren't receiving God's best.

II. Doctors are fighting sickness, but it's just through human ability.

   A. Some of what doctors do is good, and some of it's bad.

   B. There's a reason why they have the highest malpractice insurance in the world.

   C. Doctors make mistakes, but people think doctors are infallible.

   D. If the Lord tarries, people will look back on our day a hundred years from now and shake their heads at the way cancer is currently being treated.

E.   But right now, such treatment is cutting edge, and everyone is so excited about it.

F.   When you feel sick or when some kind of symptom tries to tell you that you're sick, stand on the Word of God and believe.

G.   If you aren't to that place yet, there's no condemnation (Rom. 8:1).

H.   Don't sit there and die trying to be like someone else.

I.   Do what you've got to do to get well, but you ought to turn to God first.

III.   God's Word says:

> *And Moses was an hundred and twenty years old when he died: his eye was not dim, nor his natural force abated.*
>
> Deuteronomy 34:7

A.   What we have in Christ is better than what Moses had (Heb. 8:6)!

B.   Yet if somebody today goes to believing for good eyesight without glasses, many will label them a fanatic, weirdo, or freak.

C.   We've accepted second, third, or fourth best, and we're content to live there.

D.   As long as we're content to be less, we will be.

IV.   God's eyes are searching to and fro throughout the whole earth right now (2 Chr. 16:9).

A.   He's looking for someone who will trust Him for His best—divine health. Why not you?

B.   When you decide to start believing for God's best and set that as your standard, pray this prayer: "God, don't look any further. I want Your best. I don't want second best. I don't want to just cope and survive. Lord, I want to thrive!"

C.   If you set reaching the stars as your goal, even if you miss your goal and hit the moon, that's more than most people have ever done.

D.   Most folks are shooting at nothing and hitting it every single time!

E. If you aren't walking in God's best yet, don't be condemned.

F. Take advantage of what the doctors can do, but don't be complacent; look to God for His best!

Teacher's Guide

1.   For Asa, seeking the physicians was not the same as seeking the Lord (2 Chr. 16:11-12). Many of us today do the same. Culturally, we've developed this mindset that the very first thing we should do when facing sickness is go to the physicians, depend on medicine, and submit to surgery. Seeking God is our last thought—if we even think of it at all. Many people think that God and physicians are equal; they aren't. We ought to rely on physicians only if we've prayed and the Lord has led us that way. Many people's default is to go through all of man's ways and resources first and turn to God *only* when the situation gets beyond human ability. Asa depended upon man's strength and ability. It's another indication of how he kept doing things in his own might instead of depending on God. We need to learn how to depend on God, even for our health. Many people today just take whatever others shove at them: a pill to get up and a pill to go to bed; they have a pill for everything! They rely on the flesh and then wonder why they aren't receiving God's best.

1a.   For Asa, seeking the physicians was not the _____ as seeking the Lord (2 Chr. 16:11-12).
      Same

1b.   *Discussion question:* What can you say about a culture that has made it normal to go to physicians, depend on medicine, and submit to surgery rather than seek God first?
      Discussion question

1c.   You ought to rely on physicians _____ if you've prayed and the Lord has led you that way.
      A.   Perhaps
      B.   Even
      C.   Sometimes
      D.   Only
      E.   Especially
      D.   Only

1d.   You need to _____ how to depend on God, even for your health.
      Learn

1e.   True or false: If you are relying on the flesh, you aren't receiving God's best.
      True

2.   Doctors are fighting sickness, but it's just through human ability. Some of what doctors do is good, and some of it's bad. There's a reason why they have the highest malpractice insurance in the world. Doctors make mistakes, but people think doctors are infallible. If the Lord tarries, people will look back on our day a hundred years from now and shake their heads at the way cancer is currently being treated. But right

now, such treatment is cutting edge, and everyone is so excited about it. When we feel sick or when symptoms try to tell us that we're sick, we need to stand on the Word of God and believe. If we aren't to that place yet, there's no condemnation (Rom. 8:1). We shouldn't sit there and die trying to be like someone else. We should do what we've got to do to get well, but we ought to turn to God first.

2a. *Discussion question:* What steps can you take toward receiving God's best in your health?

Discussion question

3.   God's Word says:

> *And Moses was an hundred and twenty years old when he died: his eye was not dim, nor his natural force abated.*
>
> Deuteronomy 34:7

What we have in Christ is better than what Moses had (Heb. 8:6)! Yet if somebody today goes to believing for good eyesight without glasses, many will label them a fanatic, weirdo, or freak. We've accepted second, third, or fourth best, and we're content to live there. As long as we're content to be less, we will be.

3a. What you have in Christ is _____ than what Moses had (Deut. 34:7 and Heb. 8:6).
Better

3b. *Discussion question:* What will it take for you to be discontent with second, third, or fourth best in your health?

Discussion question

4.   God's eyes are searching to and fro throughout the whole earth right now (2 Chr. 16:9). He's looking for someone who will trust Him for His best—divine health. Why not us? Let's pray this prayer and decide to start believing for God's best and set that as our standard: "God, don't look any further. I want Your best. I don't want second best. I don't want to just cope and survive. Lord, I want to thrive!" If we set reaching the stars as our goal, even if we miss our goal and hit the moon, that's more than most people have ever done. Most folks are shooting at nothing and hitting it every single time! If we aren't walking in God's best yet, we shouldn't be condemned. Let's take advantage of what the doctors can do, but not be complacent; let's look to God for His best!

4a. God is _____ for someone who will trust Him for His best—divine health (2 Chr. 16:9).
    A. Looking
    B. Weeping
    C. Thirsting
    D. Clapping
    E. Cooking
    A. Looking

4b. If you set reaching the stars as your goal, even if you miss your goal and hit the moon, that's more than _____ people have ever done.
    Most

4c. True or false: You should be condemned if you aren't walking in divine health.
    False

4d. Let's take _____ of what the doctors can do but not be _____; let's _____ to God for His best!
    Advantage / complacent / look

Discipleship Questions

1. For Asa, seeking the physicians was not the _____ as seeking the Lord (2 Chr. 16:11-12).

2. *Discussion question:* What can you say about a culture that has made it normal to go to physicians, depend on medicine, and submit to surgery rather than seek God first?

    _____

    _____

    _____

3. You ought to rely on physicians _____ if you've prayed and the Lord has led you that way.
    A. Perhaps
    B. Even
    C. Sometimes
    D. Only
    E. Especially

4. You need to _____ how to depend on God, even for your health.

5. True or false: If you are relying on the flesh, you aren't receiving God's best.

6. *Discussion question:* What steps can you take toward receiving God's best in your health?

    _____

    _____

    _____

7. What you have in Christ is _____ than what Moses had (Deut. 34:7 and Heb. 8:6).

8. *Discussion question:* What will it take for you to be discontent with second, third, or fourth best in your health?

    _____

    _____

    _____

9. God is _____ for someone who will trust Him for His best—divine health (2 Chr. 16:9).
    A. Looking
    B. Weeping
    C. Thirsting
    D. Clapping
    E. Cooking

10. If you set reaching the stars as your goal, even if you miss your goal and hit the moon, that's more than _____ people have ever done.

11. True or false: You should be condemned if you aren't walking in divine health.

12. Let's take _____ of what the doctors can do but not be _____; let's _____ to God for His best!

Answer Key

1. Same

2. *Discussion question*

3. D. Only

4. Learn

5. True

6. *Discussion question*

7. Better

8. *Discussion question*

9. A. Looking

10. Most

11. False

12. Advantage / complacent / look

Scriptures

2 CHRONICLES 16:11-12

And, behold, the acts of Asa, first and last, lo, they are written in the book of the kings of Judah and Israel. **[12]** And Asa in the thirty and ninth year of his reign was diseased in his feet, until his disease was exceeding great: yet in his disease he sought not to the LORD, but to the physicians.

1 CORINTHIANS 10:11

Now all these things happened unto them for ensamples: and they are written for our admonition, upon whom the ends of the world are come.

ROMANS 8:1

There is therefore now no condemnation to them which are in Christ Jesus, who walk not after the flesh, but after the Spirit.

DEUTERONOMY 34:7

And Moses was an hundred and twenty years old when he died: his eye was not dim, nor his natural force abated.

HEBREWS 8:6

But now hath he obtained a more excellent ministry, by how much also he is the mediator of a better covenant, which was established upon better promises.

2 CHRONICLES 16:9

For the eyes of the LORD run to and fro throughout the whole earth, to shew himself strong in the behalf of them whose heart is perfect toward him. Herein thou hast done foolishly: therefore from henceforth thou shalt have wars.

God's Kind of Love

LESSON 4

When it comes to love, we've been lied to by the world. Most people settle for lust instead of love.

First Corinthians 13 reveals to us that God's kind of love *"suffereth long, and is kind"* (1 Cor. 13:4). For most Christians, that's not even a goal. They say, "Hey, in our family, we just let our hair down. We say what we think." Or they use the excuse, "I'm just a blunt, type A personality," or "I have a prophetic gift." They have a million excuses for why they don't suffer long and aren't kind.

Well, you can be delivered of that! If you were to operate in God's kind of love, you would suffer long and be kind. You would not be critical, angry, or bitter.

"Charity [God's kind of love] *envieth not"* (1 Cor. 13:4, brackets mine). Are you jealous of other people? Do you want what they have?

Love *"vaunteth not itself, is not puffed up"* (1 Cor. 13:4). Love is not self-centered or self-promoting. If you're around somebody who's bragging about everything they've done, do you feel compelled to boast so that you'll look good in comparison, so that they'll know you're somebody special too? That's not God's kind of love.

"I'M THE BEST!"

Society today puts athletes, musicians, and movie stars on magazine covers. We look up to and idolize people like them, many of whom are arrogant to the max. I remember a certain boxer from the 1960s who declared, "I am the greatest!" Nobody talked like that back then. People didn't say such things, but this guy did, and it opened the door for many others like him. Today everybody thinks they're the greatest. They openly brag "I'm the best!" and say other boastful things. That's not God's kind of love.

Most of us have embraced this idea too, so we toot our own horns. We believe the verse that says, "He that tooteth not his own horn, the same shall not be tooted"

(Opinions 5:11). Obviously, I'm joking. That's not really in the Bible. But Proverbs 27:1-2 is:

> *Boast not thyself of to morrow; for thou knowest not what a day may bring forth. [2] Let another man praise thee, and not thine own mouth; a stranger, and not thine own lips.*

God's kind of love is self-controlled and acts properly. It *"doth not behave itself unseemly"* (1 Cor. 13:5). When a person says "Oh, we're in love. We can't wait until we're married. Let's go ahead and have sex because we're just so in love," that's not God's kind of love. It's lust. If someone can't control themselves, they are not displaying God's kind of love (Gal. 5:22-23). Yet we watch movies and hear songs all the time that say, "I love you so much; I can't close my eyes. I've just got to have you now!" That makes me want to gag. It's lust, not love!

Love was when Jesus hung on the cross (Rom. 5:8). Love is self-sacrificing, not self-indulging. If you're going to abuse, hurt, and take advantage of another person, it's not love; it's lust. God's kind of love does not behave unseemly.

NEVER FAILS

Love *"seeketh not her own"* (1 Cor. 13:5). Many people today are selfish and self-centered. I heard someone say that America is no longer a society; we're all individuals. Individuals have taken over this country, and it's all about individual rights. There's no longer a society where we get along and cooperate with one another. Now it's all about "my rights." That's not God's kind of love. We haven't even set love as a goal!

I bet most of what we're looking at right now in our study together is totally new to you, or if you've heard this before, you've rejected it and thought, *If I don't take care of myself, then who's going to take care of me? I've got to put myself first.* And then you wonder why you aren't receiving God's best. You're resisting God and have submitted to the flesh. It's supposed to be the other way around: submit to God, and resist the world, the flesh, and the devil (James 4:7).

> *[Charity] is not easily provoked, thinketh no evil; [6] Rejoiceth not in iniquity, but rejoiceth in the truth; [7] Beareth all things, believeth all things, hopeth all things, endureth all things. [8] Charity never faileth.*
> 1 Corinthians 13:5b-8a, brackets mine

God's kind of love never fails. Yet we have people today saying, "I've just taken all I can take. I can't bear anymore. I can't believe that things are going to work out anymore. I've lost my hope. I can't endure anymore." All we've done is admit that we aren't operating in God's kind of love. His love flowing to and through us can bear all things, believe all things, hope all things, and endure all things. God's kind of love never fails.

Most of us haven't even set walking in God's kind of love as a goal. We excuse ourselves, thinking, *Well, I'm only human.* You're not only human! One-third of you is wall-to-wall Holy Spirit. You can start living by the power of God. You don't have to live as a mere human being. That's awesome!

Outline

I. When it comes to love, we've been lied to by the world.

  A. First Corinthians 13 reveals to us that God's kind of love *"suffereth long, and is kind"* (1 Cor. 13:4).

  B. Many of us as Christians have a million excuses for why we don't suffer long and aren't kind.

  C. Well, we can be delivered of that!

  D. If we were to operate in God's kind of love, we would suffer long and be kind; we would not be critical, angry, or bitter.

  E. *"Charity* [God's kind of love] *envieth not"* (1 Cor. 13:4, brackets mine), but are we jealous of other people?

  F. Love *"vaunteth not itself, is not puffed up"* (1 Cor. 13:4), and love is not self-centered or self-promoting.

  G. If we're around somebody who's bragging about everything they've done, do we feel compelled to boast so that we'll look good in comparison, so that they'll know we're somebody special too?

  H. Many people toot their own horns.

  I. But Proverbs 27:1-2 says:

  Boast not thyself of to morrow; for thou knowest not what a day may bring forth. [2] *Let another man praise thee, and not thine own mouth; a stranger, and not thine own lips.*

II. God's kind of love is self-controlled and acts properly; it *"doth not behave itself unseemly"* (1 Cor. 13:5).

  A. When a person says, "Oh, we're in love. We can't wait until we're married. Let's go ahead and have sex because we're just so in love," that's not God's kind of love.

  B. If someone can't control themselves, they are not displaying God's kind of love (Gal. 5:22-23).

C. Love was when Jesus hung on the cross (Rom. 5:8).

D. If you're going to abuse, hurt, and take advantage of another person, it's not love; it's lust.

III. Love *"seeketh not her own"* (1 Cor. 13:5).

A. Many people today are selfish and self-centered.

B. I heard someone say that America is no longer a society; we're all individuals.

C. There's no longer a society where we get along and cooperate with one another; now it's all about "my rights."

IV. Most of what we're looking at right now in our study together may be totally new to you, or if you've heard this before, you might have rejected it and thought, *I've got to put myself first.*

A. And then you wonder why you aren't receiving God's best.

B. You're resisting God and have submitted to the flesh.

C. It's supposed to be the other way around: submit to God, and resist the world, the flesh, and the devil (James 4:7).

V. God's kind of love never fails:

> [Charity] *is not easily provoked, thinketh no evil;* [6] *Rejoiceth not in iniquity, but rejoiceth in the truth;* [7] *Beareth all things, believeth all things, hopeth all things, endureth all things.* [8] *Charity never faileth.*
> 1 Corinthians 13:5b-8a, brackets mine

A. Yet there are people today saying, "I've taken all I can take. I can't bear anymore. I can't believe that things are going to work out anymore. I've lost my hope. I can't endure anymore."

B. All they've done is admit that they aren't operating in God's kind of love.

C. His love flowing to and through us can bear all things, believe all things, hope all things, and endure all things.

VI. Most of us haven't even set walking in God's kind of love as a goal.

    A. We excuse ourselves, thinking, *Well, I'm only human.*

    B. We're not only human; one-third of us is wall-to-wall Holy Spirit.

    C. We can start living by the power of God.

Teacher's Guide

1. When it comes to love, we've been lied to by the world. First Corinthians 13 reveals to us that God's kind of love *"suffereth long, and is kind"* (1 Cor. 13:4). Many of us as Christians have a million excuses for why we don't suffer long and aren't kind. Well, we can be delivered of that! If we were to operate in God's kind of love, we would suffer long and be kind. We would not be critical, angry, or bitter. *"Charity* [God's kind of love] *envieth not"* (1 Cor. 13:4, brackets mine). But are we jealous of other people? Love *"vaunteth not itself, is not puffed up"* (1 Cor. 13:4). Love is not self-centered or self-promoting. If we're around somebody who's bragging about everything they've done, do we feel compelled to boast so that we'll look good in comparison, so that they'll know we're somebody special too? Many of us toot our own horns. But Proverbs 27:1-2 says:

> *Boast not thyself of to morrow; for thou knowest not what a day may bring forth.* [2] *Let another man praise thee, and not thine own mouth; a stranger, and not thine own lips.*

1a. *Discussion question:* How has the world lied to you about love?
    Discussion question
1b. _____ kind of love *"suffereth long, and is kind"* (1 Cor. 13:4).
    God's
1c. If you are critical, angry, or bitter—instead of suffering long and being kind—you are not what?
    A. Going to get any pie
    B. Operating in God's kind of love
    C. Eligible for a promotion
    D. Satisfied until you eat or sleep
    E. Apologetic for your behavior
    B. Operating in God's kind of love
1d. True or false: God's kind of love envies sometimes.
    False
1e. According to Proverbs 27:1-2, you should "_____ _____ *thyself of to morrow; for thou knowest not what a day may bring forth.* [2] *Let* _____ *man praise thee, and not thine own mouth; a stranger, and not thine own lips."*
    "Boast" / "not" / "another"

2. God's kind of love is self-controlled and acts properly. It *"doth not behave itself unseemly"* (1 Cor. 13:5). When a person says, "Oh, we're in love. We can't wait until we're married. Let's go ahead and have sex because we're just so in love," that's not God's kind of love. If someone can't control themselves, they are not displaying God's

kind of love (Gal. 5:22-23). Love was when Jesus hung on the cross (Rom. 5:8). If we're going to abuse, hurt, and take advantage of another person, it's not love. It's lust.

2a. *Discussion question:* What is an example of God's kind of love having self-control and acting properly?
 Discussion question

2b. According to 1 Corinthians 13:5, God's kind of love *"doth _____ behave itself unseemly."*
 A. Commonly
 B. Sometimes
 C. Always
 D. All of the above
 E. None of the above
 E. None of the above

2c. If someone can't control themselves, they are not displaying _____ _____ _____ _____ (Gal. 5:22-23).
 God's / kind / of / love

2d. *Discussion question:* Why is it that Jesus hanging on the cross is true love (Rom. 5:8)?
 Discussion question

2e. To abuse, hurt, and take advantage of another person is not love; it's what?
 Lust

3. Love *"seeketh not her own"* (1 Cor. 13:5). Many people today are selfish and self-centered. Andrew heard someone say that America is no longer a society; we're all individuals. There's no longer a society where we get along and cooperate with one another; now it's all about "my rights."

3a. True or false: According to 1 Corinthians 13:5, love is all about "my rights."
 False

4. Most of what we're looking at right now in our study together may be totally new to us, or if we've heard this before, we might have rejected it and thought, *I've got to put myself first.* And then we wonder why we aren't receiving God's best. We're resisting God and have submitted to the flesh. It's supposed to be the other way around: we submit to God and resist the world, the flesh, and the devil (James 4:7).

4a. True or false: If you think, *I've got to put myself first,* you aren't receiving God's best.
 True

4b. According to James 4:7, you're supposed to submit to God and resist what?
   A. The past, the present, and the future
   B. Your spirit, your soul, and your body
   C. The world, the flesh, and the devil
   D. Your family, your friends, and your neighbors
   E   The good, the bad, and the ugly
   C. The world, the flesh, and the devil

5.   God's kind of love never fails:

> [Charity] *is not easily provoked, thinketh no evil;* [6] *Rejoiceth not in iniquity, but rejoiceth in the truth;* [7] *Beareth all things, believeth all things, hopeth all things, endureth all things.* [8] *Charity never faileth.*
> 1 Corinthians 13:5b-8a, brackets mine

Yet there are people today saying, "I've taken all I can take. I can't bear anymore. I can't believe that things are going to work out anymore. I've lost my hope. I can't endure anymore." All they've done is admit that they aren't operating in God's kind of love. His love flowing to and through us can bear all things, believe all things, hope all things, and endure all things.

5a. God's love flowing _____ and _____ you can bear all things, believe all things, hope all things, and endure all things.
   To / through

6.   Most of us haven't even set walking in God's kind of love as a goal. We excuse ourselves, thinking, *Well, I'm only human.* We're not only human; one-third of us is wall-to-wall Holy Spirit! We can start living by the power of God.

6a. *Discussion question:* How is walking in God's love going to become your goal?
   Discussion question
6b. You're not only human; one-third of you is what?
   Wall-to-wall Holy Spirit

Discipleship Questions

1. *Discussion question:* How has the world lied to you about love?

   _____

   _____

   _____

2. _____ kind of love *"suffereth long, and is kind."* (1 Cor. 13:4).

3. If you are critical, angry, or bitter—instead of suffering long and being kind—you are not what?
   A. Going to get any pie
   B. Operating in God's kind of love
   C. Eligible for a promotion
   D. Satisfied until you eat or sleep
   E. Apologetic for your behavior

4. True or false: God's kind of love envies sometimes.

5. According to Proverbs 27:1-2, you should *"_____ _____ thyself of to morrow; for thou knowest not what a day may bring forth. [2] Let _____ man praise thee, and not thine own mouth; a stranger, and not thine own lips."*

6. *Discussion question:* What is an example of God's kind of love having self-control and acting properly?

   _____

   _____

   _____

7. According to 1 Corinthians 13:5, God's kind of love *"doth _____ behave itself unseemly."*
   A. Commonly
   B. Sometimes
   C. Always
   D. All of the above
   E. None of the above

8. If someone can't control themselves, they are not displaying _____ _____ _____
    _____ (Gal. 5:22-23).

9. *Discussion question:* Why is it that Jesus hanging on the cross is true love (Rom. 5:8)?

    _____

    _____

    _____

10. To abuse, hurt, and take advantage of another person is not love; it's what?

    _____

    _____

    _____

11. True or false: According to 1 Corinthians 13:5, love is all about "my rights."

12. True or false: If you think, *I've got to put myself first,* you aren't receiving God's best.

13. According to James 4:7, you're supposed to submit to God and resist what?
    A. The past, the present, and the future
    B. Your spirit, your soul, and your body
    C. The world, the flesh, and the devil
    D. Your family, your friends, and your neighbors
    E. The good, the bad, and the ugly

14. God's love flowing _____ and _____ you can bear all things, believe all things,
    hope all things, and endure all things.

15. *Discussion question:* How is walking in God's love going to become your goal?

    _____

    _____

    _____

16. You're not only human; one-third of you is what?

_____

_____

_____

Answer Key

1. *Discussion question*

2. God's

3. B. Operating in God's kind of love

4. False

5. *"Boast" / "not" / "another"*

6. *Discussion question*

7. E. None of the above

8. God's / kind / of / love

9. *Discussion question*

10. Lust

11. False

12. True

13. C. The world, the flesh, and the devil

14. To / through

15. *Discussion question*

16. Wall-to-wall Holy Spirit

Scriptures

1 CORINTHIANS 13:4-8

Charity suffereth long, and is kind; charity envieth not; charity vaunteth not itself, is not puffed up, [5] Doth not behave itself unseemly, seeketh not her own, is not easily provoked, thinketh no evil; [6] Rejoiceth not in iniquity, but rejoiceth in the truth; [7] Beareth all things, believeth all things, hopeth all things, endureth all things. [8] Charity never faileth: but whether there be prophecies, they shall fail; whether there be tongues, they shall cease; whether there be knowledge, it shall vanish away.

PROVERBS 27:1-2

Boast not thyself of to morrow; for thou knowest not what a day may bring forth. [2] Let another man praise thee, and not thine own mouth; a stranger, and not thine own lips.

GALATIANS 5:22-23

But the fruit of the Spirit is love, joy, peace, longsuffering, gentleness, goodness, faith, [23] Meekness, temperance: against such there is no law.

ROMANS 5:8

But God commendeth his love toward us, in that, while we were yet sinners, Christ died for us.

JAMES 4:7

Submit yourselves therefore to God. Resist the devil, and he will flee from you.

Until You Die?

LESSON 5

Loving security keeps us from receiving God's best. We don't want to take any risks. We play it way too safe.

> *And there were four leprous men at the entering in of the gate: and they said one to another, Why sit we here until we die? [4] If we say, We will enter into the city, then the famine is in the city, and we shall die there: and if we sit still here, we die also. Now therefore come, and let us fall unto the host of the Syrians: if they save us alive, we shall live; and if they kill us, we shall but die.*
>
> 2 Kings 7:3-4

The Syrians had come and besieged Israel. The famine became so bad in the city that in the previous chapter, the Israelites were selling animal dung for outrageous prices, and people were even eating their own children (2 Kin. 6:24-29).

These four lepers were discussing their situation at the gate of the city. They basically said, "Let's go out and ask our enemies for help. The worst they can do is kill us. We're going to die if we sit here. If we go into the city, we'll die by famine. The only chance we have is to go out to our enemies. If they kill us, we die. But if they help us, we'll live. Let's do it!"

> *And they rose up in the twilight, to go unto the camp of the Syrians: and when they were come to the uttermost part of the camp of Syria, behold, there was no man there. [6] For the Lord had made the host of the Syrians to hear a noise of chariots, and a noise of horses, even the noise of a great host: and they said one to another, Lo, the king of Israel hath hired against us the kings of the Hittites, and the kings of the Egyptians, to come upon us. [7] Wherefore they arose and fled in the twilight, and left their tents, and their horses, and their asses, even the camp as it was, and fled for their life. [8] And when these lepers came to the uttermost part of the camp, they went into one tent, and did eat and drink, and carried thence silver, and gold, and raiment, and went and hid it; and came again, and entered into another tent, and carried thence also, and went and hid it.*
>
> 2 Kings 7:5-8

ZEROS TO HEROES

Then they said one to another, We do not well: this day is a day of good tidings, and we hold our peace: if we tarry till the morning light, some mischief will come upon us: now therefore come, that we may go and tell the king's household. [10] So they came and called unto the porter of the city: and they told them, saying, We came to the camp of the Syrians, and, behold, there was no man there, neither voice of man, but horses tied, and asses tied, and the tents as they were. [11] And he called the porters; and they told it to the king's house within.

2 Kings 7:9-11

The Lord made the Syrians hear a sound, and they became so afraid that they fled. They left their food still cooking in the pots and all of their gold, silver, and fine clothes in their tents. Their animals—both horses and donkeys—were still tied up. They didn't even bother to try to saddle up and ride them away, such was their haste to escape. When these lepers arrived at the Syrian camp, there was this abundance waiting for them. Hundreds of thousands of Syrian soldiers had fled and left all their stuff behind.

The four lepers started eating and drinking. They went into a tent and took all they could possibly take, and then they went and hid their loot and came back for more. It dawned on them, "We aren't doing well. This is a day of rejoicing. We must go and tell the starving people in the besieged city what has happened!" So, they went back and told them. These four lepers went from zeros to heroes in a matter of hours because they were willing to take a risk. They asked themselves, "How long are we just going to sit here? Until we die?"

Maybe you're not content where you are, but you aren't doing anything about it because you're afraid that it might not work out. You need to understand that you'll never see a change in your situation if you're not willing to take a risk.

Personally, I'm taking a huge risk right now. This $60 million building project that I was sharing about earlier is just the tip of the iceberg. The Lord has told me to raise up a Bible college campus that has student housing, activity centers, and more. We'll be spending hundreds of millions of dollars to do it, and I haven't got any of it. I'm taking a risk. It would be easy to just sit down and stop. Right now, we have approximately 6,000 people worldwide receiving training through our various Charis Bible College campuses, our correspondence program, and online distance education programs. We are impacting nations! We've met with presidents and first ladies of different countries. We're seeing miracles happen. I'm experiencing some of the greatest things I've ever seen in my life regarding outreach and ministry. I could just stop, sit down, and camp right here. I could play it safe, but God's given me a bigger vision.

HOW LONG ARE YOU GOING TO SIT THERE?

I'm believing for more than I've ever believed for in my life! It's risky. Some people think, *Well, you could fail*. Well, I might. But so what? I believe that even if I fail, God will look at me and say, "At least you tried."

Remember when your child started to learn how to ride a bike? They didn't do everything right immediately. They made mistakes and fell a few times. They'd get on and wobble a bit, and then they'd fall off and skin their knees. But what parent would go up to their child after a fall and say, "You sorry thing! If you had done what I told you, this wouldn't have happened. You're a failure!" That's not how you would talk to your child. You would say, "Hey, you went ten feet. See, you can do it! Get up and try again." That's the way God is with us.

God encourages us. Yes, some might die trying to believe God. But when they stand before the Lord, He'll say, "That's My child. You believed Me. You didn't receive the full manifestation of what I had for you before you came home, but you believed!"

Are you a person who has never failed because you've never done anything? Anybody can live like that. Your lost neighbor can live like that, because that type of living doesn't take any faith. I'm not pointing this out to condemn you; I'm just trying to stir you up. How long are you going to sit there? Until you die? Time is ticking. You might not be a spring chicken anymore, and perhaps you're over halfway home. What have you done? What's going to change? What will make things different in the future? You're going to have to get up and do something!

Insanity is doing the same thing over and over again but expecting different results. Are you praying for different results? Are you hoping for everything to change, yet you're afraid to do anything differently? Maybe you love security so much that you won't take a chance. You'd rather be secure and miserable than make a change. You'd rather stay a slave in Egypt, eating leeks and garlic, than follow God out through the wilderness toward your promised land. Are you on the edge looking in but afraid to enter because it might mean having to fight some giant? Get up and go take your land!

ALL USED UP

This really challenges my staff and family sometimes. Jamie and I were at church one day, and the minister was preaching along the lines of needing to stir ourselves up and believe God. He said, "If you need to increase your vision, stand up, and I'm going to pray for you." My wife put her hand on my knee, leaned over, and said, "Don't you dare stand up! We're believing big enough right now." This kind of living terrifies some people, but I'm going for it!

When I die, I don't want there to be any juice left in me. I want to give everything I've got for God's kingdom—to have it ALL used up. I don't want to stand before the Lord and have to hear Him say, "I asked you to do this and that, but you didn't do it because you were afraid that it wouldn't work out." I'd rather try and trust God and risk failing and falling flat on my face than do nothing at all and be a success at it.

I believe this is ringing your bell. Before you can receive God's best, you must understand that the eyes of the Lord are looking at your heart right now. Is it fully committed to Him, or is it just embracing life the way everybody else does it? Are you choosing to aim high, or just shooting for nothing and hitting it every time? Are various fears and small thinking limiting what He can do in your life? Have you not been shooting for God's best?

The first step toward receiving God's best for you is to quit accepting less than His best. You need to raise the standard, but not through guilt and condemnation. Don't say, "O God, I'm a terrible person because I've not stepped out in faith." No, the Lord loves you just like you are, but He loves you so much that He doesn't want to leave you where you are. He wants to raise you up to a higher level. God wants you to believe for His best, but it's not going to come to pass for you accidentally. You're going to have to set God's best as your goal and pursue it.

Just like those lepers, you're going to have to stir yourself up and say, "How long am I going to sit here? Until I die?" How long are you just going to keep wishing and hoping instead of taking a step of faith? You need to do something. You need to stir yourself up, or you'll just settle back down to the bottom.

BELIEVE FOR SOMETHING BIGGER

I know this isn't comfortable. You probably weren't expecting this kind of a message; maybe you don't even like it. But I'm trying to provoke you to do the right thing and take the step of faith that God is showing you.

Before you can go any further in learning about how to receive God's best, you must change your expectancy. You have to change your aim and begin looking for something more. Don't get condemned, and don't do something stupid, but don't stay where you are. Say, "God, I want Your best. I want to accomplish everything You have for me!" We serve a big God! He thinks *big*. There's not a person alive who has tapped into everything the Lord has for them. It doesn't matter how far you've gone, how much you've believed, or how much you've received—God has more! He's huge. He's supernatural!

If your life isn't supernatural, then it's superficial. If somebody looks at you and says, "Well, how did you do that?" and you can explain how *you* did it, then you haven't tapped into God yet. If you can point to yourself and take pride in everything you've done, then you haven't come into God. He will bring you beyond yourself. He'll ask you to do something that's bigger than you so that you'll have to depend on Him. Then the only answer you can give will be, "It's not me. It's the Lord. He did it. Only the blessing of God could make these things work out this way."

Most Christians haven't stretched themselves very far. They aren't believing for much. They just want to get over this little hump so that they can go back to watching television or whatever it was they were doing. I'm telling you, there's more to life than that. You ought to be living for something that's bigger than you. You ought to be living for something worth dying for. When you wake up in the morning, you should be excited. You've got more to do than you can accomplish in a lifetime. Every day should be exciting because you're busy stretching forward in faith to fulfill what God has led you to do.

For me, it's like I'm on a roller coaster and hanging on for dear life. I'm not in control. God tells me to do things, and I say, "Okay, here we go!" Man, that's exciting!

Have you been wondering why your life isn't exciting? It's because God can't give you a sense of satisfaction, joy, and peace over what you're doing because He made you for more than that. He wants to raise your vision and lift up your head. Are you ready to believe for something bigger?

ANDREW'S RECOMMENDATIONS FOR FURTHER STUDY

The Lord spoke to me on January 31, 2002, and told me that I was limiting Him by my small thinking. I had started broadcasting on television two years before that, and from January 2000 to January 2002, our ministry had doubled. I thought that was pretty good, but then the Lord spoke to me about how I was limiting Him. You can read more about this in my book entitled *Don't Limit God*, but the point is that I decided I wasn't going to keep limiting Him that way. I started to think differently— to think bigger. That was just fourteen years ago, and our ministry has grown at least twenty times larger since then. Everything has been totally transformed. I've been living on the edge. Every time it looks like we have our feet under us and we're just about to make it, God increases my vision and I just lean a little further. Amen!

Outline

I. Loving security keeps you from receiving God's best.

    A. Second Kings 7:3-4 says,

> *And there were four leprous men at the entering in of the gate: and they said one to another, Why sit we here until we die? [4] If we say, We will enter into the city, then the famine is in the city, and we shall die there: and if we sit still here, we die also. Now therefore come, and let us fall unto the host of the Syrians: if they save us alive, we shall live; and if they kill us, we shall but die.*

    B. These four lepers basically asked themselves, "How long are we going to sit here? Until we die?"

    C. Maybe you're not content where you are, but you aren't doing anything about it because you're afraid that it might not work out.

    D. You need to understand that you'll never see a change in your situation if you're not willing to take a risk.

    E. You could play it safe, but God's given you a bigger vision.

    F. You should start believing for more than you've ever believed for in your life!

    G. Even if you fail, God will look at you and say, "At least you tried."

II. Are you a person who has never failed because you've never done anything?

    A. This is not to condemn you; this question is meant to try to stir you up.

    B. You're going to have to get up and do something!

    C. Insanity is doing the same thing over and over again but expecting different results.

    D. Are you on the edge of your promised land and looking in, but afraid to enter because it might mean having to fight a giant?

    E. Get up and go take your land!

III. You should want to give everything you've got for God's kingdom—to have your life ALL used up.

    A.   You don't want to stand before the Lord and hear Him say, "I asked you to do this and that, but you didn't do it because you were afraid that it wouldn't work out."

    B.   You should rather want to try and trust God and risk failing and falling flat on your face than do nothing at all and be a success at it.

    C.   Before you can receive God's best, you must understand that the eyes of the Lord are looking at your heart right now.

    D.   Are you fully committed to Him, or are you just embracing life the way everybody else does it?

    E.   Are various fears and small thinking limiting what He can do in your life?

    F.   Have you been shooting for God's best?

IV. The first step toward receiving God's best for you is to quit accepting less than His best.

    A.   You need to raise the standard, but not through guilt and condemnation, saying, "O God, I'm a terrible person because I've not stepped out in faith."

    B.   No, the Lord loves you just like you are, but He loves you so much that He doesn't want to leave you where you are.

    C.   He wants to raise you up to a higher level.

    D.   God wants you to believe for His best, but it's not going to come to pass for you accidentally.

    E.   You're going to have to set God's best as your goal and pursue it.

V. Just like those lepers, you're going to have to stir yourself up.

    A.   How long are you just going to keep wishing and hoping instead of taking a step of faith?

    B.   You need to stir yourself up, or you'll just settle back down to the bottom.

    C.   You probably weren't expecting this kind of a message; maybe you don't even like it.

    D.   But this lesson is meant to provoke you to do the right thing and to take the step of faith that God is showing you.

VI. Before you can go any further in learning about how to receive God's best, you must change your expectation.

    A.   You have to change your aim and begin looking for something more.

    B.   Don't get condemned, and don't do something stupid, but don't stay where you are either.

    C.   Say, "God, I want Your best. I want to accomplish everything You have for me!"

    D.   You serve a big God!

    E.   It doesn't matter how far you've gone, how much you've believed, or how much you've received—God has more!

VII. If your life isn't supernatural, then it's superficial.

    A.   If you can point to yourself and take pride in everything you've done, then you haven't come into God.

    B.   He will bring you beyond yourself.

    C.   He'll ask you to do something that's bigger than you so that you'll have to depend on Him.

    D.   Then the only answer you can give will be, "It's not me. It's the Lord. He did it. Only the blessing of God could make these things work out this way."

VIII. Many of us as Christians haven't stretched ourselves very far.

    A.   We ought to be living for something worth dying for.

    B.   We've got more to do than we can accomplish in a lifetime.

    C.   Every day should be exciting because we're busy stretching forward in faith to fulfill what God has led us to do.

IX. Have you been wondering why your life isn't exciting?

    A. It's because God can't give you a sense of satisfaction, joy, and peace over what you're doing because He made you for more than that.

    B. He wants to raise your vision and lift up your head.

    C. Are you ready to believe for something bigger?

ANDREW'S RECOMMENDATIONS FOR FURTHER STUDY

The Lord spoke to me on January 31, 2002, and told me that I was limiting Him by my small thinking. I had started broadcasting on television two years before that and from January 2000 to January 2002, our ministry had doubled. I thought that was pretty good, but then the Lord spoke to me about how I was limiting Him. You can read more about this in my book *Don't Limit God*, but the point is that I decided I wasn't going to keep limiting Him that way. I started to think differently—to think bigger. That was just fourteen years ago, and our ministry has grown at least twenty times larger since then. Everything has been totally transformed. I've been living on the edge. Every time it looks like we have our feet under us and we're just about to make it, God increases my vision, and I lean in a little further. Amen!

Teacher's Guide

1. Loving security keeps us from receiving God's best. Second Kings 7:3-4 says,

    And there were four leprous men at the entering in of the gate: and they said one to another, Why sit we here until we die? [4] If we say, We will enter into the city, then the famine is in the city, and we shall die there: and if we sit still here, we die also. Now therefore come, and let us fall unto the host of the Syrians: if they save us alive, we shall live; and if they kill us, we shall but die.

    These four lepers basically asked themselves, "How long are we just going to sit here? Until we die?" Maybe we're not content where we are, but we aren't doing anything about it because we're afraid that it might not work out. We need to understand that we'll never see a change in our situations if we're not willing to take a risk. We could play it safe, but God's given us a bigger vision. We should start believing for more than we've ever believed for in our lives! Even if we fail, God will look at us and say, "At least you tried."

    1a. True or false: Loving security keeps you from receiving God's best.
       True
    1b. What did the four lepers basically ask themselves (2 Kin. 7:3-4)?
       "How long are we just going to sit here? Until we die?"
    1c. You will never see a change in your situation if you're not willing to do what?
       A. Take a stand
       B. Take a hint
       C. Take a break
       D. Take a risk
       E. Take a bow
       D. Take a risk

2. Are we people who have never failed because we've never done anything? This is not to condemn; this question is meant to try to stir us up. We're going to have to get up and do something! Insanity is doing the same thing over and over again but expecting different results. Are we on the edge of our promised land and looking in, but afraid to enter because it might mean having to fight a giant? We need to get up and go take our land!

    2a. *Discussion question:* What will you change in order to start living more by faith?
       Discussion question
    2b. True or false: You need to sit back and receive your land.
       False

3.   We should want to give everything we've got for God's kingdom—to have our lives ALL used up. We don't want to stand before the Lord and hear Him say, "I asked you to do this and that, but you didn't do it because you were afraid that it wouldn't work out." We should rather want to try and trust God and risk failing and falling flat on our faces than do nothing at all and be a success at it. Before we can receive God's best, we must understand that the eyes of the Lord are looking at our hearts right now. Are we fully committed to Him, or are we just embracing life the way everybody else does it? Are various fears and small thinking limiting what He can do in our lives? Have we been shooting for God's best?

3a. *Discussion question:* How much are you willing to trust God even though there is the risk of failure?
     Discussion question
3b. Before you can receive God's best, you must understand what?
     That the eyes of the Lord are looking at your heart right now
3c. What is God looking to see?
     If your heart is fully committed to Him, or if you're just embracing life the way everybody else does it
3d. *Discussion question:* What are you going to do to deal with fear and small thinking?
     Discussion question

4.   The first step toward receiving God's best for us is to quit accepting less than His best. We need to raise the standard, but not through guilt and condemnation, saying, "O God, I'm a terrible person because I've not stepped out in faith." No, the Lord loves us just like we are, but He loves us so much that He doesn't want to leave us where we are. He wants to raise us up to a higher level. God wants us to believe for His best, but it's not going to come to pass for us accidentally. We're going to have to set God's best as our goal and pursue it.

4a. What is the first step toward receiving God's best for you?
     To quit accepting less than His best
4b. True or false: You need to raise the standard through guilt and condemnation.
     False
4c. True or false: God loves you so much that He wants to leave you where you are.
     False
4d. God's best is not going to come to pass for you _____.
     A.   Accidentally
     B.   Purposefully
     C.   Supernaturally
     D.   All of the above
     E.   None of the above
     A.   Accidentally

4e. You have to set God's best as your goal and then do what?
Pursue it

5. Just like those lepers, we're going to have to stir ourselves up. How long are we just going to keep wishing and hoping instead of taking a step of faith? We need to stir ourselves up, or we'll just settle back down to the bottom. We probably weren't expecting this kind of a message; maybe we don't even like it. But this lesson is meant to provoke us to do the right thing and to take the step of faith that God is showing us.

5a. True or false: You have to stir yourself up.
True
5b. What is this lesson meant to do?
Provoke you to do the right thing and to take the step of faith that God is showing you

6. Before we can go any further in learning about how to receive God's best, we must change our expectation. We have to change our aim and begin looking for something more. We shouldn't get condemned and shouldn't do something stupid, but we shouldn't stay where we are either. We need to say, "God, I want Your best. I want to accomplish everything You have for me!" We serve a big God! It doesn't matter how far we've gone, how much we've believed, or how much we've received—God has more!

6a. Before you can go any further in learning about how to receive God's best, what must you change?
Your expectation
6b. What do you need to say?
"God, I want Your best. I want to accomplish everything You have for me!"
6c. It doesn't matter how far you've gone, how much you've believed, or how much you've received—God has _____!
More

7. If our lives aren't supernatural, then they're superficial. If we can point to ourselves and take pride in everything we've done, then we haven't come into God. He will bring us beyond ourselves. He'll ask us to do something that's bigger than us so that we'll have to depend on Him. Then the only answer we can give will be, "It's not me. It's the Lord. He did it. Only the blessing of God could make these things work out this way."

7a. If your life isn't _____, then it's _____.
   A. Superabundant / superstitious
   B. Supernatural / superficial

    C. Superfluous / superlative
    D. Superior / supernal
    E. Superhuman / superb
    B. Supernatural / superficial

7b. True or false: If you can point to yourself and take pride in everything you've done, then you haven't come into God.
    True

7c. *Discussion question:* What has God asked you to do that's bigger than you?
    Discussion question

8.   Many of us as Christians haven't stretched themselves very far. We ought to be living for something worth dying for. We've got more to do than we can accomplish in a lifetime. Every day should be exciting because we're busy stretching forward in faith to fulfill what God has led us to do.

8a. You ought to be _____ for something worth _____ for.
    Living / dying

8b. You've got more to do than you can accomplish in a _____.
    A. Church service
    B. Lifetime
    C. Trip overseas
    D. All of the above
    E. None of the above
    D. All of the above

8c. Every day should be _____ because you're _____ stretching _____ in faith to fulfill what God has led you to do.
    Exciting / busy / forward

9.   Have we been wondering why our lives aren't exciting? It's because God can't give us a sense of satisfaction, joy, and peace over what we're doing because He made us for more than that. He wants to raise our vision and lift up our heads. Are we ready to believe for something bigger?

9a. *Discussion question:* What would believing for something bigger look like for you?
    Discussion question

Discipleship Questions

1. True or false: Loving security keeps you from receiving God's best.

2. What did the four lepers basically ask themselves (2 Kin. 7:3-4)?

   _____

   _____

   _____

3. You will never see a change in your situation if you're not willing to do what?
   A. Take a stand
   B. Take a hint
   C. Take a break
   D. Take a risk
   E. Take a bow

4. *Discussion question:* What will you change in order to start living more by faith?

   _____

   _____

   _____

5. True or false: You need to sit back and receive your land.

6. *Discussion question:* How much are you willing to trust God even though there is the risk of failure?

   _____

   _____

   _____

7. Before you can receive God's best, you must understand what?

   _____

   _____

   _____

8. What is God looking to see?

    _____

    _____

    _____

9. *Discussion question:* What are you going to do to deal with fear and small thinking?

    _____

    _____

    _____

10. What is the first step toward receiving God's best for you?

    _____

    _____

    _____

11. True or false: You need to raise the standard through guilt and condemnation.

12. True or false: God loves you so much that He wants to leave you where you are.

13. God's best is not going to come to pass for you _____.
    A. Accidentally
    B. Purposefully
    C. Supernaturally
    D. All of the above
    E. None of the above

14. You have to set God's best as your goal and do what?

    _____

    _____

    _____

15. True or false: You have to stir yourself up.

16. What is this lesson meant to do?

_____

_____

_____

17. Before you can go any further in learning about how to receive God's best, what must you change?

_____

_____

_____

18. What do you need to say?

_____

_____

_____

19. It doesn't matter how far you've gone, how much you've believed, or how much you've received—God has _____!

20. If your life isn't _____, then it's _____.
    A. Superabundant / superstitious
    B. Supernatural / superficial
    C. Superfluous / superlative
    D. Superior / supernal
    E. Superhuman / superb

21. True or false: If you can point to yourself and take pride in everything you've done, then you haven't come into God.

22. *Discussion question:* What has God asked you to do that's bigger than you?

_____

_____

_____

23. You ought to be _____ for something worth _____ for.

24. You've got more to do than what you can accomplish in a _____.
    A. Church service
    B. Lifetime
    C. Trip overseas
    D. All of the above
    E. None of the above

25. Every day should be _____ because you're _____ stretching _____ in faith to fulfill what God has led you to do.

26. *Discussion question:* What would believing for something bigger look like for you?

_____

_____

_____

Answer Key

1. True

2. "How long are we just going to sit here? Until we die?"

3. D. Take a risk

4. *Discussion question*

5. False

6. *Discussion question*

7. That the eyes of the Lord are looking at your heart right now

8. If your heart is fully committed to Him, or if you're just embracing life the way everybody else does it

9. *Discussion question*

10. To quit accepting less than His best

11. False

12. False

13. A. Accidentally

14. Pursue it

15. True

16. Provoke you to do the right thing and to take the step of faith that God is showing you

17. Your expectation

18. "God, I want Your best. I want to accomplish everything You have for me!"

19. More

20. B. Supernatural / superficial

21. True

22. *Discussion question*

23. Living / dying

24. D. All of the above

25. Exciting / busy / forward

26. *Discussion question*

Scriptures

2 KINGS 7:3-11

And there were four leprous men at the entering in of the gate: and they said one to another, Why sit we here until we die? [4] If we say, We will enter into the city, then the famine is in the city, and we shall die there: and if we sit still here, we die also. Now therefore come, and let us fall unto the host of the Syrians: if they save us alive, we shall live; and if they kill us, we shall but die. [5] And they rose up in the twilight, to go unto the camp of the Syrians: and when they were come to the uttermost part of the camp of Syria, behold, there was no man there. [6] For the Lord had made the host of the Syrians to hear a noise of chariots, and a noise of horses, even the noise of a great host: and they said one to another, Lo, the king of Israel hath hired against us the kings of the Hittites, and the kings of the Egyptians, to come upon us. [7] Wherefore they arose and fled in the twilight, and left their tents, and their horses, and their asses, even the camp as it was, and fled for their life. [8] And when these lepers came to the uttermost part of the camp, they went into one tent, and did eat and drink, and carried thence silver, and gold, and raiment, and went and hid it; and came again, and entered into another tent, and carried thence also, and went and hid it. [9] Then they said one to another, We do not well: this day is a day of good tidings, and we hold our peace: if we tarry till the morning light, some mischief will come upon us: now therefore come, that we may go and tell the king's household. [10] So they came and called unto the porter of the city: and they told them, saying, We came to the camp of the Syrians, and, behold, there was no man there, neither voice of man, but horses tied, and asses tied, and the tents as they were. [11] And he called the porters; and they told it to the king's house within.

2 KINGS 6:24-29

And it came to pass after this, that Benhadad king of Syria gathered all his host, and went up, and besieged Samaria. [25] And there was a great famine in Samaria: and, behold, they besieged it, until an ass's head was sold for fourscore pieces of silver, and the fourth part of a cab of dove's dung for five pieces of silver. [26] And as the king of Israel was passing by upon the wall, there cried a woman unto him, saying, Help, my lord, O king. [27] And he said, If the Lord do not help thee, whence shall I help thee? out of the barnfloor, or out of the winepress? [28] And the king said unto her, What aileth thee? And she answered, This woman said unto me, Give thy son, that we may eat him to day, and we will eat my son to morrow. [29] So we boiled my son, and did eat him: and I said unto her on the next day, Give thy son, that we may eat him: and she hath hid her son.

Already Blessed

LESSON 6

If you need to be healed, you don't need God to heal you. The Lord knew you would need healing, and He has already provided it. You don't have to pray and ask God to heal you. What you need to do is learn how to receive the healing that has already been provided. That's huge!

You might be wondering, *What's the difference?* There's a big difference. To think that you need to go and get God to do something that He hasn't yet done has an element of doubt in it, because you don't know whether He will act on your behalf or not. But how can you doubt that God will do what He's already done? If He's already provided it by grace (and in Christ, He has), then you just need to believe and receive it by faith.

See, some people say, "Oh, I believe God's going to heal me." That sounds good, but actually, it's unbelief. The Bible says, *"By whose stripes ye were healed"* (1 Pet. 2:24). According to that scripture, it's not in the future that you're going to be healed; it's in the past that you *were* healed. Jesus Christ bore your stripes on His body on the cross. God provided for your healing 2,000 years ago. It was then that He healed you. That's why this verse says you were healed. You don't need God to heal you. You just need to learn how to receive what has already been provided.

CAN DO VS. HAS DONE

It's much easier to release something that you've already got than it is to go get something that you don't yet have. This is a major shift of mindset! We're looking at how to *receive* God's best—not how to *convince* God to give you His best. In Christ, God has already done it!

Consider how the Apostle Paul prayed:

> *Wherefore I also, after I heard of your faith in the Lord Jesus, and love unto all the saints, [16] Cease not to give thanks for you, making mention of you in my prayers; [17] That the God of our Lord Jesus Christ, the Father of glory, may give unto you the spirit of wisdom and revelation in the knowledge of him.*
>
> Ephesians 1:15-17

Notice that he didn't pray, "O God, please move!" I've been traveling and ministering for almost fifty years, and throughout that time, I've been to hundreds, possibly thousands, of churches. I've heard people pray and beg God for things over and over again. A typical prayer would be, "O God, please move. O Lord, pour out Your power!"

If you were to write a prayer today for believers 2,000 years in the future, how would you pray? What kind of prayer would you record? Let me guess. It would be something along the lines of "O God, send revival. Touch these people. Pour out Your Spirit and move!" It would be, "O Lord, do something new. Stretch forth Your hand and do a new thing!"

Here we are now, 2,000 years later, reading Paul's prayer. Let's look at how the Holy Spirit inspired him to essentially pray: "God, open up their eyes to what You've already done." Wow! This is totally different than the way most Christians function today. Most Christians believe God **can do** anything but that He **has done** nothing. Seeing God work is all dependent upon our praying, asking, and begging. We think that if we do everything just right, God might move.

GOD ANTICIPATED

God anticipated every problem that you or anybody else in the entire human race would ever have. Through Christ's death, burial, and resurrection, He dealt with every problem that could ever happen—past, present, and future. It's taken care of. The Lord is now seated at the Father's right hand. Jesus is not healing, saving, and delivering people; He's already done it. His power has already been released. Now it's up to you to receive what He's done by putting faith in what is already provided, not in what God "can" do. Normally when I share this truth in a meeting, half or more of the audience just stares back at me with that "deer-in-the-headlights" look. Perhaps you need to read that over again, more slowly and prayerfully. Holy Spirit, please grant my beloved reader revelation knowledge concerning this truth.

> *The eyes of your understanding being enlightened; that ye may know what is the hope of his calling.*
>
> Ephesians 1:18a

It's not about your calling; it's His calling. Jesus has already been called and He's already provided everything. He paid the price for everything on the cross, and He has the favor of God now. We are just riding on His coattails. As born-again believers, we have favor with God because of what Jesus did, not because of what we do. It's about His calling, His anointing, His power, and His blessing that's on our lives.

Paul was praying that your eyes would be opened to understand and see *"what is the hope of his calling, and what the riches of the glory of his inheritance in the saints"*

(Eph. 1:18). God's glory isn't out there in heaven. We often sing songs with words like "when we all get to heaven, what a day that will be!" But did you know that it would bankrupt heaven to have to replace what we already have on the inside of us right now? The riches of the glory of His inheritance is in us. The glory of God is in us!

LIKE A YO-YO

Some people want to see a "glory cloud." Look on the inside! If you can't see it, it's because you're walking by sight and not by faith (2 Cor. 5:7). The truth is, you've got the glory of God.

You have been called *"to the obtaining of the glory of our Lord Jesus Christ"* (2 Thess. 2:14). That's not something that's going to happen in heaven. In heaven, you'll get a body that will reflect His glory, but right now, you have the glory of God on the inside of you. Paul prayed that your eyes would be opened to what you've already got (Eph. 1:18)!

> *And what is the exceeding greatness of his power to us-ward who believe, according to the working of his mighty power, [20] Which he wrought in Christ, when he raised him from the dead, and set him at his own right hand in the heavenly places, [21] Far above all principality, and power, and might, and dominion, and every name that is named, not only in this world, but also in that which is to come: [22] And hath put all things under his feet, and gave him to be the head over all things to the church, [23] Which is his body, the fulness of him that filleth all in all.*
>
> Ephesians 1:19-23

Paul prayed that you would see the exceeding greatness of His power *"to us-ward who believe"*—the same power God used when He raised Christ from the dead. The power that it took to raise Jesus from the dead is greater than your hangnail, greater than your cold, greater than your flu, and greater than your financial, marital, and emotional problems. He is greater! Yet again, most Christians believe that God has power, but they don't believe that He's done anything with it. They think they have to beg Him and somehow get Him to release His power. Ephesians 1:19-20 makes it clear that you already have the same power on the inside of you that raised Jesus Christ from the dead.

The only reason we accept this substandard living is because we don't believe that God has already done it. We believe that, somehow or another, all of the glory and blessings of God are reserved for heaven, and in this life, we just have to hang on and struggle through. We have to be sick, poor, and up and down like a yo-yo. Religion teaches that although God may send us up on a mountaintop, it's in the valleys where we'll grow. They think we're supposed to be up and down a lot.

CONSISTENT

John the Baptist, referring to Isaiah's prophecy, declared that *"every valley shall be filled, and every mountain and hill shall be brought low; and the crooked shall be made straight, and the rough ways shall be made smooth"* (Luke 3:5, see also Is. 40:4). This means that there should be increasingly smooth sailing. We ought to be consistent.

The number one way that people describe me when they are introducing me is to say, "He's exactly the same as he is on television." I have thought to myself, *What kind of an introduction is that*? So, I asked some people what they meant by that. I was told that many people can get in front of a group and talk victory, but then in private, they're different. This should not be! You shouldn't be one person in front of an audience and another when you're not. If you're normally a really quiet person and then you just explode and become this other person when you get behind a pulpit, you're a hypocrite.

Do you remember R. W. Schambach? He's with the Lord now, but I had the privilege of ministering with him once. When he preached, he was really animated—screaming and yelling and such. We went out for ice cream afterward in his Jaguar convertible. Guess what? He was the same way driving down the road. He even preached to the people around us while we sat there eating dessert.

There's nothing wrong with being demonstrative if that's the real you. You might have a different personality and be more animated and expressive than I am. That's fine. We need variety in the body of Christ. But if you're this meek person until you get behind a pulpit and then you just explode—you're a hypocrite. You're religious.

We shouldn't be so up and down. There ought to be consistency. We should be the same all the time, because if we're walking with Jesus, He's *"the same yesterday, and to day, and for ever"* (Heb. 13:8). If we're up sometimes and down other times, it's because sometimes we're trusting in Jesus and other times we're walking in our own flesh. We ought to be supernaturally natural. The same power that raised Christ from the dead is in us at all times (Eph. 1:19-20). It never fluctuates.

YOU DON'T KNOW

You need to find out who you are and what you have in Christ. Most Christians don't live as if they have the same power that raised Jesus from the dead on the inside of them, because they can't feel it. Looking in the mirror, it doesn't appear like they have the same power that raised Jesus from the dead. There aren't goose bumps going up and down their spines. They don't feel anything. And since they can't feel anything, they just don't believe that God has done anything.

But the truth is, Paul prayed that our eyes would be opened to see that we already have the same power that raised Christ from the dead. We aren't praying to get it. We've already got it (Eph. 1:19-20)!

God wants to bless us with His best. In Christ, He's provided everything we could ever need. It's not up to God whether or not we walk in it; it's up to us. But we've settled for less than God's best. We don't know who we are in the spirit and we don't understand our identity in Christ. I'm not only human. I'm not just a man. One-third of me is wall-to-wall Holy Ghost. I should expect to see something different than a person who doesn't know God.

You could stand the average Christian up next to an unbeliever and find that they have the same fears, the same financial problems, and the same struggles. Even before the full impact of the Great Recession, before any visible effects were seen, many Christians started planning on failure. They began expecting and anticipating problems. They acted just like people who don't know God, who don't have a covenant that says, *"My God shall supply all your need according to his riches in glory by Christ Jesus"* (Phil. 4:19). This should not be. I'm not saying this to condemn you. I'm trying to open up your eyes and help you start believing for more.

Do you have the same fears as someone who doesn't know God? When they say, "The flu season is hitting," are you afraid? If so, something is wrong with this picture. You're alive, and they're dead (spiritually). You've got the same power inside you that raised Christ from the dead (Eph. 1:19-20). Yet in many ways, you're living just like a person who doesn't know the Lord. That's wrong. It's not because God hasn't given. It's because you don't know what you have.

START PRAISING HIM!

We're sitting here begging God to do what He's already done. How does He respond to that? Let's say that I gave you my Bible, and it's sitting on your lap right now. How do you think I'd respond if you asked me, "Andrew, please pass me your Bible? Would you please hand it to me so I can look at it?" How do you respond to someone who's asking you to do something you've already done? I already gave you my Bible. It is right there on your lap. I'd probably just look at you like your elevator doesn't go all the way up to the top floor. I'd wonder, *What's wrong with you? Why are you asking me to give you something that you've already got?* This is probably similar to the reaction you're getting when you pray.

You're praying, "O God, please heal me." If God could be confused, I think He would be. I can just imagine Him looking over at Jesus and saying, "Didn't You tell them that by Your stripes they were healed (1 Pet. 2:24)? Why are they asking Me to heal them? Didn't You tell them they're blessed with all spiritual blessings (Eph. 1:3), that You became poor so that through Your poverty they could be made rich (2 Cor. 8:9)? Didn't You tell them that I would supply all of their needs according to My riches in glory—not according to the economy of their country (Phil. 4:19)? Didn't You tell them that? Why are they panicking because it's the 'Great Recession'? Why are they anxious, fearful, and worried?" It's because we don't believe that God has already done it. We're thinking that it's up to God to give and not up to us to receive. I'm telling you, it's our receivers that are messed up, not God's transmitter!

If you were watching television and all of a sudden the set turned off, the first thing you'd probably do is look to see if someone unplugged it. Then you'd troubleshoot and see if something was wrong with your set. You wouldn't just get up and call the television station, asking, "Why did you quit broadcasting?" But that's how we treat God. If we pray and don't receive something immediately, we think, *Lord, why didn't You give it?* It's never God who doesn't give; it's us who quit receiving. Something's wrong with our receivers—not God's giver. He has already blessed us with all spiritual blessings (Eph. 1:3). He has already broadcasted them to us. We just need to tune in our receivers and pray, "O Lord, help me to see and understand what You've already done!"

Believing that God has already done His part is 90 percent of the battle; then there are certain things that we must do. We need to quit doubting God and just believe, praying, "I know You've done it. If I'm not seeing the answer manifest, it's not Your fault. You've already supplied. Thank You, Lord!" Then we need to start praising God in faith, saying, "I don't know why I can't see it, but I know You're not the problem. I just want to praise You for being so faithful. Even though I'm sick and the doctor says I'm going to die, it's not Your fault. You didn't do this to me. Thank You for being a good God!" Just praise and thank Him and you'll get out of that fear, worry, griping, and complaining. Just stop murmuring and doubting God and start praising Him. I've seen many people receive healing through aggressively acknowledging, by their thanks and praise, what the Lord has already done. You can too!

ANDREW'S RECOMMENDATIONS FOR FURTHER STUDY

Blessed be the God and Father of our Lord Jesus Christ, who hath blessed us with all spiritual blessings in heavenly places in Christ.

Ephesians 1:3

Notice the terminology used in this scripture: *"who hath* [past tense] *blessed us"* (brackets mine). It's already done. God has already blessed you. By grace, He has already provided everything that you will ever need. This life-changing truth is covered in depth in my teachings entitled *You've Already Got It!* and *Living in the Balance of Grace & Faith*.

Outline

I. If you need to be healed, you don't have to pray and ask God to heal you; what you need to do is learn how to receive the healing that has already been provided.

    A To think that you need to go and get God to do something that He hasn't yet done has an element of doubt in it, because you don't know whether He will act on your behalf or not.

    B. If He's already provided it by grace (and in Christ, He has), then you just need to believe and receive it by faith.

    C. Some people say, "Oh, I believe God's going to heal me," but actually, it's unbelief.

    D. According to 1 Peter 2:24, it's not in the future that you're going to be healed; it's in the past that you *were* healed.

II. It's much easier to release something that you've already got than it is to go get something that you don't yet have.

    A. This is a major shift of mindset!

    B. You're looking at how to *receive* God's best—not how to *convince* God to give you His best.

    C. Consider how the Apostle Paul prayed:

> *Wherefore I also, after I heard of your faith in the Lord Jesus, and love unto all the saints, [16] Cease not to give thanks for you, making mention of you in my prayers; [17] That the God of our Lord Jesus Christ, the Father of glory, may give unto you the spirit of wisdom and revelation in the knowledge of him.*
>
> Ephesians 1:15-17

    D. The Holy Spirit inspired him to pray, "God, open up their eyes to what You've already done."

    E. Most Christians believe God **can do** anything but that He **has done** nothing.

    F. They think that if they do everything just right, God might move.

III. God anticipated every problem that we or anybody else in the entire human race would ever have.

    A. Through Christ's death, burial, and resurrection, He dealt with every problem that could ever happen—past, present, and future.

    B. Now it's up to us to receive what He's done by putting faith in what is already provided, not in what God "can" do.

    C. Holy Spirit, please grant us revelation knowledge concerning the truths in this lesson.

IV. Ephesians 1:18 says,

    The eyes of your understanding being enlightened; that ye may know what is the hope of his calling.

    A. It's not about our calling; it's Jesus's calling.

    B. Jesus has already been called, and He's already provided everything.

    C. He paid the price for everything on the cross, and He has the favor of God now.

    D. As born-again believers, we have favor with God because of what Jesus did, not because of what we do.

    E. It's about His calling, His anointing, His power, and His blessing that's on our lives.

V. Paul was praying that our eyes would be opened to understand and see *"what is the hope of his calling, and what the riches of the glory of his inheritance in the saints"* (Eph. 1:18).

    A. It would bankrupt heaven to have to replace what we already have on the inside of us right now.

    B. The glory of God is in us!

    C. Some people want to see a "glory cloud."

    D. We need to look on the inside!

E.   If we can't see it, it's because we're walking by sight and not by faith (2 Cor. 5:7).

F.   We have been called *"to the obtaining of the glory of our Lord Jesus Christ"* (2 Thess. 2:14).

G.   In heaven, we'll get bodies that will reflect His glory, but right now, we have the glory of God on the inside of us.

VI.   Paul prayed that we would see the exceeding greatness of His power *"to us-ward who believe"* (Eph. 1:19)—the same power God used when He raised Christ from the dead.

A.   Yet most of us as Christians think we have to beg God and somehow get Him to release His power.

B.   We may believe that, somehow or another, all the glory and blessings of God are reserved for heaven, and in this life, we just have to hang on and struggle through.

C.   Many of us believe that we have to be sick, poor, and up and down like a yo-yo.

D.   John the Baptist, referring to Isaiah's prophecy, declared that *"every valley shall be filled, and every mountain and hill shall be brought low; and the crooked shall be made straight, and the rough ways shall be made smooth"* (Luke 3:5, see also Is. 40:4).

E.   This means that there should be increasingly smooth sailing.

VII.   You ought to be consistent.

A.   The number one way that people describe me when they are introducing me is to say, "He's exactly the same as he is on television."

B.   You shouldn't be one person in front of an audience and another when you're not.

C.   If you're normally a really quiet person and then you just explode and become this other person when you get behind a pulpit, it could be because you're a hypocrite and religious.

D.   You should be the same all the time, because if you're walking with Jesus, He's *"the same yesterday, and to day, and for ever"* (Heb. 13:8).

E.   If you're up sometimes and down other times, it's because sometimes you're trusting in Jesus, and other times you're walking in your own flesh.

F.   You ought to be supernaturally natural.

G.   The same power that raised Christ from the dead is in you at all times (Eph. 1:19-20); it never fluctuates.

VIII. We need to find out who we are and what we have in Christ.

A.   Many of us as Christians don't live as if we have on the inside of us the same power that raised Jesus from the dead, because we can't feel it.

B.   Looking in the mirror, it doesn't appear like we have the same power that raised Jesus from the dead.

C.   And since we can't feel anything, we don't believe that God has done anything.

D.   It's not up to God whether or not we walk in it; it's up to us.

IX. You could stand the average Christian up next to an unbeliever and find that they have the same fears, the same financial problems, and the same struggles.

A.   They act just like people who don't know God, who don't have a covenant that says, *"My God shall supply all your need according to his riches in glory by Christ Jesus"* (Phil. 4:19).

B.   Do you have the same fears as someone who doesn't know God?

C.   If so, something is wrong with this picture.

D.   You're alive, and they're dead (spiritually).

E.   It's not because God hasn't given; it's because you don't know what you have.

X. If God could be confused, He would be.

A.   Imagine if He looked over at Jesus and said, "Didn't You tell them that by Your stripes they were healed (1 Pet. 2:24)? Why are they asking Me to heal them? Didn't You tell them they're blessed with all spiritual blessings (Eph. 1:3), that

You became poor so that through Your poverty they could be made rich (2 Cor. 8:9)? Didn't You tell them that I would supply all of their needs according to My riches in glory—not according to the economy of their country (Phil. 4:19)? Didn't You tell them that? Why are they panicking because it's the 'Great Recession'? Why are they anxious, fearful, and worried?"

B. It's because we don't believe that God has already done it.

C. We're thinking that it's up to God to give and not up to us to receive.

XI. It's our receivers that are messed up, not God's transmitter!

A. If we were watching television and all of a sudden the set turned off, the first thing we'd probably do is look to see if someone unplugged it.

B. Then we'd troubleshoot and see if something was wrong with the set.

C. We wouldn't just get up and call the television station, asking, "Why did you quit broadcasting?"

D. If we pray and don't receive something immediately, we think, *Lord, why didn't You give it?*

E. It's never God who doesn't give; it's us who quit receiving.

F. We just need to tune in our receivers and pray, "O Lord, help me to see and understand what You've already done!"

XII. Believing that God has already done His part is 90 percent of the battle; then there are certain things that we must do.

A. We need to quit doubting God and just believe, praying, "I know You've done it. If I'm not seeing the answer manifest, it's not Your fault. You've already supplied. Thank You, Lord!"

B. Then we need to start praising God in faith, saying, "I don't know why I can't see it, but I know You're not the problem. I just want to praise You for being so faithful. Even though I'm sick and the doctor says I'm going to die, it's not Your fault. You didn't do this to me. Thank You for being a good God!"

C. We need to praise and thank Him, and we'll get out of that fear, worry, griping, and complaining.

D. Let's stop murmuring and doubting God and start praising Him.

E. Many people receive healing through aggressively acknowledging, by their thanks and praise, what the Lord has already done, and we can too!

ANDREW'S RECOMMENDATIONS FOR FURTHER STUDY

Blessed be the God and Father of our Lord Jesus Christ, who hath blessed us with all spiritual blessings in heavenly places in Christ.

Ephesians 1:3

Notice the terminology used in this scripture: *"who hath* [past tense] *blessed us"* (brackets mine). It's already done. God has already blessed you. By grace, He has already provided everything that you will ever need. This life-changing truth is covered in depth in my teachings entitled *You've Already Got It!* and *Living in the Balance of Grace & Faith.*

Teacher's Guide

1. If we need to be healed, we don't have to pray and ask God to heal us; what we need to do is learn how to receive the healing that has already been provided. To think that we need to go and get God to do something that He hasn't yet done has an element of doubt in it, because we don't know whether He will act on our behalf or not. If He's already provided it by grace (and in Christ, He has), then we just need to believe and receive it by faith. Some people say, "Oh, I believe God's going to heal me," but actually, it's unbelief. According to 1 Peter 2:24, it's not in the future that we're going to be healed; it's in the past that we *were* healed.

1a. If you need to be healed, you don't have to _____ and _____ God to heal you; what you need to do is _____ how to _____ the healing that has already been provided.

   Pray / ask / learn / receive

1b. To think that you need to go and get God to do something that He hasn't yet done has an element of _____ in it, because you don't know whether He will act on your behalf or not.
   A. Expectation
   B. Doubt
   C. Comfort
   D. Power
   E. Pride
   B. Doubt

1c. True or false: It's in the future that you will be healed, not in the past (1 Pet. 2:24).

   False

2. It's much easier to release something that we've already got than it is to go get something that we don't yet have. This is a major shift of mindset! We're looking at how to *receive* God's best—not how to *convince* God to give us His best. Let's consider how the Apostle Paul prayed:

> *Wherefore I also, after I heard of your faith in the Lord Jesus, and love unto all the saints, [16] Cease not to give thanks for you, making mention of you in my prayers; [17] That the God of our Lord Jesus Christ, the Father of glory, may give unto you the spirit of wisdom and revelation in the knowledge of him.*
>
> Ephesians 1:15-17

The Holy Spirit inspired him to pray, "God, open up their eyes to what You've already done." Most Christians believe God *can do* anything but that He *has done* nothing.

They think that if they do everything just right, God might move.

2a. *Discussion question:* Why do you think it is easier to release something that you've already got than it is to go get something that you don't yet have?
   Discussion question

2b. You're looking at how to _____ God's best—not how to _____ God to give you His best.
   Receive / convince

2c. Essentially, what did the Holy Spirit inspire Paul to pray (Eph. 1:15-17)?
   "God, open up their eyes to what You've already done."

2d. *Discussion question:* In what area of life do you feel like you are waiting on God to do something that He hasn't done?
   Discussion question

2e. True or false: If you do everything just right, God might move.
   False

3. God anticipated every problem that we or anybody else in the entire human race would ever have. Through Christ's death, burial, and resurrection, He dealt with every problem that could ever happen—past, present, and future. Now it's up to us to receive what He's done by putting faith in what is already provided, not in what God "can" do. Holy Spirit, please grant us revelation knowledge concerning the truths in this lesson.

3a. God _____ every problem that you or anybody else in the entire human race would ever have.
   A. Planned
   B. Caused
   C. Anticipated
   D. All of the above
   E. None of the above
   C. Anticipated

3b. How did God deal with these problems?
   Through Christ's death, burial, and resurrection

3c. By putting faith in what is already provided, what can you do?
   Receive what God has done

4. Ephesians 1:18 says,

   The eyes of your understanding being enlightened; that ye may know what is the hope of his calling.

It's not about our calling; it's Jesus's calling. Jesus has already been called, and He's already provided everything. He paid the price for everything on the cross, and He has the favor of God now. As born-again believers, we have favor with God because of what Jesus did, not because of what we do. It's about His calling, His anointing, His power, and His blessing that's on our lives.

4a. Whose calling is it (Eph. 1:18)?
   Jesus's
4b. Since Jesus paid for everything on the cross, what does He have now?
   The favor of God
4c. As a born-again believer, what do you have now?
   A. The favor of God
   B. The toleration of God
   C. The ire of God
   D. The chagrin of God
   E. The rejection of God
   A. The favor of God
4d. It's about His _____, His _____, His _____, and His _____ that's on your life.
   Calling / anointing / power / blessing

5. Paul was praying that our eyes would be opened to understand and see *"what is the hope of his calling, and what the riches of the glory of his inheritance in the saints"* (Eph. 1:18). It would bankrupt heaven to have to replace what we already have on the inside of us right now. The glory of God is in us! Some people want to see a "glory cloud." We need to look on the inside! If we can't see it, it's because we're walking by sight and not by faith (2 Cor. 5:7). We have been called *"to the obtaining of the glory of our Lord Jesus Christ"* (2 Thess. 2:14). In heaven, we'll get bodies that will reflect His glory, but right now, we have the glory of God on the inside of us.

5a. According to Ephesians 1:18, what was Paul praying that your eyes would be opened to understand and see?
   What is the hope of His calling, and what the riches of the glory of His inheritance in the saints
5b. Whose glory is in you?
   God's
5c. You can see the glory of God inside you if you're doing what (2 Cor. 5:7)?
   A. Working hard enough
   B. Looking for it
   C. Squinting hard
   D. Walking by faith
   E. Wearing glasses
   D. Walking by faith

5d. To what have you been called (2 Thess. 2:14)?
To the obtaining of the glory of our Lord Jesus Christ

5e. *Discussion question:* What do you think about receiving a body in heaven that will reflect God's glory?
Discussion question

6.   Paul prayed that we would see the exceeding greatness of His power *"to us-ward who believe"* (Eph. 1:19)—the same power God used when He raised Christ from the dead. Yet most of us as Christians think we have to beg God and somehow get Him to release His power. We may believe that, somehow or another, all of the glory and blessings of God are reserved for heaven, and in this life, we just have to hang on and struggle through. Many of us believe that we have to be sick, poor, and up and down like a yo-yo. John the Baptist, referring to Isaiah's prophecy, declared that *"every valley shall be filled, and every mountain and hill shall be brought low; and the crooked shall be made straight, and the rough ways shall be made smooth"* (Luke 3:5, see also Is. 40:4). This means that there should be increasingly smooth sailing.

6a. According to Ephesians 1:19, what was Paul praying?
That we would see the exceeding greatness of His power *"to us-ward who believe"*—the same power God used when He raised Christ from the dead

6b. True or false: All of the glory and blessings of God are reserved for heaven.
False

6c. True or false: You don't have to be sick, poor, and up and down like a yo-yo.
True

6d. You should be experiencing increasingly smooth _____ (Luke 3:5 and Is. 40:4).
Sailing

7.   We ought to be consistent. The number one way that people describe Andrew when they are introducing him is to say, "He's exactly the same as he is on television." We shouldn't be one person in front of an audience and another when we're not. If we're normally really quiet and then we just explode and become another person when we get behind a pulpit, it could be because we're hypocrites or religious. We should be the same all the time, because if we're walking with Jesus, He's *the same yesterday, and to day, and for ever"* (Heb. 13:8). If we're up sometimes and down other times, it's because sometimes we're trusting in Jesus, and other times we're walking in our own flesh. We ought to be supernaturally natural. The same power that raised Christ from the dead is in us at all times (Eph. 1:19-20); it never fluctuates.

7a. According to Hebrews 13:8, why should you be the same all the time?
Because if you're walking with Jesus, He's *"the same yesterday, and to day, and for ever"*

7b. If you're up sometimes and down other times, why is that?

It's because sometimes you're trusting in Jesus, and other times you're walking in your own flesh

7c. *Discussion question:* How do you plan to be supernaturally natural?

Discussion question

7d. The same power that raised Christ from the dead is in you at all times; it _____ fluctuates (Eph. 1:19-20).

    A. Never
    B. Sometimes
    C. Always
    D. Randomly
    E. Seldom
    A. Never

8. We need to find out who we are and what we have in Christ. Many of us as Christians don't live as if we have on the inside of us the same power that raised Jesus from the dead, because we can't feel it. Looking in the mirror, it doesn't appear like we have the same power that raised Jesus from the dead. And since we can't feel anything, we may not believe that God has done anything. It's not up to God whether or not we walk in it; it's up to us.

8a. What do you need to find out?

Who you are and what you have in Christ

8b. Why do many Christians not live as if they have the same power on the inside of them that raised Jesus from the dead?

They can't feel it

8c. If you're going to walk in what God has done, who is it up to?

    A. God
    B. Your spouse
    C. Your pastor
    D. Your mom
    E. You
    E. You

9. We could stand the average Christian up next to an unbeliever and find that they have the same fears, the same financial problems, and the same struggles. They act just like people who don't know God, who don't have a covenant that says, *"My God shall supply all your need according to his riches in glory by Christ Jesus"* (Phil. 4:19). Do we have the same fears as someone who doesn't know God? If so, something is wrong with this picture. We're alive, and they're dead (spiritually). It's not because God hasn't given; it's because we don't know what we have.

9a. *Discussion question:* Why do you think the average Christian has the same fears, the same financial problems, and the same struggles as an unbeliever?
Discussion question

9b. According to Philippians 4:19, you have a covenant that says what?
God will supply all your need according to His riches in glory by Christ Jesus

9c. What is one major difference between you and someone who doesn't know God?
You're alive, and they're dead (spiritually)

10. If God could be confused, He would be. Imagine if He looked over at Jesus and said, "Didn't You tell them that by Your stripes they were healed (1 Pet. 2:24)? Why are they asking Me to heal them? Didn't You tell them they're blessed with all spiritual blessings (Eph. 1:3), that You became poor so that through Your poverty they could be made rich (2 Cor. 8:9)? Didn't You tell them that I would supply all of their needs according to My riches in glory—not according to the economy of their country (Phil. 4:19)? Didn't You tell them that? Why are they panicking because it's the 'Great Recession'? Why are they anxious, fearful, and worried?" It's because we don't believe that God has already done it. We're thinking that it's up to God to give and not up to us to receive.

10a.*Discussion question:* Since God has provided all spiritual blessings, what is left to pray for?
Discussion question

11. It's our receivers that are messed up, not God's transmitter! If we were watching television and all of a sudden the set turned off, the first thing we'd probably do is look to see if someone unplugged it. Then we'd troubleshoot and see if something was wrong with the set. We wouldn't just get up and call the television station, asking, "Why did you quit broadcasting?" If we pray and don't receive something immediately, we think, *Lord, why didn't You give it?* It's never God who doesn't give; it's us who quit receiving. We just need to tune in our receivers and pray, "O Lord, help me to see and understand what You've already done!"

11a.It's never God who doesn't _____; it's you who quit _____.
Give / receiving

11b.What do you need to tune in?
Your receiver

12. Believing that God has already done His part is 90 percent of the battle; then there are certain things that we must do. We need to quit doubting God and just believe, praying, "I know You've done it. If I'm not seeing the answer manifest, it's not Your

fault. You've already supplied. Thank You, Lord!" Then we need to start praising God in faith, saying, "I don't know why I can't see it, but I know You're not the problem. I just want to praise You for being so faithful. Even though I'm sick and the doctor says I'm going to die, it's not Your fault. You didn't do this to me. Thank You for being a good God!" We need to praise and thank Him, and we'll get out of that fear, worry, griping, and complaining. Let's stop murmuring and doubting God and start praising Him. Many people receive healing through aggressively acknowledging, by their thanks and praise, what the Lord has already done, and we can too!

12a.Believing that God has already done His part is _____ of the battle; then there are
   certain things that you must do.
   A.   10 percent
   B.   25 percent
   C.   50 percent
   D.   75 percent
   E.   90 percent
   E.   90 percent
12b.You need to quit doubting God and just believe, praying what?
   "I know You've done it. If I'm not seeing the answer manifest, it's not Your fault.
   You've already supplied. Thank You, Lord!"
12c.By praising and thanking Him, you'll get out of what?
   Fear, worry, griping, and complaining

Discipleship Questions

1. If you need to be healed, you don't have to _____ and _____ God to heal you; what you need to do is _____ how to _____ the healing that has already been provided.

2. To think that you need to go and get God to do something that He hasn't yet done has an element of _____ in it, because you don't know whether He will act on your behalf or not.
   A. Expectation
   B. Doubt
   C. Comfort
   D. Power
   E. Pride

3. True or false: It's in the future that you will be healed, not in the past (1 Pet. 2:24).

4. *Discussion question:* Why do you think it is easier to release something that you've already got than it is to go get something that you don't yet have?

   _____

   _____

   _____

5. You're looking at how to _____ God's best—not how to _____ God to give you His best.

6. Essentially, what did the Holy Spirit inspire Paul to pray (Eph. 1:15-17)?

   _____

   _____

   _____

7. *Discussion question:* In what area of life do you feel like you are waiting on God to do something that He hasn't done?

   _____

   _____

   _____

8. True or false: If you do everything just right, God might move.

9. God _____ every problem that you or anybody else in the entire human race would ever have.
    A. Planned
    B. Caused
    C. Anticipated
    D. All of the above
    E. None of the above

10. How did God deal with these problems?

    _____

    _____

    _____

11. By putting faith in what is already provided, what can you do?

    _____

    _____

    _____

12. Whose calling is it (Eph. 1:18)?

    _____

    _____

    _____

13. Since Jesus paid for everything on the cross, what does He have now?

    _____

    _____

    _____

14. As a born-again believer, what do you have now?
    A. The favor of God
    B. The toleration of God
    C. The ire of God
    D. The chagrin of God
    E. The rejection of God

15. It's about His _____, His _____, His _____, and His _____ that's on your life.

16. According Ephesians 1:18, what was Paul praying that your eyes would be opened to understand and see?

    _____

    _____

    _____

17. Whose glory is in you?

    _____

    _____

    _____

18. You can see the glory of God inside you if you're doing what (2 Cor. 5:7)?
    A. Working hard enough
    B. Looking for it
    C. Squinting hard
    D. Walking by faith
    E. Wearing glasses

19. To what have you been called (2 Thess. 2:14)?

    _____

    _____

    _____

20. *Discussion question:* What do you think about receiving a body in heaven that will reflect God's glory?

_____

_____

_____

21. According to Ephesians 1:19, what was Paul praying?

_____

_____

_____

22. True or false: All of the glory and blessings of God are reserved for heaven.

23. True or false: You don't have to be sick, poor, and up and down like a yo-yo.

24. You should be experiencing increasingly smooth _____ (Luke 3:5 and Is. 40:4).

25. According to Hebrews 13:8, why should you be the same all the time?

_____

_____

_____

26. If you're up sometimes and down other times, why is that?

_____

_____

_____

27. *Discussion question:* How do you plan to be supernaturally natural?

_____

_____

_____

28. The same power that raised Christ from the dead is in you at all times; it _____ fluctuates (Eph. 1:19-20).
    A. Never
    B. Sometimes
    C. Always
    D. Randomly
    E. Seldom

29. What do you need to find out?

    _____

    _____

    _____

30. Why do many Christians not live as if they have the same power on the inside of them that raised Jesus from the dead?

    _____

    _____

    _____

31. If you're going to walk in what God has done, who is it up to?
    A. God
    B. Your spouse
    C. Your pastor
    D. Your mom
    E. You

32. *Discussion question:* Why do you think the average Christian has the same fears, the same financial problems, and the same struggles as an unbeliever?

    _____

    _____

33. According to Philippians 4:19, you have a covenant that says what?

_____

_____

_____

34. What is one major difference between you and someone who doesn't know God?

_____

_____

_____

35. *Discussion question:* Since God has provided all spiritual blessings, what is left to pray for?

_____

_____

_____

36. It's never God who doesn't _____; it's you who quit _____.

37. What do you need to tune in?

_____

_____

_____

38. Believing that God has already done His part is _____ of the battle; then there are certain things that you must do.
    A. 10 percent
    B. 25 percent
    C. 50 percent
    D. 75 percent
    E. 90 percent

39. You need to quit doubting God and just believe, praying what?

_____

_____

_____

40. By praising and thanking Him, you'll get out of what?

_____

_____

_____

Answer Key

1. Pray / ask / learn / receive

2. B. Doubt

3. False

4. *Discussion question*

5. Receive / convince

6. "God, open up their eyes to what You've already done."

7. *Discussion question*

8. False

9. C. Anticipated

10. Through Christ's death, burial, and resurrection

11. Receive what God has done

12. Jesus's

13. The favor of God

14. A. The favor of God

15. Calling / anointing / power / blessing

16. What is the hope of His calling, and what the riches of the glory of His inheritance in the saints

17. God's

18. D. Walking by faith

19. To the obtaining of the glory of our Lord Jesus Christ

20. *Discussion question*

21. That we would see the exceeding greatness of His power *"to us-ward who believe"*—the same power God used when He raised Christ from the dead

22. False

23. True

24. Sailing

25. Because if you're walking with Jesus, He's *"the same yesterday, and to day, and for ever"*

26. It's because sometimes you're trusting in Jesus, and other times you're walking in your own flesh

27. *Discussion question*

28. A. Never

29. Who you are and what you have in Christ

30. They can't feel it

31. E. You

32. *Discussion question*

33. God will supply all your need according to His riches in glory by Christ Jesus

34. You're alive, and they're dead (spiritually)

35. *Discussion question*

36. Give / receiving

37. Your receiver

38. E. 90 percent

39. "I know You've done it. If I'm not seeing the answer manifest, it's not Your fault. You've already supplied. Thank You, Lord!"

40. Fear, worry, griping, and complaining

Scriptures

1 PETER 2:24
Who his own self bare our sins in his own body on the tree, that we, being dead to sins, should live unto righteousness: by whose stripes ye were healed.

EPHESIANS 1:15-23
Wherefore I also, after I heard of your faith in the Lord Jesus, and love unto all the saints, [16] Cease not to give thanks for you, making mention of you in my prayers; [17] That the God of our Lord Jesus Christ, the Father of glory, may give unto you the spirit of wisdom and revelation in the knowledge of him: [18] The eyes of your understanding being enlightened; that ye may know what is the hope of his calling, and what the riches of the glory of his inheritance in the saints, [19] And what is the exceeding greatness of his power to us-ward who believe, according to the working of his mighty power, [20] Which he wrought in Christ, when he raised him from the dead, and set him at his own right hand in the heavenly places, [21] Far above all principality, and power, and might, and dominion, and every name that is named, not only in this world, but also in that which is to come: [22] And hath put all things under his feet, and gave him to be the head over all things to the church, [23] Which is his body, the fulness of him that filleth all in all.

2 CORINTHIANS 5:7
For we walk by faith, not by sight.

2 THESSALONIANS 2:14
Whereunto he called you by our gospel, to the obtaining of the glory of our Lord Jesus Christ.

LUKE 3:5
Every valley shall be filled, and every mountain and hill shall be brought low; and the crooked shall be made straight, and the rough ways shall be made smooth.

ISAIAH 40:4
Every valley shall be exalted, and every mountain and hill shall be made low: and the crooked shall be made straight, and the rough places plain.

HEBREWS 13:8
Jesus Christ the same yesterday, and to day, and for ever.

PHILIPPIANS 4:19

But my God shall supply all your need according to his riches in glory by Christ Jesus.

EPHESIANS 1:3

Blessed be the God and Father of our Lord Jesus Christ, who hath blessed us with all spiritual blessings in heavenly places in Christ.

2 CORINTHIANS 8:9

For ye know the grace of our Lord Jesus Christ, that, though he was rich, yet for your sakes he became poor, that ye through his poverty might be rich.

Carnal

LESSON 7

We often think, *Well, I prayed and didn't see anything happen.* John 4:24 says,

> *God is a Spirit: and they that worship him must worship him in spirit and in truth.*

God moves in the spirit realm before something manifests in the physical realm. There's a process. Prayer is a process. From the time God moves and commands, there is a process. There are things that have to take place, and sometimes that takes time.

Consider Daniel 9 and 10. In chapter 9, God spoke and it took about three minutes for the answer (Gabriel) to show up (Dan. 9:20-23). Then in chapter 10, God spoke and it took three weeks for Daniel to receive the answer (Dan. 10:12-14). God wasn't the variable in these two instances. A demonic power withstood God's power the second time, so it took three weeks for what the Lord had commanded to come to pass.

When you pray, there may be a period of time in between your "amen" and when the answer shows up. But it's not God's fault. Demonic powers or your doubt could be delaying your answer, or sometimes even other people are involved in answers to prayers. Sometimes it just takes time for your answer to appear.

You can't microwave your ministry. You can't just say, "Well, Andrew is believing God, and things are working for him. So, in the name of Jesus, it's going to work for me." Well, you may not have been serving the Lord the way I've been serving Him for the past forty-seven years. Mark 4:28 says,

> *For the earth bringeth forth fruit of herself; first the blade, then the ear, after that the full corn in the ear.*

There's a growth process in the things of the Lord. It takes time to grow and see things come to pass. Some people just ignore this. They pray, and if they don't see immediate results, they think, *Well, God, You didn't answer my prayer*, and they move into unbelief.

BELIEVE YOU RECEIVE

You have to get to a place where you're practicing Mark 11:24:

> *What things soever ye desire, when ye pray, believe that ye receive them, and ye shall have them.*

You must believe you receive when you pray, and then you shall (future tense) have them. But notice, you have to believe you receive *when you pray*. How can you believe you receive something if you can't see, taste, or feel it? For instance, let's say that you have a pain in your body. You say, "God, I pray and believe that I am healed." Then you end your prayer and say, "Amen," but you still feel your pain. Most people will think, *Well, God didn't do anything*. That's because they don't understand. God is a Spirit. He's moving in the spirit realm. There are things taking place in the spiritual realm, and it may take a brief period of time before a person's body reflects that.

Jesus spoke to a fig tree, cursing it and saying, *"No man eat fruit of thee hereafter for ever"* (Mark 11:14). If someone had gone up and looked at that fig tree immediately, it wouldn't have reflected that a single thing happened. But the next day, as Jesus and His disciples were walking into Jerusalem, the disciples saw the fig tree *"dried up from the roots"* (Mark 11:20). The roots were below ground; they couldn't be seen. It took about twenty-four hours for what the Lord said to manifest itself in the physical realm, and Jesus was operating in the power of God perfectly! There was no limitation to Him and no problem with Him. Matthew's account of this reports that immediately the fig tree withered away (Matt. 21:19), but this wasn't visible, as Mark's account details, until the next day. The action happened immediately, but it happened underground where it couldn't be seen. It took about twenty-four hours for what had happened in the spiritual realm to become visible.

What would have happened if Jesus had been like us and thought, *Well, I cursed the fig tree and it still looks fine; the leaves are still good*? If He had gotten into unbelief, it would have stopped the power of God. But of course, Jesus didn't get into unbelief. He spoke and knew His words would be accomplished, even though it didn't look like it was true. It just took a brief period of time for what had happened below the surface, out of sight, to become manifest in those physical leaves.

Likewise, when you pray, you have to believe that you receive at that exact moment and that God has touched your body. Declare by faith, "I'm healed in the name of Jesus." Whether you still have pain, whether you look better, whether you feel better—anything—you just believe, saying, "I've got it right now, and it's manifesting because I've got it. It's a done deal!"

THE OPPOSITE OF LIFE

Most people are what the Bible calls *carnal*. We often think of being carnal as being ungodly, demonic, and terrible. This word normally has a really bad connotation, but it simply means to be of the flesh or dominated by the senses. Literally, the word *carnal* comes from the word *carne*. It's where we get the phrase *chili con carne*—chili with meat. According to *Strong's Concordance*, *carnal* means "flesh (as stripped of the skin)." This is not the skin but rather the flesh—the meat—part of us.

A carnally minded person is a meathead. They're just dominated by their five senses. They go by what they see, taste, hear, smell, and feel. So, carnal doesn't always refer to some terrible, ungodly God hater. A person could love the Lord with their whole heart and be carnal if they are controlled by their physical senses, if they just can't believe that anything exists that they can't see, taste, hear, smell, or feel. That's carnal.

> *For to be carnally minded is death; but to be spiritually minded is life and peace.*
>
> Romans 8:6

Carnal-mindedness equals death. It doesn't tend toward death. It's not a leading cause of death. It doesn't produce death in some people. Carnal-mindedness *is* death—the opposite of life.

I don't have to be present when you sow seed in your garden in order to know what you've planted. Just let me be there when something sprouts up. I will be able to tell what you planted because what you planted will be there growing and bearing fruit.

I don't know every person individually, and I can't tell what they have been doing, but when people come up to me and list all of the negative things they have growing in their lives, I can tell what they *haven't* been doing. They haven't been seeing who they are in Christ. They haven't taken their authority. They don't believe that it's already been done. They beg God out of desperation to "please move," but they don't believe that He's already given them power. They aren't standing their ground and resisting the devil!

WHAT YOU'VE BEEN PLANTING

> *Submit yourselves therefore to God. Resist the devil, and he will flee from you.*
>
> James 4:7

If you're being dominated and controlled by the devil, you haven't resisted him. You might argue, "Oh, no. I hate the devil and want to be free from him." I'm not saying you haven't pleaded, begged, and desired something different, but the word *resist* means to actively fight against. You haven't taken your authority in Christ and fought against Satan in the power and name of the Lord. You may have begged for help; you may be pitiful and desire help, but you haven't taken your authority. You don't know who you are. You haven't taken Ephesians 1:19-20 and said, "I've got the same power living on the inside of me that raised Jesus Christ from the dead, and I refuse to allow this sickness to stay in my body."

People come to me by the hundreds telling me just how pitiful their situations are. They try to appeal to my mercy, thinking that this will somehow or another make me feel more compassionate toward them. It just shows me what they've been planting in their lives. If you come and tell me how bad your disease is instead of telling me how awesome God is and how much greater He is than that illness, you're just revealing to me what you've been planting in your life.

There is a reason Satan is hindering us. It's not because God doesn't want to give us His best. God's eyes are going to and fro throughout the whole earth just looking for somebody to bless (2 Chr. 16:9). He wants to bless us more than we want to be blessed. He's trying to get His blessings to us, but we have settled for less. We aren't even shooting for God's best. We're begging Him to give us what He's already given us. We're carnally minded, dominated by sense knowledge. We can't believe that anything happens that we can't see, taste, hear, smell, or feel.

Yet the Word says that we should be walking in the supernatural: *"For we walk by faith, not by sight"* (2 Cor. 5:7). The normal Christian life is supernatural! But the average Christian today walks by sight and not by faith. What's normal for a born-again believer, according to the Word, is to walk by faith and not by sight.

You need to get to where what God says to you is more real than what your body says, what the doctor says, what the banker says, what the people on the news say, or what the government says. You need to get to where God's Word is the absolute, final authority, and if anyone or anything opposes it, they're wrong.

UPSIDE DOWN

It's easy to say God's Word is first place when reading an inspirational book. But if you go to work and people start ragging on you, talking bad about everything that stands for good, and countering everything moral, would you fold like a two-dollar suitcase? Or would you stand up and speak the truth in love? I'm not saying this to hurt anyone, but most Christians need a spine. They need to rise to their feet and get to where they believe, act on, and speak the Word of God. It ought to be the unbelievers who feel embarrassed instead of Christians.

If somebody asks, "Do you believe in creation instead of evolution?" your response should be "Absolutely! You don't believe that we came from slime, do you? Honestly, you don't believe that all this complexity accidentally came from goo?" Instead of us feeling weird, the people who don't believe in God ought to feel weird. Psalm 14:1 and Psalm 53:1 say the same thing: *The fool hath said in his heart, There is no God.*

When someone says "I'm an atheist" or "I'm an agnostic," we ought to be like, "You couldn't do that! That's foolish. How could you not believe in God?" My friend Duane Sheriff shared how when the Russian cosmonauts went up into space, they said, "We didn't see God." Duane suggested, "All they had to do was just step outside that space capsule and they would have met Him." It's just foolish. Our world is upside down. It's messed up. Instead of us feeling weird, the world ought to feel weird.

A long time ago I was playing basketball with a group of kids. Every time they missed a shot, they'd curse, blaspheme God, and take the name of Jesus in vain. So, when they started cursing, I'd say, "Hallelujah! Thank You, Jesus! Praise the Lord!" Boy, they just looked at me. Then they'd miss another shot, and they'd curse. I'd say, "Thank You, Father. Hallelujah!" I'd praise God. They just looked at me some more. Finally, they asked, "What are you doing?" I answered, "You praise your god, and I'll praise my God." Before long, every time they missed a shot, they'd look at me and go, "Hallelujah." And I'd say, "Hallelujah!" back. It turned the whole situation around. They ought to have felt weird for cursing and blaspheming God. I should never feel weird for praising Him. Hallelujah!

ADMISSION

God has done everything. It's not Him who isn't giving; we are just failing to receive. We're carnal. We think, *O God, I prayed. And because I didn't see anything, that means You haven't done anything.* That's just silly.

If you say, "I just don't believe anything that I can't see, taste, hear, smell, or feel," then all that means is that you aren't very smart. There are radio and television signals right there in the room where you are, but you can't see them. Just because you can't see them doesn't mean that they aren't there. If you had a receiver of some kind—a radio or television set—and plugged it in, turned it on, and tuned it in, you could perceive those signals. Now, when we see and hear signals is not when they started. They were already there, but there was no way to receive them. The signals are in a realm that we can't perceive with our little peanut-size brains, but there are lots of things that exist beyond a person's ability to see or feel. Even in the natural realm we've come to recognize that.

In the spiritual realm, there are angels right there with you. God is there. His glory is there. The same power that raised Jesus Christ from the dead is not just out in heaven someplace; it's on the inside of every born-again believer (Eph. 1:19-20). It's on the inside of you, but how do you access it?

By whom also we have access by faith into this grace wherein we stand.

Romans 5:2

According to *Strong's Concordance,* the Greek word translated *access* here literally means "admission." The way you gain admission to the grace of God is through faith. Faith is believing that something exists beyond your carnal ability to perceive.

OPERATE IN THE SUPERNATURAL

So then faith cometh by hearing, and hearing by the word of God.

Romans 10:17

The words that I speak unto you, they are spirit, and they are life.

John 6:63

If you want to know what's going on in the spirit realm, you have to go to the Word of God. God's Word is a window into the spirit world. When you ask, "Lord, what have You done for me?" look at His Word. For instance, 1 Peter 2:24 says, *"By whose stripes ye were healed."*

"But God, I don't feel healed."

If you have trouble receiving because you just can't believe anything has happened that you can't see, taste, hear, smell, or feel, then you're carnal, and carnal-mindedness equals death (Rom. 8:6). You have to get to a place where you say, "I don't feel healed, but Your Word says it and I believe it." Then your body will say, "You've got pain." You'll answer, "I don't care what I feel. I don't care what it looks like. I don't care what somebody says. This is what God's Word says, and I believe it!" When God's Word is more real to you than anything carnal, then the things that you believe will come to pass.

But you don't get to this place by being carnal and constantly feeding your five senses. You're going to have to spend time in the presence of the Lord. You're going to have to renew your mind, talk to Somebody you can't *see,* listen to Somebody you can't *hear,* and learn to operate in the supernatural realm. Very few Christians spend much time doing this. They're just bombarded with carnal, physical, natural things.

God has chosen the foolishness of preaching to save those who believe (1 Cor. 1:21). Faith comes by hearing, and hearing by the Word of God (Rom. 10:17). You do need to hear the preaching of the Word on a regular basis, but eventually, you're also going to have to go directly to God, fellowship with Him yourself, and let Him speak to you—not just through somebody else, but God Almighty talking directly with you. You need that!

FAITH WORKS

God has already provided. It's not a lack of provision on God's part that is causing our problems; it's that our receivers are messed up. We're not receiving as we should. That's because we aren't even shooting for God's best. We've settled for less, and we need to change the way we think. We need to go before the Lord, repent, and say, "God, forgive me for my doubt. Forgive me that what I see, taste, hear, smell, and feel is more real to me than You are. Forgive me that I'm more responsive to fear than I am to Your Word."

Someone came up to me recently and said that a curse was on them. They said that the curse had gone through their family, and all of these negative things had happened to them. I told that person, "Look, those curses can't have any power over you unless you believe them" (Prov. 26:2). That was a brand-new revelation for this person. In the same way that what God has provided in the spirit realm has to be accessed by faith (we access grace by faith, see Rom. 5:2), a curse has to be accessed by faith too. We call that *unbelief*.

Unbelief is nothing but faith in the wrong thing. Faith and unbelief are the same except that one is pointed toward God, believing (responding positively to) the promises in His Word, and the other is pointed away from God and is believing the wrong things, like the world, the flesh, and the devil. If Satan comes against you—including with a curse—you have to put faith in that in order for it come to pass in your life. Unbelief is having faith in the wrong things.

You're the one who empowers the devil. You're the one who believes that every time flu season comes around, you're going to catch the flu. You swallowed that lie and believed it. The same words have been spoken about me, but I don't believe them and I don't get the flu. I don't believe in getting sick. You might be thinking, *It doesn't work that way*. That's because of what you believe. You believe that you can't walk free of sickness, so you're just getting what you believe.

Faith works. If you believe that you don't have a choice about being "over the hill," that you're just obligated to start having all of these problems and you can't operate in health anymore, then you're the one who gives it power over you. You're the one who says that cancer is incurable when the Bible says that Jesus is above every name (Phil. 2:9). If you can put a name on it, Jesus is above it. It's no big deal!

Outline

I.   John 4:24 says, *"God is a Spirit: and they that worship him must worship him in spirit and in truth."*

    A. God moves in the spirit realm before something manifests in the physical realm; there's a process.

    B. From the time God moves and commands, there are things that have to take place, and sometimes that takes time.

    C. In Daniel 9, God spoke and it took about three minutes for the answer (Gabriel) to show up (Dan. 9:20-23).

    D. Then in chapter 10, God spoke and it took three weeks for Daniel to receive the answer (Dan. 10:12-14).

    E. God wasn't the variable in these two instances; a demonic power withstood God's power the second time.

    F. When you pray, there may be a period of time in between your "amen" and when the answer shows up.

    G. Demonic powers or your doubt could be delaying your answer, or sometimes even other people are involved in answers to prayers.

    H. You can't microwave your ministry.

    I. Mark 4:28 says, *"For the earth bringeth forth fruit of herself; first the blade, then the ear, after that the full corn in the ear."*

    J. There's a growth process in the things of the Lord, but some people just ignore this.

    K. They pray, and if they don't see immediate results, they think, *Well, God, You didn't answer my prayer*, and they move into unbelief.

II. You have to get to a place where you're practicing Mark 11:24: *"What things soever ye desire, when ye pray, believe that ye receive them, and ye shall have them."*

    A. For instance, let's say that you have a pain in your body.

B.   You say, "God, I pray and believe that I am healed," but you still feel pain.

C.   Many people will think, *Well, God didn't do anything.*

D.   That's because they don't understand that there are things taking place in the spirit realm.

E.   Jesus spoke to a fig tree, cursing it and saying, *"No man eat fruit of thee hereafter for ever"* (Mark 11:14).

F.   If someone had gone up and looked at that fig tree immediately, it wouldn't have reflected that a single thing happened.

G.   What would have happened if Jesus had thought, *Well, I cursed the fig tree and it still looks fine; the leaves are still good?*

H.   If He had gotten into unbelief, it would have stopped the power of God.

I.   But of course, Jesus spoke and knew His words would be accomplished, even though it didn't look like it was true.

J.   It just took a brief period of time for what had happened below the surface, out of sight, to become manifest in those physical leaves.

K.   You have to believe that you receive at that exact moment and that God has touched your body.

L.   Whether you still have pain, whether you look better, whether you feel better—anything—you just believe, saying, "I've got it right now, and it's manifesting because I've got it. It's a done deal!"

III. Many people are what the Bible calls *carnal.*

A.   We often think of being carnal as being ungodly, demonic, and terrible, but it simply means to be of the flesh or dominated by the senses.

B.   So, carnal doesn't always refer to some terrible, ungodly God hater.

C.   A person could love the Lord with their whole heart and still be carnal if they are controlled by their physical senses, if they just can't believe that anything exists that they can't see, taste, hear, smell, or feel.

D.   Carnal-mindedness equals death:

For to be carnally minded is death; but to be spiritually minded is life and peace.

Romans 8:6

    E. It doesn't tend toward death, it's not a leading cause of death, and it doesn't produce death in some people—carnal-mindedness *is* death.

IV. People don't have to be present when you sow seed in your garden in order for them to know what you've planted.

    A. Just let them be there when something sprouts up.

    B. They will be able to tell what you planted because it will be there growing and bearing fruit.

    C. When people list all of the negative things they have growing in their lives, others can tell what they *haven't* been doing:

        1. They haven't been seeing who they are in Christ.

        2. They haven't taken their authority.

        3. They don't believe that it's already been done.

        4. They beg God out of desperation to "please move," but they don't believe that He's already given them power.

        5. They aren't standing their ground and resisting the devil!

V. If you're being dominated and controlled by the devil, you haven't resisted him:

Submit yourselves therefore to God. Resist the devil, and he will flee from you.

James 4:7

    A. The word *resist* means to actively fight against.

    B. You may have begged for help; you may be pitiful and desire help, but you haven't taken your authority in Christ and fought against Satan in the power and name of the Lord.

    C. You haven't taken Ephesians 1:19-20 and said, "I've got the same power living on the inside of me that raised Jesus Christ from the dead."

VI. God's eyes are going to and fro throughout the whole earth just looking for somebody to bless (2 Chr. 16:9).

    A. He wants to bless us more than we want to be blessed, but we're carnally minded, dominated by sense knowledge.

    B. What's normal for a born-again believer, according to the Word, is to walk by faith and not by sight (2 Cor. 5:7).

    C. We need to get to where what God says to us is more real than what our bodies say, what the doctor says, what the banker says, what the people on the news say, or what the government says.

    D. We need to get to where God's Word is the absolute, final authority, and if anyone or anything opposes it, they're wrong.

VII. It's easy to say God's Word is first place when reading an inspirational book; but if you go to work and people start ragging on you, talking bad about everything that stands for good, and countering everything moral, would you fold like a two-dollar suitcase?

    A. Or would you stand up and speak the truth in love?

    B. Many Christians need to rise to their feet and get to where they believe, act on, and speak the Word of God.

    C. It ought to be the unbelievers who feel embarrassed instead of Christians.

    D. Instead of you feeling weird, the people who don't believe in God ought to feel weird.

    E. Psalm 14:1 and 53:1 say the same thing: *"The fool hath said in his heart, There is no God."*

VIII. If you say, "I just don't believe anything that I can't see, taste, hear, smell, or feel," then all that means is that you aren't very smart.

    A. There are radio and television signals right there in the room where you are, but you can't see them.

B. If you had a radio or television set, and you plugged it in, turned it on, and tuned it in, you could perceive those signals.

C. Now, when you see and hear signals is not when they started; they were already there.

D. In the spiritual realm, there are angels right there with you; God is there, and His glory is there.

E. The same power that raised Jesus Christ from the dead is not just out in heaven someplace; it's on the inside of every born-again believer, but how do you access it?

By whom also we have access by faith into this grace wherein we stand.

Romans 5:2

F. According to *Strong's Concordance,* the Greek word translated *access* here literally means "admission."

G. The way you gain admission to the grace of God is through faith.

IX. Faith is believing that something exists beyond your carnal ability to perceive:

So then faith cometh by hearing, and hearing by the word of God.

Romans 10:17

The words that I speak unto you, they are spirit, and they are life.

John 6:63

A. If you want to know what's going on in the spirit realm, you have to go to the Word of God.

B. God's Word is a window into the spirit world.

C. When you ask "Lord, what have You done for me?" look at His Word.

D. When God's Word is more real to you than anything carnal, then the things that you believe will come to pass.

E. You don't get to this place by being carnal and constantly feeding your five senses; you're going to have to spend time in the presence of the Lord; you're going to have to renew your mind, talk to Somebody you can't *see*, listen to Somebody you can't *hear*, and learn to operate in the supernatural realm.

F.   You do need to hear the preaching of the Word on a regular basis, but eventually you're also going to have to go directly to God yourself.

X.   In the same way that what God has provided in the spirit realm has to be accessed by faith, a curse has to be accessed by faith too.

A.   This is called *unbelief*.

B.   Unbelief is nothing but faith in the wrong thing.

C.   If Satan comes against you—including with a curse—you have to put faith in that in order for it come to pass in your life.

D.   You're the one who empowers the devil.

E.   Faith works.

Teacher's Guide

1.   John 4:24 says,

> *God is a Spirit: and they that worship him must worship him in spirit and in truth.*

God moves in the spirit realm before something manifests in the physical realm; there's a process. From the time God moves and commands, there are things that have to take place, and sometimes that takes time. In Daniel 9, God spoke and it took about three minutes for the answer (Gabriel) to show up (Dan. 9:20-23). Then in chapter 10, God spoke and it took three weeks for Daniel to receive the answer (Dan. 10:12-14). God wasn't the variable in these two instances; a demonic power withstood God's power the second time. When we pray, there may be a period of time in between our "amen" and when the answer shows up. Demonic powers or our doubt could be delaying our answer, or sometimes even other people are involved in answers to prayers. We can't microwave our ministry. Mark 4:28 says,

> *For the earth bringeth forth fruit of herself; first the blade, then the ear, after that the full corn in the ear.*

There's a growth process in the things of the Lord. Some people just ignore this. They pray, and if they don't see immediate results, they think, *Well, God, You didn't answer my prayer*, and they move into unbelief.

1a. Before something manifests in the physical realm, God moves where (John 4:24)?
   <u>**In the spirit realm**</u>
1b. *Discussion question:* Other than time, what does it take for a manifestation to occur in the physical realm?
   <u>***Discussion question***</u>
1c. True or false: Since it took about three minutes for God's answer to show up in the first instance and three weeks in the second instance, God was not the variable (Dan. 9:20-23 and 10:12-14).
   <u>**True**</u>
1d. When you pray and there is a period of time in between "amen" and the answer showing up, what could be the cause?
   <u>**A demonic power, your doubt, or sometimes even other people**</u>
1e. There is a _____ process in the things of the Lord (Mark 4:28).
   <u>**Growth**</u>

2.   We have to get to a place where we're practicing Mark 11:24:

What things soever ye desire, when ye pray, believe that ye receive them, and ye shall have them.

For instance, let's say we have pain in our bodies. We say "God, I pray and believe that I am healed," but we still feel the pain. Many people will think, *Well, God didn't do anything.* That's because they don't understand that there are things taking place in the spirit realm. Jesus spoke to a fig tree, cursing it and saying, *"No man eat fruit of thee hereafter for ever"* (Mark 11:14). If someone had gone up and looked at that fig tree immediately, it wouldn't have reflected that a single thing happened. What would have happened if Jesus had thought, *Well, I cursed the fig tree and it still looks fine; the leaves are still good?* If He had gotten into unbelief, it would have stopped the power of God. But of course, Jesus spoke and knew His words would be accomplished, even though it didn't look like it was true. It just took a brief period of time for what had happened below the surface, out of sight, to become manifest in those physical leaves. We have to believe that we receive at that exact moment and that God has touched our bodies. Whether we still have pain, whether we look better, whether we feel better—anything—we just believe, saying, "I've got it right now, and it's manifesting because I've got it. It's a done deal!"

2a. *Discussion question:* According to Mark 11:24, how can you believe you receive something if you can't see, taste, or feel it?
     Discussion question

3.   Many people are what the Bible calls *carnal*. We often think of being carnal as being ungodly, demonic, and terrible, but it simply means to be of the flesh or dominated by the senses. So, carnal doesn't always refer to some terrible, ungodly God hater. A person could love the Lord with their whole heart and still be carnal if they are controlled by their physical senses, if they just can't believe that anything exists that they can't see, taste, hear, smell, or feel. Carnal-mindedness equals death:

For to be carnally minded is death; but to be spiritually minded is life and peace.

Romans 8:6

It doesn't tend toward death. It's not a leading cause of death. It doesn't produce death in some people. Carnal-mindedness *is* death.

3a. What does *carnal* mean?
     To be of the flesh or dominated by the senses
3b. True or false: You can't love God with your whole heart if you're carnal.
     False

3c. *Discussion question:* What is an example of carnal-mindedness equaling death (Rom. 8:6)?
Discussion question

4. People don't have to be present when we sow seed in our gardens in order for them to know what we've planted. We can just let them be there when something sprouts up. They will be able to tell what we planted because it will be there growing and bearing fruit. When people list all of the negative things they have grown in their lives, others can tell what they *haven't* been doing: They haven't been seeing who they are in Christ. They haven't taken their authority. They don't believe that it's already been done. They beg God out of desperation to "please move," but they don't believe that He's already given them power. They aren't standing their ground and resisting the devil!

4a. When people list all of the negative things they have growing in their lives, what *haven't* they been doing?
They haven't been seeing who they are in Christ. They haven't taken their authority. They don't believe that it's already been done. They beg God out of desperation to "please move," but they don't believe that He's already given them power. They aren't standing their ground and resisting the devil!

5. If we're being dominated and controlled by the devil, we haven't resisted him:

> *Submit yourselves therefore to God. Resist the devil, and he will flee from you.*
>
> James 4:7

The word *resist* means to actively fight against. We may have begged for help; we may be pitiful and desire help, but we haven't taken our authority in Christ and fought against Satan in the power and name of the Lord. We haven't taken Ephesians 1:19-20 and said, "I've got the same power living on the inside of me that raised Jesus Christ from the dead."

5a. If you're being dominated and controlled by the devil, you haven't done what (James 4:7)?
Resisted him
5b. What does *resist* mean?
To actively fight against
5c. You have to _____ your _____ in Christ and fight against Satan in the _____ and _____ of the Lord.

A. Call / brother / night / day
B. Take / authority / power / name
C. Hold / horses / saddle / wagon
D. Take / sword / wrath / cruelty
E. Trust / feelings / mercy / kindness
B. Take / authority / power / name

6.   God's eyes are going to and fro throughout the whole earth just looking for
somebody to bless (2 Chr. 16:9). He wants to bless us more than we want to be
blessed, but we're carnally minded, dominated by sense knowledge. What's normal
for a born-again believer, according to the Word, is to walk by faith and not by sight
(2 Cor. 5:7). We need to get to where what God says to us is more real than what our
bodies say, what the doctor says, what the banker says, what the people on the news
say, or what the government says. We need to get to where God's Word is the absolute,
final authority, and if anyone or anything opposes it, they're wrong.

6a.   According to 2 Chronicles 16:9, God is just _____ for somebody to bless.
      Looking
6b.   According to 2 Corinthians 5:7, what's normal for a born-again believer?
      To walk by faith and not by sight
6c.   True or false: You need to get to where what God says to you is more real than
      what your body says, what the doctor says, what the banker says, what the people
      on the news say, or what the government says.
      True
6d.   True or false: You need to get to where God's Word is the absolute, final authority
      sometimes.
      False

7.   It's easy to say God's Word is first place when reading an inspirational book. But
if we go to work and people start ragging on us, talking bad about everything that
stands for good, and countering everything moral, would we fold like a two-dollar
suitcase? Or would we stand up and speak the truth in love? Many Christians need to
rise to their feet and get to where they believe, act on, and speak the Word of God. It
ought to be the unbelievers who feel embarrassed instead of Christians. Instead of us
feeling weird, the people who don't believe in God ought to feel weird. Psalm 14:1 and
53:1 say the same thing: *"The fool hath said in his heart, There is no God."*

7a.   *Discussion question:* How do you respond when someone talks bad about
      everything that stands for good and counters everything moral?
      Discussion question

7b. According to Psalm 14:1 and 53:1, *"The _____ hath said in his heart, There is no God."*
    A. Wise
    B. Misunderstood
    C. Well-intentioned
    D. Intelligent
    E. Fool
    E. Fool

8. If we say, "I just don't believe anything that I can't see, taste, hear, smell, or feel," then all that means is that we aren't very smart. There are radio and television signals right there in the room where we are, but we can't see them. If we had a radio or television set, and we plugged it in, turned it on, and tuned it in, we could perceive those signals. Now, when we see and hear signals is not when they started; they were already there. In the spiritual realm, there are angels right there with us. God is there, and His glory is there. The same power that raised Jesus Christ from the dead is not just out in heaven someplace; it's on the inside of every born-again believer, but how do we access it?

> *By whom also we have access by faith into this grace wherein we stand.*
>
> Romans 5:2

According to *Strong's Concordance,* the Greek word translated *"access"* here literally means "admission." The way we gain admission to the grace of God is through faith.

8a. How do you access what you can't see (Rom. 5:2)?
Through faith
8b. According to *Strong's Concordance,* what does *"access"* mean in Romans 5:2?
"Admission"

9. Faith is believing that something exists beyond our carnal ability to perceive:

> *So then faith cometh by hearing, and hearing by the word of God.*
>
> Romans 10:17

> *The words that I speak unto you, they are spirit, and they are life.*
>
> John 6:63

If we want to know what's going on in the spirit realm, we have to go to the Word of God. God's Word is a window into the spirit world. When we ask "Lord, what have You done for me?" we need to look at His Word. When God's Word is more real to us than anything carnal, then the things that we believe will come to pass. We don't get to this place by being carnal and constantly feeding our five senses. We're going to have to spend time in the presence of the Lord. We're going to have to renew our minds, talk to Somebody we can't *see*, listen to Somebody we can't *hear*, and learn to operate in the supernatural realm. We do need to hear the preaching of the Word on a regular basis, but eventually, we're also going to have to go directly to God ourselves.

9a. According to Romans 10:17 and John 6:63, what is faith?
   Believing that something exists beyond your carnal ability to perceive

9b. If you want to know what's going on in the spirit realm, you have to go where?
   To the Word of God

9c. God's Word is what?
   A.   A glimpse into the spirit world
   B.   A collage of the spirit world
   C.   A window into the spirit world
   D.   A day pass into the spirit world
   E.   A mirage of the spirit world
   C.   A window into the spirit world

9d. *Discussion question:* What do you plan to do to make God's Word more real to you than anything carnal?
   Discussion question

10. In the same way that what God has provided in the spirit realm has to be accessed by faith, a curse has to be accessed by faith too. This is called *unbelief*. Unbelief is nothing but faith in the wrong thing. If Satan comes against us—including with a curse—we have to put faith in that in order for it come to pass in our lives. We're the ones who empower the devil. Faith works.

10a. True or false: A curse has to be accessed by faith.
   True

10b. What is this called?
   Unbelief

10c. If Satan comes against you—including with a curse—you have to put faith in that in order for it to what?
   Come to pass in your life

Discipleship Questions

1. Before something manifests in the physical realm, God moves where (John 4:24)?

2. *Discussion question:* Other than time, what does it take for a manifestation to occur in the physical realm?

3. True or false: Since it took about three minutes for God's answer to show up in the first instance and three weeks in the second instance, God was not the variable (Dan. 9:20-23 and 10:12-14).

4. When you pray and there is a period of time in between "amen" and the answer showing up, what could be the cause?

5. There is a _____ process in the things of the Lord (Mark 4:28).

6. *Discussion question:* According to Mark 11:24, how can you believe you receive something if you can't see, taste, or feel it?

7. What does *carnal* mean?

    _____

    _____

    _____

8. True or false: You can't love God with your whole heart if you're carnal.

9. *Discussion question:* What is an example of carnal-mindedness equaling death (Rom. 8:6)?

    _____

    _____

    _____

10. When people list all of the negative things they have growing in their lives, what *haven't* they been doing?

    _____

    _____

    _____

11. If you're being dominated and controlled by the devil, you haven't done what (James 4:7)?

    _____

    _____

    _____

12. What does *resist* mean?

    _____

    _____

    _____

13. You have to _____ your _____ in Christ and fight against Satan in the _____ and _____ of the Lord.
    A. Call / brother / night / day
    B. Take / authority / power / name
    C. Hold / horses / saddle / wagon
    D. Take / sword / wrath / cruelty
    E. Trust / feelings / mercy / kindness

14. According to 2 Chronicles 16:9, God is just _____ for somebody to bless.

15. According to 2 Corinthians 5:7, what's normal for a born-again believer?

_____

_____

_____

16. True or false: You need to get to where what God says to you is more real than what your body says, what the doctor says, what the banker says, what the people on the news say, or what the government says.

17. True or false: You need to get to where God's Word is the absolute, final authority sometimes.

18. *Discussion question:* How do you respond when someone talks bad about everything that stands for good and counters everything moral?

_____

_____

_____

19. According to Psalm 14:1 and 53:1, "*The _____ hath said in his heart, There is no God.*"
    A. Wise
    B. Misunderstood
    C. Well-intentioned
    D. Intelligent
    E. Fool

20. How do you access what you can't see (Rom. 5:2)?

_____

_____

_____

21. According to *Strong's Concordance*, what does *"access"* mean in Romans 5:2?

_____

_____

_____

22. According to Romans 10:17 and John 6:63, what is faith?

_____

_____

_____

23. If you want to know what's going on in the spirit realm, you have to go where?

_____

_____

_____

24. God's Word is what?
    A. A glimpse into the spirit world
    B. A collage of the spirit world
    C. A window into the spirit world
    D. A day pass into the spirit world
    E. A mirage of the spirit world

25. *Discussion question:* What do you plan to do to make God's Word more real to you than anything carnal?

_____

_____

_____

26. True or false: A curse has to be accessed by faith.

27. What is this called?

_____

_____

_____

28. If Satan comes against you—including with a curse—you have to put faith in that in order for it to what?

_____

_____

_____

Answer Key

1. In the spirit realm

2. *Discussion question*

3. True

4. A demonic power, your doubt, or sometimes even other people

5. Growth

6. *Discussion question*

7. To be of the flesh or dominated by the senses

8. False

9. *Discussion question*

10. They haven't been seeing who they are in Christ. They haven't taken their authority. They don't believe that it's already been done. They beg God out of desperation to "please move," but they don't believe that He's already given them power. They aren't standing their ground and resisting the devil!

11. Resisted him

12. To actively fight against

13. B. Take / authority / power / name

14. Looking

15. To walk by faith and not by sight

16. True

17. False

18. *Discussion question*

19. E. Fool

20. Through faith

21. "Admission"

22. Believing that something exists beyond your carnal ability to perceive

23. To the Word of God

24. C. A window into the spirit world

25. *Discussion question*

26. True

27. Unbelief

28. Come to pass in your life

Scriptures

JOHN 4:24

God is a Spirit: and they that worship him must worship him in spirit and in truth.

DANIEL 9:20-23

And whiles I was speaking, and praying, and confessing my sin and the sin of my people Israel, and presenting my supplication before the Lord my God for the holy mountain of my God; [21] Yea, whiles I was speaking in prayer, even the man Gabriel, whom I had seen in the vision at the beginning, being caused to fly swiftly, touched me about the time of the evening oblation. [22] And he informed me, and talked with me, and said, O Daniel, I am now come forth to give thee skill and understanding. [23] At the beginning of thy supplications the commandment came forth, and I am come to shew thee; for thou art greatly beloved: therefore understand the matter, and consider the vision.

DANIEL 10:12-14

Then said he unto me, Fear not, Daniel: for from the first day that thou didst set thine heart to understand, and to chasten thyself before thy God, thy words were heard, and I am come for thy words. [13] But the prince of the kingdom of Persia withstood me one and twenty days: but, lo, Michael, one of the chief princes, came to help me; and I remained there with the kings of Persia. [14] Now I am come to make thee understand what shall befall thy people in the latter days: for yet the vision is for many days.

MARK 4:28

For the earth bringeth forth fruit of herself; first the blade, then the ear, after that the full corn in the ear.

MARK 11:24

Therefore I say unto you, What things soever ye desire, when ye pray, believe that ye receive them, and ye shall have them.

MARK 11:14

And Jesus answered and said unto it, No man eat fruit of thee hereafter for ever. And his disciples heard it.

MARK 11:20

And in the morning, as they passed by, they saw the fig tree dried up from the roots.

MATTHEW 21:19

And when he saw a fig tree in the way, he came to it, and found nothing thereon, but leaves only, and said unto it, Let no fruit grow on thee henceforward for ever. And presently the fig tree withered away.

ROMANS 8:6

For to be carnally minded is death; but to be spiritually minded is life and peace.

JAMES 4:7

Submit yourselves therefore to God. Resist the devil, and he will flee from you.

EPHESIANS 1:19-20

And what is the exceeding greatness of his power to us-ward who believe, according to the working of his mighty power, [20] Which he wrought in Christ, when he raised him from the dead, and set him at his own right hand in the heavenly places.

2 CHRONICLES 16:9

For the eyes of the LORD run to and fro throughout the whole earth, to shew himself strong in the behalf of them whose heart is perfect toward him. Herein thou hast done foolishly: therefore from henceforth thou shalt have wars.

2 CORINTHIANS 5:7

For we walk by faith, not by sight.

PSALM 14:1

The fool hath said in his heart, There is no God. They are corrupt, they have done abominable works, there is none that doeth good.

PSALM 53:1

The fool hath said in his heart, There is no God. Corrupt are they, and have done abominable iniquity: there is none that doeth good.

ROMANS 5:2

By whom also we have access by faith into this grace wherein we stand, and rejoice in hope of the glory of God.

ROMANS 10:17

So then faith cometh by hearing, and hearing by the word of God.

JOHN 6:63

It is the spirit that quickeneth; the flesh profiteth nothing: the words that I speak unto you, they are spirit, and they are life.

1 PETER 2:24

Who his own self bare our sins in his own body on the tree, that we, being dead to sins, should live unto righteousness: by whose stripes ye were healed.

1 CORINTHIANS 1:21

For after that in the wisdom of God the world by wisdom knew not God, it pleased God by the foolishness of preaching to save them that believe.

PROVERBS 26:2

As the bird by wandering, as the swallow by flying, so the curse causeless shall not come.

PHILIPPIANS 2:9

Wherefore God also hath highly exalted him, and given him a name which is above every name.

Words

LESSON 8

When people say the name of some sickness or disease, like cancer, it strikes fear in their hearts. Most people are more moved by what the doctor, banker, or somebody else says than they are by what God's Word says, and that's the problem; they're empowering that curse and those negative things that have been spoken. When they're told that "we're in a recession and you should plan on having problems," they believe and empower that in their lives.

Remember back in 2007-2009 when the Great Recession happened? The U.S. government started distributing all of this "stimulus" money. It was supposed to be the end of the world. Some people were even committing suicide as they anticipated all kinds of terrible things. That's the exact time God spoke to me saying that we needed to expand. He told me to begin building the new Bible college campus, and we started on the greatest expansion in the history of this ministry. Over the past five years, even during the "Great Recession" and its supposed repercussions, we built a $32 million building debt free. Now we're in the process of building a $53 million building debt free. I could have believed what was said about the Great Recession and pulled back, but I was listening to God, and He told me to do something else instead. I chose to believe what God said more than what the world said.

You might think, *This is too simplistic*, but that is just how simple it is. Although this is simple, it's not easy. The hardest thing you'll ever do is get to where the Word of God—what you hear from Him, the truth He speaks to you in your heart—is more real to you than what anything or anyone else says. It has to be more real to you than what your relatives say, what your professor says, and what the politicians say. It's really that simple. Who and what do you believe?

NO EXCUSE

Satan can't do anything to you without your consent and cooperation. Many people don't like to admit this because they take great comfort in thinking, *The devil made me do it. He's fighting against me, and I can't help it. I'm not responsible.* Satan can only do to you what you empower him to do, and you empower him through believing wrong things like, *I'm only human...I have to get sick every time illness comes around…I have to be just like everybody else…I can't prosper unless I get into debt up to my eyeballs.* You're the one who believes this stuff. You're the one who's empowering it and letting the devil run over you.

You might be saying, "Come on, Andrew! You're saying it's my fault?" Yeah, that's what I'm saying. That's exactly what I'm saying.

But you know what? That's encouraging to me. If I have an enemy out there who's bigger and stronger than me and I just can't stop him, well then, that's pitiful. Woe is me! I'm just a helpless victim. But if I'm at fault, then I can do something about it—I can change. If it's my fault that I have allowed Satan to lie to and steal from me, then I can change. I can repent and turn the other direction. Praise God! It's good news to find out that I'm the problem, because I can change me.

Quit being a victim! Do you think that the government is your problem and that everything would be okay if they'd just start giving you enough welfare? Do you believe you need more money, and you're just looking for somebody else to give it to you? Snap out of it! Nobody owes you anything. Quit being oppressed by people, and stand up and take responsibility for your life. Declare, "It's not what other people do or don't do. I'm the one who has the authority and power of God. I'm going to choose life, and through Christ, I will live and succeed!"

We have a victim mentality in America. Blacks are blaming whites. Whites find fault with blacks, Hispanics, and Asian Americans. Everybody's blaming everyone else. We've all got an ax to grind. Some say, "We need to take the money from the rich people and give it to the poor." Nobody is accepting responsibility. I'm telling you, it doesn't matter what color you are—green or even purple—find out what Jesus has done for you. Discover who you are and what you have in Christ; then take your authority and start standing on that in faith, and you will prosper.

You have no excuse for being a failure. You might have reasons, but you have no excuse. The Lord has made you the head and not the tail. You are above only and not beneath (Deut. 28:13).

WEAPONS

No weapon that is formed against thee shall prosper; and every tongue that shall rise against thee in judgment thou shalt condemn. This is the heritage of the servants of the LORD, and their righteousness is of me, saith the LORD.

Isaiah 54:17

Notice that right after the phrase *"no weapon that is formed against thee shall prosper"* is the phrase *"every tongue that shall rise against thee in judgment thou shalt condemn."* These two actions are linked. Did you know that words are weapons? When someone says, "Everybody's going to get the flu. It's going to be a pandemic," those are curses. They're weapons. So, what do you do with them? You must condemn them.

We were in Europe over a decade ago when the bird flu (avian flu) came out. While driving through England, we saw smoke rising up all over as probably millions of chickens and related fowl were being burned up and destroyed. In Scotland, I heard the leading expert for the British healthcare system being interviewed regarding this situation. The interviewer asked, "Is there a danger of this thing mutating so that it could be contagious to humans?" This expert said, "It's not a question of if, but when." He said that within two years, one-third of the world's population would die through avian flu. That was the "expert" prediction! And that was over ten years ago.

While there were deaths from the bird flu throughout the world, one-third of the world's population absolutely did not die, and there definitely wasn't mass pandemonium. Do you know what his words were? They were a curse. Someone who was respected said some things, and many people just caved in and succumbed to fear. The world says, "That's just wisdom. Even though it never came to pass, it's wise to prepare for the worst-case scenario." No, it's a curse. It's words. How do you deal with them? Isaiah 54:17 says that no weapon formed against you will prosper, and every tongue that rises against you in judgment, you shall condemn. You've got to condemn such words. You must judge them and say, "No! In the name of Jesus, that's not true for me!"

A SEED

Jesus said that the Word of God is like a seed:

> *The sower soweth the word.*
>
> Mark 4:14

> *Being born again, not of corruptible seed, but of incorruptible, by the word of God, which liveth and abideth for ever.*
>
> 1 Peter 1:23

God's Word is a seed. When you plant this seed, it germinates and begins to release the supernatural power within it. But the Word of God isn't the only seed out there. Every word that you hear is a seed—every word!

> *Death and life are in the power of the tongue.*
>
> Proverbs 18:21

Notice how this doesn't say, "Death, life, and a whole bunch of nothingness that doesn't count for anything are in the power of the tongue." No, everything you hear is either life or death, blessing or cursing. There are no non-working words. Every word is a seed that ministers either death or life.

It would be detrimental to my faith if, because I don't want to offend somebody, I just let people speak unbelief around me unchecked. If I let them say stuff around me like, "Whoa! You're believing for $53 million? That's never going to happen. You'll never make it," those words would begin to germinate and start releasing fear and doubt in my heart.

I've learned that the moment I hear something contrary to what I'm believing God for, I have to just stop the speaker right then and say, "In the name of Jesus, that's not so. I condemn it. I judge it!" I've found out that if I deal with the words right then, they roll away just like water off a duck's back. But if I don't say something right then because I don't want to offend the speaker and I wait until later when I get home, then I have to root out the unbelief that was spoken. It's already started germinating. It has already sprouted some roots, and it takes me a while to deal with it. So, I've just learned to immediately counter these words of unbelief as soon as they are spoken over me.

TALK TO THINGS

I'll do this even when I'm listening to the radio or watching television—you can ask my wife. We'll be driving along, listening to the news or something, and they'll say, "It's flu season. Have you gotten your flu shot yet?" I'll respond, "No, in the name of Jesus, I don't have a flu season. I don't have a time of the year that the Word of God doesn't work." They'll continue, "You're over forty. Have you had prostate problems yet?" I'll answer, "No, I don't have any prostate problems, in the name of Jesus. By His stripes I was healed." Then they'll ask, "Are you having pain?" I'll say, "No!" I'll talk to anything or anyone who speaks contrary to what God has said.

Jesus talked to a fig tree. The Word says that He "answered" the fig tree (Mark 11:14). This means that the fig tree had been talking to Him. Did you know that things will speak to you? Sometimes you get your bank statement and everything's in the red. It's saying, "You're in the hole. This faith stuff doesn't work." Anything that talks to you, talk back to it. Talk to your checkbook and say, "Checkbook, you are black in the name of Jesus." Speak what God's Word says to things.

You may be thinking, *Andrew's weird*. I think you're weird if you're just letting the devil run all over you without resisting him. He can't do stuff to you without your consent and cooperation. You have to be taught to accept sickness and infirmity.

One of the reasons Adam lived to be 930 years old (Gen. 5:5) is because he didn't know there was a flu season. Adam and Eve didn't know they were "over the hill" at forty. They didn't even start having children until they were in their hundreds. It took millennia for the devil to teach people to think sick and expect infirmity. People have to be taught to be sick.

IT'S YOUR CHOICE!

When you started feeling sick as a little kid, your parents put you in bed and rewarded you with the day off. They pampered you with all kinds of attention, sodas, and anything else you wanted. They made being sick feel good.

When our kids felt sick, we refused to encourage it. Instead of rewarding and pampering them, we said, "You aren't going to just lie in bed and act sick." We wouldn't let our kids be sick. We taught them that being sick isn't good, and as a result, our children weren't sick. We don't believe in being sick. God's Word says, *"There shall no evil befall thee, neither shall any plague come nigh thy dwelling"* (Ps. 91:10).

It's sad to say, but other Christians will think you're weird for believing in healing, prosperity, and victory. They'll criticize you for believing that God intends for you to walk in victory instead of defeat. One of the most popular doctrines in the body of Christ today is the belief that God controls everything—He just works "sovereignly." A person who holds to this extreme can blame all of their failure upon God, saying, "It's His fault. God must have a plan for me being sick." No, He doesn't (1 Pet. 2:24 and Ps. 91:10-11)! You don't have to be sick, poor, or depressed.

It's been forty-six years since I've been depressed. I don't believe in getting depressed—and I've had a lot of depressing things happen to me. If you say things like this, the average Christian will criticize you, saying, "You're lying." I'm not. That's my testimony, and I'm sticking with it. I've had a lot of opportunities to be depressed. My son died and many other things happened, but I just chose not to be depressed. I don't care what happens, I'm going to bless the Lord at all times (Ps. 34:1). I have love, joy, and peace in my spirit (Gal. 5:22). I don't care how I feel, I'm going to praise the Lord (Heb. 13:15)!

You can choose. It's your choice!

YOU NEED TO REPENT!

I call heaven and earth to record this day against you, that I have set before you life and death, blessing and cursing: therefore choose life, that both thou and thy seed may live.

Deuteronomy 30:19

In this verse, it's like God is giving you a multiple-choice test:

A. Life and blessing
B. Death and cursing

But then He says, "The answer is A." He gives you the answer to this test, saying, "Choose life!" It's your choice, but the right choice is to choose life.

Why would we choose death over life? Why would we choose debt over being debt free? Why would we choose sickness over being well? Why would we choose welfare over being productive? Why do we shoot for nothing and hit it every time? I'm telling you, we are the ones who are stopping the goodness and favor of God from operating in our lives.

Perhaps you have taken offense at some of the things I've addressed. You've been just embracing the standards that the world promotes today, and this is the way that you think. It doesn't bless you to hear someone say that this isn't God's best. You need to repent! When you pet a cat and all their hair stands up, it's because you're petting it the wrong way. How do you solve that? Just turn the cat around and keep petting it. If what I've shared thus far has rubbed you the wrong way, the way you solve this is to turn around. Repent, and it'll go to feeling good. Praise God!

The Lord is trying to encourage us that He's done His part. He's not the one who hasn't given; we just haven't received. We need to change us. If you approach God with humility, grace will flow and He'll show you the way (James 4:6). Just say, "Father, You're a good God. It's not Your fault that I've received less than Your best. What I don't know, please show me. Teach me. Everything's on the table before You. I'm not going to hold on to anything. I just want Your best. Show me what I need to do." God is willing and wants to show you the way, but you need to repent and turn from the things that you've been holding on to that limit and hinder God from operating in your life.

Take a moment and pray right now: "Father, thank You for speaking to me. I open my heart to Your Word. Please help me to see the areas where I've been limiting You, where I've been stopping Your goodness from operating in my life. Thank You, Father. I humble myself and receive with meekness the engrafted Word that is able to save my soul [James 1:21]. I turn from blaming You, and I take responsibility. I turn from being carnal, and I take my stand upon Your Word. Thank You, Father, for touching my life today!"

ANDREW'S RECOMMENDATIONS FOR FURTHER STUDY

Hannah—the daughter of Ashley and Carlie Terradez—was sent home to die. The doctors never expected her to come back for her next appointment. She was three and a half years old and wearing the clothes of a nine-month-old. Hannah had never eaten solid food in her life; she'd been fed a special solution through a tube in her stomach, and now her parents had been told that her body was rejecting the solution. Every time they told people how bad Hannah's condition was—even other Christians— people would say, "That's really bad!" They were more moved by what the doctors had to say than what God says.

But then Ashley and Carlie began to get hold of the Word. They heard that I was ministering near where they lived in England, so they brought Hannah to Jamie and me for prayer. When they told us about her condition, I responded, "That's a piece of cake for Jesus!" This struck a chord of faith in their hearts, and they began to have faith that the Lord was above this sickness and disease. Hannah was not expected to live through the week, but instead, she was totally healed. That was over ten years ago, and Hannah's still alive and well today. Praise God! (You can watch or read the full testimony and many others like it at our website: **www.awmi.net**.)

Outline

I. When people say the name of some sickness or disease, like cancer, it strikes fear in their hearts.

   A. Many people are more moved by what the doctor, banker, or somebody else says than they are by what God's Word says, and that's the problem; they're empowering that curse and those negative things that have been spoken.

   B. I could have believed what was said about the Great Recession back in 2007-2009 and pulled back, but I was listening to God, and He told me to do something else instead.

   C. Although this is simple, it's not easy.

   D. The hardest thing you'll ever do is get to where the Word of God—what you hear from Him, the truth He speaks to you in your heart—is more real to you than what anything or anyone else says.

II. Satan can't do anything to you without your consent and cooperation.

   A. Many people don't like to admit this because they take great comfort in thinking, *The devil made me do it. He's fighting against me, and I can't help it. I'm not responsible.*

   B. You might be saying, "Come on, Andrew! You're saying it's my fault?"

   C. That's exactly what I'm saying.

   D. If you have an enemy out there who's bigger and stronger than you and you can't stop him, well then, woe is you!

   E. But if it's your fault that you have allowed Satan to lie to and steal from you, then you can change.

   F. It's actually good news to find out that you're the problem, because you can change yourself.

III. Quit being a victim!

   A. Nobody owes you anything.

B. Quit being oppressed by people, and stand up and take responsibility for your life.

C. Declare, "It's not what other people do or don't do. I'm the one who has the authority and power of God. I'm going to choose life, and through Christ, I will live and succeed!"

D. It doesn't matter what color you are—green or even purple—find out what Jesus has done for you.

E. Discover who you are and what you have in Christ; then take your authority and start standing on that in faith, and you will prosper.

F. You might have reasons for being a failure, but you have no excuse; the Lord has made you the head and not the tail; you are above only and not beneath (Deut. 28:13).

IV. Words are weapons:

No weapon that is formed against thee shall prosper; and every tongue that shall rise against thee in judgment thou shalt condemn. This is the heritage of the servants of the LORD, *and their righteousness is of me, saith the* LORD.

Isaiah 54:17

A. Notice that right after the phrase *"no weapon that is formed against thee shall prosper"* is the phrase *"every tongue that shall rise against thee in judgment thou shalt condemn,"* which means that these two actions are linked.

B. You must condemn curses.

C. You must judge them and say, "No! In the name of Jesus, that's not true for me!"

V. God's Word is a seed:

The sower soweth the word.

Mark 4:14

Being born again, not of corruptible seed, but of incorruptible, by the word of God, which liveth and abideth for ever.

1 Peter 1:23

A. When you plant this seed, it germinates and begins to release the supernatural power within it.

B. But the Word of God isn't the only seed out there; every word that you hear is a seed—every word!

Death and life are in the power of the tongue.

Proverbs 18:21

C. Everything you hear is either life or death, blessing or cursing.

D. The moment you hear something contrary to what you're believing God for, you need to stop the speaker right then and say, "In the name of Jesus, that's not so. I condemn it. I judge it!"

E. If you don't say something right then because you don't want to offend the speaker and you wait until later when you get home, then you will have to root out the unbelief that was spoken.

F. It can take a while to deal with the unbelief.

G. Do this even while listening to the radio or watching television.

VI. The Word says that Jesus *"answered"* the fig tree (Mark 11:14).

A. This means that the fig tree had been talking to Him.

B. Speak what God's Word says to things.

C. You may think, *Andrew's weird.*

D. But *you're* weird if you're letting the devil run all over you without resisting him.

E. One of the reasons Adam lived to be 930 years old (Gen. 5:5) is because it took millennia for the devil to teach people to think sick and expect infirmity.

VII. When our kids felt sick, we refused to encourage it.

A. We taught our kids that being sick isn't good, and as a result, our children weren't sick.

B. Don't believe in being sick.

C. God's Word says, *"There shall no evil befall thee, neither shall any plague come nigh thy dwelling"* (Ps. 91:10).

VIII. It's sad to say, but other Christians will think you're weird for believing in healing, prosperity, and victory.

    A. One of the most popular doctrines in the body of Christ today is the belief that God controls everything.

    B. A person who holds to this extreme can blame all of their failure on God, saying, "It's His fault. God must have a plan for me being sick."

    C. No, you don't have to be sick, poor, or depressed (1 Pet. 2:24 and Ps. 91:10-11)!

IX. In this verse, God gives you the answer to a multiple-choice test, saying, "Choose life":

> *I call heaven and earth to record this day against you, that I have set before you life and death, blessing and cursing: therefore choose life, that both thou and thy seed may live.*
>
> Deuteronomy 30:19

    A. Why would we choose debt over being debt free?

    B. Why would we choose sickness over being well?

    C. Why would we choose welfare over being productive?

    D. Why do so many shoot for nothing and hit it every time?

X. Perhaps you've been embracing the standards that the world promotes today, and this is the way that you think.

    A. It doesn't bless you to hear someone say that this isn't God's best.

    B. You need to repent!

    C. If you approach God with humility, grace will flow, and He'll show you the way (James 4:6).

    D. Just say, "Father, You're a good God. It's not Your fault that I've received less than Your best. What I don't know, please show me. Teach me. Everything's on the table before You. I'm not going to hold on to anything. I want Your best. Show me what I need to do."

E. Take a moment and pray right now: "Father, thank You for speaking to me. I open my heart to Your Word. Please help me to see the areas where I've been limiting You, where I've been stopping Your goodness from operating in my life. Thank You, Father. I humble myself and receive with meekness the engrafted Word that is able to save my soul [James 1:21]. I turn from blaming You, and I take responsibility. I turn from being carnal, and I take my stand on Your Word. Thank You, Father, for touching my life today!"

ANDREW'S RECOMMENDATIONS FOR FURTHER STUDY

Hannah—the daughter of Ashley and Carlie Terradez—was sent home to die. The doctors never expected her to come back for her next appointment. She was three-and-a-half years old and wearing the clothes of a nine-month-old. Hannah had never eaten solid food in her life; she'd been fed a special solution through a tube in her stomach, and now her parents had been told that her body was rejecting the solution. Every time they told people how bad Hannah's condition was—even other Christians—people would say, "That's really bad!" They were more moved by what the doctors had to say than what God says.

But then Ashley and Carlie began to get hold of the Word. They heard that I was ministering near where they lived in England, so they brought Hannah to Jamie and me for prayer. When they told us about her condition, I responded, "That's a piece of cake for Jesus!" This struck a chord of faith in their hearts, and they began to have faith that the Lord was above this sickness and disease. Hannah was not expected to live through the week, but instead, she was totally healed. That was over ten years ago, and Hannah's still alive and well today. Praise God! (You can watch or read the full testimony and many others like it at our website: **www.awmi.net**.)

Teacher's Guide

1.   When people say the name of some sickness or disease, like cancer, it strikes fear in their hearts. Many people are more moved by what the doctor, banker, or somebody else says than they are by what God's Word says, and that's the problem; they're empowering that curse and those negative things that have been spoken. Andrew could have believed what was said about the Great Recession back in 2007-2009 and pulled back, but he was listening to God, and He told him to do something else instead. Although this is simple, it's not easy. The hardest thing we'll ever do is get to where the Word of God—what we hear from Him, the truth He speaks to us in our hearts—is more real to us than what anything or anyone else says.

1a. When you are more _____ by what the doctor, banker, or somebody else says than you are by what God's Word says, you're empowering that curse and those negative things that have been spoken.
Moved

1b. *Discussion question:* Who and what do you believe when it comes to your finances and your health?
Discussion question

1c. The hardest thing you'll ever do is get to where the Word of God—what you hear from Him, the truth He speaks to you in your heart—is what?
More real to you than what anything or anyone else says

2.   Satan can't do anything to us without our consent and cooperation. Many people don't like to admit this because they take great comfort in thinking, *The devil made me do it. He's fighting against me, and I can't help it. I'm not responsible.* We might be saying, "Come on, Andrew! You're saying it's my fault?" That's exactly what Andrew is saying. If we have an enemy out there who's bigger and stronger than us and we can't stop him, well then, woe is us! But if it's our fault that we have allowed Satan to lie to and steal from us, then we can change. It's actually good news to find out that we're the problem, because we can change ourselves.

2a. Satan can't do anything to you without your _____ and _____.
   A.   Consent / cooperation
   B.   Time / money
   C.   Mind / emotions
   D.   All of the above
   E.   None of the above
   A.   Consent / cooperation

2b. If it's your fault that you have allowed Satan to lie to and steal from you, then what can you do?
   A. Nothing
   B. Change
   C. Quit
   D. Run
   E. Hide
   B. Change

3. We need to quit being victims! Nobody owes us anything. Let's quit being oppressed by people, and let's stand up and take responsibility for our lives. We need to declare, "It's not what other people do or don't do. I'm the one who has the authority and power of God. I'm going to choose life, and through Christ, I will live and succeed!" It doesn't matter what color we are—green or even purple—we need to find out what Jesus has done for us. Let's discover who we are and what we have in Christ; then let's take our authority and start standing on that in faith, and we will prosper. We might have reasons for being failures, but we have no excuse. The Lord has made us the head and not the tail. We are above only and not beneath (Deut. 28:13).

3a. True or false: Somebody owes you something.
   False
3b. What do you need to declare?
   "It's not what other people do or don't do. I'm the one who has the authority and power of God. I'm going to choose life, and through Christ, I will live and succeed!"
3c. Discover who you are and what you have in Christ; then take your authority and start standing on that in faith, and you will _____.
   Prosper
3d. True or false: There is no excuse for being a failure.
   True
3e. According to Deuteronomy 28:13, you are above _____ and not beneath.
   A. Sometimes
   B. People
   C. Prayer
   D. Authority
   E. Only
   E. Only

4. Words are weapons:

   No weapon that is formed against thee shall prosper; and every tongue that shall rise against thee in judgment thou shalt condemn. This is the heritage of the servants of the LORD, *and their righteousness is of me, saith the* LORD.

Isaiah 54:17

Right after the phrase *"no weapon that is formed against thee shall prosper"* is the phrase *"every tongue that shall rise against thee in judgment thou shalt condemn,"* which means that these two actions are linked. We must condemn curses. We must judge them and say, "No! In the name of Jesus, that's not true for me!"

4a. According to Isaiah 54:17, what two actions are linked?
    "No weapon that is formed against thee shall prosper" and "every tongue that
    shall rise against thee in judgment thou shalt condemn"
4b. What must you do with curses?
    A. Accommodate them
    B. Tolerate them
    C. Accept them
    D. All of the above
    E. None of the above
    E. None of the above

5. God's Word is a seed:

    The sower soweth the word.

Mark 4:14

    Being born again, not of corruptible seed, but of incorruptible, by the word of God, which liveth and abideth for ever.

1 Peter 1:23

When we plant this seed, it germinates and begins to release the supernatural power within it. But the Word of God isn't the only seed out there; every word that we hear is a seed—every word!

    Death and life are in the power of the tongue.

Proverbs 18:21

Everything we hear is either life or death, blessing or cursing. The moment we hear something contrary to what we're believing God for, we need to stop the speaker right then and say, "In the name of Jesus, that's not so. I condemn it. I judge it!" If we don't say something right then because we don't want to offend the speaker and we wait until later when we get home, then we will have to root out the unbelief that was spoken. It can take a while to deal with it. We need to do this even while listening to the radio or watching television.

5a. According to Mark 4:14 and 1 Peter 1:23, what is God's Word?
    A seed
5b. True or false: Every word that you hear is a seed.
    True
5c. *Discussion question:* What do you do when you hear something contrary to what you're believing for?
    Discussion question

6. The Word says that Jesus *"answered"* the fig tree (Mark 11:14). This means that the fig tree had been talking to Him. We need to speak what God's Word says to things. We may think, *Andrew's weird.* But *we're* weird if we're letting the devil run all over us without resisting him. One of the reasons Adam lived to be 930 years old (Gen. 5:5) is because it took millennia for the devil to teach people to think sick and expect infirmity.

6a. Since Jesus *"answered"* the fig tree in Mark 11:14, that means what?
    The tree had been talking to Him
6b. What should you speak to things?
    What God's Word says
6c. True or false: You shouldn't let the devil run all over you without resisting him.
    True
6d. The devil had to teach people to _____ sick and _____ infirmity.
    Think / expect

7. When Andrew and Jamie's kids felt sick, they refused to encourage it. They taught their kids that being sick isn't good, and as a result, their children weren't sick. Don't believe in being sick. God's Word says, *"There shall no evil befall thee, neither shall any plague come nigh thy dwelling"* (Ps. 91:10).

7a. *Discussion question:* How will you learn not to accept sickness as normal?
    Discussion question

8. It's sad to say, but other Christians will think we're weird for believing in healing, prosperity, and victory. One of the most popular doctrines in the body of Christ today is the belief that God controls everything. A person who holds to this extreme can blame all of their failure on God, saying, "It's His fault. God must have a plan for me being sick." No, we don't have to be sick, poor, or depressed (1 Pet. 2:24 and Ps. 91:10-11)!

8a. A person who believes that God controls everything can do what?
    Blame all of their failure on Him

8b. According to 1 Peter 2:24 and Psalm 91:10-11, what don't you have to be?
Sick, poor, or depressed

9. In this verse, God gives us the answer to a multiple-choice test, saying, "Choose life":

I call heaven and earth to record this day against you, that I have set before you life and death, blessing and cursing: therefore choose life, that both thou and thy seed may live.

Deuteronomy 30:19

Why would we choose debt over being debt free? Why would we choose sickness over being well? Why would we choose welfare over being productive? Why do so many shoot for nothing and hit it every time?

9a. Read Deuteronomy 30:19. What is the answer to the multiple-choice test?
Choose life

10. Perhaps we've been embracing the standards that the world promotes today, and this is the way that we think. It doesn't bless us to hear someone say that this isn't God's best. We need to repent! If we approach God with humility, grace will flow, and He'll show us the way (James 4:6). Let's just say, "Father, You're a good God. It's not Your fault that I've received less than Your best. What I don't know, please show me. Teach me. Everything's on the table before You. I'm not going to hold on to anything. I want Your best. Show me what I need to do." Let's take a moment and pray right now: "Father, thank You for speaking to me. I open my heart to Your Word. Please help me to see the areas where I've been limiting You, where I've been stopping Your goodness from operating in my life. Thank You, Father. I humble myself and receive with meekness the engrafted Word that is able to save my soul (James 1:21). I turn from blaming You, and I take responsibility. I turn from being carnal, and I take my stand on Your Word. Thank You, Father, for touching my life today!"

10a. If you've been embracing the standards that the world promotes today, and this is the way that you think, what do you need to do?
Repent
10b. If you approach God with humility, _____ will flow, and He'll show you the way (James 4:6).
Grace
10c. *Discussion question:* Why is it important to approach God with humility?
Discussion question
10d. Discussion question: What would be a good prayer to pray right now?
Discussion question

Discipleship Questions

1. When you are more _____ by what the doctor, banker, or somebody else says than you are by what God's Word says, you're empowering that curse and those negative things that have been spoken.

2. *Discussion question:* Who and what do you believe when it comes to your finances and your health?

   _____

   _____

   _____

3. The hardest thing you'll ever do is get to where the Word of God—what you hear from Him, the truth He speaks to you in your heart—is what?

   _____

   _____

   _____

4. Satan can't do anything to you without your _____ and _____.
   A. Consent / cooperation
   B. Time / money
   C. Mind / emotions
   D. All of the above
   E. None of the above

5. If it's your fault that you have allowed Satan to lie to and steal from you, then what can you do?
   A. Nothing
   B. Change
   C. Quit
   D. Run
   E. Hide

6. True or false: Somebody owes you something.

7. What do you need to declare?

    _____

    _____

    _____

8. Discover who you are and what you have in Christ; then take your authority and start standing on that in faith, and you will _____.

9. True or false: There is no excuse for being a failure.

10. According to Deuteronomy 28:13, you are above _____ and not beneath.
    A. Sometimes
    B. People
    C. Prayer
    D. Authority
    E. Only

11. According to Isaiah 54:17, what two actions are linked?

    _____

    _____

    _____

12. What must you do with curses?
    A. Accommodate them
    B. Tolerate them
    C. Accept them
    D. All of the above
    E. None of the above

13. According to Mark 4:14 and 1 Peter 1:23, what is God's Word?

    _____

    _____

    _____

14. True or false: Every word you hear is a seed.

15. *Discussion question:* What do you do when you hear something contrary to what you're believing for?

16. Since Jesus *"answered"* the fig tree in Mark 11:14, that means what?

17. What should you speak to things?

18. True or false: You shouldn't let the devil run all over you without resisting him.

19. The devil had to teach people to _____ sick and _____ infirmity.

20. *Discussion question:* How will you learn not to accept sickness as normal?

21. A person who believes that God controls everything can do what?

22. According to 1 Peter 2:24 and Psalm 91:10-11, what don't you have to be?

_____

_____

_____

23. Read Deuteronomy 30:19. What is the answer to the multiple-choice test?

_____

_____

_____

24. If you've been embracing the standards that the world promotes today, and this is the way that you think, what do you need to do?

_____

_____

_____

25. If you approach God with humility, _____ will flow, and He'll show you the way (James 4:6.)

26. *Discussion question:* Why is it important to approach God with humility?

_____

_____

_____

27. *Discussion question:* What would be a good prayer to pray right now?

_____

_____

_____

Answer Key

1. Moved

2. *Discussion question*

3. More real to you than what anything or anyone else says

4. A. Consent / cooperation

5. B. Change

6. False

7. "It's not what other people do or don't do. I'm the one who has the authority and power of God. I'm going to choose life, and through Christ, I will live and succeed!"

8. Prosper

9. True

10. E. Only

11. *"No weapon that is formed against thee shall prosper"* and *"every tongue that shall rise against thee in judgment thou shalt condemn"*

12. E. None of the above

13. A seed

14. True

15. *Discussion question*

16. The tree had been talking to Him

17. What God's Word says

18. True

19. Think / expect

20. *Discussion question*

21. Blame all of their failure on Him

22. Sick, poor, or depressed

23. Choose life

24. Repent

25. Grace

26. *Discussion question*

27. *Discussion question*

Scriptures

DEUTERONOMY 28:13

And the LORD shall make thee the head, and not the tail; and thou shalt be above only, and thou shalt not be beneath; if that thou hearken unto the commandments of the LORD thy God, which I command thee this day, to observe and to do them.

ISAIAH 54:17

No weapon that is formed against thee shall prosper; and every tongue that shall rise against thee in judgment thou shalt condemn. This is the heritage of the servants of the LORD, and their righteousness is of me, saith the LORD.

MARK 4:14

The sower soweth the word.

1 PETER 1:23

Being born again, not of corruptible seed, but of incorruptible, by the word of God, which liveth and abideth for ever.

PROVERBS 18:21

Death and life are in the power of the tongue: and they that love it shall eat the fruit thereof.

MARK 11:14

And Jesus answered and said unto it, No man eat fruit of thee hereafter for ever. And his disciples heard it.

GENESIS 5:5

And all the days that Adam lived were nine hundred and thirty years: and he died.

PSALM 91:10-11

There shall no evil befall thee, neither shall any plague come nigh thy dwelling. [11] For he shall give his angels charge over thee, to keep thee in all thy ways.

1 PETER 2:24

Who his own self bare our sins in his own body on the tree, that we, being dead to sins, should live unto righteousness: by whose stripes ye were healed.

PSALM 34:1

I will bless the Lord at all times: his praise shall continually be in my mouth.

GALATIANS 5:22

But the fruit of the Spirit is love, joy, peace, longsuffering, gentleness, goodness, faith.

HEBREWS 13:15

By him therefore let us offer the sacrifice of praise to God continually, that is, the fruit of our lips giving thanks to his name.

DEUTERONOMY 30:19

I call heaven and earth to record this day against you, that I have set before you life and death, blessing and cursing: therefore choose life, that both thou and thy seed may live.

JAMES 4:6

But he giveth more grace. Wherefore he saith, God resisteth the proud, but giveth grace unto the humble.

JAMES 1:21

Wherefore lay apart all filthiness and superfluity of naughtiness, and receive with meekness the engrafted word, which is able to save your souls.

Natural Laws

LESSON 9

God has different ways of getting His supply to you. The two primary ways He uses are blessings and miracles. Many people have heard of these terms, but they honestly haven't given enough thought to the subject to know the difference between them.

Most Spirit-filled believers—those who speak in tongues and understand that God is real, supernatural, and can do anything—have a tendency to go for the miracles.

Let's picture two doors, side by side. One is labeled "Miracle" and the other is labeled "Blessings." Most Christians would run to the "Miracle" door every time, saying, "I want a miracle. I desire to live under the miraculous power of God!"

Miracles do happen today. I see them all the time at my meetings, at Charis Bible College, and through our ministry's Helpline. There's nothing wrong with miracles; however, they aren't God's best. A blessing is God's best for you.

Don't get me wrong; I believe in miracles and see them regularly. But I believe that miracles are for other people (unbelievers) primarily. Jesus used miracles like a bell to draw people to Himself, arrest their attention, and confirm His preaching. We need more of the supernatural miracles of God in our services to help encourage people and show them that God is real. But your life isn't going to be sustained off miracles. God wants you to walk in blessings because blessings are better than miracles in the long term.

SUPERSEDING OR SUSPENSION

By definition, a miracle involves a superseding or suspension of natural laws. If something can be explained naturally, then it's not a miracle. In medicine, they call things like the polio vaccine "a miracle." Development of a vaccine is not a miracle; it's a blessing. It's just natural. I believe people have prayed and God has given them wisdom and knowledge about how to do certain things. If it is within the natural realm, it's not a miracle.

A miracle is an event that supersedes or suspends natural laws. Walking on top of water is a miracle (Matt. 14:22-33), but it's not a miracle if the water is frozen. Miracles are supernatural.

When God created the heavens and the earth, He also spoke into being the natural laws that govern them.

> *And God said, Let there be light: and there was light. [4] And God saw the light, that it was good: and God divided the light from the darkness. [5] And God called the light Day, and the darkness he called Night. And the evening and the morning were the first day.*
>
> Genesis 1:3-5

God continued speaking and creating:

> *And God saw every thing that he had made, and, behold, it was very good. And the evening and the morning were the sixth day.*
>
> Genesis 1:31

When God created the heavens and the earth, to say that they were *"good"* (or even *"very good"*) is a gross understatement. They were awesome! His creation is wonderful! So, God created this world and all the natural laws in it, and He intended for us to live under those natural laws. Natural laws, like the law of gravity, didn't just happen. They were created.

AN EXCEPTION

Unfortunately, our world has been influenced by unbelievers to such a degree that even Christians think that creation evolved, that the earth and the heavens "just happened" naturally. They didn't. God thought everything through. When He said, *"Let there be light"* (Gen. 1:3), *"Let the dry land appear"* (Gen. 1:9), and *"Let the earth bring forth...the fruit tree yielding fruit after his kind, whose seed is in itself"* (Gen. 1:11), He had already spent much time thinking about these things and conceiving them in His heart—perhaps even eons. When He spoke, His words encapsulated everything that He had been thinking and brought those things into being. Before He spoke creation into being, every detail of it had already been conceived in His heart.

I know about the creation process because I create things. I construct buildings, make television and radio programs, and produce all kinds of teaching materials. Before I can do these things, I have to conceive them first in my imagination. God's Word says that we've been made in His image (Gen. 1:27), so I believe that our ability to create comes from Him. I believe that God thought creation through all the way down to the tiniest detail, the smallest cell and atom. He thought all of this through and then created it and said, "This is very good." He intended for us to live in this creation where everything is functioning and working together well. We are supposed to cooperate with the natural laws that He embedded into creation. He wants us to learn how they work and to live in them.

So, when God supersedes or suspends these natural laws that He created, it's an exception. It's a miracle. Miracles aren't the way God really intended for you to live. He wants you to learn how to operate within the natural laws of creation. I pray that the Lord supernaturally enables you to understand what I'm trying to communicate here.

RESEARCHERS OVERLOOK THIS

> *A merry heart doeth good like a medicine: but a broken spirit drieth the bones.*
>
> Proverbs 17:22

Choosing to rejoice does your soul and body good. This is one of God's laws in creation. He created us for fellowship with Him and to be full of joy: *"In thy presence is fulness of joy; at thy right hand there are pleasures for evermore"* (Ps. 16:11).

Stress, worry, fear, and care are all a result of the Fall. Medical science has recognized that stress shuts down the immune system, making people susceptible to all kinds of things. But if we walk in joy with the presence of the Lord, our merry hearts will be like medicine. Many of the sicknesses and health conditions we have wouldn't be able to stay in our bodies if we would just cooperate with this law God has spoken.

Exodus 20:12 says that if you honor your father and mother, it will prolong your days and cause you to live long in the land that God has given you. Ephesians 6:2-3 confirms this:

> *Honour thy father and mother; (which is the first commandment with promise;) [3] That it may be well with thee, and thou mayest live long on the earth.*

Yet there are many people who are rebellious and don't respect their parents. I'm not saying that our parents did everything right, but we can still choose to honor them. We can respect authority. Disrespect toward parents and rebellion toward authority are rampant in our country today. Most people's default is just to disrespect everything. That affects their health. The quality of a person's health is linked directly to whether or not they honor their father and mother.

I'm always surprised when researchers overlook this. They go to places where people live the longest, like Japan, and they wonder why the Japanese don't have heart disease. They analyze the people's diet and they conclude that the secret to longevity is eating fish and related omega-3s. The researchers don't even factor into it the Japanese culture that stresses honoring parents and elders. Unfortunately, researchers don't factor this in because they're only looking for physical, tangible things. They forget that these people honor their fathers and mothers. Now, I'm not saying that we're supposed to go to the extreme of worshiping our parents or ancestors, but there's great benefit to cooperating with God's laws in creation.

MISSING THE MAJORS

God's Word is life and health:

> My son, attend to my words; incline thine ear unto my sayings. [21] Let them not depart from thine eyes; keep them in the midst of thine heart. [22] For they are life unto those that find them, and health to all their flesh.
>
> Proverbs 4:20-22

Our humanistic world doesn't take into account spiritual truth. They look at things like diet and exercise for good health. In fact, many people are absolute fanatics and resort to eating all kinds of twigs and berries. That's not food. That's what food eats! Having a merry heart, honoring our parents and elders, and studying the Word of God are all major factors contributing to good health.

> He sent his word, and healed them, and delivered them from their destructions.
>
> Psalm 107:20

What I'm about to tell you is "Andyology," so you can take it or leave it—but I personally believe that diet and exercise only factor into about 20 or 25 percent of a person's overall health. I believe that the other 75 percent or more of a person's health consists of spiritual and emotional things. However, our humanistic world doesn't consider spiritual things, so they focus on diet, exercise, and other natural things—which is a part of overall health—while ignoring and overlooking these more important factors. In my opinion, they're majoring on minors and completely missing the majors.

God created both us and this world we live in. He fashioned our bodies to function a certain way. When our hearts are full of stress, fear, worry, unforgiveness, and bitterness, God's whole system is corrupted. If we would just walk in joy, peace, and freedom, meditating in the Word and keeping our minds stayed on God, we would discover that the blessing of God would just flow (Is. 26:3). We wouldn't have to deal with nearly as much sickness and other problems. Everything in life would work so much better!

RELATIONSHIP WITH GOD

Sad to say, the church has actually contributed to this problem in a large way by making people feel guilty and condemned and not telling them about the goodness and unconditional love of God. The church has twisted prayer into something it was never intended to be.

Prayer is primarily just relationship with God. Granted, there is a place to intercede for others and rebuke the devil, but that should constitute a very small percentage of our prayer lives. Prayer ought to be just loving God, thanking Him, and fellowshipping together.

Do you realize that Adam and Eve didn't have anything to pray for? That's right. In the Garden, before the Fall, they didn't have any clothes to believe for, houses to pray about, or even food to petition for. Everything was already there. The climate was perfect. They didn't have a government to gripe and complain about. There was no need to pray for revival. What does a person do if they don't have to pray about all of the stuff that we're told to pray about today? I believe that Adam and Eve just met with God every day and said, "Thank You for this beautiful day. It's awesome! I just saw some trees today that I have never seen before. I ate fruit from them and saw animals near them. God, You are awesome!" They just talked with Him about what their day was like.

After hearing my teaching entitled *A Better Way to Pray*, a certain woman testified about how she applied those truths to her life. While taking her dog on a walk, she decided to begin thanking God for just the small things. She thanked Him for how beautiful the weather was, that it was warming up and spring was coming, and for the plants she saw budding. As she started thanking God for all these things, she said that she felt the love of God very strongly. In fact, she walked twice as long as she normally did and resented having to get back to do other things. When she finished walking her dog, she wrote me an email, saying, "I'm so looking forward to tomorrow just to fellowship with Jesus and to feel His pleasure and love. I've never known that this is what prayer could be! It's always been about asking for something or repenting, rebuking, and binding."

If you just fellowship with God, you'll find that things just work supernaturally. But if you aren't walking in what God has instructed in His Word and you're stressed out, miserable, bitter, in strife, and full of unforgiveness, then you'll have all kinds of problems. You'll need a miracle! A miracle would overcome these natural laws. But if you are walking in love, joy, and peace, you won't need a miracle. God loves us so much that He will supply miracles for us, but if we would just learn how to cooperate and walk in the blessings, we wouldn't even need miracles.

Outline

I. God has different ways of getting His supply to us.

    A. The two primary ways He uses are blessings and miracles.

    B. Most Spirit-filled believers—those who speak in tongues and understand that God is real, supernatural, and can do anything—have a tendency to go for the miracles.

    C. Miracles are for other people (unbelievers) primarily.

    D. Jesus used miracles like a bell to draw people to Himself, arrest their attention, and confirm His preaching.

    E. More of the supernatural miracles of God are needed in our services to help encourage people and show them that God is real.

    F. But our lives aren't going to be sustained off miracles.

    G. God wants us to walk in blessings because blessings are better than miracles in the long term.

II. By definition, a miracle is an event that supersedes or suspends natural laws.

    A. Miracles are supernatural.

    B. When God created the heavens and the earth, He also spoke into being the natural laws that govern them (Gen. 1:3-5 and 31).

    C. Unfortunately, the world has been influenced by unbelievers to such a degree that even Christians think that creation evolved, that the earth and the heavens "just happened" naturally.

    D. When God said, *"Let there be light"* (Gen. 1:3), *"Let the dry land appear"* (Gen. 1:9), and *"Let the earth bring forth…the fruit tree yielding fruit after his kind, whose seed is in itself"* (Gen. 1:11), He had already spent much time thinking about these things and conceiving them in His heart—perhaps even eons.

    E. When He spoke, His words encapsulated everything that He had been thinking and brought those things into being.

F. I believe that God thought creation through all the way down to the tiniest detail, the smallest cell and atom.

G. So, when He supersedes or suspends these natural laws that He created, it's an exception, a miracle.

H. Miracles aren't the way God really intended for you to live.

I. He wants you to learn how to operate within the natural laws of creation.

III. Choosing to rejoice does our souls and bodies good:

> *A merry heart doeth good like a medicine: but a broken spirit drieth the bones.*
>
> Proverbs 17:22

A. This is one of God's laws in creation.

B. He created us for fellowship with Him and to be full of joy: *"In thy presence is fulness of joy; at thy right hand there are pleasures for evermore"* (Ps. 16:11).

C. Stress, worry, fear, and care are all a result of the Fall.

D. Medical science has recognized that stress shuts down the immune system, making people susceptible to all kinds of things.

E. But if we walk in joy with the presence of the Lord, our merry hearts will be like medicine.

F. Many sicknesses and health conditions won't be able to stay in our bodies when we cooperate with this law God has spoken.

IV. Exodus 20:12 says that if we honor our fathers and mothers, it will prolong our days and cause us to live long in the land that God has given us.

A. Ephesians 6:2-3 confirms this:

> *Honour thy father and mother; (which is the first commandment with promise;) [3] That it may be well with thee, and thou mayest live long on the earth.*

B. Yet there are many people who are rebellious and don't respect their parents.

C. I'm not saying that our parents did everything right, but we can still choose to honor them.

D. The quality of a person's health is linked directly to whether or not they honor their father and mother.

E. Unfortunately, researchers don't factor this in because they're only looking for physical, tangible things.

F. There's great benefit to cooperating with God's laws in creation.

V. God's Word is life and health:

My son, attend to my words; incline thine ear unto my sayings. [21] *Let them not depart from thine eyes; keep them in the midst of thine heart.* [22] *For they are life unto those that find them, and health to all their flesh.*

Proverbs 4:20-22

A. Having a merry heart, honoring our parents and elders, and studying the Word of God are all major factors contributing to good health.

B. Our humanistic world doesn't consider spiritual things, so they focus on diet, exercise, and other natural things—which is a part of overall health—while ignoring and overlooking these more important factors.

C. They're majoring on minors and completely missing the majors.

D. God fashioned our bodies to function a certain way.

E. When our hearts are full of stress, fear, worry, unforgiveness, and bitterness, God's whole system is corrupted.

F. But if we walk in joy, peace, and freedom, meditating in the Word and keeping our minds stayed on God, we would discover that the blessing of God would flow (Is. 26:3).

G. Everything in life would work so much better!

VI. The church has twisted prayer into something it was never intended to be.

    A. Prayer is primarily relationship with God.

    B. Granted, there is a place to intercede for others and rebuke the devil, but that should constitute a very small percentage of your prayer life.

    C. Prayer ought to be loving God, thanking Him, and fellowshipping together.

    D. Do you realize that Adam and Eve didn't have anything to pray for?

    E. They probably met with God every day and said, "Thank You for this beautiful day. It's awesome! I just saw some trees today that I have never seen before. I ate fruit from them and saw animals near them. God, You are awesome!"

VII. If you fellowship with God, you'll find that things work supernaturally.

    A. But if you aren't walking in what God has instructed in His Word and you're stressed out, miserable, bitter, in strife, and full of unforgiveness, then you'll have all kinds of problems.

    B. If you are walking in love, joy, and peace, you won't need a miracle.

    C. God loves you so much that He will supply miracles for you, but if you learn how to cooperate and walk in the blessings, you wouldn't even need miracles.

Teacher's Guide

1.   God has different ways of getting His supply to us. The two primary ways He uses are blessings and miracles. Most Spirit-filled believers—those who speak in tongues and understand that God is real, supernatural, and can do anything—have a tendency to go for the miracles. Miracles are for other people (unbelievers) primarily. Jesus used miracles like a bell to draw people to Himself, arrest their attention, and confirm His preaching. More of the supernatural miracles of God are needed in our services to help encourage people and show them that God is real. But our lives aren't going to be sustained off miracles. God wants us to walk in blessings because blessings are better than miracles in the long term.

1a. What are two primary ways God gets His supply to you?
     Blessings and miracles
1b. Why did Jesus use miracles?
     To draw people to Himself, arrest their attention, and confirm His preaching
1c. *Discussion question:* Since blessings are better than miracles, why are miracles needed?
     Discussion question

2.   By definition, a miracle is an event that supersedes or suspends natural laws. Miracles are supernatural. When God created the heavens and the earth, He also spoke into being the natural laws that govern them (Gen. 1:3-5 and 31). Unfortunately, the world has been influenced by unbelievers to such a degree that even Christians think that creation evolved, that the earth and the heavens "just happened" naturally. When God said, *"Let there be light"* (Gen. 1:3), *"Let the dry land appear"* (Gen. 1:9), and *"Let the earth bring forth…the fruit tree yielding fruit after his kind, whose seed is in itself"* (Gen. 1:11), He had already spent much time thinking about these things and conceiving them in His heart—perhaps even eons. When He spoke, His words encapsulated everything that He had been thinking and brought those things into being. Andrew believes that God thought creation through all the way down to the tiniest detail, the smallest cell and atom. So, when He supersedes or suspends these natural laws that He created, it's an exception, a miracle. Miracles aren't the way God really intended for you to live. He wants you to learn how to operate within the natural laws of creation.

2a. What is a miracle?
     An event that supersedes or suspends natural laws
2b. When God created the heavens and the earth, He also spoke into being the natural laws that _____ them (Gen. 1:3-5 and 31).
     Govern

2c. When God supersedes or suspends these natural laws that He created, what is it?
   A. A violation
   B. An anomaly
   C. An exception
   D. All of the above
   E. None of the above
   C. An exception
2d. Since miracles aren't the way God really intended for you to live, what does He want?
   He wants you to learn how to operate within the natural laws of creation

3. Choosing to rejoice does our souls and bodies good:

   A merry heart doeth good like a medicine: but a broken spirit drieth the bones.

   Proverbs 17:22

This is one of God's laws in creation. He created us for fellowship with Him and to be full of joy: *"In thy presence is fulness of joy; at thy right hand there are pleasures for evermore"* (Ps. 16:11). Stress, worry, fear, and care are all a result of the Fall. Medical science has recognized that stress shuts down the immune system, making people susceptible to all kinds of things. But if we walk in joy with the presence of the Lord, our merry hearts will be like medicine. Many sicknesses and health conditions won't be able to stay in our bodies when we cooperate with this law God has spoken.

3a. True or false: According to Proverbs 17:22, choosing to rejoice does your soul and body good.
   True
3b. *Discussion question:* How has this law operated in your life?
   Discussion question
3c. _____, _____, _____, and _____ are all a result of the Fall.
   Stress / worry / fear / care
3d. If you walk in joy with the presence of the Lord, what will your merry heart be like?
   A. Venom
   B. Honey
   C. Music
   D. Medicine
   E. Mush
   D. Medicine

4. Exodus 20:12 says that if we honor our fathers and mothers, it will prolong our days and cause us to live long in the land that God has given us. Ephesians 6:2-3 confirms this:

Honour thy father and mother; (which is the first commandment with promise;) [3] That it may be well with thee, and thou mayest live long on the earth.

Yet there are many people who are rebellious and don't respect their parents. Andrew isn't saying that our parents did everything right, but we can still choose to honor them. The quality of a person's health is linked directly to whether or not they honor their father and mother. Unfortunately, researchers don't factor this in because they're only looking for physical, tangible things. There's great benefit to cooperating with God's laws in creation.

4a. If you honor your father and mother, it will _____ your days and cause you to live _____ in the land that God has given you (Ex. 20:12 and Eph. 6:2-3).
   Prolong / long

4b. True or false: If your parents did something wrong, you shouldn't honor them.
   False

4c. There's great _____ to _____ with God's laws in creation.
   Benefit / cooperating

5. God's Word is life and health:

   My son, attend to my words; incline thine ear unto my sayings. [21] Let them not depart from thine eyes; keep them in the midst of thine heart. [22] For they are life unto those that find them, and health to all their flesh.
   Proverbs 4:20-22

Having a merry heart, honoring our parents and elders, and studying the Word of God are all major factors contributing to good health. Our humanistic world doesn't consider spiritual things, so they focus on diet, exercise, and other natural things—which is a part of overall health—while ignoring and overlooking these more important factors. They're majoring on minors and completely missing the majors. God fashioned our bodies to function a certain way. When our hearts are full of stress, fear, worry, unforgiveness, and bitterness, God's whole system is corrupted. But if we walk in joy, peace, and freedom, meditating in the Word and keeping our minds stayed on God, we would discover that the blessing of God would flow (Is. 26:3). Everything in life would work so much better!

5a. According to Proverbs 4:20-22, God's Word is what?
   A. Love and grace
   B. Tedious and irrelevant
   C. Yes and amen
   D. Life and health
   E. Harsh and condemning
   D. Life and health

5b. What three things are major factors contributing to good health?
A merry heart, honoring your parents and elders, and studying the Word of God

5c. *Discussion question:* Why is it important to major on the majors?
Discussion question

5d. If you walk in joy, peace, and freedom, meditating in the Word and keeping your mind stayed on God, you would discover that the blessing of God does what (Is. 26:3)?
Flows

6. The church has twisted prayer into something it was never intended to be. Prayer is primarily relationship with God. Granted, there is a place to intercede for others and rebuke the devil, but that should constitute a very small percentage of our prayer lives. Prayer ought to be loving God, thanking Him, and fellowshipping together. Adam and Eve didn't have anything to pray for. They probably met with God every day and said, "Thank You for this beautiful day. It's awesome! I just saw some trees today that I have never seen before. I ate fruit from them and saw animals near them. God, You are awesome!"

6a. True or false: Intercession for others and rebuking the devil should constitute a large percentage of your prayer life.
False

6b. Prayer ought to be _____ God, _____ Him, and _____ together.
Loving / thanking / fellowshipping

7. If we fellowship with God, we'll find that things work supernaturally. But if we aren't walking in what God has instructed in His Word and we're stressed out, miserable, bitter, in strife, and full of unforgiveness, then we'll have all kinds of problems. If we are walking in love, joy, and peace, we won't need a miracle. God loves us so much that He will supply miracles for us, but if we learn how to cooperate and walk in the blessings, we wouldn't even need miracles.

7a. True or false: If you are walking in love, joy, and peace, you won't need a miracle.
True

7b. *Discussion question:* How do you plan to better cooperate with God's natural laws?
Discussion question

Discipleship Questions

1. What are two primary ways God gets His supply to you?

    _____

    _____

    _____

2. Why did Jesus use miracles?

    _____

    _____

    _____

3. *Discussion question:* Since blessings are better than miracles, why are miracles needed?

    _____

    _____

    _____

4. What is a miracle?

    _____

    _____

    _____

5. When God created the heavens and the earth, He also spoke into being the natural laws that _____ them (Gen. 1:3-5 and 31).

6. When God supersedes or suspends these natural laws that He created, what is it?
    A. A violation
    B. An anomaly
    C. An exception
    D. All of the above
    E. None of the above

7. Since miracles aren't the way God really intended for you to live, what does He want?

_____

_____

_____

8. True or false: According to Proverbs 17:22, choosing to rejoice does your soul and body good.

9. *Discussion question:* How has this law operated in your life?

_____

_____

_____

10. _____, _____, _____, and _____ are all a result of the Fall.

11. If you walk in joy with the presence of the Lord, what will your merry heart be like?
    A. Venom
    B. Honey
    C. Music
    D. Medicine
    E. Mush

12. If you honor your father and mother, it will _____ your days and cause you to live _____ in the land that God has given you (Ex. 20:12 and Eph. 6:2-3).

13. True or false: If your parents did something wrong, you shouldn't honor them.

14. There's great _____ to _____ with God's laws in creation.

15. According to Proverbs 4:20-22, God's Word is what?
    A. Love and grace
    B. Tedious and irrelevant
    C. Yes and amen
    D. Life and health
    E. Harsh and condemning

16. What three things are major factors contributing to good health?

_____

_____

_____

17. *Discussion question:* Why is it important to major on the majors?

_____

_____

_____

18. If you walk in joy, peace, and freedom, meditating in the Word and keeping your mind stayed on God, you would discover that the blessing of God does what (Is. 26:3)?

_____

_____

_____

19. True or false: Intercession for others and rebuking the devil should constitute a large percentage of your prayer life.

20. Prayer ought to be _____ God, _____ Him, and _____ together.

21. True or false: If you are walking in love, joy, and peace, you won't need a miracle.

22. *Discussion question:* How do you plan to better cooperate with God's natural laws?

_____

_____

_____

Answer Key

1. Blessings and miracles

2. To draw people to Himself, arrest their attention, and confirm His preaching

3. *Discussion question*

4. An event that supersedes or suspends natural laws

5. Govern

6. C. An exception

7. He wants you to learn how to operate within the natural laws of creation

8. True

9. *Discussion question*

10. Stress / worry / fear / care

11. D. Medicine

12. Prolong / long

13. False

14. Benefit / cooperating

15. D. Life and health

16. A merry heart, honoring your parents and elders, and studying the Word of God

17. *Discussion question*

18. Flows

19. False

20. Loving / thanking / fellowshipping

21. True

22. *Discussion question*

Scriptures

MATTHEW 14:22-33

And straightway Jesus constrained his disciples to get into a ship, and to go before him unto the other side, while he sent the multitudes away. [23] And when he had sent the multitudes away, he went up into a mountain apart to pray: and when the evening was come, he was there alone. [24] But the ship was now in the midst of the sea, tossed with waves: for the wind was contrary. [25] And in the fourth watch of the night Jesus went unto them, walking on the sea. [26] And when the disciples saw him walking on the sea, they were troubled, saying, It is a spirit; and they cried out for fear. [27] But straightway Jesus spake unto them, saying, Be of good cheer; it is I; be not afraid. [28] And Peter answered him and said, Lord, if it be thou, bid me come unto thee on the water. [29] And he said, Come. And when Peter was come down out of the ship, he walked on the water, to go to Jesus. [30] But when he saw the wind boisterous, he was afraid; and beginning to sink, he cried, saying, Lord, save me. [31] And immediately Jesus stretched forth his hand, and caught him, and said unto him, O thou of little faith, wherefore didst thou doubt? [32] And when they were come into the ship, the wind ceased. [33] Then they that were in the ship came and worshipped him, saying, Of a truth thou art the Son of God.

GENESIS 1:3-5

And God said, Let there be light: and there was light. [4] And God saw the light, that it was good: and God divided the light from the darkness. [5] And God called the light Day, and the darkness he called Night. And the evening and the morning were the first day.

GENESIS 1:31

And God saw every thing that he had made, and, behold, it was very good. And the evening and the morning were the sixth day.

GENESIS 1:9

And God said, Let the waters under the heaven be gathered together unto one place, and let the dry land appear: and it was so.

GENESIS 1:11

And God said, Let the earth bring forth grass, the herb yielding seed, and the fruit tree yielding fruit after his kind, whose seed is in itself, upon the earth: and it was so.

GENESIS 1:27

So God created man in his own image, in the image of God created he him; male and female created he them.

PROVERBS 17:22

A merry heart doeth good like a medicine: but a broken spirit drieth the bones.

PSALM 16:11

Thou wilt shew me the path of life: in thy presence is fulness of joy; at thy right hand there are pleasures for evermore.

EXODUS 20:12

Honour thy father and thy mother: that thy days may be long upon the land which the LORD thy God giveth thee.

EPHESIANS 6:2-3

Honour thy father and mother; (which is the first commandment with promise;) [3] That it may be well with thee, and thou mayest live long on the earth.

PROVERBS 4:20-22

My son, attend to my words; incline thine ear unto my sayings. [21] Let them not depart from thine eyes; keep them in the midst of thine heart. [22] For they are life unto those that find them, and health to all their flesh.

PSALM 107:20

He sent his word, and healed them, and delivered them from their destructions.

ISAIAH 26:3

Thou wilt keep him in perfect peace, whose mind is stayed on thee: because he trusteth in thee.

Manna

LESSON 10

The same principle of learning to walk in blessings rather than beg for miracles is also true in the area of finances. There are laws that God created about how provision works.

The Lord said that He would bless the work of your hands.

> *The Lord shall command the blessing upon thee in thy storehouses, and in all that thou settest thine hand unto; and he shall bless thee in the land which the Lord thy God giveth thee.*
>
> Deuteronomy 28:8

> *The Lord shall open unto thee his good treasure, the heaven to give the rain unto thy land in his season, and to bless all the work of thine hand: and thou shalt lend unto many nations, and thou shalt not borrow.*
>
> Deuteronomy 28:12

Whatever you set your hand to will be blessed, but did you know 100 multiplied by zero equals zero? You may be living off welfare today. If you are, I'm not against you. Neither am I criticizing you. You can do whatever you want. God loves you, and I'm not mad at you. But guess what? You're praying for God's power to be released, but you aren't setting your hand to anything—and God can't bless welfare.

Some people think, *Well, I'm not going to go work at McDonald's. I get more from welfare than I would from working there.* The difference is that if you set your hand to something, God can multiply that. He can't multiply welfare. The Lord isn't going to bless you through welfare. If you need it for a brief period of time, then do what you must. Anybody could need help temporarily, but don't live there. Don't settle for less than God's best. Start believing God to be a producer and a contributor. When it comes to finances, some people just refuse to work.

WE STRUGGLED

I had this mindset of not needing to work myself. When I was first called into the ministry, I had a mistaken idea that I would be sinning against God if I worked a job. The Lord had called me to preach, and I was going to do what He called me to do. My heart was right, but my head was wrong. So, my wife and I nearly starved to death!

When Jamie was eight months pregnant, we went over two weeks with zero food—I mean nothing but water. It wasn't because I couldn't work; I just thought I was doing the right thing by not working and by pursuing the ministry instead. Looking back, I realize now that I wasn't cooperating with God's laws.

> *Even so hath the Lord ordained that they which preach the gospel should live of the gospel.*
>
> 1 Corinthians 9:14

I wasn't preaching the Gospel. I was called to it, but I didn't have a group yet. I wasn't ministering to anybody, so I shouldn't have expected to live of it.

Then I started preaching and holding a Bible study with five or ten people. Since I was only ministering to five or ten people, I shouldn't have expected to full-time "live of the Gospel." I should have been like Paul and gone out and made tents to supplement my income (Acts 18:3). But I didn't. Because of this, Jamie and I were in financial crisis for at least five years. We struggled for about ten years and nearly died because I was too stupid to figure out that until I was a full-time minister, I couldn't expect to live of the Gospel full-time.

Praise God for Jamie! There's probably not another woman on the planet who would have stayed with me through the things I put her through. If she had ever criticized me and said, "Why don't you get a job," that would have done it! I would have probably just died right there. I felt terrible as it was, but she never criticized me. Not one time did she say anything. She just followed me and did whatever I felt like God was telling us to do.

We lived from miracle to miracle. The doorbell would ring, and a sack full of food would be sitting on our front porch. Nobody was there—and there wasn't enough time for anybody to run away. I don't know where they went! We'd just have food show up, as well as surprise money in the mail. People would bless us by sending cash in an envelope with no return address. It would just show up.

NEVER DENY THEM ACCESS

We could have qualified for food stamps. Our total income during our first year of marriage was $1,253, and our rent was $100 per month. I don't know how we survived. Our second year's income was about $2,300. We could have received food stamps, welfare, or government assistance of some kind, but I just kept believing that there was something better than subsistence and government help. I was believing God. I wasn't doing a very good job of it, but at least I had the goal!

One time we took seven dollars and a coupon into the supermarket, praying and believing God because we hadn't eaten in a long time. We needed some food! Somehow, we came out with seven bags of groceries and ten dollars in coupons. We got home and tried to figure out how this happened, but we never did. Things were on special, and it was miraculous. It's a miracle that we survived!

One time we were at Christ for the Nations, listening to someone minister on prosperity. I remember standing there looking at the cassette tapes of teaching and thinking, *Those would change my life!* But I couldn't buy them. I glanced over at Jamie, and she had tears in her eyes. She also knew that those Bible teachings could help us, but she was painfully aware of our inability to purchase them. That's when I made my commitment. I prayed, "God, if You ever show me anything from Your Word that will help another person, I'll never deny them access to it because of finances." This is why we give so much of our material away for free—millions of tapes, CDs, DVDs, and books. On our website alone, we average hundreds of thousands of free downloads per month. The Lord has enabled us to give away multiple millions of different kinds of Bible teaching materials over the last four decades. Hallelujah! Glory to His name!

After that meeting on prosperity, we ran out of gas in downtown Dallas. It was around 11 p.m., and it was cold! I didn't know what to do. We didn't have any money, so I just laid my hands on that car and commanded it to run in Jesus's name. It started back up, and I drove that car for a week before I got any money to put gas in it. That was a miracle!

I didn't have enough money to put antifreeze in that same car, so the block froze and cracked. The crack could be seen, and water poured out of the block. I didn't have the money to fix the car, so I just prayed over it. We drove that car for over a year with a cracked block. It was a miracle! There's no explanation for it. We just experienced miracle after miracle.

"NO, SIR."

After moving to Colorado, I was driving and thinking about all of these things. I said, "God, we used to see miracles all the time. We'd have to pray every day or else we didn't eat. But now it's been decades since I've had a miracle. It's been a long time since I've had to lay hands on our car and see it run without gas, or since we've been hungry and received a miraculous provision of groceries." As I was praying about this, I thought, *What's wrong? I used to see a miracle every day of my life!*

Then the Lord spoke to me, asking, "Would you like to go back to those days?"

I answered, "No, Sir. I don't think I would. I like it better this way."

If something goes wrong with my car now, I go get it fixed or buy a new one. So, which is better? To be able to pray, stand, confess the Word, and—BOOM—out of the blue, somebody just gives you a brand-new car? Well, that would be a wonderful miracle, but I would rather just have enough money in the bank to go buy a car if I need one.

This is one of the differences between a blessing and a miracle. A miracle involves *a suspension or a superseding of natural laws*. God created these natural laws. He doesn't suspend them or supersede them at random, because they were originally created to be good. So, if you are going to live from miracle to miracle, you're going to be living from crisis to crisis. There has to be some desperate need in your life before God is going to grant you a miracle. Miracles aren't easy to come by, so those who are praying for miracle after miracle are living from crisis to crisis.

I see people like this all the time. They're in desperate situations and want me to pray, yet they've violated every law of God. You see, there aren't only natural, physical laws. There are also spiritual laws, such as those in the financial realm:

- What we set our hands unto, He'll bless (Deut. 28:8).
- If we don't work, we don't eat (2 Thess. 3:10).
- A hundred times zero is zero (Gen. 26:12).

On and on we could go with all of these spiritual laws. These people who come to me desperately seeking prayer aren't doing what the Word says; they aren't working. They're depressed, discouraged, and bitter. They're angry and full of unforgiveness. They're violating every spiritual law and living in crisis all the time because they're not cooperating with what God told them to do.

Does this describe you today? Are you violating spiritual laws? Are you living in crisis all the time? Have you been cooperating with what the Lord has told you to do? God loves you, just like He loves Jamie and me. He granted us miracles because He didn't want us to starve to death. But do you know what? There was a systemic problem with our finances, and chances are, there's one with yours, too.

A BETTER WAY

Are you someone who has financial problems all of the time? Do you pray and receive a miracle, but the same problem comes back again? If you cut a plant off at ground level but leave the roots intact, it will grow back again. The miracles may give you provision when you need it, but the root of your financial problem remains; it has not been dealt with. If this is the case with you, then you're going to need another miracle next month and next year because you aren't learning to cooperate and flow with the laws of God. Due to this, you live from crisis to crisis, needing miracle after miracle. There's a better way—it's living by the blessing of God. You learn what the Word of God says about how to prosper and you just put it into practice.

However, there are some natural, physical things that you need to learn and do. I've loved God my whole life. I became born again at age eight and sought the Lord continually. Though I lived in rebellion for a brief period of time, I had this miraculous encounter at age eighteen and have been serving God full-time ever since. From the start, even though I saw many good things happen, our ministry just kept struggling. We had debt, and bill collectors were constantly on our case, telling us that they were going to shut us down. We were just in crisis mode all of the time.

Paul Milligan came into my ministry in 1996 and brought his business accountant with him. He said, "We're here to help you." After two days, they reported, "Something's seriously wrong here. On the books, you're bankrupt. You shouldn't be able to function. We're just going to go through and figure out what's happening."

One of many things Paul taught me was "just-in-time" management. He took me into a storage room and said, "You have $150,000 sitting in this room." This was back when our ministry's income was probably $30,000 or $40,000 a month. I asked, "Where?" He pointed out all of the books, audio sets, and other resources we had in storage. I had a study Bible that cost about $14 to produce, but I had bought 10,000 copies of it in bulk to get the price down to about $7 per unit. I thought, *It's half price. I'm doing good because I really saved a lot!* Paul showed me that I had $150,000 of inventory sitting on those shelves. With "just-in-time" management, inventory is kept low. Even though you pay a higher price per unit, you keep that $150,000 in your pocket instead of having it sit on a shelf somewhere. Since he showed me that one principle back in 1996, our ministry has never been behind!

There were some physical, natural things that I didn't know about finances that made all the difference in the world. In addition to physical laws, there are also emotional and spiritual laws that God created. He said that they are for our good. They benefit us when we learn what they are and cooperate with them.

ABSOLUTELY SUPERNATURAL!

Walking in the blessing of God requires your cooperation. You have to access it by faith. Receiving a miracle, on the other hand, is basically dependent on how desperate you are. If you don't give up or quit and you're still looking to God, you can have a supernatural intervention, but it's going to be after a crisis. If you're going to live from miracle to miracle, you're going to live from crisis to crisis.

In contrast to a blessing, a miracle is only temporary; it's never going to become your norm. God created natural and spiritual laws for you to live by. When you get a miracle—a temporary intervention—God's going to eventually return everything back to the natural, spiritual laws.

This is what happens with some people when they get cancer or some other disease. In the natural, it's a life-or-death situation, so they have a surge of faith, believe God, and get miraculously healed. But whatever it was that allowed the illness to come in—wrong thinking, unforgiveness, bitterness, or whatever (there are multiple things that can cause this)—isn't dealt with. They leave the root intact, and over time, the physical ailment comes back with a vengeance. So, their miracle will only be temporary. It won't last because the root cause was never dealt with.

By far, the longest miracle recorded in the Bible is the miracle of the manna (Ex. 16). God's people were in a crisis situation. They were in a desert, and there wasn't any food to eat. God granted them this manna, and it was absolutely supernatural:

> *Man did eat angels' food.*
>
> Psalm 78:25

It was miraculous! Through the years, certain people have tried to come up with some natural explanation for manna, like saying it was the secretion of a beetle. It wasn't. The Israelites had to collect a certain amount of manna every day. If they collected more and tried to leave some for the next day, it bred worms and stank. But on the sixth day, just like clockwork, they could gather twice as much as normal and it wouldn't turn rotten. This enabled them to obey God's command to rest on the seventh day. It was supernatural—not natural! God miraculously supplied their needs. But it was temporary and lasted only during those forty years in the wilderness.

JUST ENOUGH

And the children of Israel encamped in Gilgal, and kept the passover on the fourteenth day of the month at even in the plains of Jericho. [11] And they did eat of the old corn of the land on the morrow after the passover, unleavened cakes, and parched corn in the selfsame day. [12] And the manna ceased on the morrow after they had eaten of the old corn of the land; neither had the children of Israel manna any more; but they did eat of the fruit of the land of Canaan that year.

Joshua 5:10-12

There came an end to manna. You can't get manna today. You can't pray for it, saying, "Well, they got it in the Bible. Bless God, I'm going to have some!" The children of Israel were in a specific crisis situation. You aren't in that crisis situation, so you won't get manna. It was temporary. It's not going to happen for you. Manna was a miracle for the time, but its time has passed away.

Here's another difference between a blessing and a miracle: a miracle is always just enough to get you by. It'll never be an abundance. This was certainly the case with the manna. The Israelites griped about it to Moses, saying, *"Our soul loatheth this light bread"* (Num. 21:5). They got sick and tired of manna—manna for breakfast, manna for lunch, manna for dinner. Manna met a need, but it wasn't an abundance.

Contrast this with the Promised Land. There, they had all kinds of fruit and meat available to eat. Consider the sample the spies returned with—one cluster of grapes so big that they had to put it on a pole and carry it between two men (Num. 13:23). That's how abundant the land was! Their cluster of grapes was huge compared to a cluster of grapes today. Perhaps the grapes were as big as apples. Can you see the abundance there?

The blessing of God comes through natural things. It grows and takes time. You have to plant a seed and then weed and water it. This takes some effort, but the blessing is much more abundant than a miracle.

TEMPORARY

I talk to a lot of folks and see these same patterns with God's people today. The Israelites crossing over into the Promised Land had grown up on nothing but manna. Other than Joshua and Caleb, everyone older than sixty had already died in the wilderness. The vast majority of those entering into the Promised Land had been born and raised during the forty years in the desert. They had never eaten anything but manna. They lived by miracles. So, when the manna ceased, some of them were out there the next day looking for the manna. Their entire lives they had lived by miracles. They weren't going to dig holes in the ground, plant seeds, water them, weed, and patiently wait for the harvest. They may have said, "You're not going to make me work. I'm a faith person! I believe in supernatural miracles!" But guess what? The day of miracles for their food supply was over. It was only temporary.

God doesn't want you to live by miracles. His plan is for you to live in the blessing. The blessing is more abundant and prevents a crisis, whereas a miracle occurs in response to a crisis. The blessing isn't temporary; it's eternal.

Later in this book, I'll show you that once you access the blessings of God, you cannot reverse it, and Satan can't stop it. Once you get into the blessing of God, it's unstoppable and so much more abundant. The abundance of the land of Canaan was so much better than that little bit of manna. Even though the manna was supernatural and was God's supply, it was temporary and not abundant.

God gives you miracles because He loves you so much, He's trying to help you. But you need a miracle because you've been violating spiritual or natural laws. God loves you and wants to keep you alive. God gave Jamie and me miracle after miracle for years because of my own stupidity. He kept me alive. But now He's taught me how to live in the blessing. He's shown me how to cooperate with the laws of God, and the blessing is much more abundant. Things are much better now. I don't want to go back to living from miracle to miracle.

Miracles should be for other people, like those who are just coming to the Lord who don't know how to walk in the blessing yet. They receive a miracle from God because they haven't gotten their hearts right and lives conformed to the Word yet. They aren't walking in joy. They still have bitterness and unforgiveness. So, praise God, we need miracles for the people who don't yet know the spiritual and natural laws and how to cooperate with them. We need miracles to take place for their sakes.

However, if you understand what I'm sharing, you ought to get to a place where you say, "God, help me to never need another miracle in my life. Father, teach me what I need to know so that I can walk in Your blessing and prevent crisis. And as I live in the abundance of Your blessing, make me a vessel through whom You can bring miracles to others who need them. Amen."

Outline

I. The same principle of learning to walk in blessings rather than beg for miracles is also true in the area of finances.

   A. There are laws that God created about how provision works.

   B. The Lord said that He would bless the work of your hands (Deut. 28:8 and 12).

   C. If you set your hand to something, God can multiply that.

   D. But don't settle for less than God's best.

   E. Start believing God to be a producer and a contributor.

II. We shouldn't have this mindset of not needing to work.

   A. Looking back, I realize now that I wasn't cooperating with God's laws:

   Even so hath the Lord ordained that they which preach the gospel should live of the gospel.

   1 Corinthians 9:14

   B. Since I wasn't ministering to anybody, I shouldn't have expected to "live of the Gospel."

   C. Jamie and I lived from miracle to miracle.

   D. After moving to Colorado, I was driving and thinking about all of these things and said, "God, we used to see miracles all the time. We'd have to pray every day or else we didn't eat. But now it's been decades since I've had a miracle. It's been a long time since I've had to lay hands on our car and see it run without gas, or since we've been hungry and received a miraculous provision of groceries."

   E. Then the Lord spoke to me, asking, "Would you like to go back to those days?"

   F. I answered, "No, Sir."

   G. If you are going to live from miracle to miracle, you're going to be living from crisis to crisis.

H. There aren't only natural, physical laws; there are also spiritual laws, such as those in the financial realm:

    1. What you set our hands unto, He'll bless (Deut. 28:8).

    2. If you don't work, you don't eat (2 Thess. 3:10).

    3. A hundred times zero is zero (Gen. 26:12).

I. The miracles may give you provision when you need it, but if the root of your financial problem remains, then you're going to need another miracle next month and next year because you aren't learning to cooperate and flow with the laws of God.

J. You learn what the Word of God says about how to prosper and you just put it into practice.

K. The spiritual laws God created are for your good.

III. Walking in the blessing of God requires your cooperation.

A. You have to access it by faith.

B. Receiving a miracle, on the other hand, is basically dependent on how desperate you are.

C. If you don't give up or quit and you're still looking to God, you can have a supernatural intervention, but it's going to be after a crisis.

IV. In contrast to a blessing, a miracle is only temporary; it's never going to become your norm.

A. When you get a miracle—a temporary intervention—God's going to eventually return everything back to the natural, spiritual laws.

B. This is what happens with some people when they get cancer or some other disease.

C. In the natural, it's a life-or-death situation, so they have a surge of faith, believe God, and get miraculously healed.

D. But whatever it was that allowed the illness to come in—wrong thinking, unforgiveness, bitterness, or whatever (there are multiple things that can cause this)—isn't dealt with.

E.   They leave the root intact, and over time, the physical ailment comes back with a vengeance.

V.   By far, the longest miracle recorded in the Bible is the miracle of the manna (Ex. 16).

A.   God's people were in a desert, and there wasn't any food to eat.

B.   God granted them this manna, and it was absolutely supernatural:

Man did eat angels' food.

Psalm 78:25

C.   But it was temporary and lasted only during those forty years in the wilderness (Josh. 5:10-12).

VI.   Here's another difference between a blessing and a miracle: a miracle is always just enough to get you by.

A.   Manna met a need, but it wasn't an abundance.

B.   Contrast this with the Promised Land: there, they had all kinds of fruit and meat available to eat.

C.   The blessing of God comes through natural things:

1.   It grows and takes time.

2.   You have to plant a seed and then weed and water it.

3.   This takes some effort.

VII.   God's plan is for you to live in the blessing.

A.   The blessing is more abundant and prevents a crisis, whereas a miracle occurs in response to a crisis.

B.   The blessing isn't temporary; it's eternal.

C. Later in this book, I'll show you that once you access the blessings of God, you cannot reverse it, and Satan can't stop it.

D. God gives you miracles because He loves you so much, He's trying to help you.

E. But you need a miracle because you've been violating spiritual or natural laws.

VIII. Miracles should be for other people, like those who are just coming to the Lord who don't know how to walk in the blessing yet.

A. They haven't gotten their hearts right and lives conformed to the Word yet.

B. They aren't walking in joy.

C. They still have bitterness and unforgiveness.

D. However, if you understand what is being shared, you ought to get to a place where you say, "God, help me to never need another miracle in my life. Father, teach me what I need to know so that I can walk in Your blessing and prevent crisis. And as I live in the abundance of Your blessing, make me a vessel through whom You can bring miracles to others who need them. Amen."

Teacher's Guide

1.   The same principle of learning to walk in blessings rather than beg for miracles is also true in the area of finances. There are laws that God created about how provision works. The Lord said that He would bless the work of our hands (Deut. 28:8 and 12). If we set our hands to something, God can multiply that. But we shouldn't settle for less than God's best. We need to start believing God to be producers and contributors.

1a.   The same principle of learning to walk in blessings rather than beg for miracles is also true in the area of _____?
      A.   Cleaning house
      B.   Ordering takeout
      C.   Finances
      D.   All of the above
      E.   None of the above
      C.   Finances

1b.   According to Deuteronomy 28:8 and 12, what did the Lord say He would do?
      Bless the work of your hands

1c.   *Discussion question:* How has the principle of being a producer and a contributor played out in your life?
      Discussion question

2.   We shouldn't have this mindset of not needing to work. Looking back, Andrew realizes now that he wasn't cooperating with God's laws:

> *Even so hath the Lord ordained that they which preach the gospel*
> *should live of the gospel.*
>
> 1 Corinthians 9:14

Since Andrew wasn't ministering to anybody, he shouldn't have expected to "live of the Gospel." He and Jamie lived from miracle to miracle. After moving to Colorado, Andrew was driving and thinking about all of these things and said, "God, we used to see miracles all the time. We'd have to pray every day or else we didn't eat. But now it's been decades since I've had a miracle. It's been a long time since I've had to lay hands on our car and see it run without gas, or since we've been hungry and received a miraculous provision of groceries." Then the Lord spoke to him, asking, "Would you like to go back to those days?" Andrew answered, "No, Sir." If we are going to live from miracle to miracle, we're going to be living from crisis to crisis. There aren't only natural, physical laws; there are also spiritual laws, such as those in the financial realm:

- What we set our hands unto, He'll bless (Deut. 28:8).
- If we don't work, we don't eat (2 Thess. 3:10).
- A hundred times zero is zero (Gen. 26:12)

The miracles may give us provision when we need it, but if the root of our financial problem remains, then we're going to need another miracle next month and next year because we aren't learning to cooperate and flow with the laws of God. We learn what the Word of God says about how to prosper and we just put it into practice. The spiritual laws that God created are for our good.

2a. According to 1 Corinthians 9:14, *"they which _____ the gospel should _____ of the gospel."*
   "Preach" / "live"

2b. True or false: If you are going to live from miracle to miracle, you're not going to be living from crisis to crisis.
   False

2c. What are some spiritual laws (Deut. 28:8, 2 Thess. 3:10, and Gen. 26:12)?
   What you set your hands unto, He'll bless (Deut. 28:8); if you don't work, you don't eat (2 Thess. 3:10); a hundred times zero is zero (Gen. 26:12)

2d. The miracles may give you provision when you need it, but if the root of your financial problem _____, then you're going to need _____ miracle next month and next year because you aren't _____ to cooperate and flow with the laws of God.
   Remains / another / learning

2e. The spiritual laws God created are for _____ _____.
   Your good

3.   Walking in the blessing of God requires our cooperation. We have to access it by faith. Receiving a miracle, on the other hand, is basically dependent on how desperate we are. If we don't give up or quit and we're still looking to God, we can have a supernatural intervention, but it's going to be after a crisis.

3a. Walking in the blessing of God _____ your cooperation.
   A.   Requires
   B.   Eliminates
   C.   Diminishes
   D.   Replaces
   E.   Multiplies
   A.   Requires

3b. What do you have to access by faith?
   The blessing of God

3c. True or false: If you don't give up or quit and you're still looking to God, you can have a supernatural intervention, but it's going to be before a crisis.
   False

4.   In contrast to a blessing, a miracle is only temporary; it's never going to become our norm. When we get a miracle—a temporary intervention—God's going to eventually return everything back to the natural, spiritual laws. This is what happens with some people when they get cancer or some other disease. In the natural, it's a life-or-death situation, so they have a surge of faith, believe God, and get miraculously healed. But whatever it was that allowed the illness to come in—wrong thinking, unforgiveness, bitterness, or whatever (there are multiple things that can cause this)— isn't dealt with. They leave the root intact, and over time, the physical ailment comes back with a vengeance.

4a. In contrast to a blessing, a miracle is what?
     Only temporary
4b. *Discussion question:* Share a story about a miracle you or someone you know has experienced.
     Discussion question

5.   By far, the longest miracle recorded in the Bible is the miracle of the manna (Ex. 16). God's people were in a desert, and there wasn't any food to eat. God granted them this manna, and it was absolutely supernatural:

> *Man did eat angels' food.*
>
> Psalm 78:25

But it was temporary and lasted only during those forty years in the wilderness (Josh. 5:10-12).

5a. How long did the miracle of the manna last?
     Forty years

6.   Here's another difference between a blessing and a miracle: a miracle is always just enough to get us by. Manna met a need, but it wasn't an abundance. We can contrast this with the Promised Land: there, they had all kinds of fruit and meat available to eat. The blessing of God comes through natural things. It grows and takes time. We have to plant a seed and then weed and water it. This takes some effort.

6a. What is another difference between a blessing and a miracle?
     A miracle is always just enough to get you by
6b. True or false: There was abundance in the Promised Land.
     True
6c. The blessing of God comes through what natural things?
     It grows and takes time; you have to plant a seed and then weed and water it; this takes some effort

7.   God's plan is for us to live in the blessing. The blessing is more abundant and prevents a crisis, whereas a miracle occurs in response to a crisis. The blessing isn't temporary; it's eternal. Later in this book, Andrew will show us that once we access the blessings of God, we cannot reverse it, and Satan can't stop it. God gives us miracles because He loves us so much, He's trying to help us. But we need a miracle because we've been violating spiritual or natural laws.

7a.   The blessing _____ a crisis, whereas a miracle occurs in _____ to a crisis.
    A.   Produces / route
    B.   Postpones / relation
    C.   Prolongs / respect
    D.   Prevents / response
    E.   Patterns / revolt
    D.   Prevents / response

7b.   Why does God give you miracles?
    A.   Because He knows He will make you pay for it later
    B.   Because He wants to appear as good sometimes
    C.   Because you caught Him at just the right time
    D.   All of the above
    E.   None of the above
    E.   None of the above

7c.   True or false: If you need a miracle, it's because you've been violating spiritual or natural laws.
    True

8.   Miracles should be for other people, like those who are just coming to the Lord who don't know how to walk in the blessing yet. They haven't gotten their hearts right and lives conformed to the Word yet. They aren't walking in joy. They still have bitterness and unforgiveness. However, if we understand what is being shared, we ought to get to a place where we say, "God, help me to never need another miracle in my life. Father, teach me what I need to know so that I can walk in Your blessing and prevent crisis. And as I live in the abundance of Your blessing, make me a vessel through whom You can bring miracles to others who need them. Amen."

8a.   True or false: Miracles should be for people who have been saved for a while.
    False

8b.   *Discussion question:* What will you do to start walking in the blessing of God?
    Discussion question

Discipleship Questions

1. The same principle of learning to walk in blessings rather than beg for miracles is also true in the area of what?
   A. Cleaning house
   B. Ordering takeout
   C. Finances
   D. All of the above
   E. None of the above

2. According to Deuteronomy 28:8 and 12, what did the Lord say He would do?

   _____

   _____

   _____

3. *Discussion question:* How has the principle of being a producer and a contributor played out in your life?

   _____

   _____

   _____

4. According to 1 Corinthians 9:14, *"they which _____ the gospel should _____ of the gospel."*

5. True or false: If you are going to live from miracle to miracle, you're not going to be living from crisis to crisis.

6. What are some spiritual laws (Deut. 28:8, 2 Thess. 3:10, and Gen. 26:12)?

   _____

   _____

   _____

7. The miracles may give you provision when you need it, but if the root of your financial problem _____, then you're going to need _____ miracle next month and next year because you aren't _____ to cooperate and flow with the laws of God.

8. The spiritual laws God created are for _____ _____.

9. Walking in the blessing of God _____ your cooperation.
    A. Requires
    B. Eliminates
    C. Diminishes
    D. Replaces
    F. Multiplies

10. What do you have to access by faith?

    _____

    _____

    _____

11. True or false: If you don't give up or quit and you're still looking to God, you can have a supernatural intervention, but it's going to be before a crisis.

12. In contrast to a blessing, a miracle is what?

    _____

    _____

    _____

13. *Discussion question:* Share a story about a miracle you or someone you know has experienced.

    _____

    _____

    _____

14. How long did the miracle of the manna last?

    _____

    _____

    _____

15. What is another difference between a blessing and a miracle?

_____

_____

_____

16. True or false: There was abundance in the Promised Land.

17. The blessing of God comes through what natural things?

_____

_____

_____

18. The blessing _____ a crisis, whereas a miracle occurs in _____ to a crisis.
    A. Produces / route
    B. Postpones / relation
    C. Prolongs / respect
    D. Prevents / response
    E. Patterns / revolt

19. Why does God give you miracles?
    A. Because He knows He will make you pay for it later
    B. Because He wants to appear as good sometimes
    C. Because you caught Him at just the right time
    D. All of the above
    E. None of the above

20. True or false: If you need a miracle, it's because you've been violating spiritual or natural laws.

21. True or false: Miracles should be for people who have been saved for a while.

22. *Discussion question:* What will you do to start walking in the blessing of God?

_____

_____

_____

Answer Key

1. C. Finances

2. Bless the work of your hands

3. *Discussion question*

4. *"Preach" / "live"*

5. False

6. What you set your hands unto, He'll bless (Deut. 28:8); if you don't work, you don't eat (2 Thess. 3:10); a hundred times zero is zero (Gen. 26:12)

7. Remains / another / learning

8. Your good

9. A. Requires

10. The blessing of God

11. False

12. Only temporary

13. *Discussion question*

14. Forty years

15. A miracle is always just enough to get you by

16. True

17. It grows and takes time; you have to plant a seed and then weed and water it; this takes some effort

18. D. Prevents / response

19. E. None of the above

20. True

21. False

22. *Discussion question*

Scriptures

DEUTERONOMY 28:8
The LORD shall command the blessing upon thee in thy storehouses, and in all that thou settest thine hand unto; and he shall bless thee in the land which the LORD thy God giveth thee.

DEUTERONOMY 28:12
The LORD shall open unto thee his good treasure, the heaven to give the rain unto thy land in his season, and to bless all the work of thine hand: and thou shalt lend unto many nations, and thou shalt not borrow.

1 CORINTHIANS 9:14
Even so hath the Lord ordained that they which preach the gospel should live of the gospel.

ACTS 18:3
And because he was of the same craft, he abode with them, and wrought: for by their occupation they were tentmakers.

2 THESSALONIANS 3:10
For even when we were with you, this we commanded you, that if any would not work, neither should he eat.

GENESIS 26:12
Then Isaac sowed in that land, and received in the same year an hundredfold: and the LORD blessed him.

PSALM 78:25
Man did eat angels' food: he sent them meat to the full.

JOSHUA 5:10-12
And the children of Israel encamped in Gilgal, and kept the passover on the fourteenth day of the month at even in the plains of Jericho. [11] And they did eat of the old corn of the land on the morrow after the passover, unleavened cakes, and parched corn in the selfsame day. [12] And the manna ceased on the morrow after they had eaten of the old corn of the land; neither had the children of Israel manna any more; but they did eat of the fruit of the land of Canaan that year.

NUMBERS 21:5

And the people spake against God, and against Moses, Wherefore have ye brought us up out of Egypt to die in the wilderness? for there is no bread, neither is there any water; and our soul loatheth this light bread.

NUMBERS 13:23

And they came unto the brook of Eshcol, and cut down from thence a branch with one cluster of grapes, and they bare it between two upon a staff; and they brought of the pomegranates, and of the figs.

Spoken Favor!

LESSON 11

The blessing of the Lord, *it maketh rich, and he addeth no sorrow with it.*
Proverbs 10:22

Did you know that you can prosper outside of the blessing of God? Sure, you can spend all of your time and energy working two or three jobs. You can make a living lying, cheating, and stealing. There are ways that you can prosper outside of God, but it takes away your life (Prov. 1:19). It makes you bitter, angry, tired, and stressed out. It gives Satan an inroad into your life. But the blessing of the Lord will make you rich, and He adds no sorrow with it.

If you understand God's blessing—what He has provided for you and how to access it—it'll make you rich. Although my wife and I lived in poverty for a time because of my own stupidity, God taught me some things, and I've now learned to cooperate with Him. Now, in our U.S. ministry office alone, we need to bring in over $40 million a year just to survive. And with this new Bible college campus that we're building, we need twice that. We're moving in the direction of needing $100 million a year—and we give our products away! Yes, there's a suggested donation amount for our products, but over 50 percent of the people who contact us don't give a penny, and we send ministry materials to them free. We give stuff away, and we're blessed!

God has taught me how to prosper. There's a way to prosper through God that is different than just working your fingers to the bone and stressing yourself out. The last time I checked, I need to bring in $5,000 an hour, 24 hours a day, 7 days a week, 365 days a year. Do you know what? I sleep well. In fact, I took a nap this afternoon. These things don't keep me awake. I don't worry or stress out about it, because it's no big deal. The blessing of the Lord will make you rich!

"YOU CHOOSE"

Consider what God said to Abraham: *"I will bless thee, and make thy name great; and thou shalt be a blessing"* (Gen. 12:2).

You can't be a blessing until you're blessed. If you aren't blessed, you can't bless others.

The blessing wasn't based on Abraham's goodness. Later in the same chapter, there was a drought, and he decided to go down into Egypt (Gen. 12:10-20). Afraid that someone would kill him to get his beautiful wife Sarah, who happened to be in her sixties at the time, Abraham lied, saying, "She's my sister." So, Pharaoh took Sarah into his harem, intending to make her his wife. And whom did God deal with over this issue?

> *And the* Lord *plagued Pharaoh and his house with great plagues because of Sarai Abram's wife.*
>
> Genesis 12:17

Abraham did this same thing a second time, with King Abimelech in Gerar (Gen. 20:1-18). Whom did God rebuke? Not Abraham, but the king. In a dream, God warned him, "You're a dead man because she's another man's wife. If you touch her, I'll kill you." The king came to Abraham and exclaimed, "Why did you say she was your sister?" Abraham answered, "Because I was afraid you would kill me." So, God rebuked Pharaoh and King Abimelech and gave Abraham servants, cattle, and sheep. Abraham not only lied about his wife, but also—in a sense—he pimped her. He gained great wealth through giving his wife to another not once, but twice! God blessed him, and he was the blessed of the Lord. Abraham became one of the richest men on the face of the earth, not because he was the most upstanding and perfect guy, but because he believed he was blessed.

Because Abraham believed he was blessed, he was able to let Lot choose the best land for himself (Gen. 13:1-11). The two of them, uncle and nephew, had so much wealth—including livestock—that they couldn't dwell together any longer. Their men were fighting over the grassland, so Abraham finally came and said, "You choose. The whole land is before you. Decide which way you want to go. If you desire to go down here to the Jordan Valley, where everything is well-watered and the vegetation is lush, then take it. It's yours, and I'll take the desert. Or if you want the desert, I'll take the other." This shows that Abraham was trusting God.

LEFTOVERS

If you've ever had animals, you'd understand this. I've had horses most of my life. I've bought places before and looked at the grass to see if it was subterranean-watered or if there was good grassland. For someone who grazes animals, it would be crazy for them to say, "Do you want the well-watered land over here that's fertile, or do you want the desert?"

I've visited this part of Israel before, where Abraham and Lot had this conversation. Down by Hebron today, you can walk five or ten feet between blades of grass. Yet it's said that the land of Sodom and Gomorrah—before God destroyed it—was like the Garden of Eden (Gen. 13:10). It was well-watered and lush. Abraham said, "Pick which way you want to go." For Lot, that was an absolute no-brainer, and he took the good land.

Why was Abraham able to do this? Because he wasn't looking just to natural things. God was his source, and he was obeying Him. Abraham believed he was blessed, so he was able to say, "You just pick whatever you want, and I'll still prosper more."

This would be comparable today to salespeople having a choice between two sales territories—one territory where anybody can make money hand over fist and one where nobody has succeeded. Instead of fighting over the good territory, one salesperson says, "Hey, you take whichever one you want. I'm blessed. Give me the leftovers, and I'll prosper more than anybody else." That person sees God as their source instead of just themselves and their own effort.

Genesis 13 shows that Abraham believed in the blessing, and because of that, he prospered. In the next chapter, he took 318 slaves who had been born in his house and who were trained soldiers (there had to have been fathers, mothers, and children too; I'm sure he had well over 1,000 slaves), and went and defeated four kings with just the slaves that were born in his house! The spoil from this victory was the equivalent of millions and millions of dollars. Abraham gave tithes to Melchizedek, the king of Salem. Then the king of Sodom said, "Just give us back our wives and children, and you can have all the spoil." Abraham answered, "I have lifted up my hand to God that I am not going to take even a shoelace from anyone lest they say that they made Abram rich. God is my source!" He gave back millions of dollars' worth of spoil that rightfully belonged to him by conquest because his faith was in God (Gen. 14:14-23). Abraham believed in the blessing, and it was the blessing of God that made him rich (Prov. 10:22).

"HOW DARE YOU!"

God has said that He will bless you (Deut. 15:6). I pray that you're getting this!

I grew up an introvert, too shy and embarrassed to look a person in the face. I never did well, and I just didn't believe I could do anything. I had already been born again before I had a supernatural encounter with the Lord on March 23, 1968. But afterward, I believed that I was blessed and that whatever I set my hand to do would prosper (Deut. 28:8). It took a while, but I began to be blessed. Because of my own stupidity, Jamie and I struggled for five or ten years, but no one would have ever known that we were poor. I never told anybody. I didn't act poor or talk poor, and I didn't go around down in the mouth and looking sad.

As a matter of fact, Jamie's dad had no idea how much we struggled. Several years ago, when we dedicated our ministry building in Colorado Springs, I was sharing some of these stories to give glory to God for what He had done. I testified how the Lord had enabled us to dedicate the building debt free. We were praising God and sharing stories from our "poverty days" to illustrate the contrast, saying, "It wasn't me but God who did it!" Jamie's dad walked up on the stage and rebuked me, saying, "How dare you! If we had known you were like this, we would have helped you. You made us look bad!" Our own relatives didn't know that we struggled. Nobody knew. We didn't tell anybody because we believed we were blessed—even when we couldn't see it.

It took me a while to figure some things out because I'm a slow learner, but do you know what? We're blessed now. I'm cooperating with God's spiritual laws much more these days, and His blessing has been made manifest in a supernatural, abundant way. But even back then, we believed we were blessed. You must believe!

NOT A THING

A blessing is not a thing. It's the favor of God spoken over you.

> *Christ hath redeemed us from the curse of the law, being made a curse for us: for it is written, Cursed is every one that hangeth on a tree: [14] That the blessing of Abraham might come on the Gentiles through Jesus Christ; that we might receive the promise of the Spirit through faith.*
>
> Galatians 3:13-14

This blessing of Abraham is now ours. This blessing that God gave Abraham made him very prosperous, but when we read about the blessing, it isn't referring to things. I don't want Abraham's 4,000-year-old tents and animals. I don't want those things that are now rotten, decayed, and even skeletons. The blessing of Abraham that is ours today as believers is the favor of God spoken over us.

When God created all of the animals, He *"blessed them, saying, Be fruitful, and multiply, and fill the waters in the seas, and let fowl multiply in the earth"* (Gen. 1:22).

God blessed by *saying.*

> *And God blessed them, and God said unto them, Be fruitful, and multiply, and replenish the earth, and subdue it: and have dominion over the fish of the sea, and over the fowl of the air, and over every living thing that moveth upon the earth.*
>
> Genesis 1:28

This is important! A blessing is not a *thing*. It's the favor of God spoken over you.

THEY'RE AFRAID OF YOU!

Do you know what the Bible is full of? Blessings—God's favor that has been spoken. The words *bless*, *blessed*, *blesseth*, and *blessing* occur about 500 times in the Bible. The words *miracle* and *miracles* occur 37 times. Certainly, there are miracles in the Bible that were recorded without using the word *miracle* or *miracles*. But there are also many blessings that were recorded without using that word either. The Bible is full of the blessings of God—His spoken favor over us!

Sadly, we live in a culture where words don't mean much. Just a generation or two ago, people would say, "I give you my word." They'd shake on it and would rather die than break their word. Nowadays, people make covenants, contracts, constitutions— whatever—and then just ignore those things and do whatever they want. Words just don't mean much to people today.

Most Christians have been raised in this kind of culture. We just don't understand the power of a blessing. Since the way that we access the blessing is through faith (Rom. 5:2), we stop that blessing from coming to pass when we don't believe in its power.

Included in the blessing of Genesis 1:28 is authority over every animal on earth. God spoke for you and me to have dominion over the animals and to subdue them. He said that with His own mouth, yet many people are afraid of animals. The truth is, the animals are afraid of you:

> *And God blessed Noah and his sons, and said unto them, Be fruitful, and multiply, and replenish the earth. [2] And the fear of you and the dread of you shall be upon every beast of the earth, and upon every fowl of the air, upon all that moveth upon the earth, and upon all the fishes of the sea; into your hand are they delivered.*
>
> Genesis 9:1-2

You have the God-given authority to rule and reign over animals, yet most Christians don't exercise it. They're afraid of all kinds of things. Is this verse true or not? Did God say it? If He did (and He did), then why do you let animals intimidate you? Are you scared of dogs? What about spiders, moths, and other bugs? If you are afraid, it's because you don't believe that you've been blessed and have dominion and authority over them.

I HAVE AUTHORITY

Personally, I used to be afraid of dogs. I jogged for decades, and one time in Alabama, I was out jogging at 5 a.m. when a whole pack of dogs treed me and kept me up there for two and a half hours! At 7:30 a.m., somebody finally came out and dispersed all of the dogs. I was bitten, chased, and intimidated by dogs until I finally got a hold of this truth. I'm blessed, and now I know that I'm the one who has the authority.

One of the major influences on me learning this was when I stayed in a friend's home while I was holding a meeting in Trinidad, Colorado. When it came time to go to bed, I found out I was staying in the room where his pit bull dog stayed. I asked what would happen if I needed to get up during the night. He said his dog wouldn't hurt me.

I looked on the shelf and there were all kinds of trophies that his dog had won as an attack dog. My friend noticed my apprehension and said, "My dog is an attack dog. He's not a mean dog. I have no mercy on a mean dog." I asked him to explain what the difference between a mean dog and an attack dog was. It sounded like the same thing to me.

He told me about an instance where a thief broke into his house while he and his wife were at work. His dog attacked the man and knocked him to the ground. He held him on the floor with his mouth around his arm for hours until the family came home, but he never even broke the skin on the thief's arm. If the man tried to move, the dog would growl and squeeze his arm, but he never hurt him. That's an attack dog. He's not a mean dog.

When I heard that, it was like a light bulb suddenly turned on in my mind. I realized that I had let fear keep me from exercising my God-given authority over dogs. My whole attitude changed. Now, I'm totally different when confronting dogs. I'll fight dogs. Dobermans used to be the ones that bothered me the most, but now I've actually gone running down the road chasing some Dobermans who were after me. I use wisdom. If a dog just had a litter, I wouldn't go in and violate their space. I'm not going to do something stupid. But if I'm out jogging or walking and a dog comes out on a public street and attacks me, that dog had best be able to defend itself, because I'm the one with authority and power. Since I've gotten that attitude, I've never had a dog stand up to me. I have authority over them because I believe I'm blessed. Amen!

I've broken horses before without breaking them—just by taking authority over them. You might think, *I don't believe that.* Well then, it won't work for you. But I'm telling you, we have much more authority than most of us realize. God has spoken so many blessings over us, and most of us just let them go because we weren't raised to believe in the power of a blessing.

Outline

I.   There are ways that you can prosper outside of God, but it takes away your life (Prov. 1:19).

   A.   The blessing of the Lord will make you rich, and He adds no sorrow with it (Prov. 10:22).

   B.   Although my wife and I lived in poverty for a time because of my own stupidity, God taught me some things, and I've learned to cooperate with Him.

   C.   There's a way to prosper through God that is different than just working your fingers to the bone and stressing yourself out.

II. Consider what God said to Abraham: *"I will bless thee, and make thy name great; and thou shalt be a blessing"* (Gen. 12:2).

   A.   If you aren't blessed, you can't bless others.

   B.   Afraid that someone would kill him to get his beautiful wife Sarah, Abraham lied, saying, "She's my sister."

   C.   So, Pharaoh took Sarah into his harem, intending to make her his wife (Gen. 12:10-20).

   D.   Abraham did this same thing a second time, with King Abimelech in Gerar (Gen. 20:1-18).

   E.   God rebuked Pharaoh and King Abimelech and gave Abraham servants, cattle, and sheep.

   F.   Abraham became one of the richest men on the face of the earth, not because he was the most upstanding and perfect guy, but because he believed he was blessed.

III. Because Abraham believed he was blessed, he was able to let Lot choose the best land for himself (Gen. 13:1-11).

   A.   This shows that Abraham was trusting God.

   B.   He wasn't looking just to natural things.

C. God was his source and he was obeying Him.

D. Abraham believed in the blessing, and it was the blessing of God that made him rich.

IV. God has said that He will bless you (Deut. 15:6).

A. It took me a while to figure some things out, but we're blessed now.

B. I'm cooperating with God's spiritual laws much more these days, and His blessing has been made manifest in a supernatural, abundant way.

C. You must believe!

V. This blessing of Abraham is now ours:

Christ hath redeemed us from the curse of the law, being made a curse for us: for it is written, Cursed is every one that hangeth on a tree: [14] That the blessing of Abraham might come on the Gentiles through Jesus Christ; that we might receive the promise of the Spirit through faith.
Galatians 3:13-14

A. This blessing that God gave Abraham made him very prosperous, but when we read about the blessing, it isn't referring to things.

B. The blessing of Abraham that is ours today as believers is the favor of God spoken over us.

C. God blessed by *saying* (Gen. 1:28).

D. This is important!

VI. The Bible is full of blessings—God's favor that has been spoken.

A. The words *bless*, *blessed*, *blesseth*, and *blessing* occur about 500 times in the Bible; the words *miracle* and *miracles* occur 37 times.

B. Sadly, we live in a culture where words don't mean much.

C. Nowadays, people make covenants, contracts, constitutions—whatever—and then just ignore those things and do whatever they want.

D. Many Christians have been raised in this kind of culture.

E. We don't understand the power of a blessing.

F. Since the way that we access the blessing is through faith (Rom. 5:2), we stop that blessing from coming to pass when we don't believe in its power.

VII. In the blessing of Genesis 1:28, God spoke for you to have dominion over the animals and to subdue them.

A. The truth is, the animals are afraid of you:

And God blessed Noah and his sons, and said unto them, Be fruitful, and multiply, and replenish the earth. [2] And the fear of you and the dread of you shall be upon every beast of the earth, and upon every fowl of the air, upon all that moveth upon the earth, and upon all the fishes of the sea; into your hand are they delivered.

Genesis 9:1-2

B. Many Christians don't exercise their God-given authority.

C. If you are afraid of dogs and bugs, it's because you don't believe that you've been blessed and have dominion and authority over them.

D. So, it won't work for you.

E. But you have much more authority than you realize.

Teacher's Guide

1.   There are ways that we can prosper outside of God, but it takes away our lives (Prov. 1:19). The blessing of the Lord will make us rich, and He adds no sorrow with it (Prov. 10:22). Although Andrew and his wife lived in poverty for a time because of his "own stupidity," God taught him some things, and he's now learned to cooperate with Him. There's a way to prosper through God that is different than just working our fingers to the bone and stressing ourselves out.

1a.   True or false: There is no way to prosper outside of God (Prov. 1:19).
      False

1b.   The blessing of the Lord will make you _____, and He adds no _____ with it (Prov. 10:22).
      A.   Pay / joy
      B.   Sorry / wealth
      C.   Rich / sorrow
      D.   Greedy / remorse
      E.   Generous / simplicity
      C.   Rich / sorrow

1c.   *Discussion question:* What are some ways to prosper God's way?
      Discussion question

2.   Let's consider what God said to Abraham: *"I will bless thee, and make thy name great; and thou shalt be a blessing"* (Gen. 12:2). If we aren't blessed, we can't bless others. Afraid that someone would kill him to get his beautiful wife Sarah, Abraham lied, saying, "She's my sister." So, Pharaoh took Sarah into his harem, intending to make her his wife (Gen. 12:10-20). Abraham did this same thing a second time, with King Abimelech in Gerar (Gen. 20:1-18). God rebuked Pharaoh and King Abimelech and gave Abraham servants, cattle, and sheep. Abraham became one of the richest men on the face of the earth, not because he was the most upstanding and perfect guy, but because he believed he was blessed.

2a.   According to Genesis 12:2, *"I will _____ thee, and make thy name great; and thou shalt be a _____."*
      "Bless" / "blessing"

2b.   True or false: If you aren't blessed, you can still be a blessing.
      False

2c.   True or false: Abraham became one of the richest men on the face of the earth because he was the most upstanding and perfect guy God could find (Gen. 12:10-20 and 20:1-18).
      False

2d. *Discussion question:* Why do you think God did not rebuke Abraham?
Discussion question

3.   Because Abraham believed he was blessed, he was able to let Lot choose the best land for himself (Gen. 13:1-11). This shows that Abraham was trusting God. He wasn't looking just to natural things. God was his source, and he was obeying Him. Abraham believed in the blessing, and it was the blessing of God that made him rich.

3a. What shows that Abraham was trusting God (Gen. 13:1-11)?
He was able to let Lot choose the best land for himself
3b. *Discussion question:* How is God your source?
Discussion question

4.   God has said that He will bless us (Deut. 15:6). We need to get this! It took Andrew a while to figure some things out, but he and Jamie are blessed now. Andrew's cooperating with God's spiritual laws much more these days, and His blessing has been made manifest in a supernatural, abundant way. We must believe!

4a. What did God say He will do (Deut. 15:6)?
Bless you
4b. What must you do with God's spiritual laws?
Cooperate with them
4c. What else must you do?
Believe

5.   This blessing of Abraham is now ours:

> *Christ hath redeemed us from the curse of the law, being made a curse for us: for it is written, Cursed is every one that hangeth on a tree:* [14] *That the blessing of Abraham might come on the Gentiles through Jesus Christ; that we might receive the promise of the Spirit through faith.*
> Galatians 3:13-14

This blessing that God gave Abraham made him very prosperous, but when we read about the blessing, it isn't referring to things. The blessing of Abraham that is ours today as believers is the favor of God spoken over us. God blessed by *saying* (Gen. 1:28). This is important!

5a. True or false: The blessing of Abraham isn't referring to things (Gal. 3:13-14).
True

5b. What is the blessing of Abraham?

The favor of God spoken over you

5c. How did God bless (Gen. 1:28)?

A. By saying
B. By pointing
C. By singing
D. By dancing
E. By crying

A. By saying

6. The Bible is full of blessings—God's favor that has been spoken. The words *bless*, *blessed*, *blesseth*, and *blessing* occur about 500 times in the Bible; the words *miracle* and *miracles* occur 37 times. Sadly, we live in a culture where words don't mean much. Nowadays, people make covenants, contracts, constitutions—whatever—and then just ignore those things and do whatever they want. Many Christians have been raised in this kind of culture. We don't understand the power of a blessing. Since the way that we access the blessing is through faith (Rom. 5:2), we stop that blessing from coming to pass when we don't believe in its power.

6a. True or false: The Bible has more to say about miracles than about blessings.

False

6b. *Discussion question:* Why do you think words don't mean much in today's culture?

Discussion question

6c. If you don't believe in the power of the blessing, you will _____ that blessing from coming to pass (Rom. 5:2).

Stop

7. In the blessing of Genesis 1:28, God spoke for us to have dominion over the animals and to subdue them. The truth is, the animals are afraid of us:

> *And God blessed Noah and his sons, and said unto them, Be fruitful, and multiply, and replenish the earth. [2] And the fear of you and the dread of you shall be upon every beast of the earth, and upon every fowl of the air, upon all that moveth upon the earth, and upon all the fishes of the sea; into your hand are they delivered.*
>
> Genesis 9:1-2

Many Christians don't exercise their God-given authority. If we are afraid of dogs and bugs, it's because we don't believe that we've been blessed and have dominion and authority over them. So, it won't work for us. But we have much more authority than we realize.

7a. According to Genesis 1:28, God spoke for you to do what?
    A. Have fun with the animals and tame them
    B. Make pets of the animals and coddle them
    C. Take captives of the animals and exploit them
    D. Have dominion over the animals and subdue them
    E. Stay away from the animals and fear them
    D. Have dominion over the animals and subdue them

7b. True or false: The animals are afraid of you (Gen. 9:1-2).
    True

7c. True or false: If you're afraid of dogs and bugs, it's because God hasn't given you dominion and authority over them.
    False

Discipleship Questions

1. True or false: There is no way to prosper outside of God (Prov. 1:19).

2. The blessing of the Lord will make you _____, and He adds no _____ with it (Prov. 10:22).
   A. Pay / joy
   B. Sorry / wealth
   C. Rich / sorrow
   D. Greedy / remorse
   E. Generous / simplicity

3. *Discussion question:* What are some ways to prosper God's way?

   _____

   _____

   _____

4. According to Genesis 12:2, "*I will _____ thee, and make thy name great; and thou shalt be a _____.*"

5. True or false: If you aren't blessed, you can still be a blessing.

6. True or false: Abraham became one of the richest men on the face of the earth because he was the most upstanding and perfect guy God could find (Gen. 12:10-20 and 20:1-18).

7. *Discussion question:* Why do you think God did not rebuke Abraham?

   _____

   _____

   _____

8. What shows that Abraham was trusting God (Gen. 13:1-11)?

   _____

   _____

   _____

9. *Discussion question:* How is God your source?

_____

_____

_____

10. What did God say He will do (Deut. 15:6)?

_____

_____

_____

11. What must you do with God's spiritual laws?

_____

_____

_____

12. What else must you do?

_____

_____

_____

13. True or false: The blessing of Abraham isn't referring to things (Gal. 3:13-14).

14. What is the blessing of Abraham?

_____

_____

_____

15. How did God bless (Gen. 1:28)?
    A. By saying
    B. By pointing
    C. By singing
    D. By dancing
    E. By crying

16. True or false: The Bible has more to say about miracles than about blessings.

17. *Discussion question:* Why do you think words don't mean much in today's culture?

    _____

    _____

    _____

18. If you don't believe in the power of the blessing, you will _____ that blessing from coming to pass (Rom. 5:2).

19. According to Genesis 1:28, God spoke for you to do what?
    A. Have fun with the animals and tame them
    B. Make pets of the animals and coddle them
    C. Take captives of the animals and exploit them
    D. Have dominion over the animals and subdue them
    E. Stay away from the animals and fear them

20. True or false: The animals are afraid of you (Gen. 9:1-2).

21. True or false: If you're afraid of dogs and bugs, it's because God hasn't given you dominion and authority over them.

Answer Key

1. False

2. C. Rich / sorrow

3. *Discussion question*

4. *"Bless" / "blessing"*

5. False

6. False

7. *Discussion question*

8. He was able to let Lot choose the best land for himself

9. *Discussion question*

10. Bless you

11. Cooperate with them

12. Believe

13. True

14. The favor of God spoken over you

15. A. By saying

16. False

17. *Discussion question*

18. Stop

19. D. Have dominion over the animals and subdue them

20. True

21. False

Scriptures

PROVERBS 10:22
The blessing of the Lord, it maketh rich, and he addeth no sorrow with it.

PROVERBS 1:19
So are the ways of every one that is greedy of gain; which taketh away the life of the owners thereof.

GENESIS 12:2
And I will make of thee a great nation, and I will bless thee, and make thy name great; and thou shalt be a blessing.

GENESIS 12:10-20
And there was a famine in the land: and Abram went down into Egypt to sojourn there; for the famine was grievous in the land. [11] And it came to pass, when he was come near to enter into Egypt, that he said unto Sarai his wife, Behold now, I know that thou art a fair woman to look upon: [12] Therefore it shall come to pass, when the Egyptians shall see thee, that they shall say, This is his wife: and they will kill me, but they will save thee alive. [13] Say, I pray thee, thou art my sister: that it may be well with me for thy sake; and my soul shall live because of thee. [14] And it came to pass, that, when Abram was come into Egypt, the Egyptians beheld the woman that she was very fair. [15] The princes also of Pharaoh saw her, and commended her before Pharaoh: and the woman was taken into Pharaoh's house. [16] And he entreated Abram well for her sake: and he had sheep, and oxen, and he asses, and menservants, and maidservants, and she asses, and camels. [17] And the Lord plagued Pharaoh and his house with great plagues because of Sarai Abram's wife. [18] And Pharaoh called Abram, and said, What is this that thou hast done unto me? why didst thou not tell me that she was thy wife? [19] Why saidst thou, She is my sister? so I might have taken her to me to wife: now therefore behold thy wife, take her, and go thy way. [20] And Pharaoh commanded his men concerning him: and they sent him away, and his wife, and all that he had.

GENESIS 20:1-18
And Abraham journeyed from thence toward the south country, and dwelled between Kadesh and Shur, and sojourned in Gerar. [2] And Abraham said of Sarah his wife, She is my sister: and Abimelech king of Gerar sent, and took Sarah. [3] But God came to Abimelech in a dream by night, and said to him, Behold, thou art but a dead man, for the woman which thou hast taken; for she is a man's wife. [4] But

Abimelech had not come near her: and he said, Lord, wilt thou slay also a righteous nation? [5] Said he not unto me, She is my sister? and she, even she herself said, He is my brother: in the integrity of my heart and innocency of my hands have I done this. [6] And God said unto him in a dream, Yea, I know that thou didst this in the integrity of thy heart; for I also withheld thee from sinning against me: therefore suffered I thee not to touch her. [7] Now therefore restore the man his wife; for he is a prophet, and he shall pray for thee, and thou shalt live: and if thou restore her not, know thou that thou shalt surely die, thou, and all that are thine. [8] Therefore Abimelech rose early in the morning, and called all his servants, and told all these things in their ears: and the men were sore afraid. [9] Then Abimelech called Abraham, and said unto him, What hast thou done unto us? and what have I offended thee, that thou hast brought on me and on my kingdom a great sin? thou hast done deeds unto me that ought not to be done. [10] And Abimelech said unto Abraham, What sawest thou, that thou hast done this thing? [11] And Abraham said, Because I thought, Surely the fear of God is not in this place; and they will slay me for my wife's sake. [12] And yet indeed she is my sister; she is the daughter of my father, but not the daughter of my mother; and she became my wife. [13] And it came to pass, when God caused me to wander from my father's house, that I said unto her, This is thy kindness which thou shalt shew unto me; at every place whither we shall come, say of me, He is my brother. [14] And Abimelech took sheep, and oxen, and menservants, and womenservants, and gave them unto Abraham, and restored him Sarah his wife. [15] And Abimelech said, Behold, my land is before thee: dwell where it pleaseth thee. [16] And unto Sarah he said, Behold, I have given thy brother a thousand pieces of silver: behold, he is to thee a covering of the eyes, unto all that are with thee, and with all other: thus she was reproved. [17] So Abraham prayed unto God: and God healed Abimelech, and his wife, and his maidservants; and they bare children. [18] For the LORD had fast closed up all the wombs of the house of Abimelech, because of Sarah Abraham's wife.

GENESIS 13:1-11

And Abram went up out of Egypt, he, and his wife, and all that he had, and Lot with him, into the south. [2] And Abram was very rich in cattle, in silver, and in gold. [3] And he went on his journeys from the south even to Bethel, unto the place where his tent had been at the beginning, between Bethel and Hai; [4] Unto the place of the altar, which he had made there at the first: and there Abram called on the name of the LORD. [5] And Lot also, which went with Abram, had flocks, and herds, and tents. [6] And the land was not able to bear them, that they might dwell together: for their substance was great, so that they could not dwell together. [7] And there was a strife between the herdmen of Abram's cattle and the herdmen of Lot's cattle: and the Canaanite and the Perizzite dwelled then in the land. [8] And Abram said unto Lot, Let there be no strife, I pray thee, between me and thee, and between my herdmen and thy herdmen; for we be brethren. [9] Is not the whole land before thee? separate thyself, I pray thee, from me: if thou wilt take the left hand, then I will go to the right; or if thou depart to the right hand, then I will go to the left. [10] And Lot lifted up his eyes, and beheld all the plain of Jordan, that it was well watered every where, before the LORD destroyed Sodom and Gomorrah, even as the garden of the LORD, like the land of Egypt, as thou comest unto Zoar. [11] Then Lot chose him all the plain of Jordan; and Lot journeyed east: and they separated themselves the one from the other.

GENESIS 14:14-23

And when Abram heard that his brother was taken captive, he armed his trained servants, born in his own house, three hundred and eighteen, and pursued them unto Dan. [15] And he divided himself against them, he and his servants, by night, and smote them, and pursued them unto Hobah, which is on the left hand of Damascus. [16] And he brought back all the goods, and also brought again his brother Lot, and his goods, and the women also, and the people. [17] And the king of Sodom went out to meet him after his return from the slaughter of Chedorlaomer, and of the kings that were with him, at the valley of Shaveh, which is the king's dale. [18] And Melchizedek king of Salem brought forth bread and wine: and he was the priest of the most high God. [19] And he blessed him, and said, Blessed be Abram of the most high God, possessor of heaven and earth: [20] And blessed be the most high God, which hath delivered thine enemies into thy hand. And he gave him tithes of all. [21] And the king of Sodom said unto Abram, Give me the persons, and take the goods to thyself. [22] And Abram said to the king of Sodom, I have lift up mine hand unto the LORD, the most high God, the possessor of heaven and earth, [23] That I will not take from a thread even to a shoelatchet, and that I will not take any thing that is thine, lest thou shouldest say, I have made Abram rich

DEUTERONOMY 15:6

For the LORD thy God blesseth thee, as he promised thee: and thou shalt lend unto many nations, but thou shalt not borrow; and thou shalt reign over many nations, but they shall not reign over thee.

DEUTERONOMY 28:8

The LORD shall command the blessing upon thee in thy storehouses, and in all that thou settest thine hand unto; and he shall bless thee in the land which the LORD thy God giveth thee.

GALATIANS 3:13-14

Christ hath redeemed us from the curse of the law, being made a curse for us: for it is written, Cursed is every one that hangeth on a tree: [14] That the blessing of Abraham might come on the Gentiles through Jesus Christ; that we might receive the promise of the Spirit through faith.

GENESIS 1:22

And God blessed them, saying, Be fruitful, and multiply, and fill the waters in the seas, and let fowl multiply in the earth.

GENESIS 1:28

And God blessed them, and God said unto them, Be fruitful, and multiply, and replenish the earth, and subdue it: and have dominion over the fish of the sea, and over the fowl of the air, and over every living thing that moveth upon the earth.

ROMANS 5:2

By whom also we have access by faith into this grace wherein we stand, and rejoice in hope of the glory of God.

GENESIS 9:1-2

And God blessed Noah and his sons, and said unto them, Be fruitful, and multiply, and replenish the earth. [2] And the fear of you and the dread of you shall be upon every beast of the earth, and upon every fowl of the air, upon all that moveth upon the earth, and upon all the fishes of the sea; into your hand are they delivered.

Curse or Blessing?

LESSON 12

Isaac's two sons, Jacob and Esau, actually fought over the blessing (Gen. 27:1-34). When Isaac was old and close to passing and wasn't seeing properly, he said this to his older son, Esau:

> *Behold now, I am old, I know not the day of my death:* [3] *Now therefore take, I pray thee, thy weapons, thy quiver and thy bow, and go out to the field, and take me some venison;* [4] *And make me savoury meat, such as I love, and bring it to me, that I may eat; that my soul may bless thee before I die.*
>
> Genesis 27:2-4

Isaac had received the blessing from his father, Abraham, and Isaac intended to speak the blessing over Esau. But Isaac's wife, Rebekah, heard him speak to Esau and she called for Jacob, their other son, and said, "Quick! Go get your brother's clothes and put them on. I'm going to slaughter these two young goats and prepare the meat the way your father likes it, that he may bless you. We'll put the goatskin on the back of your neck and hands because your brother is a hairy man." Esau must have been really hairy for a goat fleece to feel like him!

While his brother was still out hunting, Jacob went into Isaac's room, pretending to be Esau. His father, who couldn't see very well, stated, "Your voice is the voice of Jacob, but your smell and hairy feel is that of Esau." So, Isaac blessed Jacob instead of Esau.

"WHO ARE YOU?"

As soon as Jacob left, Esau came in bringing food and saying, "Arise, my father. Eat and bless me."

Isaac asked, "Who are you?"

"I am Esau, your firstborn son."

> *And Isaac trembled very exceedingly, and said, Who? where is he that*
> *hath taken venison, and brought it me, and I have eaten of all before*
> *thou camest, and have blessed him? yea, and he shall be blessed.*
>
> Genesis 27:33

Then Esau began to wail and cry because he had lost his father's blessing. Isaac said, "It's Jacob, your brother. He has come and taken away your blessing."

When you left home, did you fight with your siblings to get your father's blessing? Did you even think about it? Most folks don't even care. They'd say, "Who cares what they say over me?" I'm telling you, the attitude expressed in the Bible is the right attitude. Our society does not value words, but the Bible says,

> *Death and life are in the power of the tongue.*
>
> Proverbs 18:21

Death and life only—not death, life, and a lot of other stuff. It's death or life—one of those two.

"YOU REBEL!"

Whether you know it or not, your parents' words have had influence in your life. Maybe you left home cursed. You were told, "You rebel! You're never going to make it." Perhaps you were cursed by other people—by an extended family member or a teacher who said, "You're dumb. You're just stupid." You may not know it, but those are curses, and they do have power. Many people are still struggling today because of curses that were spoken over them instead of blessings.

The father of a very good friend of mine was just a mean man. I met him and personally knew the guy. He had twenty or thirty cars that he would use for parts. He'd take his son, my friend, with him to work on those cars. This man was so full of bitterness that he actually wound up committing suicide. He left a suicide note, blaming his family, saying, "It's your fault." He tried to make them feel guilty for his death.

He told my friend, "You're so stupid. You can't put a nut on a bolt without cross-threading it." I've worked with my friend on cars many times, and I've seen him—at forty years old—shaking while putting a nut on a bolt. He'd tighten it, and it would be just fine but he'd say, "I think I've cross-threaded it." Then he'd undo and redo it and undo and redo it. I've never seen him put a nut on a bolt that he didn't eventually cross-thread because of the curse that was spoken over him.

Maybe you were told that you would never amount to anything. It may not have been a parent who said that, but perhaps an ex from a prior relationship cursed you. They said negative things about you. Words are powerful—for life and for death. Maybe you haven't even realized what your problem is, but you were cursed. There's power in words!

I DON'T BELIEVE IT

There's also power in a blessing. And a blessing is much greater than a curse, but you have to believe it. You have to believe a curse too.

> *As the bird by wandering, as the swallow by flying, so the curse causeless shall not come.*
>
> Proverbs 26:2

A curse doesn't have any power over you unless you believe it, unless you fear it. Fear is nothing but faith in a negative. You have to empower that curse over you.

There are thousands of blogs written against me. Someone came up to me recently and shared how they had told their people back in India about me. They tried to get them to listen to my materials, but those people had gone on the internet and found something that said I'm the most dangerous man in America and so forth. People curse me and say all kinds of things, but it doesn't have any power over me because I don't believe it (Prov. 26:2).

For the words of other people to affect you and bring about life or death, you have to believe them. You don't have to be affected by negative words and curses. Likewise, the favor of God—the blessing that has been spoken over you by Him—has to be believed in order for its power to be released. The problem is, most of us just don't believe in the power of a blessing. We're quick to believe in curses and the negative. We receive bad prophecies all the time, but when it comes to good prophecies, we aren't quick to believe them. We need to reverse that!

God has spoken thousands of blessings over you, and you need to get to the place where you believe them. If He said that you have authority over animals, then you can count on the fact that you have authority over animals (Gen. 9:2). If you were in the sea, you could take authority over sharks, fish, jellyfish, and all other sea creatures. Some people say, "Well, I don't believe that." It won't work for them, but if you believe, it'll work for you!

A friend of mine heard me teach on this. He was sitting on the step of a cabin and saw a lizard crawl by, so he just spoke to the lizard, saying, "Come here, in the name of Jesus." That lizard looked at him and then crawled right over to him. Then he said,

"Now go over there," and that lizard did just what he told it to do. You have authority over animals if you believe it!

WALKING IN THE BLESSING

We have blessings spoken over us, like *"by* [His] *stripes ye were healed"* (1 Pet. 2:24, brackets mine). If you believed in the power of a blessing, it would work.

I remember an older man who was a greeter at our church. He was always a happy guy, and I enjoyed seeing him every time I went there. He was absent for a couple of weeks, so I started asking around. He was in the hospital with pneumonia and just wasn't able to get over it, so Jamie and I decided to go over and see him. He was really discouraged because he believed in the healing power of God, yet he just wasn't able to get over this illness. He had so much phlegm in his lungs that he could barely breathe and couldn't talk without coughing.

This was during the time when God taught me about the power of a blessing and the power of words, so I said, "Let me pray over you." Then I laid my hands on his chest and spoke, "Chest, in the name of Jesus, you are blessed. I bless you with health, and I curse this phlegm that's in your lungs. I command that stuff to come out now, in the name of Jesus." This guy started coughing and had to push me out of the way. He grabbed a towel and coughed up all this phlegm out of his lungs. In ten minutes, the guy was totally normal. That's the power of a blessing! But you have to believe it. Jesus said,

> *Whosoever shall say unto this mountain, Be thou removed, and be thou cast into the sea; and shall not doubt in his heart, but shall believe that those things which he saith shall come to pass; he shall have whatsoever he saith.*
>
> Mark 11:23

You have to believe in the power of your words. You must believe in the power of God's blessing. God has enabled you to bless and He has given you creative power. You have to believe in that before it'll work. If you just say words to see if it'll work, it won't. But if you can mix faith with your words, there will be creative power in your words (Heb. 4:2). You can bless!

God is the one who started everything. He created all of this. God has spoken blessings over you, and blessings are powerful. Once you begin operating in the blessing, Satan can't stop it. Once it's given, it's eternal and abundant. If you ever started living in the blessing of God, it would transform your life. You can get to a place where you never have to have another miracle. You'll believe for miracles for other people who don't yet know how to walk in the blessings of God, but you'll leave the miracles for unbelievers—you'll be walking in the blessing of God!

THE WAY IT SHOULD BE

Back in the 1970s, Mel Tari wrote a really popular book entitled *Like a Mighty Wind*, about the great revival that swept through Indonesia. People were raised from the dead, waters were parted, and people walked across on dry ground. The book detailed miracle upon miracle. Back then, Mel Tari was the biggest name in the body of Christ. He traveled around speaking, and I heard him testify in person once about all of these awesome miracles.

About seven years later, he wrote a second book entitled *The Gentle Breeze of Jesus*. It followed up with what was going on in Indonesia. He reported that now, seven years or so after this great move of God in Indonesia, they hardly ever saw a miracle in the church. They used to have miracles every service with the dead being raised, blind eyes opening, etc.

When I first heard that, I thought, *Oh, that's a shame. It's just like every other move of God. It's just waned and is passing away after seven short years.* But Mel went on to say that the miracles they saw now were out in the villages where they were doing outreach and evangelism. They didn't see miracles among the believers, because all the Christians were so blessed, healed, and prosperous that they didn't need miracles. All the miracles were happening out among the unbelievers, and that's the way it should be.

Jesus used miracles like a bell to draw people to the power of God and the message of salvation. But we as believers ought to be walking in the blessing of God so much that we don't even get sick or have any of these desperate needs. We shouldn't have to be living from crisis to crisis or pit to pit. Instead, we should be walking on the mountaintops, rejoicing.

You can receive from God through either one of these—a blessing or a miracle. As for me, I'd rather have the blessing of God than have to live from miracle to miracle.

BREAK THOSE CURSES

Perhaps you've been praying, "O God, please supply this." He's trying to bless you, but you're just waiting on a miracle. You're violating every law, not doing what He's told you to do. You aren't cooperating with the Word of God, so you'll have to have a miracle because you aren't walking in the blessing of God. There's a reason why some people prosper and others don't. These truths about the blessing of God are really important!

Father, I pray that the Holy Spirit would help us to understand. I pray for those who are living from crisis to crisis. They're violating spiritual, natural, and emotional laws and are not doing what Your Word says; yet they're believing You for a miracle. I pray that You would speak this word into their hearts right now to encourage them that it doesn't have to be this way, that they don't have to stay this way, that they can tap into Your blessing and the favor You have spoken over them through Your Word. Open their eyes to see all of these wonderful things, all of these exceedingly great and precious promises that You have given us (2 Pet. 1:4). Thank You that we don't have to just barely get by, struggling all the time. Thank You for showing us how to walk in Your blessing!

Is the Holy Spirit showing you that you've had a curse working in your life, and you're the one who empowered it because you believed it? Maybe it was an ex, a parent, a relative, a teacher, an employer, or some other person who spoke negative words—curses—over you. You've empowered them; not intentionally, but you've been fearful of them. They hurt you, and you rehearse the negative things that were said. It's become a self-fulfilling prophecy.

I'm sure you don't enjoy this curse; I'm sure you hate it. But nonetheless, you have empowered the curse through your fear. You've let those things happen. I believe that God wants to break those curses over your life and stop them from working against you, but you have to denounce them and condemn them (Is. 54:17). You have to say, "No longer will this curse dominate me. I'm going to receive the blessing of God!"

THANK YOU, JESUS!

What's stopping you from praying out loud right now?

Father, thank You for revealing the truth to me. Forgive me for empowering these curses. Forgive me for believing in what they've said. Forgive me for being hurt and offended when You've said so many wonderful things about me. You have blessed me. I am blessed above all people on the face of the earth (Deut. 7:14). Forgive me for letting these curses, these negative words, dominate me. Right now, I take my authority in Christ Jesus, and I speak death to all these curses. In the name of Jesus, I say that I am not going to let any curse that anyone has spoken over me—or that I've spoken over myself—to remain. I break them all, in Jesus's name. I can do all things through Christ who strengthens me (Phil. 4:13). You always make me to triumph in my Lord Jesus Christ (2 Cor. 2:14). I am above only and not beneath. I am the head and not the tail (Deut. 28:13).

I break the curses of doctors, bankers, lawyers, and any other person who has spoken negative things—death words—to me. I renounce these curses in the name of Jesus and refuse to allow them to dominate me anymore. Father, I believe what You have said about me. Your blessing is stronger than any curse, and right now I activate Your blessing by my faith. I put faith in You and in what You have said about me. From this time forth, I am the blessed of the Lord (Ps. 115:15). The blessing of the Lord makes me rich, and You add no sorrow with it (Prov. 10:22). I am blessed coming in and blessed going out (Deut. 28:6). I'm blessed in my basket and in my storehouse (Deut. 28:5). Thank You that everything I set my hand unto is blessed (Deut. 28:8). Thank You, Jesus!

I speak the blessing of God, and I break the curse. That curse is over. It's done. From this moment forward, the curse in my life has ended, and it's the beginning of the blessing. I declare it by faith in Jesus's name. Amen. Hallelujah!

Outline

I. Isaac's two sons, Jacob and Esau, actually fought over the blessing (Gen. 27:1-34).

    A. Isaac had received the blessing from his father, Abraham, and Isaac intended to speak the blessing over his older son, Esau.

    B. While Esau was still out hunting, the younger son, Jacob, went into Isaac's room, pretending to be Esau.

    C. So, Isaac blessed Jacob instead of Esau.

    D. When Esau found out, he began to wail and cry because he had lost his father's blessing.

    E. Most folks don't even care about their fathers' blessing.

    F. I'm telling you, the attitude expressed in the Bible is the right attitude.

    G. The Bible says,

> *Death and life are in the power of the tongue.*
>
> Proverbs 18:21

    H. Death and life only—not death, life, and a lot of other stuff—are in the *"power of the tongue."*

II. Your parents' words have had influence in your life.

    A. Perhaps you were cursed by other people—by an extended family member or a teacher.

    B. Maybe you were told that you would never amount to anything.

    C. It may not have been a parent who said that, but perhaps an ex from a prior relationship cursed you.

    D. Maybe you haven't even realized what your problem is, but you were cursed.

    E. There's power in words!

III. There's also power in a blessing.

    A. A blessing is much greater than a curse.

    B. A curse doesn't have any power over us unless we believe it, unless we fear it (Prov. 26:2).

    C. Fear is nothing but faith in a negative.

    D. The favor of God—the blessing that has been spoken over us by Him—has to be believed in order for its power to be released.

    E. Most of us are quick to believe in curses and the negative.

    F. We need to reverse that!

    G. God has spoken thousands of blessings over us, and we need to get to the place where we believe them.

    H. If we believed in the power of a blessing, it would work.

IV. You have to believe in the power of your words.

    A. Jesus said,

> *Whosoever shall say unto this mountain, Be thou removed, and be thou cast into the sea; and shall not doubt in his heart, but shall believe that those things which he saith shall come to pass; he shall have whatsoever he saith.*
>
> Mark 11:23

    B. God has enabled you to bless, and He has given you creative power.

    C. If you just say words to see if it'll work, it won't.

    D. But if you can mix faith with your words, there will be creative power in them (Heb. 4:2).

V. Once you begin operating in the blessing, Satan can't stop it.

    A. Once it's given, it's eternal and abundant.

B. If you ever started living in the blessing of God, it would transform your life.

C. You can get to a place where you never have to have another miracle.

D. You'll believe for miracles for other people who don't yet know how to walk in the blessings of God, but you'll leave the miracles for unbelievers!

E. That's the way it should be.

F. You shouldn't have to be living from crisis to crisis or pit to pit.

G. You should be walking on the mountaintops, rejoicing.

H. You can receive from God through either one of these—a blessing or a miracle.

MY PRAYER FOR YOU:

Father, I pray that the Holy Spirit would help us to understand. I pray for those who are living from crisis to crisis. They're violating spiritual, natural, and emotional laws and are not doing what Your Word says; yet they're believing You for a miracle. I pray that You would speak this word into their hearts right now to encourage them that it doesn't have to be this way, that they don't have to stay this way, that they can tap into Your blessing and the favor You have spoken over them through Your Word. Open their eyes to see all of these wonderful things, all of these exceedingly great and precious promises that You have given us (2 Pet. 1:4). Thank You that we don't have to just barely get by, struggling all the time. Thank You for showing us how to walk in Your blessing!

PRAY THIS IN FAITH:

Father, thank You for revealing the truth to me. Forgive me for empowering these curses. Forgive me for believing in what they've said. Forgive me for being hurt and offended when You've said so many wonderful things about me. You have blessed me. I am blessed above all people on the face of the earth (Deut. 7:14). Forgive me for letting these curses, these negative words, dominate me. Right now, I take my authority in Christ Jesus, and I speak death to all these curses. In the name of Jesus, I say that I am not going to let any curse that anyone has spoken over me—or that I've spoken over myself—to remain. I break them all, in Jesus's name. I can do all things through Christ who strengthens me (Phil. 4:13). You always make me to triumph in my Lord Jesus Christ (2 Cor. 2:14). I am above only and not beneath. I am the head and not the tail (Deut. 28:13).

I break the curses of doctors, bankers, lawyers, and any other person who has spoken negative things—death words—to me. I renounce these curses in the name of Jesus and refuse to allow them to dominate me anymore. Father, I believe what You have said about me. Your blessing is stronger than any curse, and right now I activate Your blessing by my faith. I put faith in You and in what You have said about me. From this time forth, I am the blessed of the Lord (Ps. 115:15). The blessing of the Lord makes me rich, and You add no sorrow with it (Prov. 10:22). I am blessed coming in and blessed going out (Deut. 28:6). I'm blessed in my basket and in my storehouse (Deut. 28:5). Thank You that everything I set my hand unto is blessed (Deut. 28:8). Thank You, Jesus!

I speak the blessing of God, and I break the curse. That curse is over. It's done. From this moment forward, the curse in my life has ended, and it's the beginning of the blessing. I declare it by faith in Jesus's name. Amen. Hallelujah!

Teacher's Guide

1.   Isaac's two sons, Jacob and Esau, actually fought over the blessing (Gen. 27:1-34). Isaac had received the blessing from his father, Abraham, and Isaac intended to speak the blessing over his older son, Esau. While Esau was still out hunting, the younger son, Jacob, went into Isaac's room, pretending to be Esau. So, Isaac blessed Jacob instead of Esau. When Esau found out, he began to wail and cry because he had lost his father's blessing. Most folks don't even care about their fathers' blessing. Andrew is telling us that the attitude expressed in the Bible is the right attitude. The Bible says,

> *Death and life are in the power of the tongue.*
>
> Proverbs 18:21

Death and life only—not death, life, and a lot of other stuff—are in the *"power of the tongue."*

1a. *Discussion question:* What in this story speaks to you about receiving God's best (Gen. 27:1-34)?
     Discussion question
1b. True or false: Death and life only are in the power of the tongue (Prov. 18:21).
     True

2.   Our parents' words have had influence in our lives. Perhaps we were cursed by other people—by an extended family member or a teacher. Maybe we were told that we would never amount to anything. It may not have been a parent who said that, but perhaps an ex from a prior relationship cursed us. Maybe we haven't even realized what our problems are, but we were cursed. There's power in words!

2a. *Discussion question:* How have you dealt with words spoken over you, whether blessings or curses?
     Discussion question

3.   There's also power in a blessing. A blessing is much greater than a curse. A curse doesn't have any power over us unless we believe it, unless we fear it (Prov. 26:2). Fear is nothing but faith in a negative. The favor of God—the blessing that has been spoken over us by Him—has to be believed in order for its power to be released. Most of us are quick to believe in curses and the negative. We need to reverse that! God has spoken thousands of blessings over us, and we need to get to the place where we believe them. If we believed in the power of a blessing, it would work.

3a. True or false: A curse has power over you even if you aren't afraid of it (Prov. 26:2).
    False

3b. The favor of God—the blessing that has been spoken over you by Him—has to be believed in order for its power to be what?
    A. Revealed
    B. Released
    C. Received
    D. All of the above
    E. None of the above
    D. All of the above

3c. *Discussion question:* How quick are you to believe in curses and the negative?
    Discussion question

3d. God has spoken _____ of blessings over you.
    Thousands

3e. What would happen if you believed in the power of a blessing?
    It would work

4. We have to believe in the power of our words. Jesus said,

    Whosoever shall say unto this mountain, Be thou removed, and be thou cast into the sea; and shall not doubt in his heart, but shall believe that those things which he saith shall come to pass; he shall have whatsoever he saith.

    Mark 11:23

God has enabled us to bless, and He has given us creative power. If we just say words to see if it'll work, it won't. But if we can mix faith with our words, there will be creative power in them (Heb. 4:2).

4a. According to Mark 11:23, "Whosoever shall _____ unto this mountain, Be thou removed, and be thou cast into the sea; and shall not doubt in his heart, but shall believe that those things which he saith shall come to pass; he shall have whatsoever he saith."
    "Say"

4b. What would happen if you just say words to see if it'll work?
    It won't

4c. If you can mix faith with your words, there will be _____ power in them (Heb. 4:2).
   A. Artificial
   B. Borrowed
   C. Creative
   D. All of the above
   E. None of the above
   C. Creative

5.   Once we begin operating in the blessing, Satan can't stop it. Once it's given, it's eternal and abundant. If we ever started living in the blessing of God, it would transform our lives. We can get to a place where we never have to have another miracle. We'll believe for miracles for other people who don't yet know how to walk in the blessings of God, but we'll leave the miracles for unbelievers! That's the way it should be. We shouldn't have to be living from crisis to crisis or pit to pit. We should be walking on the mountaintops, rejoicing. We can receive from God through either one of these—a blessing or a miracle.

5a. Once you begin operating in the blessing, _____ can't stop it.
   Satan
5b. Once a blessing is given, it's _____ and _____.
   Eternal / abundant
5c. True or false: You can get to a place where you never have to have another miracle.
   True
5d. True or false: It's better to believe for miracles for yourself than for unbelievers.
   False
5e. *Discussion question*: How are you going to start walking in the blessing instead of by miracles or by curses?
   Discussion question

Discipleship Questions

1. *Discussion question:* What in this story speaks to you about receiving God's best (Gen. 27:1-34)?

   _____

   _____

   _____

2. True or false: Death and life only are in the power of the tongue (Prov. 18:21).

3. *Discussion question:* How have you dealt with words spoken over you, whether blessings or curses?

   _____

   _____

   _____

4. True or false: A curse has power over you even if you aren't afraid of it (Prov. 26:2).

5. The favor of God—the blessing that has been spoken over you by Him—has to be believed in order for its power to be what?
   A. Revealed
   B. Released
   C. Received
   D. All of the above
   E. None of the above

6. *Discussion question:* How quick are you to believe in curses and the negative?

   _____

   _____

   _____

7. God has spoken _____ of blessings over you.

8. What would happen if you believed in the power of a blessing?

    _____

    _____

    _____

9. According to Mark 11:23, "*Whosoever shall _____ unto this mountain, Be thou removed, and be thou cast into the sea; and shall not doubt in his heart, but shall believe that those things which he saith shall come to pass; he shall have whatsoever he saith.*"

10. What would happen if you just say words to see if it'll work?

    _____

    _____

    _____

11. If you can mix faith with your words, there will be _____ power in them (Heb. 4:2).
    A. Artificial
    B. Borrowed
    C. Creative
    D. All of the above
    E. None of the above

12. Once you begin operating in the blessing, _____ can't stop it.

13. Once a blessing is given, it's _____ and _____.

14. True or false: You can get to a place where you never have to have another miracle.

15. True or false: It's better to believe for miracles for yourself than for unbelievers.

16. *Discussion question:* How are you going to start walking in the blessing instead of by miracles or by curses?

    _____

    _____

    _____

Answer Key

1. *Discussion question*

2. True

3. *Discussion question*

4. False

5. D.　All of the above

6. *Discussion question*

7. Thousands

8. It would work

9. *"Say"*

10. It won't

11. C.　Creative

12. Satan

13. Eternal / abundant

14. True

15. False

16. *Discussion question*

Scriptures

GENESIS 27:1-34

And it came to pass, that when Isaac was old, and his eyes were dim, so that he could not see, he called Esau his eldest son, and said unto him, My son: and he said unto him, Behold, here am I. [2] And he said, Behold now, I am old, I know not the day of my death: [3] Now therefore take, I pray thee, thy weapons, thy quiver and thy bow, and go out to the field, and take me some venison; [4] And make me savoury meat, such as I love, and bring it to me, that I may eat; that my soul may bless thee before I die. [5] And Rebekah heard when Isaac spake to Esau his son. And Esau went to the field to hunt for venison, and to bring it. [6] And Rebekah spake unto Jacob her son, saying, Behold, I heard thy father speak unto Esau thy brother, saying, [7] Bring me venison, and make me savoury meat, that I may eat, and bless thee before the LORD before my death. [8] Now therefore, my son, obey my voice according to that which I command thee. [9] Go now to the flock, and fetch me from thence two good kids of the goats; and I will make them savoury meat for thy father, such as he loveth: [10] And thou shalt bring it to thy father, that he may eat, and that he may bless thee before his death. [11] And Jacob said to Rebekah his mother, Behold, Esau my brother is a hairy man, and I am a smooth man: [12] My father peradventure will feel me, and I shall seem to him as a deceiver; and I shall bring a curse upon me, and not a blessing. [13] And his mother said unto him, Upon me be thy curse, my son: only obey my voice, and go fetch me them. [14] And he went, and fetched, and brought them to his mother: and his mother made savoury meat, such as his father loved. [15] And Rebekah took goodly raiment of her eldest son Esau, which were with her in the house, and put them upon Jacob her younger son: [16] And she put the skins of the kids of the goats upon his hands, and upon the smooth of his neck: [17] And she gave the savoury meat and the bread, which she had prepared, into the hand of her son Jacob. [18] And he came unto his father, and said, My father: and he said, Here am I; who art thou, my son? [19] And Jacob said unto his father, I am Esau thy firstborn; I have done according as thou badest me: arise, I pray thee, sit and eat of my venison, that thy soul may bless me. [20] And Isaac said unto his son, How is it that thou hast found it so quickly, my son? And he said, Because the LORD thy God brought it to me. [21] And Isaac said unto Jacob, Come near, I pray thee, that I may feel thee, my son, whether thou be my very son Esau or not. [22] And Jacob went near unto Isaac his father; and he felt him, and said, The voice is Jacob's voice, but the hands are the hands of Esau. [23] And he discerned him not, because his hands were hairy, as his brother Esau's hands: so he blessed him. [24]

And he said, Art thou my very son Esau? And he said, I am. [25] And he said, Bring it near to me, and I will eat of my son's venison, that my soul may bless thee. And he brought it near to him, and he did eat: and he brought him wine, and he drank. [26] And his father Isaac said unto him, Come near now, and kiss me, my son. [27] And he came near, and kissed him: and he smelled the smell of his raiment, and blessed him, and said, See, the smell of my son is as the smell of a field which the Lord hath blessed: [28] Therefore God give thee of the dew of heaven, and the fatness of the earth, and plenty of corn and wine: [29] Let people serve thee, and nations bow down to thee: be lord over thy brethren, and let thy mother's sons bow down to thee: cursed be every one that curseth thee, and blessed be he that blesseth thee. [30] And it came to pass, as soon as Isaac had made an end of blessing Jacob, and Jacob was yet scarce gone out from the presence of Isaac his father, that Esau his brother came in from his hunting. [31] And he also had made savoury meat, and brought it unto his father, and said unto his father, Let my father arise, and eat of his son's venison, that thy soul may bless me. [32] And Isaac his father said unto him, Who art thou? And he said, I am thy son, thy firstborn Esau. [33] And Isaac trembled very exceedingly, and said, Who? where is he that hath taken venison, and brought it me, and I have eaten of all before thou camest, and have blessed him? yea, and he shall be blessed. [34] And when Esau heard the words of his father, he cried with a great and exceeding bitter cry, and said unto his father, Bless me, even me also, O my father.

PROVERBS 18:21
Death and life are in the power of the tongue: and they that love it shall eat the fruit thereof.

PROVERBS 26:2
As the bird by wandering, as the swallow by flying, so the curse causeless shall not come.

GENESIS 9:2
And the fear of you and the dread of you shall be upon every beast of the earth, and upon every fowl of the air, upon all that moveth upon the earth, and upon all the fishes of the sea; into your hand are they delivered.

1 PETER 2:24
Who his own self bare our sins in his own body on the tree, that we, being dead to sins, should live unto righteousness: by whose stripes ye were healed.

MARK 11:23

For verily I say unto you, That whosoever shall say unto this mountain, Be thou removed, and be thou cast into the sea; and shall not doubt in his heart, but shall believe that those things which he saith shall come to pass; he shall have whatsoever he saith.

HEBREWS 4:2

For unto us was the gospel preached, as well as unto them: but the word preached did not profit them, not being mixed with faith in them that heard it.

2 PETER 1:4

Whereby are given unto us exceeding great and precious promises: that by these ye might be partakers of the divine nature, having escaped the corruption that is in the world through lust.

ISAIAH 54:17

No weapon that is formed against thee shall prosper; and every tongue that shall rise against thee in judgment thou shalt condemn. This is the heritage of the servants of the LORD, and their righteousness is of me, saith the LORD.

DEUTERONOMY 7:14

Thou shalt be blessed above all people: there shall not be male or female barren among you, or among your cattle.

PHILIPPIANS 4:13

I can do all things through Christ which strengtheneth me.

2 CORINTHIANS 2:14

Now thanks be unto God, which always causeth us to triumph in Christ, and maketh manifest the savour of his knowledge by us in every place.

DEUTERONOMY 28:13

And the LORD shall make thee the head, and not the tail; and thou shalt be above only, and thou shalt not be beneath; if that thou hearken unto the commandments of the LORD thy God, which I command thee this day, to observe and to do them.

PSALM 115:15

Ye are blessed of the LORD which made heaven and earth.

PROVERBS 10:22

The blessing of the LORD, it maketh rich, and he addeth no sorrow with it.

DEUTERONOMY 28:5-6

Blessed shall be thy basket and thy store. [6] Blessed shalt thou be when thou comest in, and blessed shalt thou be when thou goest out.

DEUTERONOMY 28:8

The LORD shall command the blessing upon thee in thy storehouses, and in all that thou settest thine hand unto; and he shall bless thee in the land which the LORD thy God giveth thee.

It Doesn't Matter

LESSON 13

Let's review some of the ground we've covered thus far.

Many believers have settled for less than God's best and don't even think about it. If we settle for less than God's best, we'll never experience it. Our desire to compromise, to be secure, and to not stretch ourselves out in faith is a hindrance to receiving God's best.

Receiving God's best isn't about getting the Lord to do something. The church as a whole believes that God *can do* anything, but *has done* nothing, so therefore, we have to seek, beg, plead, and somehow or another manipulate God to make Him move. This is expressed in statements like "Faith moves God." Faith does not move God. God moved by grace, and our faith only appropriates what God has already provided by grace. Now, that's a life-changing truth!

You can receive God's supply through two different delivery systems—a blessing or a miracle. Since a miracle involves a superseding or suspension of natural law, it isn't God's best. God created natural laws and said that they are good. He wants you to learn how to live by cooperating with the spiritual and natural laws He's spoken. When you violate these laws, you'll find yourself in a crisis. You can receive a miracle, but to have a miracle, you'll have to be in a crisis.

A blessing will prevent a crisis. A miracle is never as abundant as a blessing. Manna (miracle) was just enough, but the Promised Land (the blessing) was abundance. A miracle is only temporary. God isn't going to supersede or suspend natural laws long term. A blessing, once it's given, cannot be reversed.

THE REAL ASSET!

Blessings are not things. Some folks say, "That car is a blessing" or "My house is a blessing." Things you have are the result of the blessing of God, but His blessing isn't things. Galatians 3:14 reveals that the blessing of Abraham has come upon us as believers through faith. I don't want Abraham's things. I don't desire his old tents, sheep, or cattle. I want the favor of God that was spoken over him that produced such abundance. It's important to remember that blessings aren't things.

You might look at things and say, "Boy, I'm blessed! Just look at my blessings!" Things are in the physical realm, so Satan can affect them. Things come and go. The economy fluctuates. Your prosperity will fluctuate. I praise God for all of the buildings and things He's given us, but that's not the blessing of God. Those are a manifestation—a result—of the blessing of God on my life. God forbid anything should happen to them, but they're just things. It's no problem. It doesn't affect God's favor over me. If something happened and I lost everything, I'd get it back because His blessing produced those things. It would just be a matter of time.

I've got the goose that lays the golden eggs, so to speak. Who cares if something happens to one of the eggs? I have the goose! More eggs can be produced. If a person freaks out because their car gets damaged, their faith is in the wrong place. They're looking at their things. It's the favor of God that gave them their car. It's the favor of God that gave them their things. That's the real asset!

WRECKED

Due to a terrible experience, I had to buy two brand-new cars in one week. Later that same week, I drove a friend of mine up to our house to fix our satellite. Our place is located up in the mountains of Colorado, and it had just snowed. My friend marveled about how much traction my new pickup truck had in the four inches of snow that had fallen on my super steep driveway. We even stopped on the way up, and the truck never slid. He was amazed!

After finishing the repair job, I was telling my friend how our other car actually has even better traction than our truck. He commented, "I'd like to see how that works!"

So, I told him, "Okay, I'll drive you down the mountain in the other car." We got in, and I proceeded to back my brand-new Subaru into my brand-new Ford pickup. I wrecked both brand-new vehicles the same week I got them!

My friend turned white and moaned, "Oh, I'm so sorry. This is terrible!"

I responded, "Hey, they're just cars—just things. It doesn't matter."

"How could you say that? They are brand new!"

"They're just things. It doesn't matter to me. They're just machines."

Another time, we bought a brand-new car and went to church. This was the very first time we ever took it there, and a woman backed into it and dented it. She recognized me, and I could tell she just felt so bad as she said, "I can't believe I did this to you!" I told her, "Don't feel bad about it. It's just a car. It doesn't matter."

But there are some people who, if you touch their things, you've touched their hearts! It would ruin their day. That's because their faith is in the wrong place. When you have your faith in the Lord, it doesn't matter what happens to your things. They're just things.

"IT'S JUST STUFF"

We were evacuated from our house in 2002 because of a large forest fire that ultimately burned almost 140,000 acres and came within a mile of our house. This was a mandatory evacuation, so all of our neighbors were packing up moving vans and taking everything with them because they were anticipating their houses getting burned down. Jamie and I prayed over our place, blessed it, and commanded the fire not to come near our house or ruin our view. And it didn't. From where we live, you can't even see that there was a fire. God protected us.

Of course, we took our important papers, photos, and similar things that couldn't be replaced. All of our neighbors were loading up moving vans, but we just put a few things in our car. As we were driving out and leaving, Jamie said, "I agree with you. I believe we're protected. God's going to protect our place. But it's just stuff. If we lost everything we've got, it was fun getting it, and we'd have fun getting it back." What a great attitude! Praise God for a wife with that attitude.

If you were to see our house, it would take one van to move Jamie's stuff and then another one to move all of our furniture. This is our dream house. I designed it. I drew up the plans and we built it. Jamie has it customized exactly the way she wants it. She has stuff everywhere. But it's just stuff. That's the way you have to look at things.

Things are not the blessing of God. They are a result of the blessing of God. If I had everything taken away from me, I'm still blessed of God—and I'd get my possessions back with interest. Amen!

> *But if he* [a thief, see Prov. 6:30] *be found, he shall restore sevenfold; he shall give all the substance of his house.*
>
> Proverbs 6:31, brackets mine

If Satan steals something from me, I'm going to make him repay with interest!

SCAMMED

I didn't have any money to publish one of the first books that we ever published, so I went to our ministry partners and asked them to help by preselling copies of the book. We had to raise $27,000 to get 10,000 of these books printed. This was back when our ministry income was probably about $5,000 a month. We didn't have very much money, but through our partners, we raised all we needed to do the printing. I gave all the money to the publisher, and it turned out that the guy who was representing the publisher stole the money. He did the same thing to two other well-known ministries, both larger than ours at the time. We all got scammed by this guy and lost that money.

My staff came to me and said, "The $27,000 we gave this guy is gone. It's lost. He skipped the country and took the money." Not only did I lose $27,000, but then I found out it was actually going to cost $47,000 to get the books printed (this guy didn't represent the publisher very well). Add all that up—$27,000 + $47,000 = $74,000. Just like that, I had lost $74,000—almost fifteen months of income!

You can ask my staff members who were there at the time how I responded. I started to get upset, but probably no more than ten seconds elapsed before I thought of Proverbs 6:31. I took that verse and concluded, "This is nothing but the devil trying to steal from me!" I multiplied $74,000 by seven and declared, "This is how much I'm getting back this year!" Guess what? We came within a dollar or two of that exact increase that year. It was one of the best things that ever happened to me! If you believe that you're blessed, it doesn't matter what people do to you. The blessing of God isn't a thing. It's His divine favor spoken over you, and nothing and no one can take that away!

Outline

I.   Let's review some of the ground we've covered thus far.

    A.   Many believers have settled for less than God's best and don't even think about it.

    B.   Our desire to compromise, to be secure, and to not stretch ourselves out in faith is a hindrance to receiving God's best.

    C.   Receiving God's best isn't about getting the Lord to do something.

    D.   This is expressed in statements like "Faith moves God."

    E.   Faith does not move God.

    F.   God moved by grace, and our faith only appropriates what God has already provided by grace; that's a life-changing truth!

    G.   We can receive God's supply through two different delivery systems—a blessing or a miracle.

    H.   Since a miracle involves a superseding or suspension of natural law, it isn't God's best.

    I.   We can receive a miracle, but to have a miracle, we'll have to be in a crisis.

    J.   A blessing will prevent a crisis.

    K.   A miracle is never as abundant as a blessing.

    L.   A miracle is only temporary.

    M.   A blessing, once it's given, cannot be reversed.

II. Galatians 3:14 reveals that the blessing of Abraham has come upon believers through faith.

    A.   We should want the favor of God that is spoken over us that produces such abundance.

    B.   It's important to remember that blessings aren't things.

C. If something happened and I lost everything, I'd get it back because His blessing produced those things in the first place; it would just be a matter of time.

D. The favor of God is the real asset!

E. There are some people who, if you touch their things, you've touched their hearts!

F. When we have our faith in the Lord, it doesn't matter what happens to our things.

G. If Satan steals something from us, we can make him repay with interest:

> *But if he* [a thief, see Prov. 6:30] *be found, he shall restore sevenfold; he shall give all the substance of his house.*
>
> Proverbs 6:31, brackets mine

H. If we believe that we're blessed, it doesn't matter what people do to us.

I. The blessing of God is His divine favor spoken over us, and nothing and no one can take that away!

Teacher's Guide

1.   Let's review some of the ground we've covered thus far. Many believers have settled for less than God's best and don't even think about it. Our desire to compromise, to be secure, and to not stretch ourselves out in faith is a hindrance to receiving God's best. Receiving God's best isn't about getting the Lord to do something. This is expressed in statements like "Faith moves God." Faith does not move God. God moved by grace, and our faith only appropriates what God has already provided by grace. That's a life-changing truth! We can receive God's supply through two different delivery systems—a blessing or a miracle. Since a miracle involves a superseding or suspension of natural law, it isn't God's best. We can receive a miracle, but to have a miracle, we'll have to be in a crisis. A blessing will prevent a crisis. A miracle is never as abundant as a blessing. A miracle is only temporary. A blessing, once it's given, cannot be reversed.

1a. Many believers have settled for less than God's best and don't even _____ about it.
     Think
1b. What are hindrances to receiving God's best?
     Your desire to compromise, to be secure, and to not stretch yourself out in faith
1c. True or false: Faith moves God.
     False
1d. God moved by _____, and your faith only _____ what God has already provided by grace.
     A. Prayers / requires
     B. Obligation / kindles
     C. Sorrow / validates
     D. Grace / appropriates
     E. Faith / demands
     D. Grace / appropriates
1e. Why isn't a miracle God's best?
     Because it involves a superseding or suspension of natural law

2.   Galatians 3:14 reveals that the blessing of Abraham has come upon us as believers through faith. We should want the favor of God that is spoken over us that produced such abundance. It's important to remember that blessings aren't things. If something happened and we lost everything, we'd get it back because His blessing produced those things. It would just be a matter of time. The favor of God is the real asset! There are some people who, if we touch their things, we've touched their hearts! When we have our faith in the Lord, it doesn't matter what happens to our things. If Satan steals something from us, we can make him repay with interest:

But if he [a thief, see Prov. 6:30] *be found, he shall restore sevenfold; he shall give all the substance of his house.*

Proverbs 6:31, brackets mine

If we believe that we're blessed, it doesn't matter what people do to us. The blessing of God is His divine favor spoken over us, and nothing and no one can take that away!

2a. Whose blessing has come upon you as a believer (Gal. 3:14)?
    A. Moses's
    B. David's
    C. Abraham's
    D. Mary's
    E. Isaac's
    C. Abraham's

2b. What is the real asset?
    The favor of God

2c. *Discussion question:* How do you plan to have faith in the Lord versus have care for your things?
    Discussion question

2d. According to Proverbs 6:31, if a thief *"be found, he shall restore _____; he shall give all the substance of his house."*
    "Sevenfold"

2e. What or who can take away the divine favor spoken over you?
    Nothing and no one

Discipleship Questions

1. Many believers have settled for less than God's best and don't even _____ about it.

2. What are hindrances to receiving God's best?

   _____

   _____

   _____

3. True or false: Faith moves God.

4. God moved by _____, and your faith only _____ what God has already provided by grace.
   A. Prayers / requires
   B. Obligation / kindles
   C. Sorrow / validates
   D. Grace / appropriates
   E. Faith / demands

5. Why isn't a miracle God's best?

   _____

   _____

   _____

6. Whose blessing has come upon you as a believer (Gal. 3:14)?
   A. Moses's
   B. David's
   C. Abraham's
   D. Mary's
   E. Isaac's

7. What is the real asset?

   _____

   _____

   _____

8. *Discussion question:* How do you plan to have faith in the Lord versus have care for your things?

_____

_____

_____

9. According to Proverbs 6:31, if a thief *"be found, he shall restore _____; he shall give all the substance of his house."*

10. What or who can take away the divine favor spoken over you?

_____

_____

_____

Answer Key

1. Think

2. Your desire to compromise, to be secure, and to not stretch yourself out in faith

3. False

4. D. Grace / appropriates

5. Because it involves a superseding or suspension of natural law

6. C. Abraham's

7. The favor of God

8. *Discussion question*

9. *"Sevenfold"*

10. Nothing and no one

Scriptures

GALATIANS 3:14

That the blessing of Abraham might come on the Gentiles through Jesus Christ; that we might receive the promise of the Spirit through faith.

PROVERBS 6:30-31

Men do not despise a thief, if he steal to satisfy his soul when he is hungry; [31] But if he be found, he shall restore sevenfold; he shall give all the substance of his house.

Cannot Be Reversed

LESSON 14

And the children of Israel set forward, and pitched in the plains of Moab on this side Jordan by Jericho. [2] And Balak the son of Zippor saw all that Israel had done to the Amorites. [3] And Moab was sore afraid of the people, because they were many: and Moab was distressed because of the children of Israel.

Numbers 22:1-3

King Balak of Moab was distressed because of God's people. The Israelites had just defeated the Moabites' neighbors and cousins (Num. 21:21-35, see also Gen. 19:30-38).

And Moab said unto the elders of Midian, Now shall this company lick up all that are round about us, as the ox licketh up the grass of the field. And Balak the son of Zippor was king of the Moabites at that time. [5] He sent messengers therefore unto Balaam the son of Beor to Pethor, which is by the river of the land of the children of his people, to call him, saying, Behold, there is a people come out from Egypt: behold, they cover the face of the earth, and they abide over against me: [6] Come now therefore, I pray thee, curse me this people; for they are too mighty for me: peradventure I shall prevail, that we may smite them, and that I may drive them out of the land: for I wot that he whom thou blessest is blessed, and he whom thou cursest is cursed.

Numbers 22:4-6

The Moabites were afraid that the Israelites were going to conquer them, so King Balak sent to Balaam to hire him to come and curse the Israelites so that the Moabite forces could win a battle. This sounds foolish to us today. We look at things like this as being superstitious, saying, "It doesn't matter if someone curses somebody else. People don't win or lose battles because of spoken blessings or curses." But this was the attitude of the people in the Bible, and it's actually the correct attitude.

IT'S AFFECTING PEOPLE

Most people today don't properly esteem words. They just say things and curse other people, and they think that their words are not that big of a deal. People predict pandemics and huge disasters, and everyone's been conditioned to think, *You have to be cautious; it's good to be warned.*

Since Hurricane Katrina, the National Weather Service in Boulder, Colorado, has seemed to predict a terrible hurricane season every year. They've predicted up to fifteen named storms per year since then and seem to always imply that "this year" will be the worst year ever. Those things haven't come to pass. As a matter of fact, we have had only a few named hurricanes in the years since Katrina. These things haven't happened, but people think, *Well, that's okay. We're just erring on the side of caution.* It's not okay. Did you know that insurance rates go up based on these National Weather Service predictions? There are people who lose insurance or pay more for it because of those predictions. We just accept them. They're speaking curses, and it's affecting people.

Folks have gone out of business due to these cursed predictions. It reminds me of what happened in the UK because of mad cow disease. When predictions started coming out about the scope of the "epidemic," you could drive through England and see the smoke rising as hundreds of thousands of cattle were piled up and burned all around the countryside. As they slaughtered their entire herd, people would think, *We're just being cautious.* Well, that kind of thinking drove people I know totally out of business. They were raising these rare cattle that cost thousands and thousands of dollars per cow. The government only paid them a fraction of the value of each cow, so they lost nearly their whole investment! These dire "predictions" put people out of business and ruined their lives. Things were being said that were not true.

Society today doesn't have the same attitude that Bible people had about words—the proper attitude. Words are important. We can bless and we can curse. What would we think today if some country came against the United States and the President hired somebody to go curse the enemy? We'd think, *That's just superstitious. It's not going to do anything.* But there is power in words if a person believes them. Most people don't believe all this stuff today, so it stops a lot of curses from coming to pass. It also stops a lot of blessing from coming to pass too. The Bible teaches that there is power in a person's words:

> *Death and life are in the power of the tongue: and they that love it shall eat the fruit thereof.*
>
> Proverbs 18:21

THE PARENT FORCE

Jesus's disciples were awestruck at how He just spoke to a fig tree (Mark 11:12-14 and 20-21) and killed it. He never touched it. He didn't throw salt on it or anything else. If He had done something in the natural and the fig tree had died, nobody would have had a problem with that. But to think that a person could say words and kill a tree with their words… Most people think, *This is weird.* But Jesus said to His disciples,

> *Have faith in God. [23] For verily I say unto you, That whosoever shall say unto this mountain, Be thou removed, and be thou cast into the sea; and shall not doubt in his heart, but shall believe that those things which he saith shall come to pass; he shall have whatsoever he saith.*
>
> Mark 11:22-23

Jesus was telling His disciples how His words killed the fig tree. People think stuff like that won't work. That's because they doubt in their hearts. The only reason there aren't mountains moving around is because nobody has this faith. Yet that's the power of words!

Words created this physical world (Heb. 11:3). Words are the parent force. Everything on this earth will respond to words—your body, cancer, blindness—anything will respond to words *if* you believe in your heart and don't doubt. This is the proper attitude. Words are powerful, and this example shows us that God takes words very seriously.

"DON'T YOU DARE!"

King Balak sent an entourage to hire Balaam to curse the Israelites:

> *And the elders of Moab and the elders of Midian departed with the rewards of divination in their hand; and they came unto Balaam, and spake unto him the words of Balak. [8] And he said unto them, Lodge here this night, and I will bring you word again, as the LORD shall speak unto me: and the princes of Moab abode with Balaam. [9] And God came unto Balaam, and said, What men are these with thee? [10] And Balaam said unto God, Balak the son of Zippor, king of Moab, hath sent unto me, saying, [11] Behold, there is a people come out of Egypt, which covereth the face of the earth: come now, curse me them; peradventure I shall be able to overcome them, and drive them out. [12] And God said unto Balaam, Thou shalt not go with them; thou shalt not curse the people: for they are blessed.*
>
> Numbers 22:7-12

God takes cursing seriously! He said, "Don't you dare do this!" He could have answered, "It doesn't matter what you say. Do whatever you want because it doesn't make a difference." No, God takes cursing seriously and told him not to do it.

> *And Balaam rose up in the morning, and said unto the princes of Balak, Get you into your land: for the LORD refuseth to give me leave to go with you. [14] And the princes of Moab rose up, and they went unto Balak, and said, Balaam refuseth to come with us.*
>
> Numbers 22:13-14

Up until this point, Balaam had done nothing wrong. This was commendable. This was a great way to respond. Everything was fine.

> *And Balak sent yet again princes, more, and more honourable than they. [16] And they came to Balaam, and said to him, Thus saith Balak the son of Zippor, Let nothing, I pray thee, hinder thee from coming unto me: [17] For I will promote thee unto very great honour, and I will do whatsoever thou sayest unto me: come therefore, I pray thee, curse me this people.*
>
> Numbers 22:15-17

"SPEAK WHAT I SAY!"

Look at Balaam's response to this second group who presented Balak's petition:

> *And Balaam answered and said unto the servants of Balak, If Balak would give me his house full of silver and gold, I cannot go beyond the word of the LORD my God, to do less or more.*
>
> Numbers 22:18

That was an awesome answer! This was very good up to this point.

> *Now therefore, I pray you, tarry ye also here this night, that I may know what the LORD will say unto me more. [20] And God came unto Balaam at night, and said unto him, If the men come to call thee, rise up, and go with them; but yet the word which I shall say unto thee, that shalt thou do.*
>
> Numbers 22:19-20

According to the New Testament, Balaam loved the rewards of unrighteousness:

> *Woe unto them! for they…ran greedily after the error of Balaam for reward.*
>
> Jude 11

Which have forsaken the right way, and are gone astray, following the way of Balaam the son of Bosor, who loved the wages of unrighteousness.

2 Peter 2:15

Even though Balaam had said the right things up until that point, the Word reveals that he was touched by this offer of money, position, and honor. Now he wanted to go and curse the Israelites in order to receive all this gain.

And God came unto Balaam at night, and said unto him, If the men come to call thee, rise up, and go with them; but yet the word which I shall say unto thee, that shalt thou do.

Numbers 22:20

The Lord said, "All right, I'm going to let you go. But make sure you speak only what I say!" In other words, He wanted Balaam to bless the Israelites instead of curse them.

A TALKING DONKEY?

And Balaam rose up in the morning, and saddled his ass, and went with the princes of Moab. [22] And God's anger was kindled because he went.

Numbers 22:21-22

God had said that Balaam could go *if* the men came to call him in the morning (see verse 20). Since there's no mention that they did, I believe that when Balaam saw that God was willing to let him go, he just went. Apparently, he was prone to curse the Israelites. He thought, *I'm going to be able to get by with this,* so he didn't wait on the men to come call him. He was beginning to be self-willed (see 2 Pet. 2:16). He loved the wages of unrighteousness. It angered God that Balaam wasn't following His instructions, and God saw this as potentially resulting in a curse being brought against His people.

And the ass saw the angel of the LORD standing in the way, and his sword drawn in his hand: and the ass turned aside out of the way, and went into the field: and Balaam smote the ass, to turn her into the way. [24] But the angel of the LORD stood in a path of the vineyards, a wall being on this side, and a wall on that side. [25] And when the ass saw the angel of the LORD, she thrust herself unto the wall, and crushed Balaam's foot against the wall: and he smote her again. [26] And the angel of the LORD went further, and stood in a narrow place, where was no way to turn either to the right hand or to the left. [27] And when the ass saw the angel of the LORD, she fell down under Balaam: and Balaam's anger was kindled, and he smote the ass with a staff. [28] And the Lord *opened the mouth of the ass, and she said unto Balaam, What have I done unto thee, that thou hast smitten me these three times?*

Numbers 22:23-28

Amazing! The donkey started talking to Balaam, and Balaam didn't seem shocked by it at all. He just engaged in conversation with his donkey. Some folks think that this is just symbolism, but I believe that this actually happened. Parrots talk. They had an elephant in the Fort Worth Zoo that could talk. A person could say things to it, and that elephant would repeat those things like a parrot would. I believe that all animals used to talk originally. The snake spoke to Adam and Eve (Gen. 3:1-5).

And Balaam said unto the ass, Because thou hast mocked me: I would there were a sword in mine hand, for now would I kill thee. [30] And the ass said unto Balaam, Am not I thine ass, upon which thou hast ridden ever since I was thine unto this day? was I ever wont to do so unto thee? And he said, Nay.

Numbers 22:29-30

Balaam talked to his donkey like it was an everyday thing. He carried on a conversation with her, and the donkey's reasoning was better than Balaam's (2 Pet. 2:16). The donkey was smarter than the guy!

"I WON'T GO"

Then the Lord *opened the eyes of Balaam, and he saw the angel of the* Lord *standing in the way, and his sword drawn in his hand: and he bowed down his head, and fell flat on his face. [32] And the angel of the* Lord *said unto him, Wherefore hast thou smitten thine ass these three times? behold, I went out to withstand thee, because thy way is perverse before me: [33] And the ass saw me, and turned from me these three times: unless she had turned from me, surely now also I had slain thee, and saved her alive. [34] And Balaam said unto the angel of the* Lord, *I have sinned; for I knew not that thou stoodest in the way against me: now therefore, if it displease thee, I will get me back again. [35] And the angel of the* Lord *said unto Balaam, Go with the men: but only the word that I shall speak unto thee, that thou shalt speak. So Balaam went with the princes of Balak.*

Numbers 22:31-35

Finally, Balaam yielded, saying, "If it displeases You, I won't go." But the Lord said, "All right, you can go. But make sure you only speak what I say."

Upon Balaam's arrival, King Balak asked him, "Why didn't you come when I first called you?"

> *And Balaam said unto Balak, Lo, I am come unto thee: have I now any power at all to say any thing? the word that God putteth in my mouth, that shall I speak.*
>
> Numbers 22:38

In Numbers 23, Balak brought Balaam up to a high place where Balaam could see all of Israel, including their herds and livestock, spread out before him. There were millions of Israelites. Balak built seven altars, and Balaam offered a sacrifice on each one of them. Then Balaam went and prayed. When he returned, he began to bless Israel instead of cursing them. Balak got so mad! He said, "I brought you here to curse my enemies, and you're blessing them instead. The problem must be that you're seeing this vast multitude of people and you're just overwhelmed by how many there are. I'll take you to a place where you can only see a small portion of them." Balak took him to another place and built another seven altars. Seven more sacrifices were offered. Balaam went, prayed, and returned again. Then he gave a powerful blessing over the Israelites.

IT WILL COME TO PASS

> *And he took up his parable, and said, Rise up, Balak, and hear; hearken unto me, thou son of Zippor: [19] God is not a man, that he should lie; neither the son of man, that he should repent: hath he said, and shall he not do it? or hath he spoken, and shall he not make it good?*
>
> Numbers 23:18-19

That's powerful! You ought to take this passage, put it someplace prominent, memorize it, and live by it. If God has said something, it will come to pass. He is not a man; He doesn't lie. He does not repent. If God has spoken favor, it's going to come to pass. Would to God that all of us had this same attitude!

Notice what Balaam said next:

> *Behold, I have received commandment to bless: and he hath blessed; and I cannot reverse it.*
>
> Numbers 23:20

This man who was famous for his powerful words—whomever he blessed was blessed, and whomever he cursed was cursed—could not reverse the blessing of God. The greatest soothsayer of his day basically admitted, "I cannot reverse God's blessing."

What does that mean for us today? Once we receive the blessing of God, nothing and no one in Satan's kingdom—including the devil himself—can stop it. God has blessed us, and the enemy cannot reverse it!

Outline

I. King Balak of Moab was distressed because of God's people, so he sent to Balaam to come and curse the Israelites so that the Moabite forces could win a battle.

    A. This sounds foolish today.

    B. We look at things like this as being superstitious.

    C. Society today doesn't have the same attitude that Bible people had about words—the proper attitude.

    D. Words are important.

II. There is power in words if a person believes them.

    A. Most people don't believe all this stuff today, so it stops a lot of curses from coming to pass.

    B. It also stops a lot of blessing from coming to pass.

    C. Jesus's disciples were awestruck at how He just spoke to a fig tree (Matt. 21:18-20, see also Mark 11:12-14 and 20-21) and killed it.

    D. But Jesus said to His disciples,

> *Have faith in God. [23] For verily I say unto you, That whosoever shall say unto this mountain, Be thou removed, and be thou cast into the sea; and shall not doubt in his heart, but shall believe that those things which he saith shall come to pass; he shall have whatsoever he saith.*
>
> Mark 11:22-23

    E. The only reason there aren't mountains moving around is because nobody has this faith.

    F. Words created this physical world (Heb. 11:3).

    G. Words are the parent force.

    H. Everything on this earth will respond to words—your body, cancer, blindness—anything will respond to words *if* you believe in your heart and don't doubt.

III. King Balak sent an entourage to hire Balaam to curse the Israelites.

    A. God takes cursing seriously and told Balaam not to do it (Num. 22:7-12).

    B. According to the New Testament, Balaam loved the rewards of unrighteousness (Jude 11 and 2 Pet. 2:15).

    C. He was prone to curse the Israelites.

    D. It angered God that he wasn't following His instructions (Num. 22:21-22).

    E. The donkey started talking to Balaam (Num. 22:23-28), and her reasoning was better than his (2 Pet. 2:16)!

    F. Finally, Balaam yielded, saying, "If it displeases You, I won't go," but the Lord said, "All right, you can go, but make sure you only speak what I say."

    G. In Numbers 23, Balak brought Balaam up to a high place where he began to bless Israel instead of cursing them.

IV. We ought to take this verse, put it someplace prominent, memorize it, and live by it:

> *God is not a man, that he should lie; neither the son of man, that he should repent: hath he said, and shall he not do it? or hath he spoken, and shall he not make it good?*
>
> Numbers 23:19

    A. If God has said something, it will come to pass.

    B. We should all have this attitude!

    C. Balaam, the greatest soothsayer of his day, basically admitted, "I cannot reverse God's blessing" (Num. 23:20).

    D. Once we receive the blessing of God, nothing and no one in Satan's kingdom—including the devil himself—can stop it.

Teacher's Guide

1.   King Balak of Moab was distressed because of God's people, so he sent to Balaam to come and curse the Israelites so that the Moabite forces could win a battle. This sounds foolish to us today. We look at things like this as being superstitious. Society today doesn't have the same attitude that Bible people had about words—the proper attitude. Words are important.

1a. *Discussion question:* How much do you let words, positive or negative, affect what you believe?
     Discussion question

2.   There is power in words if a person believes them. Most people don't believe all this stuff today, so it stops a lot of curses from coming to pass. It also stops a lot of blessing from coming to pass. Jesus's disciples were awestruck at how He just spoke to a fig tree (Matt. 21:18-20, see also Mark 11:12-14 and 20-21) and killed it. But Jesus said to His disciples,

> *Have faith in God. [23] For verily I say unto you, That whosoever shall say unto this mountain, Be thou removed, and be thou cast into the sea; and shall not doubt in his heart, but shall believe that those things which he saith shall come to pass; he shall have whatsoever he saith.*
>
> Mark 11:22-23

The only reason there aren't mountains moving around is because nobody has this faith. Words created this physical world (Heb. 11:3). Words are the parent force. Everything on this earth will respond to words—our bodies, cancer, blindness— anything will respond to words *if* we believe in our hearts and don't doubt.

2a. True or false: When a person doesn't believe there is power in words, it stops curses and blessings from coming to pass.
     True
2b. The only reason there aren't mountains moving around is because nobody has _____ faith (Mark 11:22-23).
     This
2c. According to Hebrews 11:3, words _____ this physical world.
     A. Cracked
     B. Salvaged
     C. Broke
     D. Evolved
     E. Created
     E. Created

2d. True or false: Everything on this earth will respond to words—your body, cancer, blindness—anything will respond to words *if* you believe in your heart and don't doubt.
    True

3. King Balak sent an entourage to hire Balaam to curse the Israelites. God takes cursing seriously and told Balaam not to do it (Num. 22:7-12). According to the New Testament, Balaam loved the rewards of unrighteousness (Jude 11 and 2 Pet. 2:15). He was prone to curse the Israelites. It angered God that he wasn't following His instructions (Num. 22:21-22). The donkey started talking to Balaam (Num. 22:23-28), and her reasoning was better than his (2 Pet. 2:16)! Finally, Balaam yielded, saying, "If it displeases You, I won't go," but the Lord said, "All right, you can go, but make sure you only speak what I say." In Numbers 23, Balak brought Balaam up to a high place where he began to bless Israel instead of cursing them.

3a. True or false: According to Numbers 22:7-12, God takes cursing more seriously now than He used to.
    False
3b. Balaam was _____ to curse the Israelites because he _____ the rewards of unrighteousness (Jude 11 and 2 Pet. 2:15).
    Prone / loved
3c. True or false: God didn't care whether Balaam followed His instructions or not (Num. 22:21-22).
    False
3d. *Discussion question:* What do you think about a man having worse reasoning than an animal (Num. 22:23-28 and 2 Pet. 2:16)?
    Discussion question

4. We ought to take this verse, put it someplace prominent, memorize it, and live by it:

    God is not a man, that he should lie; neither the son of man, that he should repent: hath he said, and shall he not do it? or hath he spoken, and shall he not make it good?

    Numbers 23:19

If God has said something, it will come to pass. Let's have this attitude! Balaam, the greatest soothsayer of his day, basically admitted, "I cannot reverse God's blessing" (Num. 23:20). Once we receive the blessing of God, nothing and no one in Satan's kingdom—including the devil himself—can stop it.

4a. *Discussion question:* Why is Numbers 23:19 a good verse to put someplace prominent, memorize, and live by?

Discussion question

4b. If God has said something, it _____ come to pass.
   A. Won't
   B. Can't
   C. Has
   D. Might
   E. Will
   E. Will

4c. *Discussion question:* What does it mean to you that God has blessed you?

Discussion question

Discipleship Questions

1. *Discussion question:* How much do you let words, positive or negative, affect what you believe?

    _____

    _____

    _____

2. True or false: When a person doesn't believe there is power in words, it stops curses and blessings from coming to pass.

3. The only reason there aren't mountains moving around is because nobody has _____ faith (Mark 11:22-23).

4. According to Hebrews 11:3, words _____ this physical world.
    A. Cracked
    B. Salvaged
    C. Broke
    D. Evolved
    E. Created

5. True or false: Everything on this earth will respond to words—your body, cancer, blindness—anything will respond to words *if* you believe in your heart and don't doubt.

6. True or false: According to Numbers 22:7-12, God takes cursing more seriously now than He used to.

7. Balaam was _____ to curse the Israelites because he _____ the rewards of unrighteousness (Jude 11 and 2 Pet. 2:15).

8. True or false: God didn't care whether Balaam followed His instructions or not (Num. 22:21-22).

9. *Discussion question:* What do you think about a man having worse reasoning than an animal (Num. 22:23-28 and 2 Pet. 2:16)?

    _____

    _____

    _____

10. *Discussion question:* Why is Numbers 23:19 a good verse to put someplace prominent, memorize, and live by?

_____

_____

_____

11. If God has said something, it _____ come to pass.
    A. Won't
    B. Can't
    C. Has
    D. Might
    E. Will

12. *Discussion question:* What does it mean to you that God has blessed you?

_____

_____

_____

Answer Key

1. *Discussion question*

2. True

3. This

4. E. Created

5. True

6. False

7. Prone / loved

8. False

9. *Discussion question*

10. *Discussion question*

11. E. Will

12. *Discussion question*

Scriptures

NUMBERS 22:1-35

And the children of Israel set forward, and pitched in the plains of Moab on this side Jordan by Jericho. [2] And Balak the son of Zippor saw all that Israel had done to the Amorites. [3] And Moab was sore afraid of the people, because they were many: and Moab was distressed because of the children of Israel. [4] And Moab said unto the elders of Midian, Now shall this company lick up all that are round about us, as the ox licketh up the grass of the field. And Balak the son of Zippor was king of the Moabites at that time. [5] He sent messengers therefore unto Balaam the son of Beor to Pethor, which is by the river of the land of the children of his people, to call him, saying, Behold, there is a people come out from Egypt: behold, they cover the face of the earth, and they abide over against me: [6] Come now therefore, I pray thee, curse me this people; for they are too mighty for me: peradventure I shall prevail, that we may smite them, and that I may drive them out of the land: for I wot that he whom thou blessest is blessed, and he whom thou cursest is cursed. [7] And the elders of Moab and the elders of Midian departed with the rewards of divination in their hand; and they came unto Balaam, and spake unto him the words of Balak. [8] And he said unto them, Lodge here this night, and I will bring you word again, as the LORD shall speak unto me: and the princes of Moab abode with Balaam. [9] And God came unto Balaam, and said, What men are these with thee? [10] And Balaam said unto God, Balak the son of Zippor, king of Moab, hath sent unto me, saying, [11] Behold, there is a people come out of Egypt, which covereth the face of the earth: come now, curse me them; peradventure I shall be able to overcome them, and drive them out. [12] And God said unto Balaam, Thou shalt not go with them; thou shalt not curse the people: for they are blessed. [13] And Balaam rose up in the morning, and said unto the princes of Balak, Get you into your land: for the LORD refuseth to give me leave to go with you. [14] And the princes of Moab rose up, and they went unto Balak, and said, Balaam refuseth to come with us. [15] And Balak sent yet again princes, more, and more honourable than they. [16] And they came to Balaam, and said to him, Thus saith Balak the son of Zippor, Let nothing, I pray thee, hinder thee from coming unto me: [17] For I will promote thee unto very great honour, and I will do whatsoever thou sayest unto me: come therefore, I pray thee, curse me this people. [18] And Balaam answered and said unto the servants of Balak, If Balak would give me his house full of silver and gold, I cannot go beyond the word of the LORD my God, to do less or more. [19] Now therefore, I pray you, tarry ye also here this night, that I may know what the LORD will say unto me more. [20] And God came unto Balaam at night, and said unto him, If the men come to call thee, rise up, and go with them; but yet the word which I shall say unto thee, that shalt thou do. [21] And Balaam rose up in the morning, and saddled his ass, and went with the princes of Moab. [22] And God's anger was kindled because he went: and the angel of the LORD stood in the way for an adversary against him. Now he was riding upon his ass, and his two servants were with him. [23] And the ass saw the angel of the LORD standing in the way, and his sword drawn in his hand: and the ass turned aside out of the way, and went into the field: and Balaam smote the ass, to turn her into the way. [24] But the angel of the LORD stood in a path of the vineyards, a wall being on this side, and a wall on that side. [25] And when the ass saw the angel of the LORD, she thrust herself unto the wall, and crushed Balaam's foot against the wall: and he smote her again. [26] And the angel of the LORD went further, and stood in a narrow place, where was no way to turn either to the right hand or to the left. [27] And when the ass saw the angel of the LORD, she fell down under Balaam: and Balaam's anger was kindled, and he smote the ass with a staff. [28] And the LORD opened the mouth of the ass, and she said unto Balaam, What have I done unto thee, that thou hast smitten me these three times? [29] And Balaam said unto the ass, Because thou hast mocked me: I would there were a sword in mine hand, for now would I kill thee. [30] And the ass said unto Balaam, Am not I thine ass, upon which thou hast ridden ever since I was thine unto this day? was I ever wont to do so unto thee? And he said, Nay. [31] Then the LORD opened the eyes of Balaam, and he saw the angel of the LORD standing in the way, and his sword drawn in his hand: and he bowed down his head, and fell flat on his face. [32] And the angel of the LORD said unto him, Wherefore hast thou smitten thine ass these three times? behold, I went out to withstand thee, because thy way is perverse before me: [33] And the ass saw me, and turned from me these three times: unless she had turned from me, surely now also I had slain thee, and saved her alive. [34] And Balaam said unto the angel of the LORD, I have sinned; for I knew not that thou stoodest in the way against me: now therefore, if it displease thee, I will get me back again. [35] And the angel of the LORD said unto Balaam, Go with the men: but only the word that I shall speak unto thee, that thou shalt speak. So Balaam went with the princes of Balak.

NUMBERS 21:21-35

And Israel sent messengers unto Sihon king of the Amorites, saying, [22] Let me pass through thy land: we will not turn into the fields, or into the vineyards; we will not drink of the waters of the well: but we will go along by the king's high way, until we be past thy borders. [23] And Sihon would not suffer Israel to pass through his border: but Sihon gathered all his people together, and went out against Israel into the wilderness: and he came to Jahaz, and fought against Israel. [24] And Israel smote him with the edge of the sword, and possessed his land from Arnon unto Jabbok, even unto the children of Ammon: for the border of the children of Ammon was strong. [25] And Israel took all these cities: and Israel dwelt in all the cities of the Amorites, in Heshbon, and in all the villages thereof. [26] For Heshbon was the city of Sihon the king of the Amorites, who had fought against the former king of Moab, and taken all his land out of his hand, even unto Arnon. [27] Wherefore they that speak in proverbs say, Come into Heshbon, let the city of Sihon be built and prepared: [28] For there is a fire gone out of Heshbon, a flame from the city of Sihon: it hath consumed Ar of Moab, and the lords of the high places of Arnon. [29] Woe to thee, Moab! thou art undone, O people of Chemosh: he hath given his sons that escaped, and his daughters, into captivity unto Sihon king of the Amorites. [30] We have shot at them; Heshbon is perished even unto Dibon, and we have laid them waste even unto Nophah, which reacheth unto Medeba. [31] Thus Israel dwelt in the land of the Amorites. [32] And Moses sent to spy out Jaazer, and they took the villages thereof, and drove out the Amorites that were there. [33] And they turned and went up by the way of Bashan: and Og the king of Bashan went out against them, he, and all his people, to the battle at Edrei. [34] And the LORD said unto Moses, Fear him not: for I have delivered him into thy hand, and all his people, and his land; and thou shalt do to him as thou didst unto Sihon king of the Amorites, which dwelt at Heshbon. [35] So they smote him, and his sons, and all his people, until there was none left him alive: and they possessed his land.

GENESIS 19:30-38

And Lot went up out of Zoar, and dwelt in the mountain, and his two daughters with him; for he feared to dwell in Zoar: and he dwelt in a cave, he and his two daughters. [31] And the firstborn said unto the younger, Our father is old, and there is not a man in the earth to come in unto us after the manner of all the earth: [32] Come, let us make our father drink wine, and we will lie with him, that we may preserve seed of our father. [33] And they made their father drink wine that night: and the firstborn went in, and lay with her father; and he perceived not when she lay down, nor when she arose. [34] And it came to pass on the morrow, that the firstborn said unto the younger, Behold, I lay yesternight with my father: let us make him drink wine this night also; and go thou in, and lie with him, that we may preserve seed of our father. [35] And they made their father drink wine that night also: and the younger arose, and lay with him; and he perceived not when she lay down, nor when she arose. [36] Thus were both the daughters of Lot with child by their father. [37] And the firstborn bare a son, and called his name Moab: the same is the father of the Moabites unto this day. [38] And the younger, she also bare a son, and called his name Benammi: the same is the father of the children of Ammon unto this day.

PROVERBS 18:21

Death and life are in the power of the tongue: and they that love it shall eat the fruit thereof.

MARK 11:12-14

And on the morrow, when they were come from Bethany, he was hungry: [13] And seeing a fig tree afar off having leaves, he came, if haply he might find any thing thereon: and when he came to it, he found nothing but leaves; for the time of figs was not yet. [14] And Jesus answered and said unto it, No man eat fruit of thee hereafter for ever. And his disciples heard it.

MARK 11:20-23

And in the morning, as they passed by, they saw the fig tree dried up from the roots. [21] And Peter calling to remembrance saith unto him, Master, behold, the fig tree which thou cursedst is withered away. [22] And Jesus answering saith unto them, Have faith in God. [23] For verily I say unto you, That whosoever shall say unto this mountain, Be thou removed, and be thou cast into the sea; and shall not doubt in his heart, but shall believe that those things which he saith shall come to pass; he shall have whatsoever he saith.

HEBREWS 11:3

Through faith we understand that the worlds were framed by the word of God, so that things which are seen were not made of things which do appear.

JUDE 11

Woe unto them! for they have gone in the way of Cain, and ran greedily after the error of Balaam for reward, and perished in the gainsaying of Core.

2 PETER 2:15-16

Which have forsaken the right way, and are gone astray, following the way of Balaam the son of Bosor, who loved the wages of unrighteousness; [16] But was rebuked for his iniquity: the dumb ass speaking with man's voice forbad the madness of the prophet.

GENESIS 3:1-5

Now the serpent was more subtil than any beast of the field which the LORD God had made. And he said unto the woman, Yea, hath God said, Ye shall not eat of every tree of the garden? [2] And the woman said unto the serpent, We may eat of the fruit of the trees of the garden: [3] But of the fruit of the tree which is in the midst of the garden, God hath said, Ye shall not eat of it, neither shall ye touch it, lest ye die. [4] And the serpent said unto the woman, Ye shall not surely die: [5] For God doth know that in the day ye eat thereof, then your eyes shall be opened, and ye shall be as gods, knowing good and evil.

NUMBERS 22:38

And Balaam said unto Balak, Lo, I am come unto thee: have I now any power at all to say any thing? the word that God putteth in my mouth, that shall I speak.

NUMBERS 23:18-20

And he took up his parable, and said, Rise up, Balak, and hear; hearken unto me, thou son of Zippor: [19] God is not a man, that he should lie; neither the son of man, that he should repent: hath he said, and shall he not do it? or hath he spoken, and shall he not make it good? [20] Behold, I have received commandment to bless: and he hath blessed; and I cannot reverse it.

No Enchantment

LESSON 15

Awhile back, we had an office in Manitou Springs, Colorado. A rumor was floating around that the leading satanist in America had bought the house next door and was moving there to establish his headquarters. It turned out to be just a rumor and never came to pass, but while the rumor was circulating, people came to me and asked, "Are you putting your building up for sale? Will you be moving out of Manitou Springs?" When I asked why I would move, they answered, "Because the satanic high priest is moving in next door!"

I replied, "I hope he moves in next door. That guy needs Jesus."

"But he's the highest priest of Satan in America!"

"I don't care," I said.

People who get overwhelmed by that stuff don't understand the power of the blessing. Satan can't stop what God has said and done, unless we get into fear and believe that he can.

"WORK?"

Back when they still allowed smoking on airplanes, I sat next to a satanic high priest on a flight. He wanted to curse me, cut out my heart, and offer me for a sacrifice. We were sitting in the last row of seats, and I was in the middle seat, sandwiched in between this guy at the window and one of my employees who had the aisle seat. The satanist smoked two cigarettes while we were still parked at the gate. The stewardess came by and told him it was time to stop smoking. He just cursed her up and down. This guy was vile, vicious, and mean. He had a beard down to his waist and wore an army field jacket full of holes from cigarette burns. He stunk badly and his fingernails were about an inch long, with green and yellow crud coming out from underneath them. This fellow was grody, filthy, and nasty—and I was sitting next to him.

I started trying to talk to him, inquiring about where he was from and things like that. When I asked, "What kind of work do you do?" he answered, "*Work?*" (Remember

Maynard, the beatnik who didn't work, from the *Dobie Gillis* show? That's exactly what this guy sounded like.) He continued, "Why should I work when the government pays me a good living to get my food out of trashcans? I'm on welfare. This capitalistic system can't function without 10 percent unemployment. I'm just helping the system."

I started telling him about how God created Adam and Eve and gave them some work to do (Gen. 2:5). I said, "You need to do something, not only to be a blessing to others, but for your own self." Then I started talking to him about the Lord, but he wouldn't listen. Although he looked out the window, I kept talking to him. By this time, the plane had taken off, and we were in the air. He just turned around, stuck his nose up against mine, and screamed, "You are speaking to a disciple of the Maharishi," or something like that. He gave out this big, long name that I discovered afterward was a name for the devil. Later in our conversation, he admitted to being a satanic high priest and claimed that he had cut out the hearts of more than twenty people while offering human sacrifices. This guy was a mess! He had just screamed at me nose to nose (literally), and there was hate and fire in his demon-possessed eyes.

What would you have done in that situation? Would you have grabbed the hand of the other guy sitting next to you and said, "We need to pray! In the name of Jesus, we bind these demons…"?

This fellow had challenged me, so I just stuck my nose right up against his and screamed back at him, "You are speaking to a disciple of the Lord Jesus Christ, and my God is bigger than your god!" You should have seen what this guy did. When I said that, he freaked out! Fear and terror came on him. He jumped up, put his feet on the seat, and leaned back against the wall. He started barking like a dog, clicking his teeth, and doing all kinds of stuff. Two Filipino ladies seated in front of us were staring back at us. I could see their eyes peeking over at us from just above their seats.

"SHOOT YOUR BEST SHOT!"

I just lit into this guy. "Your god's a loser. He's a nobody!" You know, we never had a stewardess come back there, and the six rows in front of us just vacated. I don't know where the other passengers went; they were just gone.

"Your god is a loser. What a dud he planted here next to me. You're a sorry representative of your god. You have to eat out of trashcans. You stink. Who would want to serve your god?" I just let the man have it.

It was an hour-and-a-half flight, and we went back and forth the whole time. At one point he stated, "I have to go to the bathroom." He got up and went and when he returned, he was cool. I don't know what he did, but he had calmed down. He looked out the window and commented, "Beautiful day, isn't it?"

I answered, "Every day's a great day with Jesus." At the mention of the name of Jesus, he jumped right back up and started barking again. Then he threatened me, saying, "I've killed twenty-seven people, offering their hearts as a human sacrifice. I can curse you, and you'll be dead in minutes!"

I replied, "Proverbs 26:2 says that the curse causeless shall not come. I dare you. Curse me. It'll come back on you. Shoot your best shot!" I just dared the guy.

THE WITCH MOVED

He declared, "I'd die for my devil. I love my devil. I'd die for my Satan."

I countered, "You have died. You're dead and don't even know it. Who wants to be like you?" I just let this guy have it. Of course, I also told him about the goodness of God and gave him an opportunity to be saved. He didn't take it.

You need to understand that God has blessed you and that nobody can reverse that blessing unless you get into fear. You're blessed of God! He has spoken His favor over you.

R. W. Schambach told me a story about a woman who came to him for prayer. She said, "Brother Schambach, would you please pray that I could get a new place to live?"

"Why do you need a new place to live?"

"The woman next door to me is a witch. She comes over at night and puts powder in front of my door and says chants. Weird things are happening, and I've just got to leave."

Brother Schambach answered, "I will not pray for you. If anybody needs to leave, it's the witch. I'll tell you what to do." So, he whispered something to her.

That night she went home, turned the lights off, and stayed up. When the witch came over and sprinkled the powder in front of the door, this woman opened the door up, kicked off her shoes, and, in her stocking feet, started dancing and praising God, shouting, "Thank You, Jesus!" She defied the witch and the next day, the witch moved.

SATAN IS AFRAID OF YOU!

God has blessed you, and that blessing cannot be reversed unless *you* reverse it. You need to start believing in the power of a blessing!

> *Behold, I have received commandment to bless: and he hath blessed; and I cannot reverse it. [21] He hath not beheld iniquity in Jacob, neither hath he seen perverseness in Israel: the LORD his God is with him, and the shout of a king is among them.*
>
> Numbers 23:20-21

When Balaam said that God had not beheld iniquity in Jacob, it wasn't because there wasn't any. Consider what the Lord said to Moses:

> *I have seen this people, and, behold, it is a stiffnecked people: [10] Now therefore let me alone, that my wrath may wax hot against them, and that I may consume them: and I will make of thee a great nation.*
>
> Exodus 32:9-10

God got so mad at the Israelites that He told Moses, "Get out of My way; leave Me alone. I'm going to kill them all and start over, making a brand-new nation out of you!" The Lord saw perverseness and iniquity, but when it came to the enemy trying to curse Israel, their goodness or badness didn't affect Him. He dealt with them on the basis of covenant. Israel had a covenant with God, and when somebody tried to curse His people, God said, "I have not beheld iniquity in them."

Did you know that God also deals with you on the basis of covenant—your new covenant in Christ? When somebody tries to come out against you, Satan will make you think, *Well, I deserve this treatment.* The truth is, you have a covenant with God. You are blessed by God, and it doesn't matter whether you're doing everything you should or not. Even at your worst, you are better than the devil at his best. I don't care how bad you're living; you have a covenant with God, and you shouldn't be afraid of the devil. Satan is afraid of you (James 4:7)!

DEFY SICKNESS

> *Surely there is no enchantment against Jacob, neither is there any divination against Israel: according to this time it shall be said of Jacob and of Israel, What hath God wrought!*
>
> Numbers 23:23

There is no thing or enchantment that can come against God's people. If you are born again and Jesus lives in your heart, you're blessed. If you can understand and believe that you're blessed, God's favor has been spoken over you. You ought to defy sickness and disease. You should defy cancer and poverty. Those things are curses!

If you're not sure about the truth of what I'm saying, look up Deuteronomy 28 for yourself. Verses 1 through 14 list what God considers blessings, and verses 15 through 68 list all of the curses. Blessings include health, prosperity, joy, peace, abundance, and deliverance from enemies. Curses include negative things such as the botch (boils), emerods (tumors), mildew, disease, and every kind of sickness—even the ones not listed in this chapter (see verse 61). Positive things are listed as blessings, and negative things are considered curses.

Religion has come along and said, "God put this cancer on you to teach you something. He's done this to break you and make you better. It's really a blessing." Cancer is not a blessing! It's a curse.

> *Woe unto them that call evil good, and good evil; that put darkness for light, and light for darkness; that put bitter for sweet, and sweet for bitter!*
>
> Isaiah 5:20

RELIGION

Religion has made many Christians call sickness "good" and healing "of the devil." What? Religion screws everything up.

You're blessed. If you understood what I'm sharing, you would defy sickness, poverty, emotional instability, depression, discouragement, fear, and every other curse because you are not cursed; you're blessed! People aren't walking in God's best, because they've bought a lie that this is just normal and they have to live this way. It's not true. You don't have to be this way. After you have a child, you don't have to have postpartum blues. You don't have to have post-traumatic stress disorder (PTSD). That is a curse. Many people have come to me who have been totally healed of PTSD, and they had been in some bad situations! But they heard these truths, rejected the curse, and started walking in the blessing.

You have limited God. You have not been receiving His blessing. God has blessed you. There is nothing—no enchantment—that can come against you unless you empower it by your unbelief.

Outline

I.   A rumor was floating around that the leading satanist in America had bought the house next door to our ministry and was moving there to establish his headquarters.

A.   People came to me and asked, "Are you putting your building up for sale?

B.   I replied, "I hope he moves in next door. That guy needs Jesus."

C.   People who get overwhelmed by that stuff don't understand the power of the blessing.

II. Satan can't stop what God has said and done, unless you get into fear and believe that he can.

A.   I sat next to a satanic high priest on a flight.

B.   The man wanted to curse me, cut out my heart, and offer me for a sacrifice.

C.   I lit into the guy: "Your god's a loser. He's a nobody!"

D.   Then the man threatened me, saying, "I've killed twenty-seven people, offering their hearts as a human sacrifice. I can curse you, and you'll be dead in minutes!"

E.   I replied, "Proverbs 26:2 says that the curse causeless shall not come. I dare you. Curse me. It'll come back on you. Shoot your best shot!"

F.   Of course, I also told him about the goodness of God and gave him an opportunity to be saved, but he didn't take it.

III. God has blessed you, and that blessing cannot be reversed unless *you* reverse it.

A.   You need to start believing in the power of a blessing!

B.   When Balaam said that God had not beheld iniquity in Jacob, it wasn't because there wasn't any (Num. 23:20-21).

C.   The Lord saw perverseness and iniquity (Ex. 32:9-10), but when it came to the enemy trying to curse Israel, their goodness or badness didn't affect Him.

D. He dealt with them on the basis of covenant.

IV. God also deals with you on the basis of covenant—your new covenant in Christ.

A. When somebody tries to come out against you, Satan will make you think, *Well, I deserve this treatment.*

B. You are blessed by God, and it doesn't matter whether you're doing everything you should or not.

C. Even at your worst, you are better than the devil at his best.

D. No matter how bad you may be living, you have a covenant with God, and you shouldn't be afraid of the devil.

E. Satan is afraid of you (James 4:7)!

V. If you are born again and Jesus lives in your heart, you're blessed.

A. If you can understand and believe that you're blessed, you ought to defy sickness, disease, cancer, and poverty; those things are curses!

B. Deuteronomy 28:1-14 list what God considers blessings, and Deuteronomy 28:15-68 list all the curses.

C. Positive things are listed as blessings, and negative things are considered curses.

D. Religion has come along and made many Christians call sickness "good" and healing "of the devil" (Is. 5:20).

E. There is nothing—no enchantment—that can come against you (Num. 23:23) unless you empower it by your unbelief.

Teacher's Guide

1.   A rumor was floating around that the leading satanist in America had bought the house next door to Andrew's ministry and was moving there to establish his headquarters. People came to Andrew and asked, "Are you putting your building up for sale?" Andrew replied, "I hope he moves in next door. That guy needs Jesus." People who get overwhelmed by that stuff don't understand the power of the blessing.

1a. *Discussion question:* If a satanist were buying the house next door to you, what would you do?
Discussion question

2.   Satan can't stop what God has said and done, unless we get into fear and believe that he can. Andrew sat next to a satanic high priest on a flight. The man wanted to curse Andrew, cut out his heart, and offer him for a sacrifice. Andrew lit into the guy: "Your god's a loser. He's a nobody!" Then the man threatened Andrew, saying, "I've killed twenty-seven people, offering their hearts as a human sacrifice. I can curse you, and you'll be dead in minutes!" Andrew replied, "Proverbs 26:2 says that the curse causeless shall not come. I dare you. Curse me. It'll come back on you. Shoot your best shot!" Of course, Andrew also told him about the goodness of God and gave him an opportunity to be saved, but he didn't take it.

2a. *Discussion question:* If you were sitting beside a satanic high priest during an airplane flight, what would you do?
Discussion question

3.   God has blessed us, and that blessing cannot be reversed unless *we* reverse it. We need to start believing in the power of a blessing! When Balaam said that God had not beheld iniquity in Jacob, it wasn't because there wasn't any (Num. 23:20-21). The Lord saw perverseness and iniquity (Ex. 32:9-10), but when it came to the enemy trying to curse Israel, their goodness or badness didn't affect Him. He dealt with them on the basis of covenant.

3a. The blessing cannot be reversed unless who reverses it?
    A.   God
    B.   Satan
    C.   You
    D.   All of the above
    E.   None of the above
    C.   You

3b. True or false: God beheld iniquity in Jacob (Num. 23:20-21).
     False
3c. How do you know that the Lord saw perverseness and iniquity?
     Exodus 32:9-10 says that He did
3d. How did God deal with Israel?
     On the basis of covenant

4.   God also deals with us on the basis of covenant—our new covenant in Christ. When somebody tries to come out against us, Satan will make us think, *Well, I deserve this treatment.* We are blessed by God, and it doesn't matter whether we're doing everything we should or not. Even at our worst, we are better than the devil at his best. No matter how bad we may be living, we have a covenant with God, and we shouldn't be afraid of the devil. Satan is afraid of us (James 4:7)!

4a. How does God deal with you?
     On the basis of covenant—your new covenant in Christ
4b. True or false: You are blessed by God, regardless of whether you're doing everything you should.
     True
4c. Even at your _____, you are _____ than the devil at his _____.
     Worst / better / best
4d. Who is afraid of whom (James 4:7)?
     Satan is afraid of you

5.   If we are born again and Jesus lives in our hearts, we're blessed. If we can understand and believe that we're blessed, we ought to defy sickness, disease, cancer, and poverty. Those things are curses! Deuteronomy 28:1-14 list what God considers blessings, and Deuteronomy 28:15-68 list all the curses. Positive things are listed as blessings, and negative things are considered curses. Religion has come along and made many Christians call sickness "good" and healing "of the devil" (Is. 5:20). There is nothing—no enchantment—that can come against us (Num. 23:23) unless we empower it by our unbelief.

5a. True or false: If you are born again and Jesus lives in your heart, you're blessed.
     True
5b. You ought to _____ sickness, disease, cancer, and poverty.
     A. Deny
     B. Defy
     C. Decry
     D. Deep fry
     E. Retry
     B. Defy

5c. *Discussion question:* Why is it important to know which are the blessings and which are the curses (Deut. 28:1-68)?
Discussion question

5d. *Discussion question:* What does it mean to you to be blessed of God (Num. 23:23)?
Discussion question

Discipleship Questions

1. *Discussion question:* If a satanist was buying the house next door to you, what would you do?

   _____

   _____

   _____

2. *Discussion question:* If you were sitting beside a satanic high priest during an airplane flight, what would you do?

   _____

   _____

   _____

3. The blessing cannot be reversed unless who reverses it?
   A. God
   B. Satan
   C. You
   D. All of the above
   E. None of the above

4. True or false: God beheld iniquity in Jacob (Num. 23:20-21).

5. How do you know that the Lord saw perverseness and iniquity?

   _____

   _____

   _____

6. How did God deal with Israel?

   _____

   _____

   _____

7. How does God deal with you?

_____

_____

_____

8. True or false: You are blessed by God, regardless of whether you're doing everything you should.

9. Even at your _____, you are _____ than the devil at his _____.

10. Who is afraid of whom (James 4:7)?

_____

_____

_____

11. True or false: If you are born again and Jesus lives in your heart, you're blessed.

12. You ought to _____ sickness, disease, cancer, and poverty.
    A. Deny
    B. Defy
    C. Decry
    D. Deep fry
    E. Retry

13. *Discussion question:* Why is it important to know which are the blessings and which are the curses (Deut. 28:1-68)?

_____

_____

_____

14. *Discussion question:* What does it mean to you to be blessed of God (Num. 23:23)?

_____

_____

_____

Answer Key

1. *Discussion question*

2. *Discussion question*

3. C. You

4. False

5. Exodus 32:9-10 says that He did

6. On the basis of covenant

7. On the basis of covenant—your new covenant in Christ

8. True

9. Worst / better / best

10. Satan is afraid of you

11. True

12. B. Defy

13. *Discussion question*

14. *Discussion question*

Scriptures

GENESIS 2:5

And every plant of the field before it was in the earth, and every herb of the field before it grew: for the LORD God had not caused it to rain upon the earth, and there was not a man to till the ground.

PROVERBS 26:2

As the bird by wandering, as the swallow by flying, so the curse causeless shall not come.

NUMBERS 23:20-21

Behold, I have received commandment to bless: and he hath blessed; and I cannot reverse it. [21] He hath not beheld iniquity in Jacob, neither hath he seen perverseness in Israel: the LORD his God is with him, and the shout of a king is among them.

EXODUS 32:9-10

And the LORD said unto Moses, I have seen this people, and, behold, it is a stiffnecked people: [10] Now therefore let me alone, that my wrath may wax hot against them, and that I may consume them: and I will make of thee a great nation.

JAMES 4:7

Submit yourselves therefore to God. Resist the devil, and he will flee from you.

NUMBERS 23:23

Surely there is no enchantment against Jacob, neither is there any divination against Israel: according to this time it shall be said of Jacob and of Israel, What hath God wrought!

DEUTERONOMY 28:1-68

And it shall come to pass, if thou shalt hearken diligently unto the voice of the LORD thy God, to observe and to do all his commandments which I command thee this day, that the LORD thy God will set thee on high above all nations of the earth: [2] And all these blessings shall come on thee, and overtake thee, if thou shalt hearken unto the voice of the LORD thy God. [3] Blessed shalt thou be in the city, and blessed shalt thou be in the field. [4] Blessed shall be the fruit of thy body, and the fruit of thy ground, and the fruit of thy cattle, the increase of thy kine, and the flocks of thy sheep. [5] Blessed shall be thy basket and thy store. [6] Blessed shalt thou be when thou comest in, and blessed shalt thou be when thou goest out. [7] The LORD shall cause thine enemies that rise up against thee to be smitten before thy face: they shall come out against thee one way, and flee before thee seven ways. [8] The LORD shall command the blessing upon thee in thy storehouses, and in all that thou settest thine hand unto; and he shall bless thee in the land which the LORD thy God giveth thee. [9] The LORD shall establish thee an holy people unto himself, as he hath sworn unto thee, if thou shalt keep the commandments of the LORD thy God, and walk in his ways. [10] And all people of the earth shall see that thou art called by the name of the LORD; and they shall be afraid of thee. [11] And the LORD shall make thee plenteous in goods, in the fruit of thy body, and in the fruit of thy cattle, and in the fruit of thy ground, in the land which the LORD sware unto thy fathers to give thee. [12] The LORD shall open unto thee his good treasure, the heaven to give the rain unto thy land in his season, and to bless all the work of thine hand: and thou shalt lend unto many nations, and thou shalt not borrow. [13] And the LORD shall make thee the head, and not the tail; and thou shalt be above only, and thou shalt not be beneath; if that thou hearken unto the commandments of the LORD thy God, which I command thee this day, to observe and to do them: [14] And thou shalt not go aside from any of the words which I command thee this day, to the right hand, or to the left, to go after other gods to serve them. [15] But it shall come to pass, if thou wilt not hearken unto the voice of the LORD thy God, to observe to do all his commandments and his statutes which I command thee this day; that all these curses shall come upon thee, and overtake thee: [16] Cursed shalt thou be in the city, and cursed shalt thou be in the field. [17] Cursed shall be thy basket and thy store. [18] Cursed shall be the fruit of thy body, and the fruit of thy land, the increase of thy kine, and the flocks of thy sheep. [19] Cursed shalt thou be when thou comest in, and cursed shalt thou be when thou goest out. [20] The LORD shall send upon thee cursing, vexation, and rebuke, in all that thou settest thine hand unto for to do, until thou be destroyed, and until thou perish quickly; because of the wickedness of thy doings, whereby thou hast forsaken me. [21] The LORD shall make the pestilence cleave unto thee, until he have consumed thee from off the land, whither thou goest to possess it. [22] The LORD shall smite thee with a consumption, and with a fever, and with an inflammation, and with an extreme burning, and with the sword, and with blasting, and with mildew; and they shall pursue thee until thou perish. [23] And thy heaven that is over thy head shall be brass, and the earth that is under thee shall be iron. [24] The LORD shall make the rain of thy land powder and dust: from heaven shall it come down upon thee, until thou be destroyed. [25] The LORD shall cause thee to be smitten before thine enemies: thou shalt go out one way against them, and flee seven ways before them: and shalt be removed into all the kingdoms of the earth. [26] And thy carcase shall be meat unto all fowls of the air, and unto the beasts of the earth, and no man shall fray them away. [27] The LORD will smite thee with the botch of Egypt, and with the emerods, and with the scab, and with the itch, whereof thou canst not be healed. [28] The LORD shall smite thee with madness, and blindness, and astonishment of heart: [29] And thou shalt grope at noonday, as the blind gropeth in darkness, and thou shalt not prosper in thy ways: and thou shalt be only oppressed and spoiled evermore, and no man shall save thee. [30] Thou shalt betroth a wife, and another man shall lie with her: thou shalt build an house, and thou shalt not dwell therein: thou shalt plant a vineyard, and shalt not gather the grapes thereof. [31] Thine ox shall be slain before thine eyes, and thou shalt not eat thereof: thine ass shall be violently taken away from before thy face, and shall not be restored to thee: thy sheep shall be given unto thine enemies, and thou shalt have none to rescue them. [32] Thy sons and thy daughters shall be given unto another people, and thine eyes shall look, and fail with longing for them all the day long: and there shall be no might in thine hand. [33] The fruit of thy land, and all thy labours, shall a nation which thou knowest not eat up; and thou shalt be only oppressed and crushed alway: [34] So that thou shalt be mad for the sight of thine eyes which thou shalt see. [35] The LORD shall smite thee in the knees, and in the legs, with a sore botch that cannot be healed, from the sole of thy foot unto the top of thy head. [36] The LORD shall bring thee, and thy king which thou shalt set over thee, unto a nation which neither thou nor thy fathers have known; and there shalt thou serve other gods, wood and stone. [37] And thou shalt become an astonishment, a proverb, and a byword, among all nations whither the LORD shall lead thee. [38] Thou shalt carry much seed out into the field, and shalt gather but little in; for the locust shall consume it. [39] Thou shalt plant vineyards, and dress them, but shalt neither drink of the wine, nor gather the grapes; for the worms shall eat them. [40] Thou shalt have olive trees throughout all thy coasts, but thou shalt not anoint thyself with the oil; for thine olive shall cast his fruit. [41] Thou shalt beget sons and daughters, but thou shalt not enjoy them; for they shall go into captivity. [42] All thy trees and fruit of thy land shall the locust consume. [43] The stranger that is within thee shall get up above thee very high; and thou shalt come down very low. [44] He shall lend to thee, and thou shalt not lend to him: he shall be the head, and thou shalt be the tail. [45] Moreover all these curses shall come upon thee, and shall pursue thee, and overtake thee, till thou be destroyed; because thou hearkenedst not unto the voice of the LORD thy God, to keep his commandments and his statutes which he commanded thee: [46] And they shall be upon thee for a sign and for a wonder, and upon thy seed for ever [47] Because thou servedst not the

LORD thy God with joyfulness, and with gladness of heart, for the abundance of all things; [48] Therefore shalt thou serve thine enemies which the LORD shall send against thee, in hunger, and in thirst, and in nakedness, and in want of all things: and he shall put a yoke of iron upon thy neck, until he have destroyed thee. [49] The LORD shall bring a nation against thee from far, from the end of the earth, as swift as the eagle flieth; a nation whose tongue thou shalt not understand; [50] A nation of fierce countenance, which shall not regard the person of the old, nor shew favour to the young: [51] And he shall eat the fruit of thy cattle, and the fruit of thy land, until thou be destroyed: which also shall not leave thee either corn, wine, or oil, or the increase of thy kine, or flocks of thy sheep, until he have destroyed thee. [52] And he shall besiege thee in all thy gates, until thy high and fenced walls come down, wherein thou trustedst, throughout all thy land: and he shall besiege thee in all thy gates throughout all thy land, which the LORD thy God hath given thee. [53] And thou shalt eat the fruit of thine own body, the flesh of thy sons and of thy daughters, which the LORD thy God hath given thee, in the siege, and in the straitness, wherewith thine enemies shall distress thee: [54] So that the man that is tender among you, and very delicate, his eye shall be evil toward his brother, and toward the wife of his bosom, and toward the remnant of his children which he shall leave: [55] So that he will not give to any of them of the flesh of his children whom he shall eat: because he hath nothing left him in the siege, and in the straitness, wherewith thine enemies shall distress thee in all thy gates. [56] The tender and delicate woman among you, which would not adventure to set the sole of her foot upon the ground for delicateness and tenderness, her eye shall be evil toward the husband of her bosom, and toward her son, and toward her daughter, [57] And toward her young one that cometh out from between her feet, and toward her children which she shall bear: for she shall eat them for want of all things secretly in the siege and straitness, wherewith thine enemy shall distress thee in thy gates. [58] If thou wilt not observe to do all the words of this law that are written in this book, that thou mayest fear this glorious and fearful name, THE LORD THY GOD; [59] Then the LORD will make thy plagues wonderful, and the plagues of thy seed, even great plagues, and of long continuance, and sore sicknesses, and of long continuance. [60] Moreover he will bring upon thee all the diseases of Egypt, which thou wast afraid of; and they shall cleave unto thee. [61] Also every sickness, and every plague, which is not written in the book of this law, them will the LORD bring upon thee, until thou be destroyed. [62] And ye shall be left few in number, whereas ye were as the stars of heaven for multitude; because thou wouldest not obey the voice of the LORD thy God. [63] And it shall come to pass, that as the LORD rejoiced over you to do you good, and to multiply you; so the LORD will rejoice over you to destroy you, and to bring you to nought; and ye shall be plucked from off the land whither thou goest to possess it. [64] And the LORD shall scatter thee among all people, from the one end of the earth even unto the other; and there thou shalt serve other gods, which neither thou nor thy fathers have known, even wood and stone. [65] And among these nations shalt thou find no ease, neither shall the sole of thy foot have rest: but the LORD shall give thee there a trembling heart, and failing of cycs, and sorrow of mind: [66] And thy life shall hang in doubt before thee; and thou shalt fear day and night, and shalt have none assurance of thy life: [67] In the morning thou shalt say, Would God it were even! and at even thou shalt say, Would God it were morning! for the fear of thine heart wherewith thou shalt fear, and for the sight of thine eyes which thou shalt see. [68] And the LORD shall bring thee into Egypt again with ships, by the way whereof I spake unto thee, Thou shalt see it no more again: and there ye shall be sold unto your enemies for bondmen and bondwomen, and no man shall buy you.

ISAIAH 5:20
Woe unto them that call evil good, and good evil; that put darkness for light, and light for darkness; that put bitter for sweet, and sweet for bitter!

Only You

LESSON 16

Balaam blessed the Israelites three different times instead of cursing them. Look at this last verse:

> *And Balaam rose up, and went and returned to his place: and Balak also went his way.*
>
> Numbers 24:25

It appears that this is the end of Balaam's story. Many people think that the sin Balaam was rebuked for in the New Testament was when he went to meet with King Balak and the angel stood there along the way, about to kill him. Yes, Balaam was wrong, and the angel would have killed him, but the New Testament rebukes Balaam for something else.

> *And to the angel of the church in Pergamos write; These things saith he which hath the sharp sword with two edges; [13] I know thy works, and where thou dwellest, even where Satan's seat is: and thou holdest fast my name, and hast not denied my faith, even in those days wherein Antipas was my faithful martyr, who was slain among you, where Satan dwelleth. [14] But I have a few things against thee, because thou hast there them that hold the doctrine of Balaam, who taught Balac to cast a stumblingblock before the children of Israel, to eat things sacrificed unto idols, and to commit fornication.*
>
> Revelation 2:12-14

This is what the New Testament reveals that Balaam did. He taught Balak to cast a stumbling block before the Israelites—to entice them to eat things sacrificed to idols and to commit fornication. Where is that account listed? Look in the first verses of Numbers 25, immediately following when Balaam and Balak both returned to their places.

PLAGUE

> *And Israel abode in Shittim, and the people began to commit whoredom with the daughters of Moab. [2] And they called the people unto the*

sacrifices of their gods: and the people did eat, and bowed down to their gods. [3] And Israel joined himself unto Baalpeor: and the anger of the LORD was kindled against Israel.

Numbers 25:1-3

Moses commanded the elders to go through and kill all of the Israelites who had participated in this idol worship and fornication.

And those that died in the plague were twenty and four thousand.

Numbers 25:9

Here's what happened. Balaam tried to curse the Israelites, but he couldn't do it because God wouldn't let him, so he wound up speaking a blessing. But he told Balak, "You can't curse these Jews. If they are going to be defeated, they must curse themselves. They have to break covenant with their God. They're the only ones who can stop the blessing." He counseled Balak to take the Moabite women and entice the Israelites to come out and have sex with them. Their worship of Baal was a sexual worship. They actually had intercourse as part of the ritual. So, Moabite women enticed Israelite men to join with them in bowing down, eating food, and having sex in the worship of their god. Many Israelites participated, and the wrath of God came on them. The only way God's people could be overcome was if they rejected their own covenant.

This is confirmed in Numbers 31. God had commanded that Israel "take vengeance on the Midianites" (Num. 1-2) as a whole—all of Midian. This was the last instruction that God gave Moses before he died. Well, the Israelites did most of what they were commanded, but they took spoils, livestock, and kept the women and children alive. Moses was incensed.

And Moses said unto them, Have ye saved all the women alive? [16] Behold, these caused the children of Israel, through the counsel of Balaam, to commit trespass against the LORD in the matter of Peor, and there was a plague among the congregation of the LORD.

Numbers 31:15-16

UP TO YOU!

Before Christ came and established the New Covenant, people who gave themselves over to demons through idol worship had no cure. Back in the days before people could be born again, they couldn't be delivered from demonization. Like cutting out a cancer in order to save someone's life, so was purging the human race from demon-possessed individuals back then. It was actually an act of mercy toward humanity as a whole to just kill all the men, women, children, and animals who participated in demonic rituals. This helped keep the evil from spreading further and protected what purity remained.

God had commanded that all the idol-worshiping, demonized people be killed—everything that breathed. Well, these Israelites kept the women alive. They brought them back to be their wives. They kept the children alive too, along with the livestock, and they collected spoils. This ticked off Moses because he remembered how women like these, acting on the counsel of Balaam, had led many Israelite men astray. They got them involved in their demonic worship, and 24,000 people died in the plague (Num. 25:9).

Once the blessing of God is given and activated, it cannot be reversed. No enchantment can come against it. Nothing in the universe can stop the blessing of God—except you. God has given and He will not repent (Num. 23:19). He won't change. You are blessed, blessed, blessed. Satan cannot stop it. Your receiving God's blessing isn't up to Him; neither is it up to the devil. It's up to you. You are the one who establishes whether or not God's blessing comes to pass in your life. You are the one who empowers a curse. It's 100 percent up to you!

"But, Andrew, you're saying it's my fault that things in my life are the way they are." Yes, I am. I'm saying that your life is going the way of your thoughts. If you're just thinking, *I'm only human. The doctor said it's cancer. What can I do? Cancer is incurable*, you're the one who put that value on cancer. You're the one who believed the curse, received negative things, and despised God's words. Deuteronomy 28 says that no sickness, no disease, and nothing that comes against you will ever be able to stand in your way. None of your enemies will ever stand before you. God has spoken a blessing over you. If you don't see that blessing in operation, it's you who chose not to believe. You chose to believe the curse and negative things. You chose to look at things and say, "I'm only human."

I'm not only human. One-third of me is wall-to-wall Holy Ghost! I've been born again. I am supernatural. I'm not going to live like a person who doesn't know the Lord. I am not like my neighbors who don't know Jesus. I am born again. I have God's power on the inside of me. I have a choice. Am I going to believe the blessing that God has placed on me, or am I going to look at myself as just human?

STRONGER

Perhaps you haven't been able to have a child. Deuteronomy 7:14 says,

> *Thou shalt be blessed above all people: there shall not be male or female barren among you, or among your cattle.*

Exodus 23:26 says,

> *There shall nothing cast their young, nor be barren, in thy land: the*
> *number of thy days I will fulfil.*

This is talking about infertility and miscarriage. You have been blessed regarding conception and childbirth. Am I condemning someone who hasn't conceived or has suffered a miscarriage? No. There's nothing wrong with these people, except that they just don't know the blessing. They haven't believed it. The blessing has to be mixed with faith. They have to appropriate these promises by faith. These people have believed a lie that says, "Some people just can't conceive. That's just the way it is." They chose to believe that, but they could choose to believe what God's Word says instead. I have prayed with thousands of people who could not have children, and I've spoken the blessing of Deuteronomy 7:14 over them. They had given up, thinking it was impossible for them to conceive. There are now children all over the world named Andrew. There is a boy in Uganda named Andrew Wommack. Every year I go there and I have my picture taken with him sitting on my lap.

You can be free from anything. Go to the Word of God. Find out what the Lord has said about you and mix it with faith. The blessing is stronger than the curse!

SPEAK THE POSITIVE

Satan curses us. People curse us. They say bad things to us and about us all the time. But unless you respond to a curse in fear, it's causeless, and *"the curse causeless shall not come"* (Prov. 26:2).

Fear is actually faith in the wrong thing. If somebody curses you and says, "You'll never make it; you're going to die," or "It's over; you're bankrupt," you have to believe that curse before it is empowered. If you don't respond to a curse, then it's causeless. It will not come. It doesn't have any effect over you unless you submit to it. You empower the curse, and you empower the blessing.

I know that people don't empower curses intentionally. Most people wouldn't just sit there and curse themselves, but they do it all the time. When someone asks, "How are you doing?" they answer, "Well, the doctor says I'm dying. I have…" and they speak all of these things out of their mouths. They are speaking all of their doubt and unbelief.

> *Death and life are in the power of the tongue.*
>
> Proverbs 18:21

"But, Andrew, do I deny that I have a problem?" No, you don't deny that you have a problem. You see, this is where some people have been turned off and offended. If I had something wrong, you might hear me answer, "Well, I have this, but...." Then I'd turn around and speak the greater truth: "I may have this, but in the name of Jesus, I'm healed. This thing is bowing the knee." I'd speak the positive.

BLESS YOURSELF!

I don't deny the physical realm, but I do deny that the physical realm is all that there is. I don't deny that I have a problem, but I do deny that the problem is going to win. I'm going to win over it. I'm going to speak the faith of God!

So many people are hung by the tongue. They're just speaking what they feel, saying, "Well, they say it's a recession and everybody's going to be laid off. I'm sure that if they lay anyone off, I'll be one of the first." If you're talking that way, you're cursing yourself. "Well, I can't do anything right. I just don't have this. You don't understand. It's the color of my skin. I don't have the education. I came from this background. We lived on the wrong side of the tracks." These are all curses, and you're the one empowering them. Examples abound of people who have defied the odds regardless of color, background, location, or social situation.

Don't curse yourself by saying, "It's because of the color of my skin that people treat me this way." You're allowing that. You're the one empowering that. You don't have to think that way. Bless yourself!

I was in basic training in the army at a time when race relations in America were very strained. The government was coming down on the side of the blacks because of the way they had been mistreated. So, if a white person ever got into an argument or a fight with a black, the whites were always wrong. There was no way to win.

There were fifty people in my barracks—thirty-five black and fifteen white. We had a race riot. They took every white kid in there and beat their head on the concrete until the drain was stopped up with blood. I was the only white who was not attacked. That's because the black guy who instigated it all was a pimp out in the world. Our drill sergeant was ungodly, and when he discovered this fellow's former "occupation," he thought, *You're my kind of guy* and made him head over our barracks. I had witnessed to this fellow. I stood up to him and told him, "This is the wrong way to live." His father was a Baptist pastor, and he knew better. He respected me. Even though he was very ungodly, he respected me.

"GOD HELP ME"

When he and the others got to me, I was the last white guy standing. Even if the odds had been stacked in my favor, I wasn't a fighter. I was just lying in my bunk, praying, "God help me." Every other white guy in there had to be taken to the infirmary. This guy came, grabbed me, and pulled me up. When he saw me, he recognized who I was and just threw me back on my bunk. Then he lay down on his bunk and it was over. God protected me. I'm the only white fellow who didn't go to the infirmary.

The blacks in our adjoining quadrangle took an entrenching tool and beat in the face of the white field sergeant trainee. It killed him. They spat on me and did other things. This was what I encountered in my basic training. The reason I'm sharing all this is because I've had more bad things happen to me by black people than many black people have had happen to them by white people. I'm not mad, and I don't hate anyone who's black. I'm not holding anything against anyone of that color. You didn't do those things to me. I've gotten over it.

If someone has mistreated you, get over it. Release yourself by forgiving them and then move on. You took that offense long ago and you're still carrying it. Put it down. Get over it. Unforgiveness and hatred empower the curse and stop the blessing. I've been treated horribly at times by other people, but I don't have a chip on my shoulder. I'm not angry about it. I'm over it and I'm blessed. Who cares what somebody else has done to me? I refuse to be anybody's victim. Jesus has set me free! I'm focused on the blessing, not on the curse. You are the one empowering the curse over you when you won't let go of the offense you took because of how someone else treated you.

You can't control everybody else. All you can do is control yourself, and most of us could really stand to improve on that (Gal. 5:22-23). Who cares what somebody else has done to you? Jesus is the one who has set you free. You are blessed, blessed, blessed. God has blessed you, and it cannot be reversed! You are the only one who can stop the blessing of God. Whether you're male or female, whether you have an education or not, it doesn't matter what has happened to you; you're the only one who can put a limit on yourself when you believe that you can't do these things.

We need to start believing we're blessed. We need to start empowering the blessing by faith and quit fearing the curse. Let's stop fearing what people have said about us and what they have done to us. We need to start walking in the blessing of God. This is the better way to receive!

"I'M BLESSED"

Knowing that God will never take His blessing off me, even if I don't do everything right, fires me up. Even if I don't live up to His standards, He does not behold iniquity in me. Wow! God is dealing with me based on the New Covenant. I am blessed, and God will not reverse it. He's never going to take His blessing off me. Hallelujah! Praise

God! Can you see now that you are blessed?

God's blessings are voice-activated. You have to say them: *"I will say of the* L<small>ORD</small>, *He is my refuge and my fortress"* (Ps. 91:2). Words created everything (Heb. 11:3). They created you and me and everything in the physical realm that we can see. Words are the parent force. Everything will respond to words. So, start speaking your blessing!

If you ask me how I am, I'm going to answer, "I'm blessed." I've had people come to me and say, "Well, I know what the Bible says, but I want to know how you really are." I tell them, "I'm really blessed."

They say, "I want to know how you feel." Who cares how I feel? I'm blessed, blessed, blessed. I'm the head and not the tail. I'm above and not beneath. Thank You, Father!

"NOT TODAY!"

God gave His Son to bless us. Nothing the devil or any other person can do will ever undo the blessing of God in your life. You are blessed, so just believe it. Encourage yourself. Speak to yourself, saying, "I'm blessed."

When the doctor says that you're dying, say, "Not today, praise God!"

My friend was in front of a doctor who told him, "You're going to die."

He said, "Oh, no problem." The doctor said, "You aren't getting it!" This exchange continued a bit until finally the doctor said, "You're done. You're going to be dead."

My friend looked right at the doctor and declared, "So are you! We're all going to die. But I'm not going to die today!" That was years ago, and this guy is still alive and doing well today.

You're blessed. Thank You, Father, for blessing us!

Outline

I.   Many people think that the sin Balaam was rebuked for in the New Testament was when he went to meet with King Balak and the angel stood there along the way, about to kill him.

    A.   Yes, Balaam was wrong, and the angel would have killed him; but the New Testament rebukes Balaam for something else (Rev. 2:12-14).

    B.   Balaam taught Balak to cast a stumbling block before the Israelites—to entice them to eat things sacrificed to idols and to commit fornication.

    C.   Many Israelites participated, and the wrath of God came on them.

    D.   The only way God's people could be overcome was if they rejected their own covenant.

II.   Before Christ came and established the New Covenant, people who gave themselves over to demons through idol worship had no cure.

    A.   Like cutting out a cancer in order to save someone's life, so was purging the human race from demon-possessed individuals back then.

    B.   It was actually an act of mercy toward humanity as a whole to just kill all the men, women, children, and animals who participated in demonic rituals.

    C.   This helped keep the evil from spreading further and protected what purity remained.

III.   Your receiving God's blessing isn't up to Him; neither is it up to the devil.

    A.   It's up to you.

    B.   You are the one who establishes whether or not God's blessing comes to pass in your life.

    C.   You are the one who empowers a curse.

IV. Your life is going the way of your thoughts.

    A. If you're thinking, *Cancer is incurable*, you're the one who put that value on cancer.

    B. You're the one who believes the curse, receives negative things, and despises God's words.

    C. Deuteronomy 28 says that no sickness, no disease, and nothing that comes against you will ever be able to stand in your way.

    D. If you don't see that blessing in operation, it's you who chose not to believe.

V. Perhaps you haven't been able to have a child.

    A. Deuteronomy 7:14 says,

        Thou shalt be blessed above all people: there shall not be male or female barren among you, or among your cattle.

    B. Exodus 23:26 says,

        There shall nothing cast their young, nor be barren, in thy land: the number of thy days I will fulfil.

    C. You have been blessed regarding conception and childbirth.

    D. You have to appropriate these promises by faith.

    E. Go to the Word of God.

    F. Find out what the Lord has said about you and mix it with faith.

    G. The blessing is stronger than the curse!

VI. Unless you respond to a curse in fear, it's causeless, and *"the curse causeless shall not come"* (Prov. 26:2).

    A. I know that people don't empower curses intentionally.

    B. But they are speaking all of their doubt and unbelief.

    C. No, you don't deny that you have a problem.

    D. This is where some people have been turned off and offended.

    E. If I had something wrong, you might hear me answer, "Well, I have this, but...." Then I'd turn around and speak the greater truth: "In the name of Jesus, I'm healed. This thing is bowing the knee."

    F. I deny that the problem is going to win.

    G. I'm going to speak the faith of God!

VII. Examples abound of people who have defied the odds regardless of color, background, location, or social situation.

    A. If someone has mistreated us, we need to release ourselves by forgiving them and then move on.

    B. Unforgiveness and hatred empower the curse and stop the blessing.

    C. We can't control everybody else; all we can do is control ourselves, and most of us could really stand to improve on that (Gal. 5:22-23).

    D. God has blessed us, and it cannot be reversed!

    E. We need to start empowering the blessing by faith and stop fearing what people have said about us and what they have done to us.

    F. This is the better way to receive!

VIII. God's blessings are voice-activated.

    A. You have to say them.

    B. Words created you and everything in the physical realm that you can see.

    C. So, start speaking your blessing!

    D. Encourage yourself.

    E. When the doctor says that you're dying, say, "Not today, praise God!"

Teacher's Guide

1. Many people think that the sin Balaam was rebuked for in the New Testament was when he went to meet with King Balak and the angel stood there along the way, about to kill him. Yes, Balaam was wrong, and the angel would have killed him; but the New Testament rebukes Balaam for something else (Rev. 2:12-14). Balaam taught Balak to cast a stumbling block before the Israelites—to entice them to eat things sacrificed to idols and to commit fornication. Many Israelites participated, and the wrath of God came on them. The only way God's people could be overcome was if they rejected their own covenant.

1a. What was the stumbling block that Balaam taught Balak to cast before the Israelites (Rev. 2:12-14)?
   To entice them to eat things sacrificed to idols and to commit fornication
1b. What was the only way God's people could be overcome?
   If they rejected their own covenant
1c. *Discussion question:* What do you think about your covenant with God, knowing that if you reject it, you can be overcome?
   Discussion question

2. Before Christ came and established the New Covenant, people who gave themselves over to demons through idol worship had no cure. Like cutting out a cancer in order to save someone's life, so was purging the human race from demon-possessed individuals back then. It was actually an act of mercy toward humanity as a whole to just kill all the men, women, children, and animals who participated in demonic rituals. This helped keep the evil from spreading further and protected what purity remained.

2a. It was actually an act of _____ toward humanity as a whole to just kill all the men, women, children, and animals who participated in demonic rituals.
   A. Mercy
   B. Vengeance
   C. Peace
   D. Wrath
   E. Joy
   A. Mercy

3. Our receiving God's blessing isn't up to Him; neither is it up to the devil. It's up to us. We are the ones who establish whether or not God's blessing comes to pass in our lives. We are the ones who empower a curse.

3a. *Discussion question:* Knowing that you are the one who empowers God's blessing in your life, how are you going to do it?
Discussion question

4. Our lives are going the way of our thoughts. If we're thinking, *Cancer is incurable,* we're the ones who put that value on cancer. We're the ones who believe the curse, receive negative things, and despise God's words. Deuteronomy 28 says that no sickness, no disease, and nothing that comes against us will ever be able to stand in our way. If we don't see that blessing in operation, it's us who chose not to believe.

4a. Your _____ is going the way of your thoughts.
Life
4b. *Discussion question:* In what ways have you despised God's words?
Discussion question

5. Perhaps we haven't been able to have children.

Deuteronomy 7:14 says,

> *Thou shalt be blessed above all people: there shall not be male or female barren among you, or among your cattle.*

Exodus 23:26 says,

> *There shall nothing cast their young, nor be barren, in thy land: the number of thy days I will fulfil.*

As believers, we have been blessed regarding conception and childbirth. We have to appropriate these promises by faith. We need to go to the Word of God. We need to find out what the Lord has said about us and mix it with faith. The blessing is stronger than the curse!

5a. True or false: You have been blessed regarding conception and childbirth (Deut. 7:14 and Ex. 23:26).
True
5b. You have to _____ these promises by faith.
Appropriate
5c. True or false: The blessing is stronger than the curse only if you believe it.
False

6.   Unless we respond to a curse in fear, it's causeless, and *"the curse causeless shall not come"* (Prov. 26:2). People don't empower curses intentionally. But they are speaking all of their doubt and unbelief. No, we don't deny that we have a problem. This is where some people have been turned off and offended. If Andrew had something wrong, we might hear him answer, "Well, I have this, but...." Then he'd turn around and speak the greater truth: "In the name of Jesus, I'm healed. This thing is bowing the knee." Andrew denies that the problem is going to win. He's going to speak the faith of God!

6a.   Unless you respond to a curse in fear, it's _____ (Prov. 26:2).
      Causeless
6b.   True or false: You don't have to empower a curse intentionally for it to work.
      True
6c.   If you _____ all of your doubt and unbelief, you are empowering the curse.
      A.   Recall
      B.   Speak
      C.   Command
      D.   Survey
      E.   Write
      B.   Speak
6d.   *Discussion question:* Why do you think that denying the problem has turned off and offended some people?
      Discussion question
6e.   Instead of denying that you have a problem, what should you deny?
      That the problem is going to win

7.   Examples abound of people who have defied the odds regardless of color, background, location, or social situation. If someone has mistreated us, we need to release ourselves by forgiving them and then move on. Unforgiveness and hatred empower the curse and stop the blessing. We can't control everybody else; all we can do is control ourselves, and most of us could really stand to improve on that (Gal. 5:22-23). God has blessed us, and it cannot be reversed! We need to start empowering the blessing by faith and stop fearing what people have said about us and what they have done to us. This is the better way to receive!

7a.   What do you need to do if someone has mistreated you?
      You need to release yourself by forgiving them and then move on
7b.   According to Galatians 5:22-23, who can you control?
      A.   Everyone
      B.   No one
      C.   Yourself
      D.   All of the above
      E.   None of the above
      C.   Yourself

7c. *Discussion question:* In what ways have you allowed fear to stop God's blessing in your life?
   Discussion question

8. God's blessings are voice-activated. We have to say them. So, we need to start speaking our blessings and encourage yourselves. When the doctor says that we're dying, we should say, "Not today, praise God!"

8a. How do you activate God's blessings?
   With your voice
8b. What will happen if you don't speak your blessing?
   A. It will still work
   B. It won't work
   C. Nothing important
   D. Someone else will get it
   E. God will use an animal to speak it
   B. It won't work
8c. *Discussion question:* How often should you encourage yourself?
   Discussion question
8d. True or false: When the doctor says you're dying, you should believe it.
   False

Discipleship Questions

1. What was the stumbling block that Balaam taught Balak to cast before the Israelites (Rev. 2:12-14)?

   _____

   _____

   _____

2. What was the only way God's people could be overcome?

   _____

   _____

   _____

3. *Discussion question:* What do you think about your covenant with God, knowing that if you reject it, you can be overcome?

   _____

   _____

   _____

4. It was actually an act of _____ toward humanity as a whole to just kill all the men, women, children, and animals who participated in demonic rituals.
   A. Mercy
   B. Vengeance
   C. Peace
   D. Wrath
   E. Joy

5. *Discussion question:* Knowing that you are the one who empowers God's blessing in your life, how are you going to do it?

   _____

   _____

   _____

6. Your _____ is going the way of your thoughts.

7. *Discussion question:* In what ways have you despised God's words?

_____

_____

_____

8. True or false: You have been blessed regarding conception and childbirth (Deut. 7:14 and Ex. 23:26).

9. You have to _____ these promises by faith.

10. True or false: The blessing is stronger than the curse only if you believe it.

11. Unless you respond to a curse in fear, it's _____ (Prov. 26:2).

12. True or false: You don't have to empower a curse intentionally for it to work.

13. If you _____ all of your doubt and unbelief, you are empowering the curse.
    A. Recall
    B. Speak
    C. Command
    D. Survey
    E. Write

14. *Discussion question:* Why do you think that denying the problem has turned off and offended some people?

_____

_____

_____

15. Instead of denying that you have a problem, what should you deny?

_____

_____

_____

16. What do you need to do if someone has mistreated you?

_____

_____

_____

17. According to Galatians 5:22-23, who can you control?
    A. Everyone
    B. No one
    C. Yourself
    D. All of the above
    E. None of the above

18. *Discussion question:* In what ways have you allowed fear to stop God's blessing in your life?

_____

_____

_____

19. How do you activate God's blessings?

_____

_____

_____

20. What will happen if you don't speak your blessing?
    A. It will still work
    B. It won't work
    C. Nothing important
    D. Someone else will get it
    E. God will use an animal to speak it

21. *Discussion question:* How often should you encourage yourself?

_____

_____

_____

22. True or false: When the doctor says you're dying, you should believe it.

Answer Key

1. To entice them to eat things sacrificed to idols and to commit fornication

2. If they rejected their own covenant

3. *Discussion question*

4. A. Mercy

5. *Discussion question*

6. Life

7. *Discussion question*

8. True

9. Appropriate

10. False

11. Causeless

12. True

13. B. Speak

14. *Discussion question*

15. That the problem is going to win

16. You need to release yourself by forgiving them and then move on

17. C. Yourself

18. *Discussion question*

19. With your voice

20. B. It won't work

21. *Discussion question*

22. False

Scriptures

NUMBERS 24:25
And Balaam rose up, and went and returned to his place: and Balak also went his way.

REVELATION 2:12-14
And to the angel of the church in Pergamos write; These things saith he which hath the sharp sword with two edges; [13] I know thy works, and where thou dwellest, even where Satan's seat is: and thou holdest fast my name, and hast not denied my faith, even in those days wherein Antipas was my faithful martyr, who was slain among you, where Satan dwelleth. [14] But I have a few things against thee, because thou hast there them that hold the doctrine of Balaam, who taught Balac to cast a stumblingblock before the children of Israel, to eat things sacrificed unto idols, and to commit fornication.

NUMBERS 25:1-3
And Israel abode in Shittim, and the people began to commit whoredom with the daughters of Moab. [2] And they called the people unto the sacrifices of their gods: and the people did eat, and bowed down to their gods. [3] And Israel joined himself unto Baalpeor: and the anger of the LORD was kindled against Israel.

NUMBERS 25:9
And those that died in the plague were twenty and four thousand.

NUMBERS 31:15-16
And Moses said unto them, Have ye saved all the women alive? [16] Behold, these caused the children of Israel, through the counsel of Balaam, to commit trespass against the LORD in the matter of Peor, and there was a plague among the congregation of the LORD.

NUMBERS 23:19
God is not a man, that he should lie; neither the son of man, that he should repent: hath he said, and shall he not do it? or hath he spoken, and shall he not make it good?

DEUTERONOMY 7:14
Thou shalt be blessed above all people: there shall not be male or female barren among you, or among your cattle.

EXODUS 23:26

There shall nothing cast their young, nor be barren, in thy land: the number of thy days I will fulfil.

PROVERBS 26:2

As the bird by wandering, as the swallow by flying, so the curse causeless shall not come.

PROVERBS 18:21

Death and life are in the power of the tongue: and they that love it shall eat the fruit thereof.

GALATIANS 5:22-23

But the fruit of the Spirit is love, joy, peace, longsuffering, gentleness, goodness, faith, [23] Meekness, temperance: against such there is no law.

PSALM 91:2

I will say of the LORD, He is my refuge and my fortress: my God; in him will I trust.

HEBREWS 11:3

Through faith we understand that the worlds were framed by the word of God, so that things which are seen were not made of things which do appear.

Redeemed

LESSON 17

The only reason you won't prosper is if you stop the blessing of God by believing a lie.

> *I can do all things through Christ which strengtheneth me.*
>
> Philippians 4:13

This verse is a blessing. If you mix faith with what you've read in that verse, then you can do all things. You need to dream big and believe God for big things! His divine favor has been spoken over you.

> *Verily, verily, I say unto you, He that believeth on me, the works that I do shall he do also; and greater works than these shall he do; because I go unto my Father.*
>
> John 14:12

That verse is a blessing. Jesus spoke those words. He essentially declared, "Everything that I've done, you can do." Why aren't we seeing the dead raised, blind eyes opened, and deaf ears healed? Why aren't we seeing miracles happen like Jesus did? He said, "You can do the works that I do."

Almost twenty years ago, I taught on this verse at a church in Texas. From Sunday all the way through Wednesday, I ministered about and emphasized this one verse and it really convicted the pastor. So, the following Sunday morning, he stood up and preached on John 14:12 again, saying, "Do you know what? I've heard that scripture. I can quote it, but I haven't believed it. From now on, I'm believing that we can do the works that Jesus did. We're going to see the dead raised, the sick healed, and miracles happen!" He started speaking this, confessing it, and moving in that direction.

"I'M HEALED"

While he was preaching that morning, a man stood up, grabbed his chest, and fell over dead from a heart attack. A woman in the church who was a registered nurse pronounced him dead right there in front of the congregation, so they called 911. Although the fire station was just across the street, it took emergency personnel twenty minutes to get to the church. While the people were waiting, they didn't know what to do, so they were just standing around, waiting for the paramedics to come. Then all of a sudden, the pastor realized, *This is what I'm preaching about!* So, he bent down, prayed for the man, and the man sat up, raised from the dead, and was totally healed.

When the paramedics showed up, they took the man to the hospital, even though he protested, saying, "I'm healed; I don't need to go!" When the man was discharged from the emergency room and had to take a taxi back to the church so he could pick up his car, he made the pastor pay for the cab fare, saying, "I told you I didn't need to go." This church began to see miracles because somebody started believing the blessing that Jesus had spoken over them.

> *Blessed be the God and Father of our Lord Jesus Christ, who hath* [past tense] *blessed us with all spiritual blessings in heavenly places in Christ.*
>
> Ephesians 1:3, brackets mine

You are blessed with everything! You will never have a need that God didn't anticipate. The Lord is not responding to your situation. God doesn't find out about your problem when you realize that you have it. He already knew these things would happen, and before you ever had a problem, the supply was already created (Phil. 4:19). God provided for your need before you even had it.

ATTAINABLE BY FAITH

Whatever we're going through, we can choose to fix our eyes on Jesus (Heb. 12:1-3). No matter the situation or circumstance, we can decide to keep our minds on the promises in God's Word. It's comforting to know how much He loves and cares for us. It doesn't matter if the doctor says you're dying or if the world is coming to an end, the Bible says,

> *God is our refuge and strength, a very present help in trouble. [2]*
> *Therefore will not we fear, though the earth be removed, and though the mountains be carried into the midst of the sea.*
>
> Psalm 46:1-2

You can declare, "Yet I will trust in You, Lord!" You can reach a place where you say, "God, I don't care what happens: earthquake, tsunami, recession, epidemic, or attack. It doesn't matter what goes on—I'm blessed! You made the supply before I had the need, and whatever I'm going through, I'm going to keep my eyes fixed on You! Nothing will destroy me." You can reach that place. It's attainable by faith.

You're already blessed with all spiritual blessings (Eph. 1:3). It's already done. That right there ought to get you up and shouting! But for whatever reason, this truth just doesn't register with many people. So, let me give you some more specifics, starting with Deuteronomy 28.

First, you need to know how to properly interpret the Old Testament. The Old Testament is not the New Testament; there's a difference. In the Old Testament, blessings were conditional upon a person's performance. In the New Testament, everything is conditional upon Jesus's performance and whether you put faith in Him or not. If you have faith in Christ, then you get everything that God's provided, whether you deserve it or not. In the New Testament, nobody gets what they deserve. In the Old Testament, everybody got what they deserved. A person either had to live holy, or they had to make all the sacrifices and jump through all the hoops to fulfill all of the requirements to be holy. In the New Testament, everything has already been provided for you, and receiving it is just a matter of receiving Jesus. If you receive the Lord, then you receive everything He has to offer.

AVAILABLE THROUGH JESUS

So then they which be of faith are blessed with faithful Abraham…. [13] *Christ hath redeemed us from the curse of the law, being made a curse for us: for it is written, Cursed is every one that hangeth on a tree.*

Galatians 3:9 and 13

A curse was placed on anybody who hung on a tree. So when Jesus was crucified on a tree—the cross—He drew that curse onto Himself. He was made a curse for us and redeemed us from the curse, *"that the blessing of Abraham might come on the Gentiles through Jesus Christ; that we might receive the promise of the Spirit through faith"* (Gal. 3:14).

All of the Old Testament blessings that were conditional upon a person's performance have now been made available through Jesus. Even though we don't do everything right, we still are blessed because of our faith in Christ. That's huge!

"ALL"

Under the Old Covenant, the blessings were conditional upon a person's performance:

*And it shall come to pass, if thou shalt hearken diligently unto the voice of the LORD thy God, to observe and to do **all** his commandments which I command thee this day, that the LORD thy God will set thee on high* *above all nations of the earth: [2] And all these blessings shall come on thee, and overtake thee, if thou shalt hearken unto the voice of the LORD thy God.*

Deuteronomy 28:1-2, emphasis mine

I've actually heard people take these verses and say, "God wants to bless you, but you just aren't hearkening diligently enough. You have to try harder! If you're praying an hour a day, then pray two hours. If you're giving 10 percent, then give 20 percent. Love more, serve more, do more." They teach this, saying that the reason the blessing hasn't come into your life is because you just haven't lived up to it.

Notice the word *all* that I put in boldface in Deuteronomy 28:1. This word doesn't mean "as many as you can," "more than you did before," "more than somebody else," or "relative to someone else." It means that you have to do ALL of the commandments. If you don't observe and do all of the commandments, then instead of receiving the blessings listed in verses 1-14 of Deuteronomy 28, you receive the curses described in verses 15-68. This is how most New Testament Christians mistakenly interpret this, thinking, *No wonder I'm in this mess! I haven't done this and that and this or that.*

Recently a man told me how he was set free from bondage by learning that he wouldn't be sent to hell for smoking. I told him, "You don't go to hell for smoking, but you sure smell like you've been there!" This truth set him free, and now he doesn't smoke. It broke this addiction over his life.

So many people say, "If you're doing this, you're going to go to hell. You lose your salvation!" They base everything on a person's performance. That's because of scriptures like these in Deuteronomy 28:1-2, but we need to interpret this Old Testament passage in light of the New Testament. Now, through Jesus, we have been redeemed from the curse of the Law (Gal. 3:13). You and I are redeemed through Christ from the curses contained in Deuteronomy 28:15-68.

You ought to read that list of curses sometime. It describes most people's lives. Sickness and disease are on that list. Those things aren't blessings; they're curses. People are living under those things, not realizing that they are part of the curse, when they've actually been redeemed from the curse. Those who are in Christ don't have to have the curse in their lives!

NEW COVENANT EYES

The way to read Deuteronomy 28 through New Covenant eyes is to say, "All these blessings are now mine in Christ because Jesus hearkened diligently to observe and to do all of the commandments. Because He did, and because I have faith in Him, all of these blessings are coming upon me. All of the curses that are written here are now turned into blessings. Everything written here as a curse is not for me. I'm not under that curse, so I receive the opposite!"

When Jamie and I first started out in marriage and ministry, we lived in small, bad places. We once lived in a house that didn't have any insulation. When we got the house warm in the winter, the cold would come right back in. The walls would sweat and water ran down the walls, especially in the closets where there was no sunlight. So, we had mildew in our closets. Did you know that mildew is one of the curses?

> The LORD *shall smite thee...with mildew.*
>
> Deuteronomy 28:22

Mildew is a curse, so Jamie and I opened up our closets and read Deuteronomy 28:22. We said, "Mildew, you're a curse." Then we turned over to Galatians 3:13 and declared, "Christ has redeemed us from the curse, so mildew, get off our walls!" We commanded that mildew to leave. The mildew left without us having to spray it or do anything else. We cursed the curse.

You may say, "Well, I don't believe that." Then it won't work for you. You don't believe in the power of a blessing. You don't believe what Galatians 3:13 says, that Jesus has redeemed you from the curse. Jamie and I believed the Word, and because we believed, we spoke to mildew and it left.

You've been redeemed from all of the curses listed in Deuteronomy 28:15-68. You ought to read them and see for yourself the curses you can curse. All of the blessings have come upon you now through faith in Christ. You get the blessing, not because you've done everything right, but because Jesus did everything right.

Outline

I.   The only reason you won't prosper is if you stop the blessing of God by believing a lie.

   A.   This verse is a blessing:

   I can do all things through Christ which strengtheneth me.
   Philippians 4:13

   B.   If you mix faith with what you've read in that verse, then you can do all things.

   C.   You need to dream big and believe God for big things!

   D.   Jesus essentially declared, "Everything that I've done, you can do" (John 14:12).

II.   You are blessed with everything:

   Blessed be the God and Father of our Lord Jesus Christ, who hath [past tense] *blessed us with all spiritual blessings in heavenly places in Christ.*
   Ephesians 1:3, brackets mine

   A.   The Lord is not responding to your situation.

   B.   He doesn't find out about your problem when you realize that you have it.

   C.   Before you ever had a problem, the supply was already created (Phil. 4:19).

III.   No matter the situation or circumstance, we can decide to keep our minds on the promises in God's Word.

   A.   It's comforting to know how much He loves and cares for us.

   B.   The Bible says,

   God is our refuge and strength, a very present help in trouble. [2]
   Therefore will not we fear, though the earth be removed, and though the mountains be carried into the midst of the sea.
   Psalm 46:1-2

   C.   We can reach a place where we say, "God, I don't care what happens: earthquake, tsunami, recession, epidemic, or attack. It doesn't matter what goes on—I'm blessed! You made the supply before I had the need, and whatever I'm going through, I'm going to keep my eyes fixed on You! Nothing will destroy me."

D. It's attainable by faith.

IV. You're already blessed with all spiritual blessings (Eph. 1:3).

A. For whatever reason, the truth of this verse doesn't register with many people.

B. So, let's see some more specifics.

C. First, you need to know how to properly interpret the Old Testament.

D. In the Old Testament, blessings were conditional on a person's performance.

E. In the New Testament, everything is conditional upon Jesus's performance and whether you put faith in Him or not.

F. If you have faith in Christ, then you get everything that God's provided, whether you deserve it or not.

G. If you receive the Lord, then you receive everything He has to offer.

V. When Jesus was crucified on a tree—the cross—He drew that curse onto Himself (Gal. 3:13).

A. He was made a curse for us and redeemed us from the curse, *"that the blessing of Abraham might come on the Gentiles through Jesus Christ; that we might receive the promise of the Spirit through faith"* (Gal. 3:14).

B. Notice the word *all* that is put in boldface in this passage:

*And it shall come to pass, if thou shalt hearken diligently unto the voice of the LORD thy God, to observe and to do **all** his commandments which I command thee this day, that the LORD thy God will set thee on high above all nations of the earth: [2] And all these blessings shall come on thee, and overtake thee, if thou shalt hearken unto the voice of the LORD thy God.*

Deuteronomy 28:1-2, emphasis mine

C. This means that we have to do ALL of the commandments to receive the blessings.

D. Most New Testament Christians mistakenly interpret this and think, *No wonder I'm in this mess! I haven't done this and that and this or that.*

E. The way to read Deuteronomy 28 through New Covenant eyes is to say, "All these blessings are now mine in Christ because Jesus hearkened diligently to observe and to do all of the commandments. Because He did, and because I have faith in Him, all of these blessings are coming upon me. All of the curses that are written here are now turned into blessings. Everything written here as a curse is not for me. I'm not under that curse, so I receive the opposite!"

VI. When Jamie and I first started out in marriage and ministry, we had mildew in our closets.

A. Mildew is a curse (Deut. 28:22).

B. We opened our closets and cursed the curse.

C. We believed the Word, and because we believed, we spoke to mildew and it left.

D. You ought to read Deuteronomy 28:15-68 and see for yourself the curses you can curse.

E. You get the blessing, not because you've done everything right, but because Jesus did everything right.

Teacher's Guide

1. The only reason we won't prosper is if we stop the blessing of God by believing a lie. This verse is a blessing:

> *I can do all things through Christ which strengtheneth me.*
>
> Philippians 4:13

If we mix faith with what we've read in that verse, then we can do all things. We need to dream big and believe God for big things! Jesus essentially declared, "Everything that I've done, you can do" (John 14:12).

1a. If you believe a lie, you will stop the blessing of God, and you won't _____.
   A. Prosper
   B. Recover
   C. Fail
   D. Learn
   E. Yield
   A. Prosper

1b. Philippians 4:13 says, "*I can do _____ things through Christ which strengtheneth me.*"
   A. *"Some"*
   B. *"Most"*
   C. *"Other"*
   D. All of the above
   E. None of the above
   E. None of the above

1c. *Discussion question:* Why do you think miracles, like the ones Jesus did, aren't being seen today?
   Discussion question

2. We are blessed with everything:

> *Blessed be the God and Father of our Lord Jesus Christ, who hath* [past tense] *blessed us with all spiritual blessings in heavenly places in Christ.*
>
> Ephesians 1:3, brackets mine

The Lord is not responding to our situations. He doesn't find out about our problems when we realize that we have them. Before we ever had a problem, the supply was already created (Phil. 4:19).

2a. Ephesians 1:3 says, *"Blessed be the God and Father of our Lord Jesus Christ, who hath blessed us with _____ spiritual blessings in heavenly places in Christ."*
"All"

2b. True or false: The supply is not created until you have a problem (Phil. 4:19).
False

2c. *Discussion question:* Considering the way God's supply works, what does that make you think about Him?
Discussion question

3. No matter the situation or circumstance, we can decide to keep our minds on the promises in God's Word. It's comforting to know how much He loves and cares for us. The Bible says,

> *God is our refuge and strength, a very present help in trouble.* [2]
> *Therefore will not we fear, though the earth be removed, and though the mountains be carried into the midst of the sea.*
>
> Psalm 46:1-2

We can reach a place where we say, "God, I don't care what happens: earthquake, tsunami, recession, epidemic, or attack. It doesn't matter what goes on—I'm blessed! You made the supply before I had the need, and whatever I'm going through, I'm going to keep my eyes fixed on You! Nothing will destroy me." It's attainable by faith.

3a. True or false: You can't always keep your mind on the promises in God's Word (Heb. 12:1-3).
False

3b. Psalm 46:1-2 says, *"God is our refuge and strength, a very _____ help in trouble. [2] Therefore will we not _____ though the earth be removed, and though the mountains be carried into the midst of the sea."*
"Present" / "fear"

4. We're already blessed with all spiritual blessings (Eph. 1:3). For whatever reason, the truth of this verse doesn't register with many people. So, let's see some more specifics. First, we need to know how to properly interpret the Old Testament. In the Old Testament, blessings were conditional on a person's performance. In the New Testament, everything is conditional upon Jesus's performance and whether we put faith in Him or not. If we have faith in Christ, then we get everything that God's provided, whether we deserve it or not. If we receive the Lord, then we receive everything He has to offer.

4a. You're _____ blessed with all spiritual blessings (Eph. 1:3).
    Already
4b. In the Old Testament, blessings were conditional upon a _____ performance.
    Person's
4c. In the New Testament, everything is conditional on _____ performance and whether you put faith in Him or not.
    Jesus's
4d. *Discussion question:* Why do you think faith can't earn what God's provided?
    Discussion question

5.   When Jesus was crucified on a tree—the cross—He drew that curse onto Himself (Gal. 3:13). He was made a curse for us and redeemed us from the curse, *"that the blessing of Abraham might come on the Gentiles through Jesus Christ; that we might receive the promise of the Spirit through faith"* (Gal. 3:14). Let's look at the word *all* that is put in boldface in this passage:

> *And it shall come to pass, if thou shalt hearken diligently unto the voice of the* Lord *thy God, to observe and to do* **all** *his commandments which I command thee this day, that the* Lord *thy God will set thee on high above all nations of the earth:* [2] *And all these blessings shall come on thee, and overtake thee, if thou shalt hearken unto the voice of the* Lord *thy God.*
>
> Deuteronomy 28:1-2, emphasis mine

This means that we have to do ALL of the commandments. Most New Testament Christians mistakenly interpret this, thinking, *No wonder I'm in this mess! I haven't done this and that and this or that.* The way to read Deuteronomy 28 through New Covenant eyes is to say, "All these blessings are now mine in Christ because Jesus hearkened diligently to observe and to do all of the commandments. Because He did, and because I have faith in Him, all of these blessings are coming upon me. All of the curses that are written here are now turned into blessings. Everything written here as a curse is not for me. I'm not under that curse, so I receive the opposite!"

5a. Christ redeemed you from the curse so that you would be what (Gal. 3:13-14)?
    A. Satisfied
    B. Treasured
    C. Blessed
    D. Prideful
    E. Traded
    C. Blessed

5b. Deuteronomy 28:1-2 says, *"And it shall come to pass, if thou shalt hearken diligently unto the voice of the* LORD *thy God, to observe and to do _____ his commandments which I command thee this day, that the* LORD *thy God will _____ thee on high above all nations of the earth: [2] And all these blessings shall come _____ thee, and _____ thee, if thou shalt hearken unto the voice of the* LORD *thy God."*

   "All" / "set" / "on" / "overtake"

5c. True or false: As a New Testament Christian, you still must do ALL of the commandments.

   False

5d. What is the way to read Deuteronomy 28 through New Covenant eyes?

   To say, "All these blessings are now mine in Christ because Jesus hearkened diligently to observe and to do all of the commandments. Because He did, and because I have faith in Him, all of these blessings are coming upon me. All of the curses that are written here are now turned into blessings. Everything written here as a curse is not for me. I'm not under that curse, so I receive the opposite!"

6. When Jamie and Andrew first started out in marriage and ministry, they had mildew in their closets. Mildew is a curse (Deut. 28:22). They opened their closets and cursed the curse. They believed the Word, and because they believed, they spoke to the mildew and it left. We ought to read Deuteronomy 28:15-68 and see for ourselves the curses we can curse. We get the blessing, not because we've done everything right, but because Jesus did everything right.

6a. Why should you read Deuteronomy 28:15-68?

   To see for yourself the curses you can curse

6b. True or false: You get the blessing, not because you've done everything right, but because Jesus did everything right.

   True

Discipleship Questions

1. If you believe a lie, you will stop the blessing of God, and you won't _____.
    A. Prosper
    B. Recover
    C. Fail
    D. Learn
    E. Yield

2. Philippians 4:13 says, "*I can do _____ things through Christ which strengtheneth me.*"
    A. "*Some*"
    B. "*Most*"
    C. "*Other*"
    D. All of the above
    E. None of the above

3. *Discussion question:* Why do you think miracles, like the ones Jesus did, aren't being seen today?

    _____

    _____

    _____

4. Ephesians 1:3 says, "*Blessed be the God and Father of our Lord Jesus Christ, who hath blessed us with _____ spiritual blessings in heavenly places in Christ.*"

5. True or false: The supply is not created until you have a problem (Phil. 4:19).

6. *Discussion question:* Considering the way God's supply works, what does that make you think about Him?

    _____

    _____

    _____

7. True or false: You can't always keep your mind on the promises in God's Word (Heb. 12:1-3).

8. Psalm 46:1-2 says, "*God is our refuge and strength, a very _____ help in trouble.* [2] *Therefore will we not _____ though the earth be removed, and though the mountains be carried into the midst of the sea.*"

9. You're _____ blessed with all spiritual blessings (Eph. 1:3).

10. In the Old Testament, blessings were conditional upon a _____ performance.

11. In the New Testament, everything is conditional upon _____ performance and whether you put faith in Him or not.

12. *Discussion question:* Why do you think faith can't earn what God's provided?

_____

_____

_____

13. Christ redeemed you from the curse so that you would be what (Gal. 3:13-14)?
    A. Satisfied
    B. Treasured
    C. Blessed
    D. Prideful
    E. Traded

14. Deuteronomy 28:1-2 says, "*And it shall come to pass, if thou shalt hearken diligently unto the voice of the* LORD *thy God, to observe and to do _____ his commandments which I command thee this day, that the* LORD *thy God will _____ thee on high above all nations of the earth:* [2] *And all these blessings shall come _____ thee, and _____ thee, if thou shalt hearken unto the voice of the* LORD *thy God.*"

15. True or false: As a New Testament Christian, you still must do ALL of the commandments.

16. What is the way to read Deuteronomy 28 through New Covenant eyes?

_____

_____

_____

17. Why should you read Deuteronomy 28:15-68?

_____

_____

_____

18. True or false: You get the blessing, not because you've done everything right, but because Jesus did everything right.

Answer Key

1. A. Prosper

2. E. None of the above

3. *Discussion question*

4. *"All"*

5. False

6. *Discussion question*

7. False

8. *"Present" / "fear"*

9. Already

10. Person's

11. Jesus's

12. *Discussion question*

13. C. Blessed

14. *"All" / "set" / "on" / "overtake"*

15. False

16. To say, "All these blessings are now mine in Christ because Jesus hearkened diligently to observe and to do all of the commandments. Because He did, and because I have faith in Him, all of these blessings are coming upon me. All of the curses that are written here are now turned into blessings. Everything written here as a curse is not for me. I'm not under that curse, so I receive the opposite!"

17. To see for yourself the curses you can curse

18. True

Scriptures

PHILIPPIANS 4:13
I can do all things through Christ which strengtheneth me.

JOHN 14:12
Verily, verily, I say unto you, He that believeth on me, the works that I do shall he do also; and greater works than these shall he do; because I go unto my Father.

EPHESIANS 1:3
Blessed be the God and Father of our Lord Jesus Christ, who hath blessed us with all spiritual blessings in heavenly places in Christ.

PHILIPPIANS 4:19
But my God shall supply all your need according to his riches in glory by Christ Jesus.

HEBREWS 12:1-3
Wherefore seeing we also are compassed about with so great a cloud of witnesses, let us lay aside every weight, and the sin which doth so easily beset us, and let us run with patience the race that is set before us, [2] Looking unto Jesus the author and finisher of our faith; who for the joy that was set before him endured the cross, despising the shame, and is set down at the right hand of the throne of God. [3] For consider him that endured such contradiction of sinners against himself, lest ye be wearied and faint in your minds.

PSALM 46:1-2
God is our refuge and strength, a very present help in trouble. [2] Therefore will not we fear, though the earth be removed, and though the mountains be carried into the midst of the sea

GALATIANS 3:9
So then they which be of faith are blessed with faithful Abraham.

GALATIANS 3:13-14
Christ hath redeemed us from the curse of the law, being made a curse for us: for it is written, Cursed is every one that hangeth on a tree: [14] That the blessing of Abraham might come on the Gentiles through Jesus Christ; that we might receive the promise of the Spirit through faith.

DEUTERONOMY 28:1-68

And it shall come to pass, if thou shalt hearken diligently unto the voice of the LORD thy God, to observe and to do all his commandments which I command thee this day, that the LORD thy God will set thee on high above all nations of the earth: [2] And all these blessings shall come on thee, and overtake thee, if thou shalt hearken unto the voice of the LORD thy God. [3] Blessed shalt thou be in the city, and blessed shalt thou be in the field. [4] Blessed shall be the fruit of thy body, and the fruit of thy ground, and the fruit of thy cattle, the increase of thy kine, and the flocks of thy sheep. [5] Blessed shall be thy basket and thy store. [6] Blessed shalt thou be when thou comest in, and blessed shalt thou be when thou goest out. [7] The LORD shall cause thine enemies that rise up against thee to be smitten before thy face: they shall come out against thee one way, and flee before thee seven ways. [8] The LORD shall command the blessing upon thee in thy storehouses, and in all that thou settest thine hand unto; and he shall bless thee in the land which the LORD thy God giveth thee. [9] The LORD shall establish thee an holy people unto himself, as he hath sworn unto thee, if thou shalt keep the commandments of the LORD thy God, and walk in his ways. [10] And all people of the earth shall see that thou art called by the name of the LORD; and they shall be afraid of thee. [11] And the LORD shall make thee plenteous in goods, in the fruit of thy body, and in the fruit of thy cattle, and in the fruit of thy ground, in the land which the LORD sware unto thy fathers to give thee. [12] The LORD shall open unto thee his good treasure, the heaven to give the rain unto thy land in his season, and to bless all the work of thine hand: and thou shalt lend unto many nations, and thou shalt not borrow. [13] And the LORD shall make thee the head, and not the tail; and thou shalt be above only, and thou shalt not be beneath; if that thou hearken unto the commandments of the LORD thy God, which I command thee this day, to observe and to do them: [14] And thou shalt not go aside from any of the words which I command thee this day, to the right hand, or to the left, to go after other gods to serve them. [15] But it shall come to pass, if thou wilt not hearken unto the voice of the LORD thy God, to observe to do all his commandments and his statutes which I command thee this day; that all these curses shall come upon thee, and overtake thee: [16] Cursed shalt thou be in the city, and cursed shalt thou be in the field. [17] Cursed shall be thy basket and thy store. [18] Cursed shall be the fruit of thy body, and the fruit of thy land, the increase of thy kine, and the flocks of thy sheep. [19] Cursed shalt thou be when thou comest in, and cursed shalt thou be when thou goest out. [20] The LORD shall send upon thee cursing, vexation, and rebuke, in all that thou settest thine hand unto for to do, until thou be destroyed, and until thou perish quickly; because of the wickedness of thy doings, whereby thou hast forsaken me. [21] The

LORD shall make the pestilence cleave unto thee, until he have consumed thee from off the land, whither thou goest to possess it. [22] The LORD shall smite thee with a consumption, and with a fever, and with an inflammation, and with an extreme burning, and with the sword, and with blasting, and with mildew; and they shall pursue thee until thou perish. [23] And thy heaven that is over thy head shall be brass, and the earth that is under thee shall be iron. [24] The LORD shall make the rain of thy land powder and dust: from heaven shall it come down upon thee, until thou be destroyed. [25] The LORD shall cause thee to be smitten before thine enemies: thou shalt go out one way against them, and flee seven ways before them: and shalt be removed into all the kingdoms of the earth. [26] And thy carcase shall be meat unto all fowls of the air, and unto the beasts of the earth, and no man shall fray them away. [27] The LORD will smite thee with the botch of Egypt, and with the emerods, and with the scab, and with the itch, whereof thou canst not be healed. [28] The LORD shall smite thee with madness, and blindness, and astonishment of heart: [29] And thou shalt grope at noonday, as the blind gropeth in darkness, and thou shalt not prosper in thy ways: and thou shalt be only oppressed and spoiled evermore, and no man shall save thee. [30] Thou shalt betroth a wife, and another man shall lie with her: thou shalt build an house, and thou shalt not dwell therein: thou shalt plant a vineyard, and shalt not gather the grapes thereof. [31] Thine ox shall be slain before thine eyes, and thou shalt not eat thereof: thine ass shall be violently taken away from before thy face, and shall not be restored to thee: thy sheep shall be given unto thine enemies, and thou shalt have none to rescue them. [32] Thy sons and thy daughters shall be given unto another people, and thine eyes shall look, and fail with longing for them all the day long: and there shall be no might in thine hand. [33] The fruit of thy land, and all thy labours, shall a nation which thou knowest not eat up; and thou shalt be only oppressed and crushed alway: [34] So that thou shalt be mad for the sight of thine eyes which thou shalt see. [35] The LORD shall smite thee in the knees, and in the legs, with a sore botch that cannot be healed, from the sole of thy foot unto the top of thy head. [36] The LORD shall bring thee, and thy king which thou shalt set over thee, unto a nation which neither thou nor thy fathers have known; and there shalt thou serve other gods, wood and stone. [37] And thou shalt become an astonishment, a proverb, and a byword, among all nations whither the LORD shall lead thee. [38] Thou shalt carry much seed out into the field, and shalt gather but little in; for the locust shall consume it. [39] Thou shalt plant vineyards, and dress them, but shalt neither drink of the wine, nor gather the grapes; for the worms shall eat them. [40] Thou shalt have olive trees throughout all thy coasts, but thou shalt not anoint thyself with the oil; for thine olive shall cast his fruit. [41] Thou shalt beget sons and daughters, but thou shalt not enjoy them; for they shall go into captivity. [42] All thy trees and fruit of thy land shall the locust consume. [43] The stranger that is within thee shall get up above thee very high; and thou shalt come down very low. [44] He shall lend to thee, and thou shalt not lend to him: he shall be the head, and thou shalt be the tail. [45] Moreover all these curses shall come upon thee, and shall pursue thee, and overtake thee, till thou be destroyed; because thou hearkenedst not unto the voice of the Lord thy God, to keep his commandments and his statutes which he commanded thee: [46] And they shall be upon thee for a sign and for a wonder, and upon thy seed for ever [47] Because thou servedst not the Lord thy God with joyfulness, and with gladness of heart, for the abundance of all things; [48] Therefore shalt thou serve thine enemies which the Lord shall send against thee, in hunger, and in thirst, and in nakedness, and in want of all things: and he shall put a yoke of iron upon thy neck, until he have destroyed thee. [49] The Lord shall bring a nation against thee from far, from the end of the earth, as swift as the eagle flieth; a nation whose tongue thou shalt not understand; [50] A nation of fierce countenance, which shall not regard the person of the old, nor shew favour to the young: [51] And he shall eat the fruit of thy cattle, and the fruit of thy land, until thou be destroyed: which also shall not leave thee either corn, wine, or oil, or the increase of thy kine, or flocks of thy sheep, until he have destroyed thee. [52] And he shall besiege thee in all thy gates, until thy high and fenced walls come down, wherein thou trustedst, throughout all thy land: and he shall besiege thee in all thy gates throughout all thy land, which the Lord thy God hath given thee. [53] And thou shalt eat the fruit of thine own body, the flesh of thy sons and of thy daughters, which the Lord thy God hath given thee, in the siege, and in the straitness, wherewith thine enemies shall distress thee: [54] So that the man that is tender among you, and very delicate, his eye shall be evil toward his brother, and toward the wife of his bosom, and toward the remnant of his children which he shall leave: [55] So that he will not give to any of them of the flesh of his children whom he shall eat: because he hath nothing left him in the siege, and in the straitness, wherewith thine enemies shall distress thee in all thy gates. [56] The tender and delicate woman among you, which would not adventure to set the sole of her foot upon the ground for delicateness and tenderness, her eye shall be evil toward the husband of her bosom, and toward her son, and toward her daughter, [57] And toward her young one that cometh out from between her feet, and toward her children which she shall bear: for she shall eat them for want of all things secretly in the siege and straitness, wherewith thine enemy shall distress thee in thy gates. [58] If thou wilt not observe to do all the words of this law that are written in this book, that thou mayest fear this glorious and fearful name, THE LORD THY GOD; [59] Then the

LORD will make thy plagues wonderful, and the plagues of thy seed, even great plagues, and of long continuance, and sore sicknesses, and of long continuance. [60] Moreover he will bring upon thee all the diseases of Egypt, which thou wast afraid of; and they shall cleave unto thee. [61] Also every sickness, and every plague, which is not written in the book of this law, them will the LORD bring upon thee, until thou be destroyed. [62] And ye shall be left few in number, whereas ye were as the stars of heaven for multitude; because thou wouldest not obey the voice of the LORD thy God. [63] And it shall come to pass, that as the LORD rejoiced over you to do you good, and to multiply you; so the LORD will rejoice over you to destroy you, and to bring you to nought; and ye shall be plucked from off the land whither thou goest to possess it. [64] And the LORD shall scatter thee among all people, from the one end of the earth even unto the other; and there thou shalt serve other gods, which neither thou nor thy fathers have known, even wood and stone. [65] And among these nations shalt thou find no ease, neither shall the sole of thy foot have rest: but the LORD shall give thee there a trembling heart, and failing of eyes, and sorrow of mind: [66] And thy life shall hang in doubt before thee; and thou shalt fear day and night, and shalt have none assurance of thy life: [67] In the morning thou shalt say, Would God it were even! and at even thou shalt say, Would God it were morning! for the fear of thine heart wherewith thou shalt fear, and for the sight of thine eyes which thou shalt see. [68] And the LORD shall bring thee into Egypt again with ships, by the way whereof I spake unto thee, Thou shalt see it no more again: and there ye shall be sold unto your enemies for bondmen and bondwomen, and no man shall buy you.

Choose Life

LESSON 18

Blessed shalt thou be in the city, and blessed shalt thou be in the field.

Deuteronomy 28:3

Regardless of where you live, you're blessed. Some people think, *Well, I can't prosper and make it out here in the country. I have to move into the city to find a job.* If you'd believe the Word of God, you could be blessed in the field. Others think, *I live in the city, and it's so poor. There's such hardship here. I need to leave the city.* No, you're blessed in the city, and you're blessed in the field. It doesn't matter where you are. Your location doesn't determine your prosperity if you would believe God (Deut. 28:3).

Blessed shall be the fruit of thy body, and the fruit of thy ground, and the fruit of thy cattle, the increase of thy kine, and the flocks of thy sheep.

Deuteronomy 28:4

This verse is saying that you and all that's yours will be fruitful in every way. You'll have children. Your ground will be blessed. Your crops and trees will be blessed. Your animals will be blessed. You can use this verse to pray over your dog, cat, goldfish, or whatever else you have. They're blessed because they belong to you!

PECAN TREES

When Jamie and I first got married, we didn't have any money. My mother actually kept us alive, but she didn't know it. We didn't tell her our situation. I'd go over and mow the lawn for her, and she'd fix us a meal. Sometimes that was the only time we'd eat for days. I was just so grateful and appreciative.

There were twenty-three pecan trees in my mother's yard. When my dad was alive, he pruned, fertilized, and sprayed them. We would harvest 300 or 400 pounds of pecans every year. But after my dad died, my mother just let the trees go. They got bagworms in them and only produced about 50 pounds of pecans one year.

As I was mowing my mother's yard, I stood on this scripture in Deuteronomy 28:4 and combined it with Deuteronomy 28:8:

The LORD shall command the blessing upon thee in thy storehouses, and in all that thou settest thine hand unto; and he shall bless thee in the land which the LORD thy God giveth thee.

I declared, "Blessed is the fruit of my ground. Everything I set my hands unto is blessed!" As I mowed around those trees, I laid my hands on them and blessed them. I cursed the bagworms and commanded them to get out. Even though we didn't spray the trees or fertilize or do anything like that, over 600 pounds of pecans were harvested that year. You might say, "Well, I don't believe that." Then it won't work for you. But I'm telling you how to operate in the blessing.

According to Deuteronomy 28:8, everything you set your hand unto is blessed. If you would believe that, you could bless your plants and speak life over your flowers. Maybe you're someone who has a black thumb instead of a green thumb and everything you plant dies. You could reverse that curse. Quit saying, "I can't grow anything!" Start speaking a blessing instead and declare, "I don't care what I do, it'll be blessed!" You could begin growing things. Some folks have spent decades cursing themselves, yet they wonder why things are the way they say they are. It's because they're hung by their tongues!

YOUR STOREHOUSE

Blessed shall be thy basket and thy store.

Deuteronomy 28:5

God can't bless your storehouse if you don't have one. If you don't have any extra set aside somewhere, the Lord can't bless it.

God taught Al Jandl, a friend of mine from Texas, this truth in a very personal and powerful way. He's even written a book about it entitled *The Storehouse Principle*. The Lord told Al that He couldn't bless his storehouse because he didn't have one. At that time, Al was living hand to mouth, so do you know what he did? He took one dollar and opened up a savings account. Then every week, he put another dollar in it. Most people would look at this and say, "That won't amount to anything much—just fifty-two dollars in a year. What'll that do?" Well, it's a storehouse, and God can bless it. But one hundred times zero is zero.

Al started putting one dollar a week in his savings account, and within a short period of time, God began to bless him supernaturally. Now he has a facility that seats over 2,000 people (my estimate) set on something like 150 acres near Houston, Texas. He's got something like an amusement park on his land, as well as dormitories. He has what is probably a $40 or $50 million facility that's completely debt free because he started taking one dollar a week, putting it aside, and letting God bless it.

The Lord will bless your savings—your storehouse (Deut. 28:5). However, He can't bless what you don't have. You need to start some savings (Deut. 28:8). The Lord will bless your basket and your storehouse!

COMING OR GOING

Blessed shalt thou be when thou comest in, and blessed shalt thou be when thou goest out.

Deuteronomy 28:6

We used to have doormats at the entrance to our ministry that read "Blessed Coming In" on one side of the door and "Blessed Going Out" on the other. What a great reminder. Every time we walked in or out of those doors, we saw the mats. You need to remind yourself that it doesn't matter whether you are coming or going—you're blessed. You are blessed anywhere you are (Deut. 28:3 and 6).

Every time someone asks me how I am, I answer, "I'm blessed." I've said that probably twenty times a day for thirty years. Figure that out: 20 x 365 x 30 = 219,000. I believe what I say, and I've spoken this over and over again for many years. Do you know what? I'm blessed!

You may think, *But, Andrew, I'm not blessed.* Well, that's what you believe. If you're born again, then you're blessed through Jesus whether you know it and believe it or not. God told you to choose:

I call heaven and earth to record this day against you, that I have set before you life and death, blessing and cursing: therefore choose life.

Deuteronomy 30:19

God gives you the answer: Choose life. Choose blessing. It's your choice. Since we get to choose, I've chosen—and continue to choose—to be blessed.

VOICE-ACTIVATED

"Well, Andrew, I didn't choose to be cursed." Yes, you did. You may not have welcomed it or liked it, but you chose to think that you're only human. You chose to believe, "I can't choose between life and death, blessing and cursing. I can't help it." You can choose to believe that you're blessed. It's up to you. You can be blessed coming in and blessed going out (Deut. 28:6).

> *The LORD shall cause thine enemies that rise up against thee to be smitten before thy face: they shall come out against thee one way, and flee before thee seven ways.*
>
> Deuteronomy 28:7

That's powerful, and *"thine enemies"* isn't only talking about people. *"Thine enemies"* could be poverty, sickness, worry, stress, and anything else that's against you. It will not prosper! (See Ephesians 6:11-13.)

> *No weapon that is formed against thee shall prosper; and every tongue that shall rise against thee in judgment thou shalt condemn. This is the heritage of the servants of the LORD, and their righteousness is of me, saith the LORD.*
>
> Isaiah 54:17

This blessing is yours!

> *The LORD shall command the blessing upon thee.*
>
> Deuteronomy 28:8a

I like that. Verse 8 agrees with verse 2 of the same chapter:

> *And all these blessings shall come on thee, and overtake thee.*
>
> Deuteronomy 28:2

This doesn't mean we run from meeting to meeting with our tongues hanging out, chasing the blessing and saying, "I'm worn out trying to get blessed." No, the blessings will chase us! They'll come upon and overtake us. We can't outrun the blessing of God. The blessing of God is pursuing us, chasing us, and trying to get us blessed. But we have to cooperate. We have to believe and start speaking it. The blessings of God are voice-activated.

"DEPART FROM US"

> *The LORD shall command the blessing upon thee in thy storehouses, and in all that thou settest thine hand unto.*
>
> Deuteronomy 28:8

I've already mentioned this, but God doesn't have anything to bless if you aren't setting your hand unto something. One hundred times zero is zero. Some people collect welfare, unemployment, and things like that, and they won't work. That's because in the United States, a person can make more money off of welfare than by going out and getting a job at McDonald's. The difference is, God can't bless welfare and unemployment because the person collecting it isn't doing anything. A person can prosper more by working at McDonald's—even though they may take a cut in their welfare payment—because they're doing something and God can multiply that, but He can't multiply welfare. It's the truth. You can reject it if you want to, but I'm not going to reject it for you. I'm telling you the truth from God's Word.

> *The LORD shall establish thee an holy people unto himself, as he hath sworn unto thee, if thou shalt keep the commandments of the LORD thy God, and walk in his ways. [10] And all people of the earth shall see that thou art called by the name of the LORD; and they shall be afraid of thee.*
>
> Deuteronomy 28:9-10

How many people have come up to you and said, "You're one of those Christians. I can tell because you're blessed of God"? Isaac had a king ask him to leave because he was mightier and wealthier than that king's whole nation (Gen. 26:12-17). The king said, "Depart from us. We can't handle it." This is the way it's supposed to be. People should be able to recognize the blessing and power of God operating in your life.

God wants you to be so blessed that other people can see it. It may take a while because there's got to be a time of renewing your mind and of sowing and reaping. You don't just jump into this automatically, but this ought to be your goal. You ought to be saying, "I'm blessed of God, and everybody's going to see it. It will manifest, and they'll recognize the Lord's blessing in my life." All glory to Jesus!

BREAK THAT DROUGHT

> *And the LORD shall make thee plenteous in goods, in the fruit of thy body, and in the fruit of thy cattle, and in the fruit of thy ground, in the land which the LORD sware unto thy fathers to give thee. [12] The LORD shall open unto thee his good treasure, the heaven to give the rain unto thy land in his season, and to bless all the work of thine hand: and thou shalt lend unto many nations, and thou shalt not borrow.*
>
> Deuteronomy 28:11-12

These verses are powerful! God will open up the rain. There's no reason for a drought. You can break droughts. Jamie and I have done this in different places where we've pastored. We've prayed and broken droughts.

When our kids were little, we had a picnic at John Martin Reservoir. Normally the reservoir was a huge body of water because the Arkansas River ran through it; a person could hardly see to the other side. But Colorado was in a drought at that time, so we actually walked down into the reservoir and stepped across the Arkansas River. It was just a trickle.

I got our church together, and we started praying. We took authority, stood on this verse, and broke that drought. I remember standing there and specifically saying, "John Martin Reservoir will never be empty again," and I blessed that place. Guess what? It started raining. That was back in 1978. The reservoir filled up and has never been empty again. It's blessed!

You can do that too. "Yeah, sure, Andrew. You think your prayers did that?" Yes, I certainly do! What's the point in praying if I don't think that God is going to answer me? I may not have been the only one who prayed, but I believe that my prayer and faith made a difference. Yours can too.

LEAD DOG

And the Lord *shall make thee the head, and not the tail; and thou shalt be above only, and thou shalt not be beneath; if that thou hearken unto the commandments of the* Lord *thy God, which I command thee this day, to observe and to do them.*

Deuteronomy 28:13

You are supposed to be the head and not the tail. It's like those dogs that pull sleds; if a dog isn't the lead dog, the scenery never changes. Think about that. You need to be at the head of the parade. That's the only way you'll ever get a different view of anything. You need to be the head and not the tail.

You should be above and not beneath. When I ask someone how they're doing and they answer "Not too bad, under the circumstances," it makes me wonder, *Well, what are you doing down there UNDER the circumstances?* You're supposed to be above only and not beneath. You have no business being **under** the circumstances!

Are you the head and not the tail? Are you above and not beneath? That's what the Lord says you are to be, and those are blessings. Why don't you receive them? You choose between life or death, a blessing or a curse (Deut. 30:19). You can choose to be the head and not the tail. You can choose to be above and not beneath. You don't have to let life knock the wind out of you, keeping you down and under, the way it does other people. You are the blessed of the Lord!

"WHY DID YOU LET THIS HAPPEN?"

People come to me all the time with their sob stories. On the verge of tears, they tell me how pitiful their situations are, hoping to solicit some sympathy, compassion, and help from me. Instead, the spirit of slap comes all over me. I look at them and say something like, "Why did you let this happen? Why did you let things get out of hand?" They respond, "Oh, I don't have any control over that!"

If that's you, then you don't believe that you're blessed, and that is why you're letting all of these things oppress you. You believe you just have to live under the curse and do with less because, after all, you're only human. I'm not only human. One-third of me is wall-to-wall Holy Ghost. I'm the head and not the tail. I'm above and not beneath. I'm blessed!

I encourage you to read all of Deuteronomy 28, mining it for all of the blessings. And remember, anything you can see that was a curse, you don't have to have it. Through Christ, the curses have been turned into blessings. You can believe and receive the opposite. You're blessed!

Outline

I. Regardless of where you live, you're blessed:

Blessed shalt thou be in the city, and blessed shalt thou be in the field.
Deuteronomy 28:3

    A. Your location doesn't determine your prosperity if you would believe God.

    B. You and all that's yours will be fruitful in every way:

Blessed shall be the fruit of thy body, and the fruit of thy ground, and the fruit of thy cattle, the increase of thy kine, and the flocks of thy sheep.
Deuteronomy 28:4

    C. You can use this verse to pray over your dog, cat, goldfish, or whatever else you have.

    D. They're blessed because they belong to you!

II. God can't bless your storehouse if you don't have one:

Blessed shall be thy basket and thy store.
Deuteronomy 28:5

    A. If you don't have any extra set aside somewhere, the Lord can't bless it.

    B. The Lord will bless your savings—your storehouse.

    C. You need to start some savings.

III. We need to remind ourselves that it doesn't matter whether we are coming or going—we're blessed:

Blessed shalt thou be when thou comest in, and blessed shalt thou be when thou goest out.
Deuteronomy 28:6

    A. We are blessed anywhere we are.

    B. If we're born again, then we're blessed through Jesus whether or not we know it and believe it.

C. God told us to choose (Deut. 30:19).

D. Since we get to choose, we must choose—and continue to choose—to be blessed.

IV. This is powerful:

> *The LORD shall cause thine enemies that rise up against thee to be smitten before thy face: they shall come out against thee one way, and flee before thee seven ways.*
>
> Deuteronomy 28:7

A. *"Thine enemies"* isn't only talking about people.

B. *"Thine enemies"* could be poverty, sickness, worry, stress, and anything else that's against you.

C. They will not prosper (Is. 54:17)!

V. Verse 8 agrees with verse 2 of the same chapter:

> *The LORD shall command the blessing upon thee.*
>
> Deuteronomy 28:8a

> *And all these blessings shall come on thee, and overtake thee.*
>
> Deuteronomy 28:2

A. We can't outrun the blessing of God.

B. The blessing of God is pursuing us, chasing us, and trying to get us blessed.

C. But we have to cooperate.

D. We have to believe and start speaking it.

E. The blessings of God are voice-activated.

VI. God doesn't have anything to bless if you aren't setting your hand unto something:

> *The LORD shall command the blessing upon thee in thy storehouses, and in all that thou settest thine hand unto.*
>
> Deuteronomy 28:8

A. One hundred times zero is zero.

B. A person can prosper more by working at McDonald's—even though they may take a cut in their welfare payment—because they're doing something, and God can multiply that.

C. But He can't multiply welfare.

D. You can reject it if you want to, but it's the truth.

VII. Isaac had a king ask him to leave because he was mightier and wealthier than that king's whole nation (Gen. 26:12-17).

A. This is the way it's supposed to be.

B. God wants you to be so blessed that other people can see it:

> *The LORD shall establish thee an holy people unto himself, as he hath sworn unto thee, if thou shalt keep the commandments of the LORD thy God, and walk in his ways. [10] And all people of the earth shall see that thou art called by the name of the LORD; and they shall be afraid of thee.*
>
> Deuteronomy 28:9-10

C. It may take a while because there's got to be a time of renewing your mind and of sowing and reaping.

D. You don't just jump into this automatically, but this ought to be your goal.

E. You ought to be saying, "I'm blessed of God, and everybody's going to see it. It will manifest, and they'll recognize the Lord's blessing in my life."

F. All glory to Jesus!

VIII. These verses are powerful:

> *And the LORD shall make thee plenteous in goods, in the fruit of thy body, and in the fruit of thy cattle, and in the fruit of thy ground, in the land which the LORD sware unto thy fathers to give thee. [12] The LORD*

shall open unto thee his good treasure, the heaven to give the rain unto thy land in his season, and to bless all the work of thine hand: and thou shalt lend unto many nations, and thou shalt not borrow.

Deuteronomy 28:11-12

    A. You can break droughts.

    B. Jamie and I have prayed and broken droughts.

    C. We may not have been the only ones who prayed, but I believe that our prayer and faith made a difference.

    D. Yours can too.

IX. You are supposed to be the head and not the tail:

And the Lord *shall make thee the head, and not the tail; and thou shalt be above only, and thou shalt not be beneath; if that thou hearken unto the commandments of the* Lord *thy God, which I command thee this day, to observe and to do them.*

Deuteronomy 28:13

    A. When I ask someone how they're doing, and they answer, "Not too bad, under the circumstances," it makes me wonder, *Well, what are you doing down there?*

    B. You're supposed to be above only and not beneath.

    C. You have no business being **under** the circumstances!

    D. The head and not the tail, above and not beneath—that's what the Lord says you are to be, and those are blessings.

    E. You don't have to let life knock the wind out of you, keeping you down and under, the way it does other people.

X. Read all of Deuteronomy 28 to mine it for all of the blessings.

    A. And remember, anything you can see that was a curse, you don't have to have it.

    B. Through Christ, the curses have been turned into blessings.

C. You can believe and receive the opposite.

D. You're blessed!

Teacher's Guide

1.   Regardless of where we live, we're blessed:

Blessed shalt thou be in the city, and blessed shalt thou be in the field.
Deuteronomy 28:3

Our locations don't determine our prosperity if we would believe God. We and all that's ours will be fruitful in every way:

Blessed shall be the fruit of thy body, and the fruit of thy ground, and the fruit of thy cattle, the increase of thy kine, and the flocks of thy sheep.
Deuteronomy 28:4

We can use this verse to pray over our dogs, cats, goldfish, or whatever else we have. They're blessed because they belong to us!

1a. True or false: According to Deuteronomy 28:3, your location doesn't determine your prosperity.
True

1b. Deuteronomy 28:4 says, *"Blessed shall be the _____ of thy body, and the _____ of thy ground, and the _____ of thy cattle, the increase of thy kine, and the flocks of thy sheep."*
"Fruit" / "fruit" / "fruit"

1c. All you have is blessed. Why?
Because it belongs to you

2.   God can't bless our storehouses if we don't have them:

Blessed shall be thy basket and thy store.
Deuteronomy 28:5

If we don't have any extra set aside somewhere, the Lord can't bless it. The Lord will bless our savings—our storehouses. We need to start some savings.

2a. *Discussion question:* What is the purpose of a storehouse?
Discussion question

2b. Deuteronomy 28:5 says, *"Blessed _____ be thy basket and thy store."*
"Shall"

3.   We need to remind ourselves that it doesn't matter whether we are coming or going—we're blessed:

Blessed shalt thou be when thou comest in, and blessed shalt thou be when thou goest out.

Deuteronomy 28:6

We are blessed anywhere we are. If we're born again, then we're blessed through Jesus whether or not we know it and believe it. God told us to choose (Deut. 30:19). Since we get to choose, we must choose—and continue to choose—to be blessed.

3a. You need to _____ yourself that it doesn't matter whether you are coming or going—you're blessed.
  A. Thank
  B. Remind
  C. Nag
  D. All of the above
  E. None of the above
  B. Remind
3b. True or false: Deuteronomy 28:6 says, *"Blessed shalt thou be when thou comest in, and blessed shalt thou be when thou goest out."*
  True
3c. *Discussion question*: Since God has blessed you, how does your choice determine whether you actually are blessed (Deut. 30:19)?
  Discussion question

4. This is powerful:

The Lord shall cause thine enemies that rise up against thee to be smitten before thy face: they shall come out against thee one way, and flee before thee seven ways.

Deuteronomy 28:7

"Thine enemies" isn't only talking about people. *"Thine enemies"* could be poverty, sickness, worry, stress, and anything else that's against us. They will not prosper (Is. 54:17)!

4a. Deuteronomy 28:7 says, *"The Lord shall cause thine enemies that rise up against thee to be _____ before thy face: they shall come out against thee _____ way, and _____ before thee _____ ways."*
  "Smitten" / "one" / "flee" / "seven"
4b. Besides people, what could "thine enemies" be?
  Poverty, sickness, worry, stress, and anything else that's against you
4c. According to Isaiah 54:17, your enemies will not _____.
  Prosper

5.   Verse 8 agrees with verse 2 of the same chapter:

The Lord shall command the blessing upon thee.
                                                    Deuteronomy 28:8a

And all these blessings shall come on thee, and overtake thee.
                                                    Deuteronomy 28:2

We can't outrun the blessing of God. The blessing of God is pursuing us, chasing us, and trying to get us blessed. But we have to cooperate. We have to believe and start speaking it. The blessings of God are voice-activated.

5a. True or false: You can outrun the blessing of God.
     False
5b. *Discussion question:* What do you see when you imagine the blessing pursuing, chasing, and trying to get you blessed?
     Discussion question
5c. How do you cooperate with the blessing of God?
     By believing and starting to speak it
5d. The blessings of God are _____.
     Voice-activated

6.   God doesn't have anything to bless if we aren't setting our hands unto something:

The Lord shall command the blessing upon thee in thy storehouses, and in all that thou settest thine hand unto.
                                                    Deuteronomy 28:8

One hundred times zero is zero. A person can prosper more by working at McDonald's—even though they may take a cut in their welfare payment—because they're doing something, and God can multiply that. But He can't multiply welfare. We can reject it if we want to, but it's the truth.

6a. True or false: God doesn't have anything to bless if you aren't setting your hand unto something.
     True
6b. Deuteronomy 28:8 says, "*The Lord shall _____ the blessing upon thee in thy storehouses, and in all that thou settest thine hand unto.*"
     "Command"
6c. Why can a person prosper more by working at McDonald's than by welfare?
     Because they are doing something, and God can multiply that

7. Isaac had a king ask him to leave because he was mightier and wealthier than that king's whole nation (Gen. 26:12-17). This is the way it's supposed to be. God wants us to be so blessed that other people can see it:

> *The LORD shall establish thee an holy people unto himself, as he hath sworn unto thee, if thou shalt keep the commandments of the LORD thy God, and walk in his ways. [10] And all people of the earth shall see that thou art called by the name of the LORD; and they shall be afraid of thee.*
>
> Deuteronomy 28:9-10

It may take a while because there's got to be a time of renewing our minds and of sowing and reaping. We don't just jump into this automatically, but this ought to be our goal. We ought to be saying, "I'm blessed of God, and everybody's going to see it. It will manifest, and they'll recognize the Lord's blessing in my life." All glory to Jesus!

7a. Why did a king ask Isaac to leave (Gen. 26:12-17)?
Because he was mightier and wealthier than that king's whole nation

7b. Why might it take a while for you to be so blessed that other people can see it?
Because there's got to be a time of renewing your mind and of sowing and reaping

7c. Deuteronomy 28:9-10 says, "*The LORD shall establish thee an holy people unto himself, as he hath _____ unto thee, if thou shalt keep the commandments of the LORD thy God, and walk in his ways. [10] And all people of the earth shall _____ that thou art _____ by the name of the LORD; and they shall be _____ of thee.*"
"Sworn" / "see" / "called" / "afraid"

8. These verses are powerful:

> *And the LORD shall make thee plenteous in goods, in the fruit of thy body, and in the fruit of thy cattle, and in the fruit of thy ground, in the land which the LORD sware unto thy fathers to give thee. [12] The LORD shall open unto thee his good treasure, the heaven to give the rain unto thy land in his season, and to bless all the work of thine hand: and thou shalt lend unto many nations, and thou shalt not borrow.*
>
> Deuteronomy 28:11-12

We can break droughts. Jamie and Andrew have prayed and broken droughts. They may not have been the only ones who prayed, but Andrew believes that their prayer and faith made a difference. Ours can too.

8a. Deuteronomy 28:11-12 says, "*And the LORD shall make thee _____ in goods, in the fruit of thy body, and in the fruit of thy cattle, and in the fruit of thy ground, in the land which the LORD sware unto thy fathers to give thee. [12] The LORD shall open unto thee his _____ treasure, the heaven to give the rain unto thy land in his*

season, and TO *bless all the work of thine hand: and thou shalt _____ unto many nations, and thou shalt not _____."*
"Plenteous" / "good" / "lend" / "borrow"

8b. With your prayer and faith, what can you break?
A. Bread
B. Traditions
C. Fasts
D. Droughts
E. Eggs
D. Droughts

9. We are supposed to be the head and not the tail:

And the LORD *shall make thee the head, and not the tail; and thou shalt be above only, and thou shalt not be beneath; if that thou hearken unto the commandments of the* LORD *thy God, which I command thee this day, to observe and to do them.*

Deuteronomy 28:13

When Andrew asks someone how they're doing, and they answer, "Not too bad, under the circumstances," it makes him wonder, *Well, what are you doing down there?* We're supposed to be above only and not beneath. We have no business being **under** the circumstances! The head and not the tail, above and not beneath—that's what the Lord says we are to be, and those are blessings. We don't have to let life knock the wind out of us, keeping us down and under, the way it does other people.

9a. According to Deuteronomy 28:13, you are supposed to be the _____ and not the _____.
Head / tail

9b. You have no business being where?
Under the circumstances

9c. *Discussion question:* How do you plan to overcome obstacles to receive your blessings?
Discussion question

10. We can read all of Deuteronomy 28 to mine it for all of the blessings. And let's remember, anything we can see that was a curse, we don't have to have it. Through Christ, the curses have been turned into blessings. We can believe and receive the opposite. We're blessed!

10a.Through _____, the curses have been turned into blessings.

Christ

10b.You can believe and receive the opposite of what?

 A. The curses

 B. The blessings

 C. The circumstances

 D. All of the above

 E. None of the above

 A. The curses

Discipleship Questions

1. True or false: According to Deuteronomy 28:3, your location doesn't determine your prosperity.

2. Deuteronomy 28:4 says, "*Blessed shall be the _____ of thy body, and the _____ of thy ground, and the _____ of thy cattle, the increase of thy kine, and the flocks of thy sheep.*"

3. All you have is blessed. Why?

   _____

   _____

   _____

4. *Discussion question:* What is the purpose of a storehouse?

   _____

   _____

   _____

5. Deuteronomy 28:5 says, "*Blessed _____ be thy basket and thy store.*"

6. You need to _____ yourself that it doesn't matter whether you are coming or going—you're blessed.
   A. Thank
   B. Remind
   C. Nag
   D. All of the above
   E. None of the above

7. True or false: Deuteronomy 28:6 says, "*Blessed shalt thou be when thou comest in, and blessed shalt thou be when thou goest out.*"

8. *Discussion question:* Since God has blessed you, how does your choice determine whether you actually are blessed (Deut. 30:19)?

   _____

   _____

   _____

9. Deuteronomy 28:7 says, "*The* Lord *shall cause thine enemies that rise up against thee to be* _____ *before thy face: they shall come out against thee* _____ *way, and* _____ *before thee* _____ *ways.*"

10. Besides people, what could "thine enemies" be?

    _____

    _____

    _____

11. According to Isaiah 54:17, your enemies will not _____.

12. True or false: You can outrun the blessing of God.

13. *Discussion question:* What do you see when you imagine the blessing pursuing, chasing, and trying to get you blessed?

    _____

    _____

    _____

14. How do you cooperate with the blessing of God?

    _____

    _____

    _____

15. The blessings of God are _____.

16. True or false: God doesn't have anything to bless if you aren't setting your hand unto something.

17. Deuteronomy 28:8 says, "*The* Lord *shall* _____ *the blessing upon thee in thy storehouses, and in all that thou settest thine hand unto.*"

18. Why can a person prosper more by working at McDonald's than by welfare?

_____

_____

_____

19. Why did a king ask Isaac to leave (Gen. 26:12-17)?

_____

_____

_____

20. Why might it take a while for you to be so blessed that other people can see it?

_____

_____

_____

21. Deuteronomy 28:9-10 says, "*The Lord shall establish thee an holy people unto himself, as he hath _____ unto thee, if thou shalt keep the commandments of the Lord thy God, and walk in his ways. [10] And all people of the earth shall _____ that thou art _____ by the name of the Lord; and they shall be _____ of thee.*"

22. Deuteronomy 28:11-12 says, "*And the Lord shall make thee _____ in goods, in the fruit of thy body, and in the fruit of thy cattle, and in the fruit of thy ground, in the land which the Lord sware unto thy fathers to give thee. [12] The Lord shall open unto thee his _____ treasure, the heaven to give the rain unto thy land in his season, and to bless all the work of thine hand: and thou shalt _____ unto many nations, and thou shalt not _____.*"

23. With your prayer and faith, what can you break?
    A. Bread
    B. Traditions
    C. Fasts
    D. Droughts
    E. Eggs

24. According to Deuteronomy 28:13, you are supposed to be the _____ and not the _____.

25. You have no business being where?

    _____

    _____

    _____

26. *Discussion question:* How do you plan to overcome obstacles to receive your blessings?

    _____

    _____

    _____

27. Through _____, the curses have been turned into blessings.

28. You can believe and receive the opposite of what?
    A. The curses
    B. The blessings
    C. The circumstances
    D. All of the above
    E. None of the above

Answer Key

1. True

2. *"Fruit" / "fruit" / "fruit"*

3. Because it belongs to you

4. *Discussion question*

5. *"Shall"*

6. B. Remind

7. True

8. *Discussion question*

9. *"Smitten" / "one" / "flee" / "seven"*

10. Poverty, sickness, worry, stress, and anything else that's against you

11. Prosper

12. False

13. *Discussion question*

14. By believing and starting to speak it

15. Voice-activated

16. True

17. *"Command"*

18. Because they are doing something, and God can multiply that

19. Because he was mightier and wealthier than that king's whole nation

20. Because there's got to be a time of renewing your mind and of sowing and reaping

21. *"Sworn" / "see" / "called" / "afraid"*

22. *"Plenteous" / "good" / "lend" / "borrow"*

23. D.   Droughts

24. Head / tail

25. Under the circumstances

26. *Discussion question*

27. Christ

28. A.   The curses

Scriptures

DEUTERONOMY 28:2-13

And all these blessings shall come on thee, and overtake thee, if thou shalt hearken unto the voice of the Lord thy God. [3] Blessed shalt thou be in the city, and blessed shalt thou be in the field. [4] Blessed shall be the fruit of thy body, and the fruit of thy ground, and the fruit of thy cattle, the increase of thy kine, and the flocks of thy sheep. [5] Blessed shall be thy basket and thy store. [6] Blessed shalt thou be when thou comest in, and blessed shalt thou be when thou goest out. [7] The Lord shall cause thine enemies that rise up against thee to be smitten before thy face: they shall come out against thee one way, and flee before thee seven ways. [8] The Lord shall command the blessing upon thee in thy storehouses, and in all that thou settest thine hand unto; and he shall bless thee in the land which the Lord thy God giveth thee. [9] The Lord shall establish thee an holy people unto himself, as he hath sworn unto thee, if thou shalt keep the commandments of the Lord thy God, and walk in his ways. [10] And all people of the earth shall see that thou art called by the name of the Lord; and they shall be afraid of thee. [11] And the Lord shall make thee plenteous in goods, in the fruit of thy body, and in the fruit of thy cattle, and in the fruit of thy ground, in the land which the Lord sware unto thy fathers to give thee. [12] The Lord shall open unto thee his good treasure, the heaven to give the rain unto thy land in his season, and to bless all the work of thine hand: and thou shalt lend unto many nations, and thou shalt not borrow. [13] And the Lord shall make thee the head, and not the tail; and thou shalt be above only, and thou shalt not be beneath; if that thou hearken unto the commandments of the Lord thy God, which I command thee this day, to observe and to do them.

DEUTERONOMY 30:19

I call heaven and earth to record this day against you, that I have set before you life and death, blessing and cursing: therefore choose life, that both thou and thy seed may live.

EPHESIANS 6:11-13

Put on the whole armour of God, that ye may be able to stand against the wiles of the devil. [12] For we wrestle not against flesh and blood, but against principalities, against powers, against the rulers of the darkness of this world, against spiritual wickedness in high places. [13] Wherefore take unto you the whole armour of God, that ye may be able to withstand in the evil day, and having done all, to stand.

ISAIAH 54:17

No weapon that is formed against thee shall prosper; and every tongue that shall rise against thee in judgment thou shalt condemn. This is the heritage of the servants of the LORD, and their righteousness is of me, saith the LORD.

GENESIS 26:12-17

Then Isaac sowed in that land, and received in the same year an hundredfold: and the LORD blessed him. [13] And the man waxed great, and went forward, and grew until he became very great: [14] For he had possession of flocks, and possession of herds, and great store of servants: and the Philistines envied him. [15] For all the wells which his father's servants had digged in the days of Abraham his father, the Philistines had stopped them, and filled them with earth. [16] And Abimelech said unto Isaac, Go from us; for thou art much mightier than we. [17] And Isaac departed thence, and pitched his tent in the valley of Gerar, and dwelt there.

Delight

LESSON 19

Blessed is the man that walketh not in the counsel of the ungodly, nor standeth in the way of sinners, nor sitteth in the seat of the scornful.

Psalm 1:1

Most of us have swallowed the lies of this world even more than we realize. We've let the world tell us, "You can't do this, and you can't do that," "It's the season for you to get sick," "You have to have this," or "You're a certain age, so you have to have that." That's walking in the counsel of the ungodly and expecting negative things, just like an ungodly person does.

We need to look at people in the Bible like Moses. He lived to be 120 years old, and his natural force wasn't abated and his eyesight wasn't dim (Deut. 34:7). If Moses could do that, and what we have is better than what he had, then what he had ought to be the minimum that we expect (Heb. 8:6). Many people are only expecting to make it to 60 or 70 years of age. They're told that they have one foot in the grave and should start slowing down. No, we need to stay active and do things. We're the ones who curse ourselves and stop the blessing. God won't ever stop it, and Satan can't. We're the ones who determine whether or not the blessing is working in our lives!

By and large, our universities today are producing ungodliness. I've heard David Barton reference a statistic that something like 90 percent of Christian youth renounce their faith after one year in a secular college. That's because secular colleges are out to destroy faith in God. Even those institutions that started out more as divinity schools, like Harvard, Yale, and Princeton, are now anti-God.

Our first-year program at Charis Bible College is designed to get believers grounded in foundational truths. It's ideal for the student whose calling from God requires them to go to a secular college. This way, before they go train to become a lawyer, a doctor, or whatever they may be called to become, they're mentally and spiritually prepared for what they will face in school. They can come for one year and get their faith built up so that they aren't just thrown to the wolves without a sure foundation. It's bad out there!

ALL THE TIME

Our society was once a Christian society founded on biblical principles. However, it's not functioning that way today. People are systematically coming against everything that God is for. It's ungodly.

Sad to say, there are Christians walking in the counsel of the ungodly (Ps. 1:1). They're endorsing homosexual marriage, supporting abortion, and buying into all kinds of other ungodly things. Those who do that stop the blessing because they are walking in the counsel of the ungodly. They're standing in the ways of sinners and sitting in the seat of the scornful.

As believers in Christ, this should describe us:

> *But his delight is in the law of the* Lord *[the Word of God]; and in his law doth he meditate day and night.*
>
> Psalm 1:2, brackets mine

This is speaking of meditating in God's Word more than just every once in a while. It's meditating in God's Word more than just once a week when you go to church for a service or just ten minutes a day when you do a little devotional. Certainly, listening to the Word at church and using a daily devotional is a beginning, but this verse is talking about meditating in God's Word day and night. It's referring to God's Word being in your ears, in your eyes, on your mind, and in your mouth all the time.

> *This book of the law shall not depart out of thy mouth; but thou shalt meditate therein day and night, that thou mayest observe to do according to all that is written therein: for then thou shalt make thy way prosperous, and then thou shalt have good success.*
>
> Joshua 1:8

In other words, if you delight in God's Word and meditate on it day and night, then you'll be blessed. You will see the blessing of God begin to manifest in your life.

UP AND DOWN

There are many people all around the world who are Christians in name only. The Bible says that true believers—the just—shall live by faith (Hab. 2:4, Rom. 1:17, Gal. 3:11, and Heb.10:38). Most Christians just visit faith, but they don't live there. It's not the address where they reside. They just visit faith and maybe spend a weekend there every once in a while. They go to church on Sunday and perhaps even Wednesday too, but they don't live in faith. You need to live there!

In order to actually live in faith, you must meditate constantly in the Word. It's a day-and-night process, but when you do it, you will make your way prosperous and you will have good success (Josh. 1:8). That's another blessing!

> *And he shall be like a tree planted by the rivers of water, that bringeth forth his fruit in his season; his leaf also shall not wither; and whatsoever he doeth shall prosper.*
>
> Psalm 1:3

When you meditate on the Word day and night, whatsoever you do will prosper. What part of "whatsoever" do you not understand? *Whatsoever* you do will prosper. You might say, "I'm going to claim that one!" Well, are you going to quit walking in the counsel of the ungodly, standing in the way of sinners, and sitting in the seat of the scornful? Are you going to meditate in God's Word day and night? Those things are all linked together.

Although it's not based on your holiness, it does take a total commitment for you to see God's blessing manifest in your life. As long as you can settle for less than God's best, you will. You must be committed to receiving His best. This verse paints a picture of a tree that is planted next to water. Even in a drought, that tree will still flourish because its roots draw nourishment from the river. There won't be recession for you. There won't be ups and downs. God will speak to you!

LIKE A PINBALL

The Holy Spirit will show you things to come. That's another blessing!

> *Howbeit when he, the Spirit of truth, is come, he will guide you into all truth: for he shall not speak of himself; but whatsoever he shall hear, that shall he speak: and he will shew you things to come.*
>
> John 16:13

You don't have to be like a pinball that just bounces off things, going round and round again. You can hear from God (John 10:3-5)! God spoke to Jamie in January 2008 and led us to take out of the stock market the little bit of inheritance that we had received from her father. We did, and then the stock market crashed a short time later. The crash didn't affect us because we're like trees planted by rivers of water, and we hear the voice of God (Ps. 1:3 and John 10:27).

We invested that money back into the stock market after it crashed and had gone down 50 percent. We made 61 percent profit during that time. If you're asking, "What's your broker's name?" then you missed it. It's the Holy Spirit! We do have a broker, and as a matter of fact, he told us that everybody he was working for prospered during that time, but he reported that we prospered more than anybody! He commented, "I don't know why it worked for you." I know why. It's because Jamie and I are blessed. Everything we set our hands unto is blessed (Deut. 28:8)! Praise God.

WIPED OUT

Jeremiah 17 agrees with and confirms Psalm 1:

> *Blessed is the man that trusteth in the* LORD, *and whose hope the* LORD *is. [8] For he shall be as a tree planted by the waters, and that spreadeth out her roots by the river, and shall not see when heat cometh, but her leaf shall be green; and shall not be careful in the year of drought, neither shall cease from yielding fruit.*
>
> Jeremiah 17:7-8

The Bible is full of blessings—God's spoken favor over you. All you have to do is activate the blessings through faith.

> *Blessed is he whose transgression is forgiven, whose sin is covered. [2] Blessed is the man unto whom the* LORD *imputeth not iniquity, and in whose spirit there is no guile.*
>
> Psalm 32:1-2

We say we're forgiven, but many of us don't even understand what that means. To have our sins atoned for and wiped out is a huge blessing! Many people don't understand the magnitude of this blessing because religion has hidden this truth, saying, "Yeah, when you got born again, your sins up to that point were forgiven. But every time you sin after that, you have to get that sin confessed and under the blood." This makes forgiveness conditional upon having every sin confessed.

> *For whatsoever is not of faith is sin.*
>
> Romans 14:23

"I'M NOT WORTHY"

Sin isn't only the wrong things we do. There's more to it than that.

> *Therefore to him that knoweth to do good, and doeth it not, to him it is sin.*
>
> James 4:17

Sin is also not doing the good things that we should be doing but fail to do. If we use that definition of sin, which is the Bible's definition, then not loving a mate properly is sin. Not studying the Word enough is sin. Not being gracious to people and not thinking of others—just getting caught up in our own worlds and forgetting about others—is also sin. If we use a Bible definition of sin, then we sin all the time. Because of this, our own consciences condemn us, saying, "You're not worthy. You're separated from God." But that's not what the Word teaches.

ANDREW'S RECOMMENDATIONS FOR FURTHER STUDY

For a full exposition of this important truth, refer to my teachings entitled *Redemption* and *Spirit, Soul & Body*. I'm only able to scratch the surface in these lessons.

Outline

I. Many of us have swallowed the lies of this world even more than we realize.

    A. We've let the world tell us, "You can't do this and you can't do that," "It's the season for you to get sick," "You have to have this," or "You're a certain age, so you have to have that."

    B. That's walking in the counsel of the ungodly and expecting negative things, just like an ungodly person does:

> *Blessed is the man that walketh not in the counsel of the ungodly, nor standeth in the way of sinners, nor sitteth in the seat of the scornful.*
>
> Psalm 1:1

    C. We need to look at people in the Bible like Moses. He lived to be 120 years old, and his natural force wasn't abated and his eyesight wasn't dim (Deut. 34:7).

    D. If Moses could do that, and what we have is better than what he had, then what he had ought to be the minimum that we expect (Heb. 8:6).

    E. We're the ones who determine whether or not the blessing is working in our lives!

II. As believers in Christ, this should describe us:

> *But his delight is in the law of the LORD [the Word of God]; and in his law doth he meditate day and night.*
>
> Psalm 1:2, brackets mine

    A. This is speaking of meditating in God's Word more than just every once in a while.

    B. Certainly, listening to the Word at church and using a daily devotional is a beginning, but this verse is talking about meditating in God's Word day and night.

    C. It's referring to God's Word being in our ears, in our eyes, on our minds, and in our mouths all the time.

    D. In other words, if we delight in God's Word and meditate on it day and night, then we'll be blessed.

III. The Bible says that true believers—the just—shall live by faith (Hab. 2:4, Rom. 1:17, Gal. 3:11, and Heb. 10:38).

    A. Many Christians just visit faith, but they don't live there.

    B. In order to actually live in faith, you must meditate constantly in the Word.

    C. It's a day-and-night process, but when you do it, you will make your way prosperous and you will have good success (Josh. 1:8).

    D. That's another blessing!

IV. When you meditate on the Word day and night, whatsoever you do will prosper:

And he shall be like a tree planted by the rivers of water, that bringeth forth his fruit in his season; his leaf also shall not wither; and whatsoever he doeth shall prosper.

Psalm 1:3

    A. You might say, "I'm going to claim that one!"

    B. Well, are you going to quit walking in the counsel of the ungodly, standing in the way of sinners, and sitting in the seat of the scornful?

    C. Are you going to meditate in God's Word day and night?

    D. Those things are all linked together.

    E. Although it's not based on your holiness, it does take a total commitment for you to see God's blessing manifest in your life.

    F. This verse paints a picture of a tree that is planted next to water.

    G. Even in a drought, that tree will still flourish because its roots draw nourishment from the river.

V. The Holy Spirit will show you things to come:

Howbeit when he, the Spirit of truth, is come, he will guide you into all truth: for he shall not speak of himself; but whatsoever he shall hear, that shall he speak: and he will shew you things to come.

John 16:13

A. That's another blessing!

B. You don't have to be like a pinball that just bounces off things, going round and round again.

C. You can hear from God (John 10:3-5)!

VI. We say we're forgiven, but many of us don't even understand what that means.

A. To have our sins atoned for and wiped out is a huge blessing:

> *Blessed is he whose transgression is forgiven, whose sin is covered.* [2]
> *Blessed is the man unto whom the* Lord *imputeth not iniquity, and in whose spirit there is no guile.*
>
> Psalm 32:1-2

B. Many people don't understand the magnitude of this blessing because religion has hidden this truth, saying, "Yeah, when you got born again, your sins up to that point were forgiven. But every time you sin after that, you have to get that sin confessed and under the blood."

C. This makes forgiveness conditional upon having every sin confessed.

VII. Sin isn't only the wrong things we do:

> *For whatsoever is not of faith is sin.*
>
> Romans 14:23

> *Therefore to him that knoweth to do good, and doeth it not, to him it is sin.*
>
> James 4:17

A. Sin is also not doing the good things that we should be doing but fail to do.

B. If we use a Bible definition of sin, then we sin all the time.

C. Because of this, our own consciences condemn us, saying, "You're not worthy. You're separated from God."

D. But that's not what the Word teaches.

ANDREW'S RECOMMENDATIONS FOR FURTHER STUDY

For a full exposition of this important truth, refer to my teachings entitled *Redemption* and *Spirit, Soul & Body*. I'm only able to scratch the surface in these lessons.

Teacher's Guide

1. Many of us have swallowed the lies of this world even more than we realize. We've let the world tell us, "You can't do this and you can't do that," "It's the season for you to get sick," "You have to have this," or "You're a certain age, so you have to have that." That's walking in the counsel of the ungodly and expecting negative things, just like an ungodly person does:

> *Blessed is the man that walketh not in the counsel of the ungodly, nor standeth in the way of sinners, nor sitteth in the seat of the scornful.*
>
> Psalm 1:1

We need to look at people in the Bible like Moses. He lived to be 120 years old, and his natural force wasn't abated and his eyesight wasn't dim (Deut. 34:7). If Moses could do that, and what we have is better than what he had, then what he had ought to be the minimum that we expect (Heb. 8:6). We're the ones who determine whether or not the blessing is working in our lives!

1a. *Discussion question:* How have you walked in the counsel of the godly rather than the counsel of the ungodly?
   Discussion question

1b. According to Psalm 1:1, "_____ *is the man that walketh not in the counsel of the ungodly, nor standeth in the way of sinners, nor sitteth in the seat of the scornful.*"
   A. *"Humbled"*
   B. *"Gifted"*
   C. *"Blessed"*
   D. *"Scared"*
   E. *"Cursed"*
   C. *"Blessed"*

1c. True or false: Moses lived to be 120 years old, and his natural force wasn't abated and his eyesight wasn't dim (Deut. 34:7).
   True

1d. What Moses had ought to be the _____ that you can expect (Heb. 8:6).
   A. Limit
   B. Maximum
   C. Most
   D. All of the above
   E. None of the above
   E. None of the above

2.   As believers in Christ, this should describe us:

> *But his delight is in the law of the* LORD *[the Word of God]; and in his law doth he meditate day and night.*
>
> Psalm 1:2, brackets mine

This is speaking of meditating in God's Word more than just every once in a while. Certainly, listening to the Word at church and using a daily devotional is a beginning, but this verse is talking about meditating in God's Word day and night. It's referring to God's Word being in our ears, in our eyes, on our minds, and in our mouths all the time. In other words, if we delight in God's Word and meditate on it day and night, then we'll be blessed.

2a.   Psalm 1:2 says, "*But his _____ is in the law of the* LORD *[the Word of God]; and in his law doth he _____ day and night.*"
      "Delight" / "meditate"
2b.   Psalm 1:2 is referring to God's Word being where?
      In your ears, in your eyes, on your mind, and in your mouth all the time
2c.   True or false: If you delight in God's Word and meditate on it day and night, then you'll be blessed.
      True

3.   The Bible says that true believers—the just—shall live by faith (Hab. 2:4, Rom. 1:17, Gal. 3:11, and Heb. 10:38). Many Christians just visit faith, but they don't live there. In order to actually live in faith, we must meditate constantly in the Word. It's a day-and-night process, but when we do it, we will make our way prosperous and we will have good success (Josh. 1:8). That's another blessing!

3a.   True believers—the just—shall _____ by faith (Hab. 2:4, Rom. 1:17, Gal. 3:11, and Heb. 10:38).
      Live
3b.   In order to actually live in faith, you must do what?
      Meditate constantly in the Word
3c.   If you will meditate in the Word day and night, what will happen (Josh. 1:8)?
      You will make your way prosperous and you will have good success
3d.   Prosperity and good success is considered one of God's _____.
      Blessings

4.   When we meditate on the Word day and night, whatsoever we do will prosper:

And he shall be like a tree planted by the rivers of water, that bringeth forth his fruit in his season; his leaf also shall not wither; and whatsoever he doeth shall prosper.

Psalm 1:3

We might say, "I'm going to claim that one!" Well, are we going to quit walking in the counsel of the ungodly, standing in the way of sinners, and sitting in the seat of the scornful? Are we going to meditate in God's Word day and night? Those things are all linked together. Although it's not based on our holiness, it does take a total commitment for us to see God's blessing manifest in our lives. This verse paints a picture of a tree that is planted next to water. Even in a drought, that tree will still flourish because its roots draw nourishment from the river.

4a.   Psalm 1:3 says, *"And he shall be like a _____ planted by the rivers of water, that bringeth forth his fruit in his season; his _____ also shall not wither; and _____ he doeth shall prosper."*
   "Tree" / "leaf" / "whatsoever"

4b.   *Discussion question:* What does a total commitment look like to you?
   Discussion question

4c.   Why would a tree that's planted by a river flourish?
   Because its roots draw nourishment from the river

5.   The Holy Spirit will show us things to come:

Howbeit when he, the Spirit of truth, is come, he will guide you into all truth: for he shall not speak of himself; but whatsoever he shall hear, that shall he speak: and he will shew you things to come.

John 16:13

That's another blessing! We don't have to be like a pinball that just bounces off things, going round and round again. We can hear from God (John 10:3-5)!

5a.   According to John 16:13, *"Howbeit when he, the Spirit of truth, is come, he will _____ you into all truth: for he shall not speak of himself; but whatsoever he shall hear, that shall he _____: and he will _____ you things to come."*
   "Guide" / "speak" / "shew"

5b.   Another blessing is the guidance of the _____ _____.
   Holy Spirit

5c.   True or false: Only Jesus could hear from God (John 10:3-5).
   False

6.   We say we're forgiven, but many of us don't even understand what that means. To have our sins atoned for and wiped out is a huge blessing:

> *Blessed is he whose transgression is forgiven, whose sin is covered.* [2]
> *Blessed is the man unto whom the* Lord *imputeth not iniquity, and in whose spirit there is no guile.*
>
> Psalm 32:1-2

Many people don't understand the magnitude of this blessing because religion has hidden this truth, saying, "Yeah, when you got born again, your sins up to that point were forgiven. But every time you sin after that, you have to get that sin confessed and under the blood." This makes forgiveness conditional upon having every sin confessed.

6a.   To have your _____ atoned for and wiped out is a huge blessing.
      Sins
6b.   True or false: Forgiveness is conditional on having every sin confessed.
      False

7.   Sin isn't only the wrong things we do:

> *For whatsoever is not of faith is sin.*
>
> Romans 14:23

> *Therefore to him that knoweth to do good, and doeth it not, to him it is sin.*
>
> James 4:17

Sin is also not doing the good things that we should be doing but fail to do. If we use a Bible definition of sin, then we sin all the time. Because of this, our own consciences condemn us, saying, "You're not worthy. You're separated from God." But that's not what the Word teaches.

7a.   True or false: Sin is only doing the wrong things.
      False
7b.   According to Romans 14:23, "_____ *is not of faith is sin.*"
      "Whatsoever"
7c.   According to James 4:17, "*To him that* _____ *to do good, and doeth it not, to him it is sin.*"
      "Knoweth"
7d.   *Discussion question:* When is it good to trust your conscience, and when is it good not to trust it?
      Discussion question

Discipleship Questions

1. *Discussion question:* How have you walked in the counsel of the godly rather than the counsel of the ungodly?

   _____

   _____

   _____

2. According to Psalm 1:1, "_____ *is the man that walketh not in the counsel of the ungodly, nor standeth in the way of sinners, nor sitteth in the seat of the scornful.*"
   A. "*Humbled*"
   B. "*Gifted*"
   C. "*Blessed*"
   D. "*Scared*"
   E. "*Cursed*"

3. True or false: Moses lived to be 120 years old, and his natural force wasn't abated and his eyesight wasn't dim (Deut. 34:7).

4. What Moses had ought to be the _____ that you can expect (Heb. 8:6).
   A. Limit
   B. Maximum
   C. Most
   D. All of the above
   E. None of the above

5. Psalm 1:2 says, "*But his _____ is in the law of the* LORD [the Word of God]; *and in his law doth he _____ day and night.*"

6. Psalm 1:2 is referring to God's Word being where?

   _____

   _____

   _____

7. True or false: If you delight in God's Word and meditate on it day and night, then you'll be blessed.

8. True believers—the just—shall _____ by faith (Hab. 2:4, Rom. 1:17, Gal. 3:11, and Heb. 10:38).

9. In order to actually live in faith, you must do what?

    _____

    _____

    _____

10. If you will meditate in the Word day and night, what will happen (Josh. 1:8)?

    _____

    _____

    _____

11. Prosperity and good success is considered one of God's _____.

12. Psalm 1:3 says, *"And he shall be like a _____ planted by the rivers of water, that bringeth forth his fruit in his season; his _____ also shall not wither; and _____ he doeth shall prosper."*

13. *Discussion question:* What does a total commitment look like to you?

    _____

    _____

    _____

14. Why would a tree that's planted by a river flourish?

    _____

    _____

    _____

15. According to John 16:13, *"Howbeit when he, the Spirit of truth, is come, he will _____ you into all truth: for he shall not speak of himself; but whatsoever he shall hear, that shall he _____: and he will _____ you things to come.*

16. Another blessing is the guidance of the _____ _____.

17. True or false: Only Jesus could hear from God (John 10:3-5).

18. To have your _____ atoned for and wiped out is a huge blessing.

19. True or false: Forgiveness is conditional on having every sin confessed.

20. True or false: Sin is only doing the wrong things.

21. According to Romans 14:23, "_____ *is not of faith is sin.*"

22. According to James 4:17, "*To him that _____ to do good, and doeth it not, to him it is sin.*"

23. *Discussion question:* When is it good to trust your conscience, and when is it good not to trust it?

_____

_____

_____

Answer Key

1. *Discussion question*

2. C. *"Blessed"*

3. True

4. E.   None of the above

5. *"Delight" / "meditate"*

6. In your ears, in your eyes, on your mind, and in your mouth all the time

7. True

8. Live

9. Meditate constantly in the Word

10. You will make your way prosperous and you will have good success

11. Blessings

12. *"Tree" / "leaf" / "whatsoever"*

13. *Discussion question*

14. Because its roots draw nourishment from the river

15. *"Guide" / "speak" / "shew"*

16. Holy Spirit

17. False

18. Sins

19. False

20. False

21. *"Whatsoever"*

22. *"Knoweth"*

23. *Discussion question*

Scriptures

PSALM 1:1-3
Blessed is the man that walketh not in the counsel of the ungodly, nor standeth in the way of sinners, nor sitteth in the seat of the scornful. [2] But his delight is in the law of the Lord; and in his law doth he meditate day and night. [3] And he shall be like a tree planted by the rivers of water, that bringeth forth his fruit in his season; his leaf also shall not wither; and whatsoever he doeth shall prosper.

DEUTERONOMY 34:7
And Moses was an hundred and twenty years old when he died: his eye was not dim, nor his natural force abated.

HEBREWS 8:6
But now hath he obtained a more excellent ministry, by how much also he is the mediator of a better covenant, which was established upon better promises.

JOSHUA 1:8
This book of the law shall not depart out of thy mouth; but thou shalt meditate therein day and night, that thou mayest observe to do according to all that is written therein: for then thou shalt make thy way prosperous, and then thou shalt have good success.

HABAKKUK 2:4
Behold, his soul which is lifted up is not upright in him: but the just shall live by his faith.

ROMANS 1:17
For therein is the righteousness of God revealed from faith to faith: as it is written, The just shall live by faith.

GALATIANS 3:11
But that no man is justified by the law in the sight of God, it is evident: for, The just shall live by faith.

HEBREWS 10:38
Now the just shall live by faith: but if any man draw back, my soul shall have no pleasure in him.

JOHN 16:13

Howbeit when he, the Spirit of truth, is come, he will guide you into all truth: for he shall not speak of himself; but whatsoever he shall hear, that shall he speak: and he will shew you things to come.

JOHN 10:3-5

To him the porter openeth; and the sheep hear his voice: and he calleth his own sheep by name, and leadeth them out. [4] And when he putteth forth his own sheep, he goeth before them, and the sheep follow him: for they know his voice. [5] And a stranger will they not follow, but will flee from him: for they know not the voice of strangers.

JOHN 10:27

My sheep hear my voice, and I know them, and they follow me.

DEUTERONOMY 28:8

The LORD shall command the blessing upon thee in thy storehouses, and in all that thou settest thine hand unto; and he shall bless thee in the land which the LORD thy God giveth thee.

JEREMIAH 17:7-8

Blessed is the man that trusteth in the LORD, and whose hope the LORD is. [8] For he shall be as a tree planted by the waters, and that spreadeth out her roots by the river, and shall not see when heat cometh, but her leaf shall be green; and shall not be careful in the year of drought, neither shall cease from yielding fruit.

PSALM 32:1-2

Blessed is he whose transgression is forgiven, whose sin is covered. [2] Blessed is the man unto whom the LORD imputeth not iniquity, and in whose spirit there is no guile.

ROMANS 14:23

And he that doubteth is damned if he eat, because he eateth not of faith: for whatsoever is not of faith is sin.

JAMES 4:17

Therefore to him that knoweth to do good, and doeth it not, to him it is sin.

He's Not Mad

LESSON 20

You were forgiven of all sin—past, present, and future. God has forgiven you of all sin, even the sins you haven't committed yet. You might be tempted to think, *That's heresy, Andrew*, but I can prove it to you from the following scriptures:

Neither by the blood of goats and calves, but by his own blood he entered in once into the holy place, having obtained eternal redemption for us.... [15] And for this cause he is the mediator of the new testament, that by means of death, for the redemption of the transgressions that were under the first testament, they which are called might receive the promise of eternal inheritance.

Hebrews 9:12 and 15

For the law having a shadow of good things to come, and not the very image of the things, can never with those sacrifices which they offered year by year continually make the comers thereunto perfect. [2] For then would they not have ceased to be offered? because that the worshippers once purged should have had no more conscience of sins.

Hebrews 10:1-2

By the which will we are sanctified through the offering of the body of Jesus Christ once for all.... [14] For by one offering he hath perfected for ever them that are sanctified.

Hebrews 10:10 and 14

But ye are come unto mount Sion, and unto the city of the living God, the heavenly Jerusalem, and to an innumerable company of angels, [23] To the general assembly and church of the firstborn, which are written in heaven, and to God the Judge of all, and to the spirits of just men made perfect.

Hebrews 12:22-23

AN INROAD OF SATAN

Those verses confirm that you are forgiven of all past, present, and future sin. *But, Andrew, how can God forgive a sin before I commit it?* Well, you'd better pray that He can forgive a sin before you commit it because He only died for your sins one time 2,000 years ago, long before you ever committed them. You are forgiven of all sin. If you're born again, sin is not an issue between you and God.

You're probably wondering, *Does this mean that I can just go live in sin?* No, because sin is still an inroad of Satan into your life.

> *Know ye not, that to whom ye yield yourselves servants to obey, his servants ye are to whom ye obey; whether of sin unto death, or of obedience unto righteousness?*
>
> Romans 6:16

God has forgiven *all* of your sin—past, present, and future—but if you go out and live in sin, you're just inviting Satan in. You're throwing open the door to your life and saying, "Shoot your best shot! Destroy me. Have at me."

> *The thief cometh not, but for to steal, and to kill, and to destroy.*
>
> John 10:10

If you go live in sin, Satan's going to eat your lunch and pop the bag. You don't want to live in sin.

STUPID

Sin is stupid. If you're living in sin, you're stupid. But God loves you, stupid. He's not holding your sin against you, but you are inviting the devil in. You aren't going to prosper if you live in sin. You'll stop the blessing because you aren't cooperating with God.

> *Blessed is the man unto whom the* LORD *imputeth not iniquity.*
>
> Psalm 32:2

Speaking of God's grace, Paul quoted these verses in Romans:

> *Even as David also describeth the blessedness of the man, unto whom God imputeth righteousness without works, [7] Saying, Blessed are they whose iniquities are forgiven, and whose sins are covered. [8] Blessed is the man to whom the Lord will not* [future tense] *impute sin.*
>
> Romans 4:6-8, brackets mine

Verse 8 doesn't say "did not" or "does not," but *will not.* When you were born again, all of your sin—past, present, and even future tense sin—was laid upon Jesus. All of your sin was dealt with and forgiven. God will never hold sin against you!

This goes against over 90 percent of all religious teaching. Nearly all such teaching holds sin over a person's head, saying, "God won't bless you. God won't move. God won't answer your prayer if you're in sin." Now, it's true that if you're in sin, you won't prosper, but that's not because God isn't blessing you. It's because you are allowing the devil to come into your life and destroy, kill, and steal (John 10:10).

YOUR OWN CONSCIENCE

You might be saying, "Come on, Andrew. What's the difference? Either way, I'm not prospering!" The difference is that if you think God is angry with you and is imputing your sins unto you, then you'll never have any boldness, confidence, or faith. But if you understand this truth, you can say, "God, thank You that You never turned away from me. You never took the blessing back. I stopped it through my own stupidity. I gave Satan this place in my life. I welcomed him in. How dumb can I get and still breathe? Thank You, God, that You still love me." Then you can just turn on the devil and say, "I don't care what I've done. Jesus is still my Lord, and I refuse to allow you to dominate me" (James 4:7). This is a big difference.

It's huge for you to understand that your transgressions have been forgiven and that all your iniquity has been taken away (Ps. 103:11-12). God will not impute sin unto you (Heb. 8:12 and 10:17).

I'm so glad that God's covenant with Noah was an unconditional covenant. God told him, "I'll never destroy the earth again with a flood." He didn't add, "As long as you never tick me off again," or "As long as you never do anything wrong again." It wasn't conditional. He just said, "I'm swearing by Myself that I'll never destroy the earth again with a flood." If the covenant had been conditional, God would've already destroyed the earth again with a flood. We deserve it. But it was an unconditional covenant.

> *For this is as the waters of Noah unto me: for as I have sworn that the waters of Noah should no more go over the earth; so have I sworn that I would not be wroth with thee, nor rebuke thee.*
>
> Isaiah 54:9

God has never been angry with you since you became born again. He has never rebuked you, regardless of what you think. Your own conscience smites you, and Satan—the accuser of the brethren—condemns you (Rev. 12:10), but God does not.

NO CONDEMNATION

There is therefore now no condemnation to them which are in Christ Jesus.... [34] Who is he that condemneth?

Romans 8:1 and 34

God isn't the one condemning you (Rom. 8:31-35). Your own heart is condemning you, and you've blamed it on God. God is not mad at you. In fact, He's not even in a bad mood. God loves you!

ANDREW'S RECOMMENDATIONS FOR FURTHER STUDY

For further assistance with overcoming condemnation, check out my teaching entitled *The War Is Over*. It'll help you become more confident in your relationship with God.

Outline

I.   You were forgiven of all sin—past, present, and future.

    A.   You might be tempted to think, *That's heresy, Andrew*, but I can prove it to you from the following scriptures:

> *Neither by the blood of goats and calves, but by his own blood he entered in once into the holy place, having obtained eternal redemption for us…. [15] And for this cause he is the mediator of the new testament, that by means of death, for the redemption of the transgressions that were under the first testament, they which are called might receive the promise of eternal inheritance.*
>
> Hebrews 9:12 and 15

> *For the law having a shadow of good things to come, and not the very image of the things, can never with those sacrifices which they offered year by year continually make the comers thereunto perfect. [2] For then would they not have ceased to be offered? because that the worshippers once purged should have had no more conscience of sins.*
>
> Hebrews 10:1-2

> *By the which will we are sanctified through the offering of the body of Jesus Christ once for all…. [14] For by one offering he hath perfected for ever them that are sanctified.*
>
> Hebrews 10:10 and 14

> *But ye are come unto mount Sion, and unto the city of the living God, the heavenly Jerusalem, and to an innumerable company of angels, [23] To the general assembly and church of the firstborn, which are written in heaven, and to God the Judge of all, and to the spirits of just men made perfect.*
>
> Hebrews 12:22-23

    B.   You might wonder, *But, Andrew, how can God forgive a sin before I commit it?*

    C.   Well, you'd better pray that He can forgive a sin before you commit it because He only died for your sins one time 2,000 years ago, long before you ever committed them.

    D.   If you're born again, sin is not an issue between you and God.

II. If you go out and live in sin, you're just inviting Satan in (Rom. 6:16).

   A. You're throwing open the door to your life and saying, "Shoot your best shot! Destroy me. Have at me."

   The thief cometh not, but for to steal, and to kill, and to destroy.
   John 10:10

   B. If you're living in sin, you're stupid.

   C. But God loves you, stupid.

III. Speaking of God's grace, Paul quoted these verses in Romans:

   Even as David also describeth the blessedness of the man, unto whom God imputeth righteousness without works, [7] Saying, Blessed are they whose iniquities are forgiven, and whose sins are covered. [8] Blessed is the man to whom the Lord will not [future tense] impute sin.
   Romans 4:6-8, brackets mine

   A. Verse 8 doesn't say "did not" or "does not," but *"will not."*

   B. God will never hold sin against you!

   C. Now, it's true that if you're in sin, you won't prosper, but that's not because God isn't blessing you.

   D. You might be saying, "Come on, Andrew. What's the difference? Either way, I'm not prospering!"

   E. The difference is that if you think God is angry with you and is imputing your sins unto you, then you'll never have any boldness, confidence, or faith.

   F. But if you understand this truth, you can say, "God, thank You that You never turned away from me. You never took the blessing back. I stopped it through my own stupidity. I gave Satan this place in my life. I welcomed him in. How dumb can I get and still breathe? Thank You, God, that You still love me."

   G. Then you can just turn on the devil and say, "I don't care what I've done. Jesus is still my Lord, and I refuse to allow you to dominate me" (James 4:7).

   H. It's huge for you to understand that your transgressions have been forgiven and that all your iniquity has been taken away (Ps. 103:11-12).

IV. We should be glad that God's covenant with Noah was an unconditional covenant.

    A. God told him, "I'll never destroy the earth again with a flood."

    B. He didn't add, "As long as you never do anything wrong again."

    C. If the covenant had been conditional, God would've already destroyed the earth again with a flood.

    D. We deserve it.

    E. But it was an unconditional covenant (Is. 54:9).

V. God has never been angry with you since you became born again.

    A. He has never rebuked you, regardless of what you think.

    B. Your own conscience smites you, and Satan—the accuser of the brethren—condemns you (Rev. 12:10), but God does not (Rom. 8:31-35).

    C. Your own heart is condemning you, and you've blamed it on God.

    D. God is not mad at you.

    E. He's not even in a bad mood.

ANDREW'S RECOMMENDATIONS FOR FURTHER STUDY

For further assistance with overcoming condemnation, check out my teaching entitled *The War Is Over*. It'll help you become more confident in your relationship with God.

Teacher's Guide

1. We were forgiven of all sin—past, present, and future. We might be tempted to think, *That's heresy*, but this can be proven with the following scriptures:

> *Neither by the blood of goats and calves, but by his own blood he entered in once into the holy place, having obtained eternal redemption for us....* [15] *And for this cause he is the mediator of the new testament, that by means of death, for the redemption of the transgressions that were under the first testament, they which are called might receive the promise of eternal inheritance.*
>
> Hebrews 9:12 and 15

> *For the law having a shadow of good things to come, and not the very image of the things, can never with those sacrifices which they offered year by year continually make the comers thereunto perfect.* [2] *For then would they not have ceased to be offered? because that the worshippers once purged should have had no more conscience of sins.*
>
> Hebrews 10:1-2

> *By the which will we are sanctified through the offering of the body of Jesus Christ once for all....* [14] *For by one offering he hath perfected for ever them that are sanctified.*
>
> Hebrews 10:10 and 14

> *But ye are come unto mount Sion, and unto the city of the living God, the heavenly Jerusalem, and to an innumerable company of angels,* [23] *To the general assembly and church of the firstborn, which are written in heaven, and to God the Judge of all, and to the spirits of just men made perfect.*
>
> Hebrews 12:22-23

We might wonder, *But how can God forgive a sin before I commit it?* Well, we'd better pray that He can forgive a sin before we commit it because He only died for our sins one time 2,000 years ago, long before we ever committed them. If we're born again, sin is not an issue between us and God.

1a. You were forgiven of _____ sin—past, present, and future.
    <u>All</u>
1b. *Discussion question:* How does it feel knowing you are forgiven?
    <u>Discussion question</u>
1c. True or false: Sin is still an issue between you and God.
    <u>False</u>

2. If we go out and live in sin, we're just inviting Satan in (Rom. 6:16). We're throwing open the door to our lives and saying, "Shoot your best shot! Destroy me. Have at me."

>   *The thief cometh not, but for to steal, and to kill, and to destroy.*
>
>   John 10:10

If you're living in sin, you're stupid. But God loves you, stupid.

2a. Why shouldn't you go out and live in sin (Rom. 6:16)?
    Because you're just inviting Satan in
2b. According to John 10:10, "The _____ cometh not, but for to steal, and to kill, and to destroy."
    "Thief"
2c. If you're living in sin, you're _____.
    Stupid
2d. True or false: God loves you whether you're living in sin or not.
    True

3. Speaking of God's grace, Paul quoted these verses in Romans:

>   *Even as David also describeth the blessedness of the man, unto whom God imputeth righteousness without works, [7] Saying, Blessed are they whose iniquities are forgiven, and whose sins are covered. [8] Blessed is the man to whom the Lord will not [future tense] impute sin.*
>
>   Romans 4:6-8, brackets mine

Verse 8 doesn't say "did not" or "does not," but *"will not."* God will never hold sin against us! Now, it's true that if we're in sin, we won't prosper, but that's not because God isn't blessing us. We might be saying, "Come on. What's the difference? Either way, I'm not prospering!" The difference is that if we think God is angry with us and is imputing our sins unto us, then we'll never have any boldness, confidence, or faith. But if we understand this truth, we can say, "God, thank You that You never turned away from me. You never took the blessing back. I stopped it through my own stupidity. I gave Satan this place in my life. I welcomed him in. How dumb can I get and still breathe? Thank You, God, that You still love me." Then we can just turn on the devil and say, "I don't care what I've done. Jesus is still my Lord, and I refuse to allow you to dominate me" (James 4:7). It's huge for us to understand that our transgressions have been forgiven and that all our iniquity has been taken away (Ps. 103:11-12).

3a. Romans 4:6-8 says, *"Even as David also describeth the _____ of the man, unto whom God imputeth righteousness without works, [7] Saying, _____ are they whose iniquities are forgiven, and whose sins are covered. [8] _____ is the man to whom the Lord will _____ impute sin."*
"Blessedness" / "blessed" / "blessed" / "not"

3b. True or false: If you're in sin, you will still prosper.
False

3c. Why is it important to understand that God will never hold sin against you?
Because if you think God is angry with you and is imputing your sins unto you, then you'll never have any boldness, confidence, or faith

3d. If you understand this truth, what can you say to God?
"God, thank You that You never turned away from me. You never took the blessing back. I stopped it through my own stupidity. I gave Satan this place in my life. I welcomed him in. How dumb can I get and still breathe? Thank You, God, that You still love me"

3e. What can you say to the devil (James 4:7)?
"I don't care what I've done. Jesus is still my Lord, and I refuse to allow you to dominate me"

3f. *Discussion question:* Since God has taken away your iniquity, how do you want to respond to Him (Ps. 103:11-12)?
Discussion question

4. We should be glad that God's covenant with Noah was an unconditional covenant. God told him, "I'll never destroy the earth again with a flood." He didn't add, "As long as you never do anything wrong again." If the covenant had been conditional, God would've already destroyed the earth again with a flood. We deserve it. But it was an unconditional covenant (Is. 54:9).

4a. God's covenant with Noah was what kind of covenant?
    A. Unconventional
    B. Conditional
    C. Conventional
    D. Unconditional
    E. Circumstantial
    D. Unconditional

4b. If the covenant had been conditional, why would God have already destroyed the earth again with a flood?
Because we deserve it

4c. *Discussion question:* Why do you think God swore He would never flood the earth again (Is. 54:9)?
Discussion question

5. God has never been angry with us since we became born again. He has never rebuked us, regardless of what we think. Our own consciences smite us, and Satan—the accuser of the brethren—condemns us (Rev. 12:10), but God does not (Rom. 8:31-35). Our own hearts are condemning us, and we've blamed it on God. God is not mad at us. He's not even in a bad mood.

5a. True or false: God has been angry with you since you became born again.
    False
5b. What smites you?
    Your own conscience
5c. According to Romans 8:31-35, who condemns you?
    A. Satan
    B. God
    C. People
    D. Angels
    E. Demons
    A. Satan
5d. What else condemns you?
    Your own heart
5e. True or false: God is not mad at you; He's not even in a bad mood.
    True

Discipleship Questions

1. You were forgiven of _____ sin—past, present, and future.

2. *Discussion question:* How does it feel knowing you are forgiven?

   _____

   _____

   _____

3. True or false: Sin is still an issue between you and God.

4. Why shouldn't you go out and live in sin (Rom. 6:16)?

   _____

   _____

   _____

5. According to John 10:10, *"The _____ cometh not, but for to steal, and to kill, and to destroy."*

6. If you're living in sin, you're _____.

7. True or false: God loves you whether you're living in sin or not.

8. Romans 4:6-8 says, *"Even as David also describeth the _____ of the man, unto whom God imputeth righteousness without works, [7] Saying, _____ are they whose iniquities are forgiven, and whose sins are covered. [8] _____ is the man to whom the Lord will _____ impute sin."*

9. True or false: If you're in sin, you will still prosper.

10. Why is it important to understand that God will never hold sin against you?

   _____

   _____

   _____

11. If you understand this truth, what can you say to God?

_____

_____

_____

12. What can you say to the devil (James 4:7)?

_____

_____

_____

13. *Discussion question:* Since God has taken away your iniquity, how do you want to respond to Him (Ps. 103:11-12)?

_____

_____

_____

14. God's covenant with Noah was what kind of covenant?
    A. Unconventional
    B. Conditional
    C. Conventional
    D. Unconditional
    E. Circumstantial

15. If the covenant had been conditional, why would God have already destroyed the earth again with a flood?

_____

_____

_____

16. *Discussion question:* Why do you think God swore He would never flood the earth again (Is. 54:9)?

_____

_____

_____

17. True or false: God has been angry with you since you became born again.

18. What smites you?

_____

_____

_____

19. According to Romans 8:31-35, who condemns you?
    A. Satan
    B. God
    C. People
    D. Angels
    E. Demons

20. What else condemns you?

_____

_____

_____

21. True or false: God is not mad at you; He's not even in a bad mood.

Answer Key

1. All

2. *Discussion question*

3. False

4. Because you're just inviting Satan in

5. *"Thief"*

6. Stupid

7. True

8. *"Blessedness" / "blessed" / "blessed" / "not"*

9. False

10. Because if you think God is angry with you and is imputing your sins unto you, then you'll never have any boldness, confidence, or faith

11. "God, thank You that You never turned away from me. You never took the blessing back. I stopped it through my own stupidity. I gave Satan this place in my life. I welcomed him in. How dumb can I get and still breathe? Thank You, God, that You still love me"

12. "I don't care what I've done. Jesus is still my Lord, and I refuse to allow you to dominate me"

13. *Discussion question*

14. D. Unconditional

15. Because we deserve it

16. *Discussion question*

17. False

18. Your own conscience

19. A. Satan

20. Your own heart

21. True

Scriptures

HEBREWS 9:12
Neither by the blood of goats and calves, but by his own blood he entered in once into the holy place, having obtained eternal redemption for us.

HEBREWS 9:15
And for this cause he is the mediator of the new testament, that by means of death, for the redemption of the transgressions that were under the first testament, they which are called might receive the promise of eternal inheritance.

HEBREWS 10:1-2
For the law having a shadow of good things to come, and not the very image of the things, can never with those sacrifices which they offered year by year continually make the comers thereunto perfect. [2] For then would they not have ceased to be offered? because that the worshippers once purged should have had no more conscience of sins.

HEBREWS 10:10
By the which will we are sanctified through the offering of the body of Jesus Christ once for all.

HEBREWS 10:14
For by one offering he hath perfected for ever them that are sanctified.

HEBREWS 12:22-23
But ye are come unto mount Sion, and unto the city of the living God, the heavenly Jerusalem, and to an innumerable company of angels, [23] To the general assembly and church of the firstborn, which are written in heaven, and to God the Judge of all, and to the spirits of just men made perfect.

ROMANS 6:16
Know ye not, that to whom ye yield yourselves servants to obey, his servants ye are to whom ye obey; whether of sin unto death, or of obedience unto righteousness?

JOHN 10:10
The thief cometh not, but for to steal, and to kill, and to destroy: I am come that they might have life, and that they might have it more abundantly.

PSALM 32:2

Blessed is the man unto whom the LORD imputeth not iniquity, and in whose spirit there is no guile.

ROMANS 4:6-8

Even as David also describeth the blessedness of the man, unto whom God imputeth righteousness without works, [7] Saying, Blessed are they whose iniquities arc forgivcn, and whose sins are covered. [8] Blessed is the man to whom the Lord will not impute sin.

JAMES 4:7

Submit yourselves therefore to God. Resist the devil, and he will flee from you.

PSALM 103:11-12

For as the heaven is high above the earth, so great is his mercy toward them that fear him. [12] As far as the east is from the west, so far hath he removed our transgressions from us.

HEBREWS 8:12

For I will be merciful to their unrighteousness, and their sins and their iniquities will I remember no more.

HEBREWS 10:17

And their sins and iniquities will I remember no more.

ISAIAH 54:9

For this is as the waters of Noah unto me: for as I have sworn that the waters of Noah should no more go over the earth; so have I sworn that I would not be wroth with thee, nor rebuke thee.

REVELATION 12:10

And I heard a loud voice saying in heaven, Now is come salvation, and strength, and the kingdom of our God, and the power of his Christ: for the accuser of our brethren is cast down, which accused them before our God day and night.

ROMANS 8:1

There is therefore now no condemnation to them which are in Christ Jesus, who walk not after the flesh, but after the Spirit.

ROMANS 8:31-35

What shall we then say to these things? If God be for us, who can be against us? [32] He that spared not his own Son, but delivered him up for us all, how shall he not with him also freely give us all things? [33] Who shall lay any thing to the charge of God's elect? It is God that justifieth. [34] Who is he that condemneth? It is Christ that died, yea rather, that is risen again, who is even at the right hand of God, who also maketh intercession for us. [35] Who shall separate us from the love of Christ? shall tribulation, or distress, or persecution, or famine, or nakedness, or peril, or sword?

Every Evil Work

LESSON 21

O taste and see that the Lord *is good: blessed is the man that trusteth in him.*

Psalm 34:8

Did you know that when you trust in God, there's a blessing that comes upon you? It's better to rely on Him instead of trusting in yourself, because when you do, you're blessed!

Thou wilt keep him in perfect peace, whose mind is stayed on thee: because he trusteth in thee.

Isaiah 26:3

Peace is one of the blessings that comes through trusting in God, yet most Christians struggle with peace. They're stressed-out and worried. Do you know why? They aren't trusting in the Lord. They're afraid He won't come through. They feel like they've failed and deserve whatever is happening to them—that God is holding sin against them. These things add up and compound upon each other.

You need to understand that you are forgiven of all sin. God is not holding anything against you, so He'll certainly do whatever else you need. If God forgave you of your sins, which is the greatest miracle that could ever happen, how could you believe that He won't heal you? If He loved you enough to forgive you of your sins, then He loves you enough to heal your body. If you would just trust Him enough to understand that your sins are forgiven, then your body would be healed. You'd be able to recover from this illness or infirmity. He'd keep you in perfect peace (Is. 26:3)!

YOUR CHILDREN'S PEACE

The children of the righteous will never go hungry. Great shall be their peace. They shall be mighty and blessed.

I have been young, and now am old; yet have I not seen the righteous forsaken, nor his seed begging bread. [26] He is ever merciful, and

427

lendeth; and his seed is blessed.

Psalm 37:25-26

And all thy children shall be taught of the LORD; and great shall be the peace of thy children. [14] In righteousness shalt thou be established: thou shalt be far from oppression; for thou shalt not fear: and from terror; for it shall not come near thee.

Isaiah 54:13-14

Praise ye the LORD. Blessed is the man that feareth the LORD, that delighteth greatly in his commandments. [2] His seed shall be mighty upon earth: the generation of the upright shall be blessed.

Psalm 112:1-2

He will bless them that fear the LORD, both small and great. [14] The LORD shall increase you more and more, you and your children. [15] Ye are blessed of the LORD which made heaven and earth.

Psalm 115:13-15

God will increase both you and your children. All these verses are about your children being blessed. Now, this doesn't rule out the fact that they have a choice of their own to make, to trust God or not. This doesn't mean that they will automatically be forced to do the right thing, but your children will be blessed.

UNITY

When our kids became teenagers, it seemed as if aliens had abducted them and sucked their brains out. Raising kids is harder than raising the dead. I know, because I've had to do both with our family. Raising my son from the dead was a piece of cake compared to raising him to be an adult. He didn't fight, resist, or anything when he was dead.

Our kids have done some weird things, but because Jamie and I love God, are seeking Him, and are praying for our children, our kids have been blessed. With the choices they were making, things could have gone much, much worse. Our kids have escaped problems over and over again because our seed is blessed. That's one of the blessings that come upon us!

Blessed is that man that maketh the LORD his trust, and respecteth not the proud, nor such as turn aside to lies.

Psalm 40:4

You're blessed if you make the Lord your trust.

Behold, how good and how pleasant it is for brethren to dwell together in unity! [2] It is like the precious ointment upon the head, that ran down upon the beard, even Aaron's beard: that went down to the skirts of his garments. [3] As the dew of Hermon, and as the dew that descended upon the mountains of Zion: for there the LORD commanded the blessing, even life for evermore.

Psalm 133:1-3

Aaron was the high priest, and he was anointed with oil, which symbolizes the Holy Spirit. The power and anointing of the Holy Spirit were dumped on his head and ran down on his beard and through his garments. It's the holy anointing oil, the power of the Holy Spirit.

What occasioned this blessing? On whom did God command this blessing? On those who dwell together in unity. These verses say that there is a blessing that comes when people are in unity that won't manifest any other way.

"WE TRUSTED HIM"

Strife is an inroad of Satan!

For where envying and strife is, there is confusion and every evil work.

James 3:16

Did you see that? Every evil work! Some people think, *Well, I'm not giving place to the devil*, yet they're mad, in strife, and bitter.

For rebellion is as the sin of witchcraft, and stubbornness is as iniquity and idolatry.

1 Samuel 15:23

Perhaps you know better than to allow a Ouija board in your house, and you wouldn't dare participate in a séance. But if you're self-willed and stubborn, those are the same as the sins of witchcraft and idolatry. Maybe you were raised to think that living in strife is just the way it has to be. That's not true. Where envying and strife is, so is confusion and every evil work (James 3:16).

Remember that church where the pastor received a revelation of John 14:12 and they saw a man raised from the dead on Sunday morning? This same church had been really struggling with discouragement earlier that week. A certain family was trying to believe for their son to be healed. He was in a coma, and the whole church got involved with fasting and praying for him. Despite what they did, the boy died, and the funeral took place the week before I got there. They were really struggling.

When I arrived, the pastor told me what had happened, and I visited with the parents of the boy who had died. They were saying, "We just can't understand why this happened. We believed God. We trusted Him, doing everything we knew to do, and yet our son died."

PLAYING RUSSIAN ROULETTE

I didn't know what to tell these parents except, "Look, it's not God who failed. He didn't do this. I don't know where the problem is, but it's not God. He didn't fail you." I didn't know this couple very well, so I went out to eat with them every single day. By the end of that time, I discovered that there had been a lot of strife in that home. The father and mother were talking about divorce. The day the boy's accident happened, the boy and his mother had gotten into a fight.

She had said, "I hate you! Get out of this house and don't ever come back!" The young man left the home, went to school, and broke the school's rules. He left during lunch and went over to a friend's house. They were playing Russian roulette with a gun. This young man held the gun to his head and pulled the trigger. That was the reason he was in a coma. He shot himself in the head. It wasn't suicide, but it was stupid. His parents just couldn't understand how it happened. It happened because of all the strife in the home. There's a reason that things happen. We don't always know the reason, but it's never God who fails.

However, God commands a blessing where there is unity (Ps. 133).

> *And when the day of Pentecost was fully come, they were all with one accord in one place. [2] And suddenly there came a sound from heaven as of a rushing mighty wind, and it filled all the house where they were sitting.*
>
> Acts 2:1-2

When the believers were all together in unity, the power of the Holy Spirit fell. Unfortunately, the body of Christ is so divided today. We're separated from and angry with each other. There are Baptists and Methodists, Catholics and Pentecostals, Lutherans, Episcopalians, Presbyterians, and charismatics—and nobody will fellowship with anybody who's different than they are. Often, there's disunity even in a single local church. We have all this strife, yet we wonder why we're struggling.

THE ONLY REASON

For where envying and strife is, there is confusion and every evil work.

James 3:16

This verse says there is *"every evil work."* Not some, but *every*. You just turn Satan loose when you are angry. You might say, "But, Andrew, I just need to get it off my chest." No, you just need to repent and get over it.

Only by pride cometh contention.

Proverbs 13:10

Pride is the only reason for this strife. It's not your personality type. It's not what other people do to you. It's what is inside of you—your pride, your selfishness—that makes you angry. Although God commands His blessing on unity, it's not even a goal for most people.

Many folks have someone they hate. They're mad, and they just don't care. They don't want to get over it. They think that they're hurting this other person by harboring unforgiveness. No, they're hurting themselves.

CHANGE THE HEARTS

When you hate someone and live in unforgiveness, it's as if you're drinking poison and thinking, *That'll sure teach them!* No, drinking poison hurts you. It isn't going to hurt them. Having unforgiveness toward somebody isn't hurting them; it's hurting you. It destroys you. Satan uses that as an inroad into your life. It stops the blessing of God. You need to forgive and start walking in love.

We as the church need to be in unity. There are some things that just aren't going to happen in the body of Christ until we get into unity. Some things just cannot be done on an individual basis.

I and several other ministers and pastors visited with Oral Roberts in his home just a couple of months before he died. One of the pastors asked him, "Oral, how can we turn our nation back to God?" Oral Roberts then said one of the wisest things I've ever heard: "You can't turn the nation back to God. Nobody can do that. One person can't turn a nation to God. All you can do is what the Lord tells you to do. Then if other people do what He tells them to do, God can knit these things together and turn a nation. But you can't do that. Don't try to take that responsibility on yourself." Profound!

You can't do some things by yourself. America isn't going to turn back to God because of one person. We could elect to the White House the godliest individual there is—someone who is totally committed to the Lord and makes every decision based on His Word. Do you know what would happen? There would be civil war. America would destroy itself because we have lost the battle out amongst the people.

Many Americans now don't care about morality. They hate God and everything moral. If we put somebody in as president and started enforcing morals, there would be a revolution in this country. It's not one person in the White House who's going to turn anything around. We must reach our fellow countrymen. We have to change the hearts of people. American voters elect people into office who reflect their morals.

GOVERNMENT IS A REFLECTION

John Adams, the first vice president and the second president of the United States, basically said that democracy is totally unfit or unsuited for anybody but a moral people. If America ever ceases to be moral, democracy will destroy us. That's what we see happening today. America has ceased to be moral. We are ungodly. Our culture is embracing and promoting ungodly things.

> *Righteousness exalteth a nation: but sin is a reproach to any people.*
> Proverbs 14:34

People can't just put one person in government and expect that to change a nation. The hearts of individual people must be changed. If a revival occurred among the people of a country, the government of that country would change as a byproduct. Right now, the American government is a reflection of American culture. If you're an American, then you ought to exercise your right to vote because it's irresponsible not to, and when you do, be sure to vote according to godliness, not outward appearance. Compared to righteousness, things like good looks, gender, and color just aren't important.

Each person must do their own part. I'm doing what the Lord is telling me to do. Although I'm trying to influence as many people as I can, I can't turn this nation to God by myself. But if I do what I'm supposed to do, and if you do what God is leading you to do, and if every other Christian goes out as salt and light and does what the Lord wants them to do, this nation could turn back to God (Matt. 5:13-16). But it'll have to be through unity. We must quit fighting each other and come into unity. That's where the Lord commands the blessing.

There is a God-given blessing on unity, and right now, we aren't seeing it. Our society is more fragmented than we've probably ever been.

ANDREW'S RECOMMENDATIONS FOR FURTHER STUDY

If you struggle with pride, anger, or being in strife, I encourage you to get hold of my teachings entitled *Self-Centeredness: The Source of All Grief* and *Anger Management.* They'll help you!

Outline

I.   When you trust in God, there's a blessing that comes upon you:

O taste and see that the LORD *is good: blessed is the man that trusteth in him.*
Psalm 34:8

   A.   It's better to rely on Him instead of trusting in yourself, because when you do, you're blessed!

   B.   Peace is one of the blessings that comes through trusting in God:

Thou wilt keep him in perfect peace, whose mind is stayed on thee: because he trusteth in thee.
Isaiah 26:3

   C.   Many Christians struggle with peace.

   D.   They're stressed-out and worried.

   E.   They feel like they've failed and deserve whatever is happening to them—that God is holding sin against them.

   F.   These things add up and compound upon each other.

II. You need to understand that you are forgiven of all sin.

   A.   If God forgave you of your sins, which is the greatest miracle that could ever happen, how could you believe that He won't heal you?

   B.   If He loved you enough to forgive you of your sins, then He loves you enough to heal your body.

   C.   He'd keep you in perfect peace!

III. Psalm 37:25-26, Isaiah 54:13-14, Psalm 112:1-2, and Psalm 115:13-15 are about your children being blessed.

   A.   God will increase both you and your children.

   B.   Now, this doesn't rule out the fact that your children have a choice of their own to make, to trust God or not.

C. This doesn't mean that they will automatically be forced to do the right thing, but your children will be blessed.

IV. Aaron was the high priest, and he was anointed with oil, which symbolizes the Holy Spirit.

Behold, how good and how pleasant it is for brethren to dwell together in unity! [2] It is like the precious ointment upon the head, that ran down upon the beard, even Aaron's beard: that went down to the skirts of his garments. [3] As the dew of Hermon, and as the dew that descended upon the mountains of Zion: for there the Lord *commanded the blessing, even life for evermore.*

Psalm 133:1-3

A. On whom did God command this blessing?

B. On those who dwell together in unity.

C. These verses say that there is a blessing that comes on people when they are in unity that won't manifest any other way.

V. Strife is an inroad of Satan:

For where envying and strife is, there is confusion and every evil work.

James 3:16

A. Some people think, *Well, I'm not giving place to the devil*, yet they're mad, in strife, and bitter.

B. If you're self-willed and stubborn, those are the same as the sins of witchcraft and idolatry:

For rebellion is as the sin of witchcraft, and stubbornness is as iniquity and idolatry.

1 Samuel 15:23

C. Maybe you were raised to think that living in strife is just the way it has to be.

D. That's not true.

VI. When the believers were all together in unity, the power of the Holy Spirit fell:

> *And when the day of Pentecost was fully come, they were all with one accord in one place. [2] And suddenly there came a sound from heaven as of a rushing mighty wind, and it filled all the house where they were sitting.*
>
> Acts 2:1-2

    A. Unfortunately, the body of Christ is so divided today.

    B. The body is separated from and angry with each other.

    C. Nobody will fellowship with anybody who's different than they are.

    D. The church has all this strife, yet we wonder why we're struggling.

VII. You turn Satan loose when you are angry (James 3:16).

    A. You might say, "But, Andrew, I just need to get it off my chest."

    B. No, you just need to repent and get over it.

    C. Pride is the only reason for this strife:

> *Only by pride cometh contention.*
>
> Proverbs 13:10

    D. It's what is inside of you—your pride, your selfishness—that makes you angry.

    E. Although God commands His blessing on unity, it's not even a goal for most people.

    F. They're mad, and they just don't care.

    G. They think that they're hurting this other person by harboring unforgiveness.

    H. No, they're hurting themselves.

    I. Satan uses that as an inroad into their lives.

    J. It stops the blessing of God.

    K. They need to forgive and start walking in love.

VIII. We as the church need to be in unity.

    A. Some things just cannot be done on an individual basis.

    B. America isn't going to turn back to God because of one person.

    C. We as the church have to change the hearts of people.

    D. American voters elect people into office who reflect their morals.

IX. John Adams, the first vice president and the second president of the United States, basically said that democracy is totally unfit or unsuited for anybody but a moral people.

    A. If America ever ceases to be moral, democracy will destroy its people.

    B. That's what is happening today.

> *Righteousness exalteth a nation: but sin is a reproach to any people.*
> Proverbs 14:34

    C. If you're an American, then you ought to exercise your right to vote because it's irresponsible not to, and when you do, be sure to vote according to godliness, not outward appearance.

    D. Compared to righteousness, things like good looks, gender, and color aren't important.

    E. If you do what God is leading you to do, and if every other Christian goes out as salt and light and does what the Lord wants them to do, this nation could turn back to God (Matt. 5:13-16).

ANDREW'S RECOMMENDATIONS FOR FURTHER STUDY

If you struggle with pride, anger, or being in strife, I encourage you to get hold of my teachings entitled *Self-Centeredness: The Source of All Grief* and *Anger Management*. They'll help you!

Teacher's Guide

1. When we trust in God, there's a blessing that comes upon us:

    O taste and see that the L ORD is good: blessed is the man that trusteth in him.

    Psalm 34:8

    It's better to rely on Him instead of trusting in ourselves, because when we do, we're blessed! Peace is one of the blessings that comes through trusting in God:

    Thou wilt keep him in perfect peace, whose mind is stayed on thee: because he trusteth in thee.

    Isaiah 26:3

    Many Christians struggle with peace. They're stressed-out and worried. They feel like they've failed and deserve whatever is happening to them—that God is holding sin against them. These things add up and compound upon each other.

    1a. When you trust in God, what comes upon you?
    A. A zeal
    B. A thirst
    C. A power
    D. All of the above
    E. None of the above
    E. None of the above
    1b. Psalm 34:8 says, "*O taste and see that the _____ is good: blessed is the man that trusteth in him.*
    "L ORD "
    1c. What is one of the blessings that comes through trusting in God?
    Peace
    1d. According to Isaiah 26:3, "*Thou wilt keep him in _____ peace, whose mind is stayed on thee: because he trusteth in thee.*"
    "Perfect"
    1e. *Discussion question:* How have you learned to experience peace?
    Discussion question

2. We need to understand that we are forgiven of all sin. If God forgave us of our sins, which is the greatest miracle that could ever happen, how could we believe that He won't heal us? If He loved us enough to forgive us of our sins, then He loves us enough to heal our bodies. He'd keep us in perfect peace!

2a. *Discussion question:* When you consider that God would forgive and heal you, what do you think about God's love?
<u>*Discussion question*</u>

3.   Psalm 37:25-26, Isaiah 54:13-14, Psalm 112:1-2, and Psalm 115:13-15 are about our children being blessed. God will increase both us and our children. Now, this doesn't rule out the fact that our children have a choice of their own to make, to trust God or not. This doesn't mean that they will automatically be forced to do the right thing, but our children will be blessed.

3a. Psalm 37:25-26, Isaiah 54:13-14, Psalm 112:1-2, and Psalm 115:13-15 are about what?
<u>Your children being blessed</u>

3b. True or false: This rules out the fact that your children have a choice to make, to trust God or not.
<u>False</u>

3c. True or false: Your children will not automatically be forced to do the right thing, even though they are blessed.
<u>True</u>

4.   Aaron was the high priest, and he was anointed with oil, which symbolizes the Holy Spirit.

> *Behold, how good and how pleasant it is for brethren to dwell together in unity! [2] It is like the precious ointment upon the head, that ran down upon the beard, even Aaron's beard: that went down to the skirts of his garments. [3] As the dew of Hermon, and as the dew that descended upon the mountains of Zion: for there the* Lord *commanded the blessing, even life for evermore.*
>
> Psalm 133:1-3

On whom did God command this blessing? On those who dwell together in unity. These verses say that there is a blessing that comes on people when they are in unity that won't manifest any other way.

4a. Psalm 133:1-3 says, "*Behold, how _____ and how _____ it is for brethren to dwell together in _____! [2] It is like the precious _____ upon the head, that ran down upon the beard, even Aaron's beard: that went down to the skirts of his garments. [3] As the dew of Hermon, and as the dew that descended upon the mountains of Zion: for there the* Lord _____ *the* _____, *even life for evermore.*"
<u>*"Good" / "pleasant" / "unity" / "ointment" / "commanded" / "blessing"*</u>

4b. On whom did God command this blessing?
     On those who dwell together in unity

5.   Strife is an inroad of Satan:

     For where envying and strife is, there is confusion and every evil work.

     James 3:16

Some people think, *Well, I'm not giving place to the devil*, yet they're mad, in strife, and bitter. If we're self-willed and stubborn, those are the same as the sins of witchcraft and idolatry:

     For rebellion is as the sin of witchcraft, and stubbornness is as iniquity and idolatry.

     1 Samuel 15:23

Maybe we were raised to think that living in strife is just the way it has to be. That's not true.

5a. What is an inroad of Satan?
     Strife
5b. According to James 3:16, "*For where envying and strife is, there is confusion and _____ evil work.*"
     "Every"
5c. What are the same as the sins of witchcraft and idolatry?
     Being self-willed and stubborn
5d. What verse says that?
     1 Samuel 15:23
5e. True or false: Living in strife is just the way it has to be.
     False

6.   When the believers were all together in unity, the power of the Holy Spirit fell:

     And when the day of Pentecost was fully come, they were all with one accord in one place. [2] And suddenly there came a sound from heaven as of a rushing mighty wind, and it filled all the house where they were sitting.

     Acts 2:1-2

Unfortunately, the body of Christ is so divided today. The body is separated from and angry with each other. Nobody will fellowship with anybody who's different than they are. The church has all this strife, yet we wonder why we're struggling.

6a. When did the power of the Holy Spirit fall?
    A. When the believers lived in the same house
    B. When the believers agreed on everything
    C. When the believers cooked together
    D. When the believers were all together in unity
    E. When the believers attended the same local church
    D. When the believers were all together in unity

6b. Acts 2:1-2 says, *"And when the day of Pentecost was fully come, they were all with one _____ in one place. [2] And suddenly there came a sound from heaven as of a rushing mighty wind, and it filled all the house where they were sitting."*
    "Accord"

6c. *Discussion question:* Why do you think the body of Christ is so divided today?
    Discussion question

7.   We turn Satan loose when we are angry (James 3:16). We might say, "But I just need to get it off my chest." No, we just need to repent and get over it. Pride is the only reason for this strife:

> *Only by pride cometh contention.*
>
> Proverbs 13:10

It's what is inside of us—our pride, our selfishness—that makes us angry. Although God commands His blessing on unity, it's not even a goal for most people. They're mad, and they just don't care. They think that they're hurting this other person by harboring unforgiveness. No, they're hurting themselves. Satan uses that as an inroad into their lives. It stops the blessing of God. They need to forgive and start walking in love.

7a. You turn Satan loose when you are what (James 3:16)?
    A. Angry
    B. Quiet
    C. Happy
    D. Loud
    E. Late
    A. Angry

7b. If you say you need to get something off your chest, what do you really need to do?
    A. Receive and get a blessing
    B. Respire and get a nap
    C. Repent and get over it
    D. Relax and get a pizza
    E. Relent and get some therapy
    C. Repent and get over it

7c. According to Proverbs 13:10, "_____ *by pride cometh contention.*"
"Only"
7d. What makes you angry?
What is inside of you—your pride, your selfishness
7e. *Discussion question:* How do you forgive and start walking in love?
Discussion question

8.   We as the church need to be in unity. Some things just cannot be done on an individual basis. America isn't going to turn back to God because of one person. We as the church have to change the hearts of people. American voters elect people into office who reflect their morals.

8a. *Discussion question:* What does a unified church look like?
Discussion question

9.   John Adams, the first vice president and the second president of the United States, basically said that democracy is totally unfit or unsuited for anybody but a moral people. If America ever ceases to be moral, democracy will destroy its people. That's what is happening today.

> *Righteousness exalteth a nation: but sin is a reproach to any people.*
>
> Proverbs 14:34

If we're Americans, then we ought to exercise our right to vote because it's irresponsible not to. When we do, we should be sure to vote according to godliness, not outward appearance. Compared to righteousness, things like good looks, gender, and color aren't important. If we do what God is leading us to do, and if every other Christian goes out as salt and light and does what the Lord wants them to do, this nation could turn back to God (Matt. 5:13-16).

9a. If America ever ceases to be moral, democracy will _____ its people.
Destroy
9b. According to Proverbs 14:34, "_____ *exalteth a nation: but* _____ *is a* _____ *to any people.*"
"Righteousness" / "sin" / "reproach"
9c. *Discussion question:* How are you going to be salt and light (Matt. 5:13-16)?
Discussion question

Discipleship Questions

1. When you trust in God, what comes upon you?
    A. A zeal
    B. A thirst
    C. A power
    D. All of the above
    E. None of the above

2. Psalm 34:8 says, "*O taste and see that the* _____ *is good: blessed is the man that trusteth in him.*

3. What is one of the blessings that comes through trusting in God?

    _____

    _____

    _____

4. According to Isaiah 26:3, "*Thou wilt keep him in* _____ *peace, whose mind is stayed on thee: because he trusteth in thee.*"

5. *Discussion question:* How have you learned to experience peace?

    _____

    _____

    _____

6. *Discussion question:* When you consider that God would forgive and heal you, what do you think about God's love?

    _____

    _____

    _____

7.	Psalm 37:25-26, Isaiah 54:13-14, Psalm 112:1-2, and Psalm 115:13-15 are about what?

_____

_____

_____

8.	True or false: This rules out the fact that your children have a choice to make, to trust God or not.

9.	True or false: Your children will not automatically be forced to do the right thing, even though they are blessed.

10.	Psalm 133:1-3 says, *"Behold, how _____ and how _____ it is for brethren to dwell together in _____! [2] It is like the precious _____ upon the head, that ran down upon the beard, even Aaron's beard: that went down to the skirts of his garments. [3] As the dew of Hermon, and as the dew that descended upon the mountains of Zion: for there the* LORD _____ *the _____, even life for evermore."*

11.	On whom did God command this blessing?

_____

_____

_____

12.	What is an inroad of Satan?

_____

_____

_____

13.	According to James 3:16, *"For where envying and strife is, there is confusion and _____ evil work."*

14.	What are the same as the sins of witchcraft and idolatry?

_____

_____

_____

15. What verse says that?

_____

_____

_____

16. True or false: Living in strife is just the way it has to be.

17. When did the power of the Holy Spirit fall?
    A. When the believers lived in the same house
    B. When the believers agreed on everything
    C. When the believers cooked together
    D. When the believers were all together in unity
    E. When the believers attended the same local church

18. Acts 2:1-2 says, *"And when the day of Pentecost was fully come, they were all with one _____ in one place. [2] And suddenly there came a sound from heaven as of a rushing mighty wind, and it filled all the house where they were sitting."*

19. *Discussion question:* Why do you think the body of Christ is so divided today?

_____

_____

_____

20. You turn Satan loose when you are what (James 3:16)?
    A. Angry
    B. Quiet
    C. Happy
    D. Loud
    E. Late

21. If you say you need to get something off your chest, what do you really need to do?
    A. Receive and get a blessing
    B. Respire and get a nap
    C. Repent and get over it
    D. Relax and get a pizza
    E. Relent and get some therapy

22. According to Proverbs 13:10, *"_____ by pride cometh contention."*

23. What makes you angry?

_____

_____

_____

24. *Discussion question:* How do you forgive and start walking in love?

_____

_____

_____

25. *Discussion question:* What does a unified church look like?

_____

_____

_____

26. If America ever ceases to be moral, democracy will _____ its people.

27. According to Proverbs 14:34, "_____ *exalteth a nation: but* _____ *is a* _____ *to any people.*"

28. *Discussion question:* How are you going to be salt and light (Matt. 5:13-16)?

_____

_____

_____

Answer Key

1. E. None of the above

2. *"Lord"*

3. Peace

4. *"Perfect"*

5. *Discussion question*

6. *Discussion question*

7. Your children being blessed

8. False

9. True

10. *"Good"* / *"pleasant"* / *"unity"* / *"ointment"* / *"commanded"* / *"blessing"*

11. On those who dwell together in unity

12. Strife

13. *"Every"*

14. Being self-willed and stubborn

15. 1 Samuel 15:23

16. False

17. D. When the believers were all together in unity

18. *"Accord"*

19. *Discussion question*

20. A. Angry

21. C. Repent and get over it

22. *"Only"*

23. What is inside of you—your pride, your selfishness

24. *Discussion question*

25. *Discussion question*

26. Destroy

27. *"Righteousness" / "sin" / "reproach"*

28. *Discussion question*

Scriptures

PSALM 34:8
O taste and see that the LORD is good: blessed is the man that trusteth in him.

ISAIAH 26:3
Thou wilt keep him in perfect peace, whose mind is stayed on thee: because he trusteth in thee.

PSALM 37:25-26
I have been young, and now am old; yet have I not seen the righteous forsaken, nor his seed begging bread. [26] He is ever merciful, and lendeth; and his seed is blessed.

ISAIAH 54:13-14
And all thy children shall be taught of the LORD; and great shall be the peace of thy children. [14] In righteousness shalt thou be established: thou shalt be far from oppression; for thou shalt not fear: and from terror; for it shall not come near thee.

PSALM 112:1-2
Praise ye the LORD. Blessed is the man that feareth the LORD, that delighteth greatly in his commandments. [2] His seed shall be mighty upon earth: the generation of the upright shall be blessed.

PSALM 115:13-15
He will bless them that fear the LORD, both small and great. [14] The LORD shall increase you more and more, you and your children. [15] Ye are blessed of the LORD which made heaven and earth.

PSALM 40:4
Blessed is that man that maketh the LORD his trust, and respecteth not the proud, nor such as turn aside to lies.

PSALM 133:1-3
Behold, how good and how pleasant it is for brethren to dwell together in unity! [2] It is like the precious ointment upon the head, that ran down upon the beard, even Aaron's beard: that went down to the skirts of his garments; [3] As the dew of Hermon, and as the dew that descended upon the mountains of Zion: for there the LORD commanded the blessing, even life for evermore.

JAMES 3:16

For where envying and strife is, there is confusion and every evil work.

1 SAMUEL 15:23

For rebellion is as the sin of witchcraft, and stubbornness is as iniquity and idolatry. Because thou hast rejected the word of the LORD, he hath also rejected thee from being king.

JOHN 14:12

Verily, verily, I say unto you, He that believeth on me, the works that I do shall he do also; and greater works than these shall he do; because I go unto my Father.

ACTS 2:1-2

And when the day of Pentecost was fully come, they were all with one accord in one place. [2] And suddenly there came a sound from heaven as of a rushing mighty wind, and it filled all the house where they were sitting.

PROVERBS 13:10

Only by pride cometh contention: but with the well advised is wisdom.

PROVERBS 14:34

Righteousness exalteth a nation: but sin is a reproach to any people.

MATTHEW 5:13-16

Ye are the salt of the earth: but if the salt have lost his savour, wherewith shall it be salted? it is thenceforth good for nothing, but to be cast out, and to be trodden under foot of men. [14] Ye are the light of the world. A city that is set on an hill cannot be hid. [15] Neither do men light a candle, and put it under a bushel, but on a candlestick; and it giveth light unto all that are in the house. [16] Let your light so shine before men, that they may see your good works, and glorify your Father which is in heaven.

Great Faith

LESSON 22

Now therefore hearken unto me [wisdom], O ye children: for blessed are they that keep my ways. [33] Hear instruction, and be wise, and refuse it not. [34] Blessed is the man that heareth me, watching daily at my gates, waiting at the posts of my doors. [35] For whoso findeth me findeth life, and shall obtain favour of the LORD. [36] But he that sinneth against me wrongeth his own soul: all they that hate me love death.

Proverbs 8:32-36, brackets mine

My son, if thou wilt receive my words, and hide my commandments with thee; [2] So that thou incline thine ear unto wisdom, and apply thine heart to understanding.

Proverbs 2:1-2

To know wisdom and instruction; to perceive the words of understanding; [3] To receive the instruction of wisdom, justice, and judgment, and equity; [4] To give subtilty to the simple, to the young man knowledge and discretion. [5] A wise man will hear, and will increase learning; and a man of understanding shall attain unto wise counsels.

Proverbs 1:2-5

We have been forsaking wisdom. God's Word has been given to people for wisdom, yet society has been rejecting it. Specifically, the book of Proverbs is full of wisdom for everyday life.

I recognize that I'm preaching to the choir here. You're reading this book and are almost done with it, but most people in our country and many different countries around the world have rejected godly wisdom. They've embraced the wisdom of this world, and they love death (Prov. 8:36). They hate their own souls and are destroying themselves. If you want to see the blessing of God manifest, you need to walk in wisdom—the wisdom that's revealed in the Word of God!

SOMEBODY MISSES ME

The memory of the just is blessed: but the name of the wicked shall rot.

Proverbs 10:7

If you live a righteous life, you'll have a godly legacy. People will talk about you when you're gone, saying, "What a great person they were. They really made a difference." But the memory of the wicked will rot. People will say, "Good riddance! Glad they're gone. They were taking up too much space." I know that many don't like to consider this, but how will people talk about you when you're gone?

We just had a funeral for one of my employees who died in a car wreck. There's a saying that goes "Live your life so that the preacher won't have to lie at your funeral." This man certainly did that. He loved the Lord and lived a godly life, and everything people said about him was awesome.

What about you? What if you died right now? Would there be a lot of good things to say about you? I'm not asking this to agitate or hurt you in any way. We each need to confront ourselves with this truth. What will our legacies be? If you want people to miss you, give them something to miss. Live a godly life and your memory will be blessed (Prov. 10:7). Isn't that awesome? I sure hope somebody misses me when I'm gone!

LEAP FOR JOY

When you're persecuted, you ought to shout and leap for joy. Why? Because there's a special blessing on every person who has been persecuted for righteousness' sake.

> *Blessed are they which are persecuted for righteousness' sake: for theirs is the kingdom of heaven. [11] Blessed are ye, when men shall revile you, and persecute you, and shall say all manner of evil against you falsely, for my sake. [12] Rejoice, and be exceeding glad: for great is your reward in heaven: for so persecuted they the prophets which were before you.*

Matthew 5:10-12

Someday you will stand before God, and He will honor you in front of all creation. People who have never heard of you will see you rewarded because you stood up for the Lord and suffered the criticism, rejection, and persecution of other people. If you understood this, you could rejoice. You could be like the Apostle Paul, who said he longed for the fellowship of Christ's sufferings (Phil. 3:10). When you understand that when you're persecuted for righteousness' sake, it's like a crown that you could wear, then you'll look forward to persecution. Now, I'm not saying that you should be unwise and cause persecution to come your way, but when it does due to your godly life, you can look forward to it because you know that the Lord will bless you for it.

Mary, the mother of Jesus, was a blessed lady. Large groups of people today still talk about how great she was. Now, it was awesome that Mary was chosen to give birth to Jesus, but by our Lord's own words, we who hear the Word of God and keep it are more blessed than even she was!

> *And it came to pass, as he spake these things, a certain woman of the company lifted up her voice, and said unto him, Blessed is the womb that bare thee, and the paps which thou hast sucked. [28] But he said, Yea rather, blessed are they that hear the word of God, and keep it.*
>
> Luke 11:27-28

We're blessed! Jesus said that those who respond to His Word and keep it are more blessed than our Lord's own mother.

MIND IN THE WAY

Givers are more blessed than receivers. Jesus said,

> *It is more blessed to give than to receive.*
>
> Acts 20:35

If you truly understood this, you would choose to be a generous giver because you get blessed when you give.

Jesus appeared to His disciples after He rose from the dead, but Thomas wasn't with them. So, the rest of the disciples told Thomas when they saw him, "The Lord's alive! We've seen Him."

> *But he said unto them, Except I shall see in his hands the print of the nails, and put my finger into the print of the nails, and thrust my hand into his side, I will not believe.*
>
> John 20:25

If you can't believe, it's because you willed not to believe. You chose to believe something else instead of the report of the Lord. You might think, *I just struggle to believe*. It's because you've decided to be that way. Your mind is in the way. You've educated yourself right out of faith. You made a choice not to believe.

FEELING SOMETHING PHYSICAL

Jesus wasn't there when Thomas asked for proof that He had risen from the dead, yet when He showed up eight days later, He walked right over to him. He knew everything that Thomas had said.

> *And after eight days again his disciples were within, and Thomas with them: then came Jesus, the doors being shut, and stood in the midst, and said, Peace be unto you. [27] Then saith he to Thomas, Reach hither thy finger, and behold my hands; and reach hither thy hand, and thrust it into my side: and be not faithless, but believing.*
>
> John 20:26-27

Thomas knew that this was Jesus and knew that He knew everything he had said. Look at Thomas's response:

> *And Thomas answered and said unto him, My Lord and my God.*
>
> John 20:28

There's no indication that Thomas ever stuck his finger into the print of the nails or his hand into Jesus's side. When he knew that it was Jesus, he just fell down and declared Him Lord and God.

> *Jesus saith unto him, Thomas, because thou hast seen me, thou hast believed: blessed are they that have not seen, and yet have believed.*
>
> John 20:29

There is a greater blessing on believing the Word than there is in seeing or feeling something physical. That's powerful!

SPEAK THE WORD ONLY

Growing up in the Baptist church, we were told that miracles had passed away and didn't happen anymore. We didn't have any tangible, physical experience of God. It was all about believing to get saved, and then we were saved and stuck until we went to heaven. We would sing, "When we all get to heaven, what a day that will be," but there was no expectation of encountering God in the rough here and now. There was no steak on the plate while we wait, but it was all pie in the sky by and by. We were told miracles don't happen today.

When I finally got turned on to the Lord, I started hearing about people like Kenneth E. Hagin. He had fire in his hands, saw visions, heard the Lord's voice, and flowed in the power of God. Miracles would happen, and people would experience things and often fall out under God's power. Goose bumps would go up and down their spines. When I heard about all this, I started pressing in. I desired to have a vision. I wanted the Lord to speak to me, so I was praying and asking God to do all of these things.

The Lord took me to Thomas's encounter with the risen Christ in John 20. He said, "If you keep pressuring Me, you can get into the spirit and see some things. But there's a greater blessing on those who will just believe My Word—not because they've had an angel come and tell them something." He contrasted this with Matthew 8, where the centurion said, "Lord, I don't need You to come into my house," but *speak the word only, and my servant shall be healed*" (Matt. 8:8). Jesus marveled at the faith of the centurion and told His disciples, *"Verily I say unto you, I have not found so great faith, no, not in Israel"* (Matt. 8:10).

AGAINST THEIR WILL

Jesus had never found a Jew who believed this strongly, but this Gentile believed so strongly that Jesus marveled at his faith. The greatest faith that the Lord ever saw was a faith that simply took Him at His Word. The least faith that Jesus ever saw was Thomas's faith. Jesus told Thomas to put his finger into the print of the nail (John 20:27); then Thomas basically answered, "Lord, I believe" (John 20:28). Jesus responded that there is a greater blessing on those who will just believe the Word than there is on those who believe because it's been proven to them in some natural, physical way (John 20:29).

I know people who claim to have been inside the remains of Noah's Ark. They say that they've even taken a piece of wood from it. They reason, "We could release a movie on this and make everybody believe." You can't make people believe. Faith is a choice. You can't argue a person into faith. You can't just use something in the natural to force people to believe. It won't work.

There were people who refused to believe even after seeing Lazarus rise from the dead. He had been dead for four days and buried. He came out of the tomb, bound hand and foot with grave clothes that had been wrapped around him. Lazarus couldn't walk, yet he came to the front of the tomb, raised from the dead (John 11:44). People had to take those grave clothes off him. Many of those who saw this miracle believed, but some didn't. They went to report this to the Pharisees, who conspired together with the chief priests about how they could kill both Jesus and Lazarus (John 11:45-53 and 12:10-11).

A rich man died and went to hell. He pleaded that Lazarus (same name, but different man than in John 11) be sent back to witness to his brothers so that they wouldn't come to the terrible place in which he now found himself.

> *And he said unto him, If they hear not Moses and the prophets, neither will they be persuaded, though one rose from the dead.*
>
> Luke 16:31

You can't do something to make people believe against their will. They have to choose to believe.

WALK BY FAITH

Are you waiting until God proves something to you so that there's no faith required on your part? Are you waiting until something is just physical and natural to the point where all your doubts are removed? That doesn't please God.

> *But without faith it is impossible to please him.*
>
> Hebrews 11:6

God could write His name on every cloud that goes over your head if He wanted to. He could have a dog walk up to you and say, "Hey, this is what you're supposed to do today." He used Balaam's donkey to speak, didn't He? God could do anything, but faith is what pleases Him (Heb. 11:6). He's not going to force anyone to believe.

Are you saying, "O God, prove it to me; remove all my doubt"? He's not going to do that. The Lord loves you so much that He wants you to come into His best, and that is to believe without seeing. His best is for you to believe His promises simply because the Holy Spirit bears witness and there's a quickening in your heart. God's best is for you to walk by faith (2 Cor. 5:7). God is a God of faith!

It's not that He won't come down to us, but He's already come down to us in Jesus. He proved everything through Christ. There is more proof that Jesus lived, died, and resurrected than there is that Caesar lived. There's more proof of Jesus's existence than any other fact in history. Do the research. It's there. Since He's already come down to our level and ministered to us, now He's trying to bring us up to His level. He's trying to get us to walk in the supernatural faith that is available to each one of us. There is a blessing on those who will take the Word and believe it, regardless of what they feel (John 20:29).

LIFE WILL BECOME BETTER

There are so many blessings! God has truly provided everything. You just need to choose to believe in the power of His spoken favor. You need to find out what these blessings are and then activate them with your voice. Begin to speak the blessings.

Start acting on the Word. If you cooperate with what He's said, the blessing of God will manifest itself in your life, and your life will become better than you could ever have believed.

God's plans for you are awesome. Your future is so bright, you have to squint to look at it. God loves you, and you're blessed. Receive His very best!

Outline

I. The book of Proverbs is full of wisdom for everyday life (Prov. 1:2-5; 2:1-2; and 8:32-36).

   A. Many people in the United States and different countries around the world have rejected godly wisdom.

   B. They've embraced the wisdom of this world.

   C. If we want to see the blessing of God manifest, we need to walk in wisdom—the wisdom that's revealed in the Word of God!

II. If you live a righteous life, you'll have a godly legacy:

   The memory of the just is blessed: but the name of the wicked shall rot.

   Proverbs 10:7

   A. Many don't like to consider this, but how will people talk about you when you're gone?

   B. Would there be a lot of good things to say about you?

   C. You need to confront yourself with this truth.

   D. If you want people to miss you, give them something to miss.

III. There's a special blessing on every person who has been persecuted for righteousness' sake:

   Blessed are they which are persecuted for righteousness' sake: for theirs is the kingdom of heaven. [11] Blessed are ye, when men shall revile you, and persecute you, and shall say all manner of evil against you falsely, for my sake. [12] Rejoice, and be exceeding glad: for great is your reward in heaven: for so persecuted they the prophets which were before you.

   Matthew 5:10-12

   A. Someday you will stand before God, and He will honor you in front of all creation.

   B. People who have never heard of you will see you rewarded because you stood up for the Lord and suffered the criticism, rejection, and persecution of other people.

C. If you understood this, you could rejoice.

D. When you understand that when you're persecuted for righteousness' sake, it's like a crown that you could wear, then you'll look forward to persecution (Phil. 3:10).

E. You should not be unwise and cause persecution to come your way, but when it does come due to your godly life, you can look forward to it because you know that the Lord will bless you for it.

IV. By Jesus's own words, we who hear the Word of God and keep it are more blessed than even His mother was:

And it came to pass, as he spake these things, a certain woman of the company lifted up her voice, and said unto him, Blessed is the womb that bare thee, and the paps which thou hast sucked. [28] But he said, Yea rather, blessed are they that hear the word of God, and keep it.

Luke 11:27-28

A. We're blessed!

B. Givers are more blessed than receivers:

It is more blessed to give than to receive.

Acts 20:35

C. If we truly understood this, we would choose to be generous givers because we get blessed when we give.

V. If you can't believe, it's because you willed not to believe (John 20:25).

A. You chose to believe something else instead of the report of the Lord.

B. Your mind is in the way.

C. You've educated yourself right out of faith.

D. The greatest faith that the Lord ever saw was a faith that simply took Him at His Word (Matt. 8:10).

E. The least faith that Jesus ever saw was Thomas's faith (John 20:29), who basically said "Lord, I believe" (John 20:28) only after he saw Jesus risen from the dead.

F. There is a greater blessing on those who will just believe the Word than there is on those who believe because it's been proven to them in some natural, physical way.

VI. You can't argue a person into faith.

   A. You can't just use something in the natural to force people to believe (Luke 16:31); it won't work.

   B. Everyone has to choose to believe.

VII. God could do anything, but faith is what pleases Him (Heb. 11:6).

   A. The Lord loves you so much that He wants you to come into His best, and that is to believe without seeing.

   B. His best is for you to believe His promises simply because the Holy Spirit bears witness and there's a quickening in your heart.

   C. God's best is for you to walk by faith (2 Cor. 5:7).

   D. It's not that He won't come down to you, but He's already come down to you in Jesus.

   E. Now He's trying to bring you up to His level.

VIII. There are so many blessings!

   A. God has truly provided everything.

   B. You need to choose to believe in the power of His spoken favor and to find out what these blessings are and then activate them with your voice.

   C. Start acting on the Word.

   D. If you cooperate with what He's said, the blessing of God will manifest itself in your life, and your life will become better than you could ever have believed.

   E. God's plans for you are awesome.

F.   Your future is so bright, you have to squint to look at it.

G.   God loves you, and you're blessed.

H.   Receive His very best!

Teacher's Guide

1.   The book of Proverbs is full of wisdom for everyday life (Prov. 1:2-5; 2:1-2; and 8:32-36). Many people in the United States and different countries around the world have rejected godly wisdom. They've embraced the wisdom of this world. If we want to see the blessing of God manifest, we need to walk in wisdom—the wisdom that's revealed in the Word of God!

1a.   What is the book of Proverbs full of (Prov. 1:2-5; 2:1-2; and 8:32-36)?
Wisdom

1b.   *Discussion question:* What are some examples of how people have rejected godly wisdom?
Discussion question

1c.   If you want to see the blessing of God manifest, you need to _____ in wisdom—the wisdom that's revealed in the Word of God!
A.   Pay
B.   Grow
C.   Walk
D.   Sit
E.   Rest
C.   Walk

2.   If we live righteous lives, we'll have godly legacies:

> *The memory of the just is blessed: but the name of the wicked shall rot.*
>
> Proverbs 10:7

Many don't like to consider this, but how will people talk about us when we're gone? Would there be a lot of good things to say about us? We need to confront ourselves with this truth. If we want people to miss us, we need to give them something to miss.

2a.   If you _____ a righteous life, you'll have a godly legacy.
Live

2b.   According to Proverbs 10:7, "*The _____ of the just is blessed: but the _____ of the wicked shall rot.*"
"Memory" / "name"

2c.   *Discussion question:* What can you do to leave a godly legacy?
Discussion question

3.   There's a special blessing on every person who has been persecuted for righteousness' sake:

Blessed are they which are persecuted for righteousness' sake: for theirs is the kingdom of heaven. [11] Blessed are ye, when men shall revile you, and persecute you, and shall say all manner of evil against you falsely, for my sake. [12] Rejoice, and be exceeding glad: for great is your reward in heaven: for so persecuted they the prophets which were before you.

Matthew 5:10-12

Someday we will stand before God, and He will honor us in front of all creation. People who have never heard of us will see us rewarded because we stood up for the Lord and suffered the criticism, rejection, and persecution of other people. If we understood this, we could rejoice. When we understand that when we're persecuted for righteousness' sake, it's like a crown that we could wear, then we'll look forward to persecution (Phil. 3:10). We should not be unwise and cause persecution to come our way, but when it does come due to our godly lives, we can look forward to it because we know that the Lord will bless us for it.

3a. What is on every person who has been persecuted for righteousness' sake?
   A special blessing
3b. Where does it say that in the Bible?
   Matthew 5:10-12
3c. Someday you will stand before God, and He will do what?
   A. Reject you in front of all creation
   B. Acknowledge you in front of all creation
   C. Condemn you in front of all creation
   D. Embarrass you in front of all creation
   E. Honor you in front of all creation
   E. Honor you in front of all creation
3d. True or false: You shouldn't cause persecution to come your way.
   True
3e. When persecution comes due to your godly life, why can you look forward to it (Phil. 3:10)?
   Because you know that the Lord will bless you for it

4. By Jesus's own words, we who hear the Word of God and keep it are more blessed than even His mother was:

And it came to pass, as he spake these things, a certain woman of the company lifted up her voice, and said unto him, Blessed is the womb that bare thee, and the paps which thou hast sucked. [28] But he said, Yea rather, blessed are they that hear the word of God, and keep it.

Luke 11:27-28

We're blessed! Givers are more blessed than receivers:

> *It is more blessed to give than to receive.*

Acts 20:35

If we truly understood this, we would choose to be generous givers because we get blessed when we give.

4a. Luke 11:27-28 says, *"And it came to pass, as he spake these things, a certain woman of the company lifted up her voice, and said unto him, _____ is the womb that bare thee, and the paps which thou hast sucked. [28] But he said, Yea _____, blessed are they that hear the word of God, and keep it."*
"Blessed" / "rather"

4b. According to Acts 20:35, *"It is more blessed to _____ than to _____."*
   A. "Receive" / "give"
   B. "Work" / "play"
   C. "Walk" / "run"
   D. "Give" / "receive"
   E. "Eat" / "sleep"
   D. "Give" / "receive"

5. If we can't believe, it's because we willed not to believe (John 20:25). We chose to believe something else instead of the report of the Lord. Our minds are in the way. We've educated ourselves right out of faith. The greatest faith that the Lord ever saw was a faith that simply took Him at His Word (Matt. 8:10). The least faith that Jesus ever saw was Thomas's faith (John 20:29), who basically said "Lord, I believe" (John 20:28) only after he saw Jesus risen from the dead. There is a greater blessing on those who will just believe the Word than there is on those who believe because it's been proven to them in some natural, physical way.

5a. If you can't believe, it's because you _____ not to believe (John 20:25).
Willed

5b. What did you choose to believe instead?
Something other than the report of the Lord

5c. When that happens, what is in the way?
   A. Your brain
   B. Your thoughts
   C. Your mind
   D. All of the above
   E. None of the above
   D. All of the above

5d. True or false: The greatest faith that the Lord ever saw was a faith that simply took Him at His Word (Matt. 8:10).
True

5e. True or false: The least faith that Jesus ever saw was Thomas's faith, who basically said "Lord, I believe" only after he saw Jesus risen from the dead (John 20:28-29).
True

5f. What kind of blessing is on those who will just believe the Word?
A greater blessing

6. We can't argue a person into faith. We can't just use something in the natural to force people to believe (Luke 16:31). It won't work. They have to choose to believe.

6a. True or false: You can argue a person into faith.
False

6b. *Discussion question:* Why do you think a person won't believe even when there is proof (Luke 16:31)?
Discussion question

7. God could do anything, but faith is what pleases Him (Heb. 11:6). The Lord loves us so much that He wants us to come into His best, and that is to believe without seeing. His best is for us to believe His promises simply because the Holy Spirit bears witness and there's a quickening in our hearts. God's best is for us to walk by faith (2 Cor. 5:7). It's not that He won't come down to us, but He's already come down to us in Jesus. Now He's trying to bring us up to His level.

7a. According to Hebrews 11:6, what pleases God?
    A. Faith
    B. Fasting
    C. Giving
    D. All of the above
    E. None of the above
A. Faith

7b. The Lord loves you so much that He wants you to come into His best, which is what?
To believe without seeing

7c. True or false: His best is for you to believe His promises simply because the Holy Spirit bears witness and there's a quickening in your heart.
True

7d. *Discussion question:* How do you walk by faith (2 Cor. 5:7)?
Discussion question

7e. Since God has already come down to you in Jesus, what is He trying to do?
Bring you up to His level

8.   There are so many blessings! God has truly provided everything. We need to choose to believe in the power of His spoken favor and to find out what these blessings are and then activate them with our voices. Let's start acting on the Word. If we cooperate with what He's said, the blessing of God will manifest itself in our lives, and our lives will become better than we could ever have believed. God's plans for us are awesome. Our future is so bright, we have to squint to look at it. God loves us, and we're blessed. Let's receive His very best!

8a. *Discussion question:* Now that you've reached the end of the book, how will your approach to receiving, walking, and living in God's best be the same or different from what it was at the beginning of the book?

   Discussion question

Discipleship Questions

1. What is the book of Proverbs full of (Prov. 1:2-5; 2:1-2; and 8:32-36)?

   _____

   _____

   _____

2. *Discussion question:* What are some examples of how people have rejected godly wisdom?

   _____

   _____

   _____

3. If you want to see the blessing of God manifest, you need to _____ in wisdom—the wisdom that's revealed in the Word of God!
   A. Pay
   B. Grow
   C. Walk
   D. Sit
   E. Rest

4. If you _____ a righteous life, you'll have a godly legacy.

5. According to Proverbs 10:7, "*The _____ of the just is blessed: but the _____ of the wicked shall rot.*"

6. *Discussion question:* What can you do to leave a godly legacy?

   _____

   _____

   _____

7. What is on every person who has been persecuted for righteousness' sake?

_____

_____

_____

8. Where does it say that in the Bible?

_____

_____

_____

9. Someday you will stand before God, and He will do what?
    A. Reject you in front of all creation
    B. Acknowledge you in front of all creation
    C. Condemn you in front of all creation
    D. Embarrass you in front of all creation
    E. Honor you in front of all creation

10. True or false: You shouldn't cause persecution to come your way.

11. When persecution comes due to your godly life, why can you look forward to it (Phil. 3:10)?

_____

_____

_____

12. Luke 11:27-28 says, _"And it came to pass, as he spake these things, a certain woman of the company lifted up her voice, and said unto him, _____ is the womb that bare thee, and the paps which thou hast sucked. [28] But he said, Yea _____, blessed are they that hear the word of God, and keep it."_

13. According to Acts 20:35, _"It is more blessed to _____ than to _____."_
    A. _"Receive" / "give"_
    B. _"Work" / "play"_
    C. _"Walk" / "run"_
    D. _"Give" / "receive"_
    E. _"Eat" / "sleep"_

14. If you can't believe, it's because you _____ not to believe (John 20:25).

15. What did you choose to believe instead?

   _____

   _____

   _____

16. When that happens, what is in the way?
   A. Your brain
   B. Your thoughts
   C. Your mind
   D. All of the above
   E. None of the above

17. True or false: The greatest faith that the Lord ever saw was a faith that simply took Him at His Word (Matt. 8:10).

18. True or false: The least faith that Jesus ever saw was Thomas's faith, who basically said "Lord, I believe" only after he saw Jesus risen from the dead (John 20:28-29).

19. What kind of blessing is on those who will just believe the Word?

   _____

   _____

   _____

20. True or false: You can argue a person into faith.

21. *Discussion question:* Why do you think a person won't believe even when there is proof (Luke 16:31)?

   _____

   _____

   _____

22. According to Hebrews 11:6, what pleases God?
    A. Faith
    B. Fasting
    C. Giving
    D. All of the above
    E. None of the above

23. The Lord loves you so much that He wants you to come into His best, which is what?

    _____

    _____

    _____

24. True or false: His best is for you to believe His promises simply because the Holy Spirit bears witness and there's a quickening in your heart.

25. *Discussion question:* How do you walk by faith (2 Cor. 5:7)?

    _____

    _____

    _____

26. Since God has already come down to you in Jesus, what is He trying to do?

    _____

    _____

    _____

27. *Discussion question:* Now that you've reached the end of the book, how will your approach to receiving, walking, and living in God's best be the same or different from what it was at the beginning of the book?

    _____

    _____

    _____

Answer Key

1. Wisdom

2. *Discussion question*

3. C. Walk

4. Live

5. *"Memory" / "name"*

6. *Discussion question*

7. A special blessing

8. Matthew 5:10-12

9. E. Honor you in front of all creation

10. True

11. Because you know that the Lord will bless you for it

12. *"Blessed" / "rather"*

13. D. *"Give" / "receive"*

14. Willed

15. Something other than the report of the Lord

16. D. All of the above

17. True

18. True

19. A greater blessing

20. False

21. *Discussion question*

22. A. Faith

23. To believe without seeing

24. True

25. *Discussion question*

26. Bring you up to His level

27. *Discussion question*

Scriptures

PROVERBS 8:32-36
Now therefore hearken unto me, O ye children: for blessed are they that keep my ways. [33] Hear instruction, and be wise, and refuse it not. [34] Blessed is the man that heareth me, watching daily at my gates, waiting at the posts of my doors. [35] For whoso findeth me findeth life, and shall obtain favour of the LORD. [36] But he that sinneth against me wrongeth his own soul: all they that hate me love death.

PROVERBS 2:1-2
My son, if thou wilt receive my words, and hide my commandments with thee; [2] So that thou incline thine ear unto wisdom, and apply thine heart to understanding.

PROVERBS 1:2-5
To know wisdom and instruction; to perceive the words of understanding; [3] To receive the instruction of wisdom, justice, and judgment, and equity; [4] To give subtilty to the simple, to the young man knowledge and discretion. [5] A wise man will hear, and will increase learning; and a man of understanding shall attain unto wise counsels.

PROVERBS 10:7
The memory of the just is blessed: but the name of the wicked shall rot.

MATTHEW 5:10-12
Blessed are they which are persecuted for righteousness' sake: for theirs is the kingdom of heaven. [11] Blessed are ye, when men shall revile you, and persecute you, and shall say all manner of evil against you falsely, for my sake. [12] Rejoice, and be exceeding glad: for great is your reward in heaven: for so persecuted they the prophets which were before you.

PHILIPPIANS 3:10
That I may know him, and the power of his resurrection, and the fellowship of his sufferings, being made conformable unto his death.

LUKE 11:27-28
And it came to pass, as he spake these things, a certain woman of the company lifted up her voice, and said unto him, Blessed is the womb that bare thee, and the paps which thou hast sucked. [28] But he said, Yea rather, blessed are they that hear the word of God, and keep it.

ACTS 20:35

I have shewed you all things, how that so labouring ye ought to support the weak, and to remember the words of the Lord Jesus, how he said, It is more blessed to give than to receive.

JOHN 20:25-29

The other disciples therefore said unto him, We have seen the Lord. But he said unto them, Except I shall see in his hands the print of the nails, and put my finger into the print of the nails, and thrust my hand into his side, I will not believe. [26] And after eight days again his disciples were within, and Thomas with them: then came Jesus, the doors being shut, and stood in the midst, and said, Peace be unto you. [27] Then saith he to Thomas, Reach hither thy finger, and behold my hands; and reach hither thy hand, and thrust it into my side: and be not faithless, but believing. [28] And Thomas answered and said unto him, My Lord and my God. [29] Jesus saith unto him, Thomas, because thou hast seen me, thou hast believed: blessed are they that have not seen, and yet have believed.

MATTHEW 8:8

The centurion answered and said, Lord, I am not worthy that thou shouldest come under my roof: but speak the word only, and my servant shall be healed.

MATTHEW 8:10

When Jesus heard it, he marvelled, and said to them that followed, Verily I say unto you, I have not found so great faith, no, not in Israel.

JOHN 11:44-53

And he that was dead came forth, bound hand and foot with graveclothes: and his face was bound about with a napkin. Jesus saith unto them, Loose him, and let him go. [45] Then many of the Jews which came to Mary, and had seen the things which Jesus did, believed on him. [46] But some of them went their ways to the Pharisees, and told them what things Jesus had done. [47] Then gathered the chief priests and the Pharisees a council, and said, What do we? for this man doeth many miracles. [48] If we let him thus alone, all men will believe on him: and the Romans shall come and take away both our place and nation. [49] And one of them, named Caiaphas, being the high priest that same year, said unto them, Ye know nothing at all, [50] Nor consider that it is expedient for us, that one man should die for the people, and that the whole nation perish not. [51] And this spake he not of himself: but being high priest that year, he prophesied that Jesus should die for that nation; [52] And not for that nation only, but that also he should gather together in one the children of God that were scattered abroad. [53] Then from that day forth they took counsel together for to put him to death.

JOHN 12:10-11

But the chief priests consulted that they might put Lazarus also to death; [11] Because that by reason of him many of the Jews went away, and believed on Jesus.

LUKE 16:31

And he said unto him, If they hear not Moses and the prophets, neither will they be persuaded, though one rose from the dead.

HEBREWS 11:6

But without faith it is impossible to please him: for he that cometh to God must believe that he is, and that he is a rewarder of them that diligently seek him.

2 CORINTHIANS 5:7

For we walk by faith, not by sight.

Receive Jesus as Your Savior

Choosing to receive Jesus Christ as your Lord and Savior is the most important decision you'll ever make!

God's Word promises that *"if thou shalt confess with thy mouth the Lord Jesus, and shalt believe in thine heart that God hath raised him from the dead, thou shalt be saved. [10] For with the heart man believeth unto righteousness; and with the mouth confession is made unto salvation"* (Rom. 10:9-10). *"For whosoever shall call upon the name of the Lord shall be saved"* (Rom. 10:13).

By His grace, God has already done everything to provide salvation. Your part is simply to believe and receive.

Pray out loud, "Jesus, I confess that You are my Lord and Savior. I believe in my heart that God raised You from the dead. By faith in Your Word, I receive salvation now. Thank You for saving me!"

The very moment you commit your life to Jesus Christ, the truth of His Word instantly comes to pass in your spirit. Now that you're born again, there's a brand-new you!

Please contact our Helpline (719-635-1111) and let us know that you've prayed to receive Jesus as your Savior. We would like to rejoice with you and help you understand more fully what has taken place in your life. We'll send you a free gift that will help you understand and grow in your new relationship with the Lord. *Welcome to your new life!*

Receive the Holy Spirit

As His child, your loving heavenly Father wants to give you the supernatural power you need to live this new life.

> *For every one that asketh receiveth; and he that seeketh findeth; and to him that knocketh it shall be opened. . . . [13] How much more shall your heavenly Father give the Holy Spirit to them that ask him?*
>
> Luke 11:10 and 13b

All you have to do is ask, believe, and receive!

Pray, "Father, I recognize my need for Your power to live this new life. Please fill me with Your Holy Spirit. By faith, I receive it right now! Thank You for baptizing me. Holy Spirit, You are welcome in my life!"

Congratulations! Now you're filled with God's supernatural power!

Some syllables from a language you don't recognize will rise up from your heart to your mouth (1 Cor. 14:14). As you speak them out loud by faith, you're releasing God's power from within and building yourself up in your spirit (1 Cor. 14:4). You can do this whenever and wherever you like.

It doesn't really matter whether you felt anything or not when you prayed to receive the Lord and His Spirit. If you believed in your heart that you received, then God's Word promises that you did. *"Therefore I say unto you, What things soever ye desire, when ye pray, believe that ye receive them, and ye shall have them"* (Mark 11:24). God always honors His Word—believe it!

Please contact our Helpline (719-635-1111) and let us know that you've prayed to be filled with the Holy Spirit. We would like to rejoice with you and send you a free gift that will help you understand more fully what has taken place in your life.

About the Author

Andrew Wommack's life was forever changed the moment he encountered the supernatural love of God on March 23, 1968. As a renowned Bible teacher and author, Andrew has made it his mission to change the way the world sees God.

Andrew's vision is to go as far and deep with the Gospel as possible. His message goes far through the *Gospel Truth* television and radio program, which is available to over half the world's population. The message goes deep through discipleship at Charis Bible College, founded in 1994, which has campuses across the United States and around the globe.

Andrew's Teaching Recommendations in This Study Guide

LESSON 5

Don't Limit God

How do you see yourself? Most of the Israelites didn't enter the Promised Land because they saw themselves as less than they really were. The Bible says they *"limited the Holy One of Israel"* (Ps. 78:41). If you are truly going to experience God's will for your life, you need to see yourself the way He sees you. Be inspired and challenged as Andrew reveals how he took the limits off God. You can too!

CD series
Item Code: 1096-C

As-Seen-on-TV DVD series
Item Code: 1096-D

Paperback
Item Code: 340

Study Guide
Item Code: 440

Spanish Spiral-Bound Book
Item Code: 763

Spanish Study Guide
Item Code: 768

LESSON 6

You've Already Got It!

Many Christians try to get God to heal, deliver, and prosper them, without realizing that He's already done it. Quit waiting on God, and receive what He has already provided!

CD series
Item Code: 1033-C

As-Seen-on-TV DVD series
Item Code: 1033-D

Paperback
Item Code: 320

Study Guide
Item Code: 420i

Spanish Paperback
Item Code: 732

Living in the Balance of Grace & Faith

Grace and faith—emphasize one at the expense of the other and the imbalance will make it difficult to receive from God. If you have been struggling with confusion, frustration, and disappointment in your relationship with God, this teaching is for you.

CD series
Item Code: 1064-C

As-Seen-on-TV DVD series
Item Code: 1064-D

Live DVD series
Item Code: 3208-D

Paperback
Item Code: 328

Study Guide
Item Code: 428

Spanish Spiral-Bound Book   **Spanish Study Guide**
Item Code: 737   Item Code: 746

LESSON 8

Watch or read Hannah Terradez's testimony and many others like it on our website: **www.awmi.net.**

LESSON 19

Redemption

It's more than theology; it's practical. Your understanding of redemption will determine what you are able to receive from God—not just in eternity, but here and now.

CD series   **As-Seen-on-TV DVD series**   **Live DVD series**
Item Code: 1056-C   Item Code: 1056-D   Item Code: 3201-D

Spirit, Soul & Body

A spiritual realm exists inside every person. You are a spirit being who has a soul and lives in a body. *Spirit, Soul & Body* answers the questions "Who am I, really?" and "What changed when I became born again?" This foundational teaching will help you unlock your identity in Jesus Christ.

CD series   **As-Seen-on-TV DVD series**   **Live DVD series**   **Paperback**
Item Code: 1027-C   Item Code: 1027-D   Item Code: 3227-D   Item Code: 318

Audiobook   **Study Guide**
Item Code: 318-A   Item Code: 418

Spanish Spiral-Bound Book   **Spanish Study Guide**
Item Code: 701   Item Code: 770

LESSON 20

The War Is Over

Many wars have been fought throughout history, and more are yet to come. However, the most important one—the one between God and man—is over, and most Christians don't even know it.

CD series
Item Code: 1053-C

As-Seen-on-TV DVD series
Item Code: 1053-D

Paperback
Item Code: 326

Study Guide
Item Code: 426

Spanish Spiral-Bound Book
Item Code: 733

Spanish Study Guide
Item Code: 759

LESSON 21

Self-Centeredness: The Source of All Grief

It's not other people, it's not your circumstances, and it's not the devil. It's the only thing you have the power to change.

Paperback
Item Code: 315

Spanish Spiral-Bound Book
Item Code: 772

Anger Management

Every person deals with anger. But what does the Bible say about it? You might be surprised to learn that anger can be good!

CD series
Item Code: 1044-C